Cambridge Tracts in Theoretical Computer Science

Titles in the series

1. G. Chaitin *Algorithmic Information Theory*
2. L.C. Paulson *Logic and Computation*
3. M. Spivey *Understanding Z*
4. G. Revesz *Lambda Calculus, Combinators and Logic Programming*
5. S. Vickers *Topology via Logic*
6. A. Ramsay *Formal Methods in Artificial Intelligence*
7. J-Y. Girard, Y. Lafont & P. Taylor *Proofs and Types*
8. J. Clifford *Formal Semantics & Pragmatics for Natural Language Processing*
9. M. Winslett *Updating Logical Databases*
10. K. McEvoy & J.V. Tucker (eds) *Theoretical Foundations of VLSI Design*
12. G. Brewka *Nonmonotonic Reasoning*
13. G. Smolka *Logic Programming over Polymorphically Order-Sorted Types*

APPLICATIONS OF PROCESS ALGEBRA

Edited by
J. C. M. BAETEN
CWI, Amsterdam

The right of the University of Cambridge to print and sell all manner of books was granted by Henry VIII in 1534. The University has printed and published continuously since 1584.

CAMBRIDGE UNIVERSITY PRESS

Cambridge

New York   Port Chester   Melbourne   Sydney

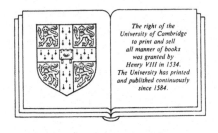

PUBLISHED BY THE PRESS SYNDICATE OF THE UNIVERSITY OF CAMBRIDGE
The Pitt Building, Trumpington Street, Cambridge, United Kingdom

CAMBRIDGE UNIVERSITY PRESS
The Edinburgh Building, Cambridge CB2 2RU, UK
40 West 20th Street, New York NY 10011–4211, USA
477 Williamstown Road, Port Melbourne, VIC 3207, Australia
Ruiz de Alarcón 13, 28014 Madrid, Spain
Dock House, The Waterfront, Cape Town 8001, South Africa

http://www.cambridge.org

First published 1990
First paperback edition 2004

A catalogue record for this book is available from the British Library

ISBN 0 521 40028 7 hardback
ISBN 0 521 60750 7 paperback

Preface

In this book, we give applications of the theory of process algebra, known by the acronym ACP (Algebra of Communicating Processes), as it has been developed since 1982 at the Centre for Mathematics and Computer Science, Amsterdam (see [7]), since 1985 in cooperation with the University of Amsterdam and the University of Utrecht. An important stimulus for this book was given by the ESPRIT contract no. 432, An Integrated Formal Approach to Industrial Software Development (Meteor). The theory itself is treated in [3], which will be revised, translated and published in this series. The theory is briefly reviewed in the first article in this book, *An introduction to process algebra,* by J.A. Bergstra and J.W. Klop.

This book gives applications of the theory of process algebra. By the term process algebra we mean the study of concurrent or communicating processes in an algebraic framework. We endeavour to treat communicating processes in an axiomatic way, just as for instance the study of mathematical objects as groups or fields starts with an axiomatization of the intended objects. The axiomatic method which will concern us, is algebraic in the sense that we consider structures which are models of some set of (mostly) equational axioms; these structures are equipped with several operators. Thus we use the term 'algebra' in the sense of model theory.

There is ample motivation for such an axiomatic-algebraic approach to the theory of communicating processes. An important reason is that there is not one definite notion of process. There is a staggering amount of properties which one may or may not attribute to processes, there are dozens of views ('semantics') which one may have on processes, and there are infinitely many models of processes. So an attempt to organize this field of process theories leads very naturally to an axiomatic methodology.

The aspect of the axiomatic-algebraic approach that is most prominent in this book, is the obvious computational aspect. Much more than in mathematics or mathematical logic, in computer science it is 'algebra' that counts - the well-known etymology of the word 'algebra' should be convincing enough. In system verification, the use of transition diagrams is very illuminating, but especially for larger systems it is desirable to have a formalized mathematical language at our disposal in which specifications, computations, proofs can be given in what is in principle a linear notation. Only then can we expect something of attempts to mechanize our dealings with the objects of interest. In our case the mathematical language is algebraic, with basic constants, operators to construct larger processes and equations defining the nature of the processes under consideration. (The format of pure equations will not be enough, though. We also will use conditional equations and some infinitary proof-rules.)

Of course, the present axiomatizations for communicating processes do not cover the entire spectrum of interest. Several aspects of processes are as yet not well treated in the algebraic framework. The most notable examples are real-time behaviour of processes, and what sometimes is called 'true concurrency' (non-interleaving semantics).

The first system verifications that were done using this theory were [9] and [8]. The verification of the Alternating Bit Protocol of the first article is (in a revised version) part of the second article of this book, *Two simple protocols,* by F.W. Vaandrager. The second article, dealing with FIFO queues, contains problems, that are at this moment not yet well understood. This is the reason that it is not included in this book. From these articles, it became clear that more structuring mechanisms, more operators, were needed to deal with the verification of larger systems. The article [4] was written in order to provide more structuring power. Most of the operators introduced were then used in [28]. Parts of this article can be found in this book: The verification of the Positive Acknowledgement with Retransmission protocol is the second protocol discussed in *Two simple protocols,* and the modularization tool of redundancy in context is discussed (in an extensively revised form) in *Some observations on redundancy in a context,* the tenth article in this book. Other parts of [28], most notably the verification of a One Bit Sliding Window protocol, will appear elsewhere. In the meantime, another approach to modularization was pursued in [18]. The last article in this book is a revision of this paper. Later, more complicated protocol verifications were attempted. [12] gives a verification of a Sliding Window protocol, that takes over 100 pages. Further investigation is necessary, in order to incorporate Hoare-style proof-rules into the theory.

This book presents examples of algorithms other than communication protocols. The third article, a revision of [24], considers Peterson's protocol for ensuring mutual exclusion. Some properties are shown to hold for the process algebra specification. Interesting is the idea of considering global variables as processes communicating with all components in a system. Assigning a value to a variable is done by sending it the value, testing for an equality by reading its value. In the following article, a revision of [20], an example is given of an automated plant (a CIM-architecture), and it is verified that the design goals were met. Next, [6] introduces the concept of process creation, that is used in the following articles. An example is given in the specification of the Sieve of Eratosthenes, an algorithm to generate prime numbers. Recently, in [29], we find a verification of this specification.

An application of the process creation operator is given in the following article, a revision of [16]. Here, a verification is given of two so-called systolic algorithms, an algorithm for recognizing palindromes, and an algorithm for sorting sequences of numbers. Systolic systems consist of regular configurations of simple components, which make them very suitable for chip design. The next article, a revision of [22], also considers a systolic algorithm. Two other articles about such algorithms in the present theory are [17] and [30].

The following article is the recent [21], that considers the distributed operating system Amoeba. It is found that there is a mistake in the description of this system in [23], and it is indicated how this mistake can be corrected. The corrected version is verified. Finally, there is an article in this book about the object-oriented programming language POOL, which is a revision of [27]. A translation is given to the language of ACP, which gives a number of different semantics for POOL. A direction that is not represented in this book is the investigation of circuit architecture, see [5].

Of course, we do not mean to imply that the verification techniques presented in this book constitute the only approach to these problems. In fact, there are many other approaches. From some we have benefited, others have inspired us. To mention just a few verifications in other theories, there are [19] and [25] in the context of CCS, [14] by Hennessy, [26] and [15] in the context of trace theory, [10] in the context of LOTOS, [11] in the context of ASL, [13] using knowledge-based reasoning, and [1,2] using denotational and operational semantics. However, I think this is the first time a collection of articles in this area is collected together, where a single approach is followed in all articles.

Finally, I would like to thank all authors, and all other participants of the PAM seminar, for their cooperation. Also, my thanks goes to the typing staff of the Centre for Mathematics and Computer Science and the desk editor W.A.M. Aspers.

J.C.M. BAETEN

REFERENCES

1. P. AMERICA, J.W. DE BAKKER, J.N. KOK, J.J.M.M. RUTTEN (1986). Operational semantics of a parallel object-oriented language. *Conference Record of the 13th ACM Symposium of Principles of Programming Languages,* St. Petersburg, Florida, 194-208.
2. P. AMERICA, J.W. DE BAKKER, J.N. KOK, J.J.M.M. RUTTEN (1986). *A Denotational Semantics of a Parallel Object-oriented Language,* CWI Report

CS-R8626, Centre for Mathematics and Computer Science, Amsterdam. To appear in *Information and Computation.*
3. J.C.M. BAETEN (1986). *Procesalgebra,* Kluwer Programmatuurkunde, Deventer (in Dutch).
4. J.C.M. BAETEN, J.A. BERGSTRA (1988). Global renaming operators in concrete process algebra. *Information and Computation 78(3),* 205-245.
5. J.C.M. BAETEN, F.W. VAANDRAGER (1988). *Specification and Verification of a Circuit in ACP,* Report P8803, Programming Research Group, University of Amsterdam.
6. J.A. BERGSTRA (1985). *A Process Creation Mechanism in Process Algebra,* Logic Group Preprint Series Nr. 2, CIF, State University of Utrecht.
7. J.A. BERGSTRA, J.W. KLOP (1982). *Fixed Point Semantics in Process Algebras,* MC Report IW 206, Centre for Mathematics and Computer Science, Amsterdam.
8. J.A. BERGSTRA, J.W. KLOP (1984). *Fair FIFO Queues Satisfy an Algebraic Criterion for Protocol Correctness,* CWI Report CS-R8405, Centre for Mathematics and Computer Science, Amsterdam.
9. J.A. BERGSTRA, J.W. KLOP (1986). Verification of an Alternating Bit Protocol by means of process algebra. W. BIBEL, K.P. JANTKE (eds.). *Math. Methods of Spec. and Synthesis of Software Systems '85, Math. Research 31,* Akademie-Verlag, Berlin, 9-23. Also appeared as CWI Report CS-R8404, Centre for Mathematics and Computer Science, Amsterdam, 1984.
10. F. BIEMANS, P. BLONK (1986). On the formal specification and verification of CIM architectures using LOTOS. *Computers in Industry 7(6),* 491-504.
11. M. BROY (1987). *Views of Queues,* Report MIP-8704, Fakultät für Mathematik und Informatik, Universität Passau.
12. R.A. GROENVELD (1987). *Verification of a Sliding Window Protocol by Means of Process Algebra,* Report P8701, Programming Research Group, University of Amsterdam.
13. J.Y. HALPERN, L.D. ZUCK (1987). *A Little Knowledge Goes a Long Way: Simple Knowledge-based Derivations and Correctness Proofs for a Family of Protocols* (extended abstract), IBM Almaden Research Center.
14. M. HENNESSY (1986). Proving systolic systems correct. *TOPLAS 8(3),* 344-387.
15. A. KALDEWAIJ (1987). The translation of processes into circuits. J.W. DE BAKKER, A.J. NIJMAN, P.C. TRELEAVEN (eds.). *Proceedings PARLE Conference, Eindhoven, Volume I (Parallel Architectures),* LNCS 258, Springer-Verlag, 195-212.
16. L. KOSSEN, W.P. WEIJLAND (1987). *Correctness Proofs for Systolic Algorithms: Palindromes and Sorting,* Report FVI 87-04, Computer Science Department, University of Amsterdam.
17. L. KOSSEN, W.P. WEIJLAND (1987). *Verification of a Systolic Algorithm for String Comparison,* CWI Report CS-R8734, Centre for Mathematics and Computer Science, Amsterdam.

18. C.P.J. Koymans, J.C. Mulder (1989). *A Modular Approach to Protocol Verification using Process Algebra.* This volume.
19. K.G. Larsen, R. Milner (1987). A complete protocol verification using relativized bisimulation. Th. Ottmann (ed.). *Proceedings 14th ICALP, Karlsruhe,* LNCS 267, Springer-Verlag, 126-135.
20. S. Mauw (1987). *Process Algebra as a Tool for the Specification and Verification of CIM-Architectures,* Report P8708, Programming Research Group, University of Amsterdam.
21. J.C. Mulder (1988). *On the Amoeba Protocol,* CWI Report CS-R8827, Centre for Mathematics and Computer Science, Amsterdam.
22. J.C. Mulder, W.P. Weijland (1987). *Verification of an Algorithm for Log-time Sorting by Square Comparison,* CWI Report CS-R8729, Centre for Mathematics and Computer Science, Amsterdam.
23. S.J. Mullender (1985). *Principles of Distributed Operating System Design,* Ph.D. Thesis, Free University, Amsterdam.
24. E.R. Nieuwland (1987). *Proving Mutual Exclusion with Process Algebra,* Report FVI 87-10, Department of Computer Science, University of Amsterdam.
25. J. Parrow (1985). *Fairness Properties in Process Algebra - with Applications in Communication Protocol Verification,* DoCS 85/03, Ph.D. Thesis, Department of Computer Systems, Uppsala University.
26. M. Rem (1987). Trace theory and systolic computations. J.W. de Bakker, A.J. Nijman, P.C. Treleaven (eds.). *Proceedings PARLE Conference, Eindhoven, Volume I (Parallel Architectures),* LNCS 258, Springer-Verlag, 14-33.
27. F.W. Vaandrager (1986). *Process Algebra Semantics of POOL,* CWI Report CS-R8629, Centre for Mathematics and Computer Science, Amsterdam.
28. F.W. Vaandrager (1986). *Verification of Two Communication Protocols by means of Process Algebra,* CWI Report CS-R8608, Centre for Mathematics and Computer Science, Amsterdam.
29. J.L.M. Vrancken (1988). *The Implementation of Process Algebra Specifications in POOL-T,* Report P8807, Programming Research Group, University of Amsterdam.
30. W.P. Weijland (1987). A systolic algorithm for matrix-vector multiplication. *Proceedings SION Conference CSN 87,* Centre for Mathematics and Computer Science, Amsterdam, 143-160.

Contents

An Introduction to Process Algebra

J.A. Bergstra
Programming Research Group, University of Amsterdam
P.O. Box 41882, 1009 DB Amsterdam, The Netherlands
Department of Philosophy, State University of Utrecht
Heidelberglaan 2, 3584 CS Utrecht, The Netherlands

J.W. Klop
Department of Software Technology, Centre for Mathematics and Computer Science
P.O. Box 4079, 1009 AB Amsterdam, The Netherlands
Department of Mathematics and Computer Science, Free University
P.O. Box 7161, 1007 MC Amsterdam, The Netherlands

This article serves as an introduction to the basis of the theory, that will be used in the rest of this book. To be more precise, we will discuss the axiomatic theory ACP_τ (Algebra of Communicating Processes with abstraction), with additional features added, which is suitable for both specification and verification of communicating processes. As such, it can be used as background material for the other articles in the book, where all basic axioms are gathered. But we address ourselves not exclusively to readers with previous exposure to algebraic approaches to concurrency (or, as we will call it, process algebra). Also newcomers to this type of theory could find enough here, to get started. For a more thorough treatment of the theory, we refer to [1], which will be revised, translated and published in this CWI Monograph series. There, most proofs can also be found; we refer also to the original papers where the theory was developed. This article is an abbreviated version of reference [11].

Our presentation will concentrate on process algebra as it has been developed since 1982 at the Centre for Mathematics and Computer Science, Amsterdam (see [7]), since 1985 in cooperation with the University of Amsterdam and the University of Utrecht. This means that we make no attempt to give a survey of related approaches though there will be references to some of the main ones.

This paper is not intended to give a survey of the whole area of activities in process algebra.

We acknowledge the help of Jos Baeten in the preparation of this paper.

Partial support received from the European Community under ESPRIT project no. 432, An Integrated Formal Approach to Industrial Software Development (METEOR).

1. THE BASIC CONSTRUCTORS

The processes that we will consider are capable of performing atomic steps or actions $a,b,c,...,$ with the idealization that these actions are events without positive duration in time; it takes only one moment to execute an action. The actions are combined into composite processes by the operations + and $\cdot$, with the interpretation that $(a+b)\cdot c$ is the process that first chooses between executing a or b and, second, performs the action c after which it is finished. (We will often suppress the dot and write $(a+b)c$.) These operations, 'alternative composition' and 'sequential composition' (or just sum and product), are the basic constructors of processes. Since time has a direction, multiplication is not commutative; but addition is, and in fact it is stipulated that the options (summands) possible at some stage of the process form a *set*. Formally, we will require that processes $x,y,$ ... satisfy the following axioms:

BPA
$x+y=y+x$
$(x+y)+z=x+(y+z)$
$x+x=x$
$(x+y)z=xz+yz$
$(xy)z=x(yz)$

TABLE 1

Thus far we used 'process algebra' in the generic sense of denoting the area of algebraic approaches to concurrency, but we will also adopt the following technical meaning for it: any model of these axioms will be a *process algebra.* The simplest process algebra, then, is the term model of BPA (Basic Process Algebra), whose elements are BPA-expressions (built from the atoms $a,b,c,...$ by means of the basic constructors) modulo the equality generated by the axioms. This process algebra contains only finite processes; things get more lively if we admit recursion enabling us to define infinite processes. Even at this stage one can define, recursively, interesting processes:

COUNTER
$X=(zero+up\cdot Y)\cdot X$
$Y=down+up\cdot Y\cdot Y$

TABLE 2

where 'zero' is the action that asserts that the counter has value 0, and 'up' and 'down' are the actions of incrementing resp. decrementing the counter by one unit. The process COUNTER is now represented by X; Y is an auxiliary process. COUNTER is a 'perpetual' process, that is, all its execution traces are infinite. Such a trace is e.g. zero-zero-up-down-zero-up-up-up-....

Equations as in Table 2 are also called fixed point equations. An important property of such equations is whether or not they are guarded. A fixed point equation is *guarded* if every occurrence of a recursion variable in the right hand side is preceded ('guarded') by an occurrence of an action. For instance, the occurrence of X in the RHS of $X=(zero+up\cdot Y)\cdot X$ is guarded since, when this X is accessed, one has to pass either the guard zero or the guard up. A non-example: the equation $X=X+a\cdot X$ is not guarded.

Before proceeding to the next section, let us assure the reader that the omission of the other distributive law, $z(x+y)=zx+zy$, is intentional. The reason will become clear after the introduction of 'deadlock'.

2. Deadlock

A vital element in the present set-up of process algebra is the process δ, signifying 'deadlock'. The process ab performs its two steps and then stops, silently and happily; but the process $ab\delta$ deadlocks (with a crunching sound, one may imagine) after the a- and b-action: it wants to do a proper action but it cannot. So δ is the acknowledgement of stagnation. With this in mind, the axioms to which δ is subject, should be clear:

DEADLOCK
$\delta+x=x$
$\delta\cdot x=\delta$

Table 3

(In fact, it can be argued that 'deadlock' is not the most appropriate name for the process constant δ. In the sequel we will encounter a process which can more rightfully claim this name: $\tau\delta$, where τ is the silent step. We will stick to the present terminology, however.)

The axiom system of BPA (Table 1) together with the present axioms for δ is called BPA_δ. Now suppose that the distributive law $z(x+y)=zx+zy$ is added to BPA_δ. Then: $ab=a(b+\delta)=ab+a\delta$. This means that a process with deadlock possibility is equal to one without; and that conflicts with our intention to model also deadlock behaviour of processes.

3. Interleaving or free merge

If x, y are processes, their 'parallel composition' $x \| y$ is the process that first chooses whether to do a step in x or in y, and proceeds as the parallel composition of the remainders of x, y. In other words, the steps of x, y are interleaved. Using an auxiliary operator $\lfloor\!\lfloor$ (with the interpretation that $x \lfloor\!\lfloor y$ is like $x \| y$ but with the commitment of choosing the initial step from x) the operation $\|$ can be succinctly defined by the axioms:

FREE MERGE
$x\|y=x\mathbin{\|\!\!\lfloor}y+y\mathbin{\|\!\!\lfloor}x$
$a\mathbin{\|\!\!\lfloor}x=ax$
$ax\mathbin{\|\!\!\lfloor}y=a(x\|y)$
$(x+y)\mathbin{\|\!\!\lfloor}z=x\mathbin{\|\!\!\lfloor}z+y\mathbin{\|\!\!\lfloor}z$

TABLE 4

One can show that an equivalent axiomatization of $\|$ without an auxiliary operator like $\mathbin{\|\!\!\lfloor}$, would require infinitely many axioms.

The system of nine axioms consisting of BPA and the four axioms for free merge will be called PA. Moreover, if the axioms for δ are added, the result will be PA_δ. The operators $\|$ and $\mathbin{\|\!\!\lfloor}$ will also be called *merge* and *left-merge* respectively.

An example of a process recursively defined in PA, is: $X=a(b\|X)$. It turns out that this process can already be defined in BPA, by the two fixed point equations $X=aYX$, $Y=b+aYY$. (This is a simplified version of the counter in Table 2, without the action zero.) To see that both ways of defining X yield the same process, one may 'unwind' according to the given equations:

$$X=a(b\|X)=a(b\mathbin{\|\!\!\lfloor}X+X\mathbin{\|\!\!\lfloor}b)=a(bX+a(b\|X)\mathbin{\|\!\!\lfloor}b)$$
$$=a(bX+a((b\|X)\|b))=a(bX+a...),$$

while on the other hand

$$X=aYX=a(b+aYY)X=a(bX+aYYX)=a(bX+a...);$$

so at least up to level 2 the processes are equal. In fact they can be proved equal up to each finite level. Later on, we will introduce an infinitary proof rule enabling us to infer that, therefore, the processes are equal.

So, is the defining power (or expressibility) of PA greater than that of BPA? Indeed it is, as is shown by the following process:

BAG
$X=in(0)(out(0)\|X)+in(1)(out(1)\|X)$

TABLE 5

This equation describes the process behaviour of a 'bag' or 'multiset' that may contain finitely many instances of data 0, 1. The actions $in(0)$, $out(0)$ are: putting a 0 in the bag resp. getting a 0 from the bag, and likewise for 1. This process does not have a finite specification in BPA, that is, a finite specification without merge ($\|$).

If we want to define a bag over a general finite data set D (instead of just over $\{0,1\}$) we use a sum notation as an abbreviation, so

$$X = \sum_{d\in D} in(d)\cdot(out(d)\|X).$$

4. Fixed points

We have already alluded to the existence of infinite processes; this raises the question how one can actually construct process algebras (for BPA or PA) containing infinite processes in addition to finite ones. Such models can be obtained by means of:

(1) projective limits ([8,10]);
(2) complete metrical spaces, as in the work of De Bakker and Zucker [5,6];
(3) quotients of graph domains (a graph domain is a set of process graphs or transition diagrams), as in Milner [18], Baeten, Bergstra and Klop [4]; or Van Glabbeek [14];
(4) the 'explicit' models of Hoare [16];
(5) ultraproducts of finite models (Kranakis [17]).

In Section 12 we will discuss a model as in (3).

5. Communication

So far, the parallel composition or merge ($\|$) did not involve communication in the process $x\|y$: x and y are 'freely' merged. However, some actions in one process may need an action in another process for an actual execution, like the act of shaking hands requires simultaneous acts of two persons. In fact, 'hand shaking' is the paradigm for the type of communication which we will introduce now. If $A = \{a,b,c, ...,\}$ is the action alphabet, let us adopt a partial binary function γ on A, that is required to be commutative and associative. If $\gamma(a,b)$ is defined, a and b communicate, and $\gamma(a,b)$ is the result of the communication; if $\gamma(a,b)$ is not defined, a and b do not communicate. We can extend γ to a total function $|$ on $A \cup \{\delta\}$, by putting $a|b=\delta$ whenever $\gamma(a,b)$ is not defined (so also when one of a,b equals δ). The result is a binary communication function $|$ on $A \cup \{\delta\}$ satisfying

COMMUNICATION FUNCTION
$a\|b=b\|a$
$(a\|b)\|c=a\|(b\|c)$
$\delta\|a=\delta$

TABLE 6

(Here a,b vary over $A \cup \{\delta\}$.) We can now specify *merge with communication*; we use the same notation $\|$ as for the free merge, since in fact free merge is an instance of merge with communication (by choosing the communication function trivial, i.e. $a|b=\delta$ for all a,b). There are now two auxiliary operators, allowing a finite axiomatization: left-merge ($⌊\!⌊$) as before and $|$ (communication merge or 'bar'), which is an extension of the communication function to all processes, not only the constants. The axioms for $\|$ and its auxiliary operators are:

MERGE WITH COMMUNICATION
$x \Vert y = x ⌊\!⌊ y + y ⌊\!⌊ x + x \vert y$
$a ⌊\!⌊ x = ax$
$ax ⌊\!⌊ y = a(x \Vert y)$
$(x+y) ⌊\!⌊ z = x ⌊\!⌊ z + y ⌊\!⌊ z$
$ax \vert b = (a \vert b)x$
$a \vert bx = (a \vert b)x$
$ax \vert by = (a \vert b)(x \Vert y)$
$(x+y) \vert z = x \vert z + y \vert z$
$x \vert (y+z) = x \vert y + x \vert z$

TABLE 7

We also need the so-called *encapsulation* operators $\partial_H (H \subseteq A)$ for removing unsuccessful attempts at communication:

ENCAPSULATION
$\partial_H(a) = a$ if $a \notin H$
$\partial_H(a) = \delta$ if $a \in H$
$\partial_H(x+y) = \partial_H(x) + \partial_H(y)$
$\partial_H(xy) = \partial_H(x) \cdot \partial_H(y)$

TABLE 8

The axioms for BPA, DEADLOCK together with the present ones constitute the axiom system ACP (Algebra of Communicating Processes). Typically, a system of communicating processes $x_1, ..., x_n$ is now represented in ACP by the expression $\partial_H(x_1 \Vert \cdots \Vert x_n)$. Prefixing the encapsulation operator says that the system $x_1, ..., x_n$ is to be perceived as a separate unit w.r.t. the communication actions mentioned in H; no communications between actions in H with an environment are expected or intended.

We will often adopt the following special format for the communication function, called *read/write (receive/send) communication.* Let a finite set D of *data* d and a set $\{1, ..., p\}$ of *ports* be given. Then the alphabet consists of *read* actions $ri(d)$ and *send* actions $si(d)$, for $i = 1, ..., p$ and $d \in D$. The interpretation is: read datum d at port i, resp. send datum d at port i. Furthermore, the alphabet contains actions $ci(d)$ for $i = 1, ..., p$ and $d \in D$, with interpretation: *communicate d at i.* These actions will be called *transactions.* The only non-trivial communications (i.e. not resulting in δ) are: $si(d) \vert ri(d) = ci(d)$. Instead of $si(d)$ we will also see the notation $wi(d)$ (write d along i).

6. ABSTRACTION

A fundamental issue in the design and specification of hierarchical (or modularized) systems of communicating processes is *abstraction.* Without having an abstraction mechanism enabling us to abstract from the inner workings of modules to be composed to larger systems, specification of all but very small systems would be virtually impossible. We will now extend the axiom system ACP, obtained thus far, with such an abstraction mechanism. Consider two bags B_{12}, B_{23} (cf. Section 3) with action alphabets $\{r1(d), s2(d) | d \in D\}$ resp. $\{r2(d), s3(d) | d \in D\}$. That is, B_{12} is a bag-like channel reading data d at port 1, sending them at port 2; B_{23} reads data at 2 and sends them to 3. (That the channels are bags means that, unlike the case of a queue, the order of incoming data is lost in the transmission.) Suppose the bags are connected at 2; that is, we adopt communications $s2(d)|r2(d) = c2(d)$ where $c2(d)$ is the transaction of d at 2.

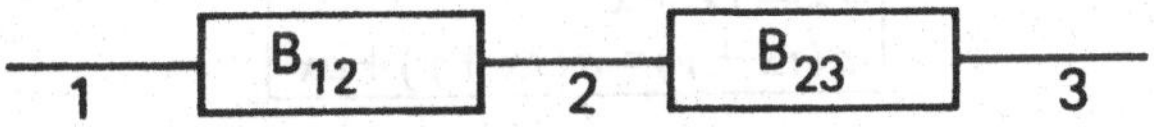

FIGURE 1

The composite system $\mathbf{B}_{13} = \partial_H(B_{12} \| B_{23})$ where $H = \{s2(d),\ r2(d) | d \in D\}$ should, intuitively, be again a bag between locations 1, 3. However, some (rather involved) calculations learn that $\mathbf{B}_{13} = \Sigma_{d \in D} r1(d) \cdot ((c2(d)s3(d)) \| \mathbf{B}_{13})$; so $\mathbf{B}_{13}$ is a 'transparant' bag: the passage of d through 2 is visible as the transaction event $c2(d)$.

How can we *abstract* from such internal details, if we are only interested in the external behaviour at 1, 3? The first step to obtain such an abstraction is to remove the distinctive identity of the actions to be abstracted, that is, to rename them all into one designated action which we call, after Milner, τ: the *silent* action (this is called 'pre-abstraction' in [2]). This renaming operator is the *abstraction operator* τ_I, parameterized by a set of actions $I \subseteq A$ and subject to the following axioms:

ABSTRACTION
$\tau_I(\tau) = \tau$
$\tau_I(a) = a$ if $a \notin I$
$\tau_I(a) = \tau$ if $a \in I$
$\tau_I(x+y) = \tau_I(x) + \tau_I(y)$
$\tau_I(xy) = \tau_I(x) \cdot \tau_I(y)$

TABLE 9

The second step is to attempt to devise axioms for the silent step τ by means of which τ can be removed from expressions, as e.g. in the equation $a\tau b = ab$.

However, it is not possible (nor desirable) to remove *all* τ's in an expression if one is interested in a faithful description of deadlock behaviour of processes. For, consider the process (expression) $a+\tau\delta$; this process can deadlock, namely if it chooses to perform the silent action. Now, if one would propose naively the equations $\tau x = x\tau = x$, then $a+\tau\delta = a+\delta = a$, and the latter process has no deadlock possibility. It turns out that one of the proposed equations, $x\tau = x$, can safely be adopted, but the other one is wrong. Fortunately, Milner [19] has devised some simple axioms which can be used to give a complete description of the properties of the silent step (complete w.r.t. a certain semantical notion of process equivalence called bisimulation, which does respect deadlock behaviour; this notion is discussed in the sequel), as follows.

SILENT STEP
$x\tau = x$
$\tau x = \tau x + x$
$a(\tau x + y) = a(\tau x + y) + ax$

TABLE 10

To return to our example of the transparant bag $\mathbf{B}_{13}$, after abstraction of the set of transactions $I = \{c2(d) | d \in D\}$ the result is indeed an 'ordinary' bag:

$$\tau_I(\mathbf{B}_{13}) = \tau_I(\Sigma r1(d)(c2(d)\cdot s3(d) \| \mathbf{B}_{13})) \overset{(*)}{=} \Sigma r1(d)(\tau\cdot s3(d) \| \tau_I(\mathbf{B}_{13}))$$
$$= \Sigma(r1(d)\cdot\tau\cdot s3(d)) \mathbin{\|\!\!\_}\, \tau_I(\mathbf{B}_{13}) = \Sigma(r1(d)\cdot s3(d)) \mathbin{\|\!\!\_}\, \tau_I(\mathbf{B}_{13})$$
$$= \Sigma r1(d)(s3(d) \| \tau_I(\mathbf{B}_{13}))$$

from which it follows that $\tau_I(\mathbf{B}_{13}) \overset{(**)}{=} B_{13}$, the bag defined by

$$B_{13} = \Sigma r1(d)(s3(d) \| B_{13}).$$

Here we were able to eliminate all silent actions, but this will not always be the case. In fact, this computation is not as straightforward as was maybe suggested: to justify the equations marked with (*) and (**) we need more powerful principles, which we will discuss in the sequel. (Specifically, in (*) an appeal to the 'alphabet calculus' of Section 9 is needed and (**) requires the principle RSP, see Section 8 below.)

7. Projection and auxiliary axioms

First, we define the projection operators $\pi_n (n \geq 1)$, cutting off a process at level n:

PROJECTION	
$\pi_n(a) = a$	$\pi_n(x+y) = \pi_n(x) + \pi_n(y)$
$\pi_1(ax) = a$	$\pi_n(\tau) = \tau$
$\pi_{n+1}(ax) = a\pi_n(x)$	$\pi_n(\tau x) = \tau\cdot\pi_n(x)$

TABLE 11

E.g., for X defining BAG as in Table 5:

$$\pi_2(X) = in(0)(out(0) + in(0) + in(1)) + in(1)(out(1) + in(0) + in(1)).$$

We have that τ-steps do not add to the depth; this is enforced by the τ-laws (since, e.g. $a\tau b = ab$ and $\tau a = \tau a + a$).

By means of these projections a distance between processes x, y can be defined: $d(x,y) = 2^{-n}$ where n is the least natural number such that $\pi_n(x) \neq \pi_n(y)$, and $d(x,y) = 0$ if there is no such n. If the term model of BPA (or PA) as in Section 1 is equipped with this distance function, the result is an ultrametrical space. By metrical completion we obtain a model of BPA (resp. PA) in which all systems of guarded recursion equations have a unique solution. This model construction has been employed in various settings by De Bakker and Zucker [5,6].

In the articles of Vaandrager in this volume a slightly different definition of the projection operators is used, which lead to the same theorems below, but which have the advantage that they also can be defined for $n = 0$, and are definable in our theory ACP_τ (see Section 11). We present the new axioms below.

PROJECTION, Second version
$\pi_0(ax) = \delta$
$\pi_{n+1}(ax) = a\pi_n(x)$
$\pi_n(x+y) = \pi_n(x) + \pi_n(y)$
$\pi_n(\tau) = \tau$
$\pi_n(\tau x) = \tau \cdot \pi_n(x)$

TABLE 12

In ACP_τ, systems are described as the parallel composition of their components, and so a system of communicating processes $x_1, ..., x_n$ is represented by the expression $\partial_H(x_1 \| \cdots \| x_n)$. When we want to focus on the external actions of such a system, we apply an abstraction operator, that abstracts from all communications between actions from H. A useful theorem to break down these expressions is the *Expansion Theorem* which holds under the assumption of the *handshaking axiom* $x|y|z = \delta$. This axiom says that all communications are binary.

THEOREM (EXPANSION THEOREM).

$$x_1 \| \cdots \| x_k = \sum_i x_i \lfloor\!\lfloor X_k^i + \sum_{i \neq j} (x_i | x_j) \lfloor\!\lfloor X_k^{i,j}.$$

Here X_k^i denotes the merge of $x_1, ..., x_k$ except x_i, and $X_k^{i,j}$ denotes the same merge except $x_i, x_j (k \geq 3)$. In order to prove the Expansion Theorem, one first proves by simultaneous induction on term complexity that for all closed ACP_τ-terms (i.e. terms without free variables) the following holds:

AXIOMS OF STANDARD CONCURRENCY
$(x \lfloor\!\lfloor y) \lfloor\!\lfloor z = x \lfloor\!\lfloor (y \| z)$
$(x \mid ay) \lfloor\!\lfloor z = x \mid (ay \lfloor\!\lfloor z)$
$x \mid y = y \mid x$
$x \| y = y \| x$
$x \mid (y \mid z) = (x \mid y) \mid z$
$x \| (y \| z) = (x \| y) \| z$

TABLE 13

8. PROOF RULES FOR RECURSIVE SPECIFICATIONS

We have now presented a survey of ACP_τ; we refer to [9] for an analysis of this proof system. Note that ACP_τ (displayed in full in Section 11) is entirely equational. Without further proof rules it is not possible to deal (in an algebraical way) with infinite processes, obtained by recursive specifications, such as BAG; in the derivation above we tacitly used such proof rules which will be made explicit now.

(i) RDP, the Recursive Definition Principle: *Every guarded and abstraction-free recursive specification has a solution.*

(ii) RSP, the Recursive Specification Principle: *Every guarded and abstraction-free recursive specification has at most one solution.*

(iii) AIP, the Approximation Induction Principle: *A process is determined by its finite projections.*

In a more formal notation, AIP can be rendered as the infinitary rule

$$\frac{\forall n \quad \pi_n(x) = \pi_n(y)}{x = y}.$$

As to (i), the restriction to guarded specifications is not very important (for the definition of 'guarded' see Section 1); in the process algebras that we have encountered and that satisfy RDP, also the same principle without the guardedness condition is true. More delicate is the situation in principle (ii): first, *τ-steps may not act as guards*: e.g. the recursion equation $X = \tau X + a$ has infinitely many solutions, namely $\tau(a+q)$ is a solution for arbitrary q; and second, the *recursion equations must not contain occurrences of abstraction operators τ_I*. That is, they are 'abstraction-free' (but there may be occurrences of τ in the equations). The latter restriction is in view of the fact that, surprisingly, the recursion equation $X = a \cdot \tau_{\{a\}}(X)$ possesses infinitely many solutions, even though it looks very guarded. (The solutions are: $a \cdot q$ where q satisfies $\tau_{\{a\}}(q) = q$.) That the presence of abstraction operators in recursive specifications causes trouble, was first noticed by Hoare [15,16].

The unrestricted form of AIP as in (iii) will turn out to be too strong in some circumstances; it does not hold in one of the main models of ACP_τ, namely the graph model which is introduced in Section 12. Therefore we also introduce the following weaker form.

(iv) AIP$^-$ (Weak Approximation Induction Principle): *Every process which has an abstraction-free guarded specification is determined by its finite projections.*

Roughly, a process which can be specified without abstraction operators is one in which there are no infinite τ-traces (and which is definable). E.g. the process X_0 defined by the infinite specification $\{X_0=bX_1, X_{n+1}=bX_{n+2}+a^n\}$, where a^n is $a \cdot a \cdot \cdots \cdot a$ (n times), contains an infinite trace of b-actions; after abstraction w.r.t. b, the resulting process, $Y=\tau_{\{b\}}(X_0)$, has an infinite trace of τ-steps; and (at least in the main model of ACP$_\tau$ of Section 12) this Y is not definable without abstraction operators.

Even the Weak Approximation Induction Principle is rather strong. In fact a short argument shows the following:

THEOREM. AIP$^-$ $\Rightarrow$RSP.

As a rule, we will be very careful in admitting abstraction operators in recursive specifications. Yet there are processes which can be elegantly specified by using abstraction inside recursion.

9. Alphabet calculus

In computations with infinite processes one often needs information about the *alphabet* $\alpha(x)$ of a process x. E.g. if x is the process uniquely defined by the recursion equation $X=aX$, we have $\alpha(x)=\{a\}$. An example of the use of this alphabet information is given by the implication $\alpha(x)\cap H=\emptyset \Rightarrow \partial_H(x)=x$. For finite closed process expressions this fact can be proved with induction to the structure, but for infinite processes we have to require such a property axiomatically. In fact, the example will be one of the 'conditional axioms' below (conditional, in contrast with the purely equational axioms we have introduced thus far). First we have to define the alphabet:

ALPHABET
$\alpha(\delta)=\emptyset$
$\alpha(\tau)=\emptyset$
$\alpha(a)=\{a\}$ (if $a\neq\delta$)
$\alpha(\tau x)=\alpha(x)$
$\alpha(ax)=\{a\}\cup\alpha(x)$ (if $a\neq\delta$)
$\alpha(x+y)=\alpha(x)\cup\alpha(y)$
$\alpha(x)=\cup_{n\geq 1}\alpha(\pi_n(x))$
$\alpha(\tau_I(x))=\alpha(x)-I$

TABLE 14

To appreciate the non-triviality of the concept $\alpha(x)$, let us mention that a finite specification can be given of a process for which the alphabet is uncomputable (see [3] for an example).

Now the following conditional axioms will be adopted:

CONDITIONAL AXIOMS
$\alpha(x)\|(\alpha(y)\cap H)\subseteq H \Rightarrow \partial_H(x\|y)=\partial_H(x\|\partial_H(y))$
$\alpha(x)\|(\alpha(y)\cap I)=\emptyset \Rightarrow \tau_I(x\|y)=\tau_I(x\|\tau_I(y))$
$\alpha(x)\cap H=\emptyset \Rightarrow \partial_H(x)=x$
$\alpha(x)\cap I=\emptyset \Rightarrow \tau_I(x)=x$
$H=H_1\cup H_2 \Rightarrow \partial_H(x)=\partial_{H_1}\circ\partial_{H_2}(x)$
$I=I_1\cup I_2 \Rightarrow \tau_I(x)=\tau_{I_1}\circ\tau_{I_2}(x)$
$H\cap I=\emptyset \Rightarrow \tau_I\circ\partial_H(x)=\partial_H\circ\tau_I(x)$

TABLE 15

Using these axioms, one can derive for instance the following fact: if communication is of the read-write format and I is disjoint from the set of transactions (communication results) as well as disjoint from the set of communication actions, then the abstraction τ_I distributes over merges $x\|y$.

10. Koomen's Fair Abstraction Rule

Suppose the following statistical experiment is performed: somebody flips a coin, repeatedly, until head comes up. This process is described by the recursion equation $X=flip\cdot(tail\cdot X+head)$. Suppose further that the experiment takes place in a closed room, and all information to be obtained about the process in the room is that we can hear the experimenter shout joyfully: 'Head!'. That is, we observe the process $\tau_I(X)$ where $I=\{flip,tail\}$. Now, if the coin is 'fair', it is to be expected that sooner or later (i.e., after a τ-step) the action 'head' will be perceived. Hence, intuitively, $\tau_I(X)=\tau\cdot head$. (This vivid example is from Vaandrager [21].)

Koomen's Fair Abstraction Rule (KFAR) is an algebraic rule enabling us to arrive at such a conclusion formally. The rule was introduced in this form in Bergstra and Klop [12]. (For an extensive analysis of the rule see [4].) The simplest form is

$$\frac{x=ix+y \quad (i\in I)}{\tau_I(x)=\tau\cdot\tau_I(y)} \ \mathrm{KFAR}_1.$$

So, KFAR_1 expresses the fact that the 'τ-loop' (originating from the i-loop) in $\tau_I(x)$ will not be taken infinitely often. In case this 'τ-loop' is of length 2, the same conclusion is expressed in the rule

$$\frac{x_1=i_1x_2+y_1,\ x_2=i_2x_1+y_2 \quad (i_1,i_2\in I)}{\tau_I(x_1)=\tau\cdot\tau_I(y_1+y_2)} \ \mathrm{KFAR}_2$$

and it is not hard to guess what the general formulation (KFAR_n, $n\geqslant 1$) will be. In fact, we will need an even more general formulation, CFAR (the Cluster Fair Abstraction Rule). This principle was introduced by Vaandrager [21]. There, he showed that CFAR can already be derived from KFAR_1 (at least in the framework to be discussed below).

Suppose E is a recursive specification (a system of fixed point equations) over variables V, and suppose I is the set of atomic actions to be abstracted from. We call a subset C of V a *cluster of I in E* if for all X in C the equation for X in E has the form

$$X = \sum_{k=1}^{m} i_k \cdot X_k + \sum_{l=1}^{n} Y_l,$$

where $m \geq 1$, $n \geq 0$, $i_1,...,i_m \in I \cup \{\tau\}$, $X_1,...,X_m \in C$, $Y_1,...,Y_n \in V-C$. The variables in C are called *cluster variables.* For variables $X,Y \in V$ we write $X \rightsquigarrow Y$ if Y occurs in the right hand side of the equation of X. Then, the *exits* of the cluster are those variables outside C, that can be reached from C, i.e.

$$exits(C) = \{Y \in V-C : X \rightsquigarrow Y \text{ for some } X \in C\}.$$

Let $\rightsquigarrow^*$ be the transitive and reflexive closure of $\rightsquigarrow$. We call a cluster C of I in E *conservative* if every exit can be reached from every cluster variable, i.e. for all $X \in C$ and all $Y \in exits(C)$ we have $X \rightsquigarrow^* Y$. Now we can formulate the rule CFAR as follows.

DEFINITION. The *Cluster Fair Abstraction Rule* is the following statement: let E be a guarded recursive specification; let $I \subseteq A$ be such that $|I| \geq 2$; let C be a finite conservative cluster of I in E; and let $X \in C$. Then:

$$\tau_I(X) = \tau \cdot \sum_{Y \in exits(C)} \tau_I(Y).$$

We see that CFAR can only be applied when we are dealing with a conservative cluster. In practice, most specifications will not contain conservative clusters. If, in such a situation, we state that a certain result is obtained by the use of CFAR, we mean that there is a specification which is equivalent to the one we are dealing with (using RSP), which contains a conservative cluster, and that the result follows when we apply CFAR to this second specification.

KFAR and CFAR are of great help in protocol verifications. As an example, KFAR can be used to abstract from a cycle of internal steps which is due to a defective communication channel; the underlying fairness assumption is that this channel is not defective forever, but will function properly after an undetermined period of time. (Just as in the coin flipping experiment the wrong option, tail, is not chosen infinitely often.)

An interesting peculiarity of the present framework is the following. Call the process τ^ω ($=\tau\cdot\tau\cdot\tau\cdots$) *livelock.* Formally, this is the process $\tau_{\{i\}}(x)$ where x is uniquely defined by the recursion equation $X = i \cdot X$. Noting that $x = i \cdot x = i \cdot x + \delta$ and applying $KFAR_1$ we obtain $\tau^\omega = \tau_{\{i\}}(x) = \tau\delta$. In words: *livelock = deadlock.* There are other semantical frameworks for processes, also in the scope of process algebra but not in the scope of this paper, where this equality does not hold (see [13]).

11. A FRAMEWORK FOR PROCESS SPECIFICATION AND VERIFICATION

We have now arrived at a framework which contains all the axioms and proof rules introduced so far. In Table 16 the list of all components of this system is given; Table 17 contains the equational system ACP_τ and Table 18 contains the extra features and furthermore the proof principles which were introduced. Note that for *specification* purposes one only needs ACP_τ; for *verification* one will need the whole system. Also, it is important to notice that this framework resides entirely on the level of syntax and formal specifications and verification using that syntax - even though some proof rules are infinitary. No semantics has been provided yet; this will be done in Section 12. The idea is that 'users' can stay in the realm of this formal system and execute algebraical manipulations, without the need for an excursion into the semantics. That this can be done is demonstrated throughout this book. This does not mean that the semantics is unimportant; it does mean that the user needs only be concerned with formula manipulation. The underlying semantics is of great interest for the theory, if only to guarantee the consistency of the formal system; but applications should not be burdened with it, in our intention.

A PROCESS SPECIFICATION AND VERIFICATION FRAMEWORK	
Basic Process Algebra	A1-5
Deadlock	A6,7
Communication Function	C1-3
Merge with Communication	CM1-9
Encapsulation	D1-4
Silent Step	T1-3
Silent Step: Auxiliary Axioms	TM1,2; TC1-4
Abstraction	DT; TI1-5
Projection	PR1-6
Hand Shaking	HA
Standard Concurrency	SC
Expansion Theorem	ET
Alphabet Calculus	CA
Recursive Definition Principle	RDP
Recursive Specification Principle	RSP
Weak Approximation Induction Principle	AIP^-
Cluster Fair Abstraction Rule	CFAR

TABLE 16

ACP$_\tau$			
$x+y=y+x$	A1	$x\tau=x$	T1
$(x+y)+z=x+(y+z)$	A2	$\tau x=\tau x+x$	T2
$x+x=x$	A3	$a(\tau x+y)=a(\tau x+y)+ax$	T3
$(x+y)z=xz+yz$	A4		
$(xy)z=x(yz)$	A5		
$x+\delta=x$	A6		
$\delta x=\delta$	A7		
$a \mid b=b \mid a$	C1		
$(a \mid b) \mid c=a \mid (b \mid c)$	C2		
$\delta \mid a=\delta$	C3		
$x \parallel y=x \lfloor\!\lfloor y+y \lfloor\!\lfloor x+x \mid y$	CM1		
$a \lfloor\!\lfloor x=ax$	CM2	$\tau \lfloor\!\lfloor x=\tau x$	TM1
$ax \lfloor\!\lfloor y=a(x \parallel y)$	CM3	$\tau x \lfloor\!\lfloor y=\tau(x \parallel y)$	TM2
$(x+y) \lfloor\!\lfloor z=x \lfloor\!\lfloor z+y \lfloor\!\lfloor z$	CM4	$\tau \mid x=\delta$	TC1
$ax \mid b=(a \mid b)x$	CM5	$x \mid \tau=\delta$	TC2
$a \mid bx=(a \mid b)x$	CM6	$\tau x \mid y=x \mid y$	TC3
$ax \mid by=(a \mid b)(x \parallel y)$	CM7	$x \mid \tau y=x \mid y$	TC4
$(x+y) \mid z=x \mid z+y \mid z$	CM8		
$x \mid (y+z)=x \mid y+x \mid z$	CM9	$\partial_H(\tau)=\tau$	DT
		$\tau_I(\tau)=\tau$	TI1
$\partial_H(a)=a$ if $a \notin H$	D1	$\tau_I(a)=a$ if $a \notin I$	TI2
$\partial_H(a)=\delta$ if $a \in H$	D2	$\tau_I(a)=\tau$ if $a \in I$	TI3
$\partial_H(x+y)=\partial_H(x)+\partial_H(y)$	D3	$\tau_I(x+y)=\tau_I(x)+\tau_I(y)$	TI4
$\partial_H(xy)=\partial_H(x)\cdot\partial_H(y)$	D4	$\tau_I(xy)=\tau_I(x)\cdot\tau_I(y)$	TI5

TABLE 17

REMAINING AXIOMS AND RULES

$\pi_1(ax)=a$	PR1
$\pi_{n+1}(ax)=a\cdot\pi_n(x)$	PR2
$\pi_n(a)=a$	PR3
$\pi_n(x+y)=\pi_n(x)+\pi_n(y)$	PR4
$\pi_n(\tau)=\tau$	PR5
$\pi_n(\tau x)=\tau\cdot\pi_n(x)$	PR6
$x\|y\|z=\delta$	HA
$x\|y=y\|x$	SC1
$x\,\|\,y=y\,\|\,x$	SC2
$x\|(y\|z)=(x\|y)\|z$	SC3
$(x \lfloor\!\lfloor y)\lfloor\!\lfloor z=x\lfloor\!\lfloor(y\,\|\,z)$	SC4
$(x\|ay)\lfloor\!\lfloor z=x\|(ay\lfloor\!\lfloor z)$	SC5
$x\,\|\,(y\,\|\,z)=(x\,\|\,y)\,\|\,z$	SC6

$$x_1\,\|\cdots\|\,x_n=\sum_{1\leqslant i\leqslant n} x_i\lfloor\!\lfloor\Big(\mathop{\|}_{\substack{1\leqslant k\leqslant n\\ k\neq i}} x_k\Big)+\sum_{1\leqslant i<j\leqslant n}(x_i|x_j)\lfloor\!\lfloor\Big(\mathop{\|}_{\substack{1\leqslant k\leqslant n\\ k\neq i,k\neq j}} x_k\Big)\quad(n\geqslant 3)\qquad \text{ET}$$

$\alpha(\delta)=\varnothing$	AB1
$\alpha(\tau)=\varnothing$	AB2
$\alpha(a)=\{a\}$ (if $a\neq\delta$)	AB3
$\alpha(\tau x)=\alpha(x)$	AB4
$\alpha(ax)=\{a\}\cup\alpha(x)$ (if $a\neq\delta$)	AB5
$\alpha(x+y)=\alpha(x)\cup\alpha(y)$	AB6
$\alpha(x)=\cup_{n\geqslant 1}\alpha(\pi_n(x))$	AB7
$\alpha(\tau_I(x))=\alpha(x)-I$	AB8
$\alpha(x)\|(\alpha(y)\cap H)\subseteq H\Rightarrow\partial_H(x\,\|\,y)=\partial_H(x\,\|\,\partial_H(y))$	CA1
$\alpha(x)\|(\alpha(y)\cap I)=\varnothing\Rightarrow\tau_I(x\,\|\,y)=\tau_I(x\,\|\,\tau_I(y))$	CA2
$\alpha(x)\cap H=\varnothing\Rightarrow\partial_H(x)=x$	CA3
$\alpha(x)\cap I=\varnothing\Rightarrow\tau_I(x)=x$	CA4
$H=H_1\cup H_2\Rightarrow\partial_H(x)=\partial_{H_1}\circ\partial_{H_2}(x)$	CA5
$I=I_1\cup I_2\Rightarrow\tau_I(x)=\tau_{I_1}\circ\tau_{I_2}(x)$	CA6
$H\cap I=\varnothing\Rightarrow\tau_I\circ\partial_H(x)=\partial_H\circ\tau_I(x)$	CA7

RDP	*Every guarded and abstraction-free specification has a solution*
RSP	*Every guarded and abstraction-free specification has at most one solution*
AIP$^-$	*Every process which has an guarded abstraction-free specification is determined by its finite projections*
CFAR	*If E is a guarded recursive specification, and C a finite conservative cluster of I in E, then for each $X\in C$:* $\tau_I(X)=\tau\sum_{Y\in exits(C)}\tau_I(Y)$.

TABLE 18

It should be noted that there is redundancy in this presentation; as we already stated, AIP^- implies RSP and there are other instances where we can save some axioms or rules (for instance, the axioms CM2,5,6 turn out to be derivable from the other axioms). This would however not enhance clarity.

So we have here a medium for formal process specifications and verifications; let us note that we also admit infinite specifications. As the system is meant to have practical applications, we will only encounter *computable* specifications.

12. The graph model for ACP_τ

We will give a quick introduction to what we consider to be the 'main' model of ACP_τ. The basic building material consists of the domain of *countably branching, labeled, rooted, connected, directed multigraphs.* Such a graph, also called a process graph, consists of a possibly infinite set of nodes s with one distinguished node s_0, the root. The edges, also called transitions or steps, between the nodes are labeled with an element from the action alphabet; also δ and τ may be edge labels. We use the notation $s \rightarrow_a t$ for an a-transition from node s to node t; likewise $s \rightarrow_\tau t$ is a τ-transition and $s \rightarrow_\delta t$ is a δ-step. That the graph is connected means that every node must be accessible by finitely many steps from the root node.

Corresponding to the operations $+, \cdot, \|, \lfloor\!\lfloor, |, \partial_H, \tau_I, \pi_n, \alpha$ in our theory we define operations in this domain of process graphs. Precise definitions can be found in [1,4]; we will sketch some of them here. The sum $g+h$ of two process graphs g,h is obtained by glueing together the roots of g and h (see Figure 2(i)); there is one caveat: if a root is cyclic (i.e. lying on a cycle of transitions leading back to the root), then the initial part of the graph has to be 'unwound' first so as to make the root acyclic (see Figure 2(ii)). The product $g \cdot h$ is obtained by appending copies of h to each terminal node of g; alternatively, one may first identify all terminal nodes of g and then append one copy of h to the unique terminal node if it exists (see Figure 2 (iii)). The merge $g \| h$ is obtained as a cartesian product of both graphs, with 'diagonal' edges for communications (see Figure 2(v) for an example without communication, and Figure 2(vi) for an example with communication action $a|b$). Definitions of the auxiliary operators are somewhat more complicated and not discussed here. The encapsulation and abstraction operators are simply renamings, that replace the edge labels in H resp. in I by δ resp. τ. Definitions of the projection operators π_n and α should be clear from the axioms by which they are specified. As to the projection operators, it should be emphasized that τ-steps are 'transparent': they do not increase the depth.

OPERATIONS ON PROCESS GRAPHS

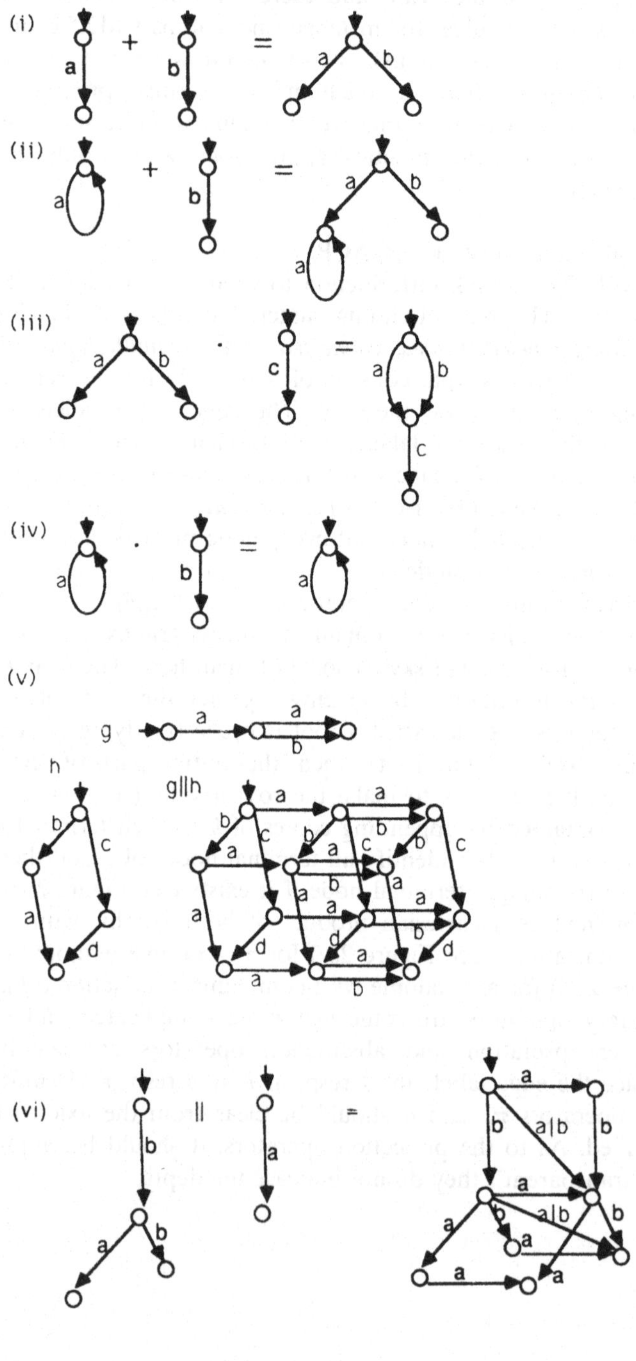

FIGURE 2

This domain of process graphs equipped with the operations just introduced, is not yet a model of ACP_τ: for instance the axiom $x+x=x$ does not hold. In order to obtain a model, we define an equivalence on the process graphs which is moreover a congruence w.r.t. the operations. This equivalence is called *bisimulation congruence* or *bisimilarity*. (The original notion is due to Park [20]; it was anticipated by Milner's observational equivalence, see [18].) In order to define this notion, let us first introduce the notation $s \Rightarrow_a t$ for nodes s, t of graph g, indicating that from node s to node t there is a finite path consisting of zero or more τ-steps and one a-step followed by zero or more τ-steps. Let us say that in this situation there is a 'generalized a-step' from s to t. Likewise with 'a' replaced by 'τ'. Next, let a *coloring* of process graph g be a surjective mapping from a set of 'colors' C to the node set of g, such that the color assigned to the root of g is different from all other colors, and furthermore, such that all end nodes are assigned the same color which is different from other colors. Now two process graphs g, h are bisimilar if there are colorings of g, h such that (1) the roots of g, h have the same color and (2) whenever *somewhere* in the two graphs a generalized a-step is possible from a node with color c to a node with color c', then *every* c-colored node admits a generalized a-step to a c'-colored node (be it in g or in h). We use the notation $g \leftrightarrows h$ to indicate that g, h are bisimilar. One can prove that $\leftrightarrows$ is a congruence and, if **G** is the original domain of countably branching process graphs:

THEOREM ([4]). *$\mathbf{G}/\leftrightarrows$ is a model of all axioms in Tables 17 and 18.*

Remarkably, this graph model does not satisfy the unrestricted Approximation Induction Principle. A counterexample is given (in a self-explaining notation) by the two graphs $g=\Sigma_{n\geq 1}a^n$ and $h=\Sigma_{n\geq 1}a^n+a^\omega$; while g and h have the same finite projections $\pi^n(g)= \pi^n(h)= a+a^2+a^3+\cdots+a^n$, they are not bisimilar due to the presence of the infinite trace of a-steps in h. It might be thought that it would be helpful to restrict the domain of process graphs to finitely branching graphs, in order to obtain a model which satisfies AIP, but there are two reasons why this is not the case: (1) the finitely branching graph domain would not be closed under the operations, in particular the communication merge (|); (2) a similar counterexample can be obtained by considering the finitely branching graphs $g'=\tau_{\{t\}}(g'')$ where g'' is the graph defined by $\{X_n= a^n+tX_{n+1} | n\geq 1\}$ and $h'=g'+a^\omega$.

REFERENCES

1. J.C.M. BAETEN (1986). *Procesalgebra,* Kluwer Programmatuurkunde, Deventer (in Dutch).
2. J.C.M. BAETEN, J.A. BERGSTRA (1988). Global renaming operators in concrete process algebra. *Information and Computation 78(3),* 205-245.
3. J.C.M. BAETEN, J.A. BERGSTRA, J.W. KLOP (1987). Conditional axioms and α/β calculus in process algebra. M. WIRSING (ed.). *Proc. IFIP Conf. on Formal Description of Programming Concepts - III,* Ebberup 1986, North-Holland, Amsterdam, 53-75.

4. J.C.M. BAETEN, J.A. BERGSTRA, J.W. KLOP (1987). On the consistency of Koomen's Fair Abstraction Rule. *Theoretical Computer Science 51 (1/2),* 129-176.
5. J.W. DE BAKKER, J.I. ZUCKER (1982). Denotational semantics of concurrency. *Proc. 14th ACM Symp. Theory of Comp.,* 153-158.
6. J.W. DE BAKKER, J.I. ZUCKER (1982). Processes and the denotational semantics of concurrency. *Information and Control 54 (1/2),* 70-120.
7. J.A. BERGSTRA, J.W. KLOP (1982). *Fixed Point Semantics in Process Algebras,* MC Report IW 206, Centre for Mathematics and Computer Science, Amsterdam.
8. J.A. BERGSTRA, J.W. KLOP (1984). Process algebra for synchronous communication. *Information and Control 60 (1/3),* 109-137.
9. J.A. BERGSTRA, J.W. KLOP (1985). Algebra of communicating processes with abstraction. *Theoretical Computer Science 37 (1),* 77-121.
10. J.A. BERGSTRA, J.W. KLOP (1986). Algebra of communicating processes. J.W. DE BAKKER, M. HAZEWINKEL, J.K. LENSTRA (eds.). *Mathematics and Computer Science,* CWI Monograph 1, North-Holland, Amsterdam, 89-138.
11. J.A. BERGSTRA, J.W. KLOP (1986). Process algebra: specification and verification in bisimulation semantics. M. HAZEWINKEL, J.K. LENSTRA, L.G.L.T. MEERTENS (eds.). *Mathematics and Computer Science II,* CWI Monograph 4, North-Holland, Amsterdam, 61-94.
12. J.A. BERGSTRA, J.W. KLOP (1986) Verification of an Alternating Bit Protocol by means of process algebra. W. BIBEL, K.P. JANTKE (eds.). *Math. Methods of Spec. and Synthesis of Software Systems '85, Math. Research 31,* Akademie-Verlag Berlin, 9-23. Also appeared as CWI Report CS-R8404, Centre for Mathematics and Computer Science, Amsterdam, 1984.
13. J.A. BERGSTRA, J.W. KLOP, E.-R. OLDEROG (1987). Failures without chaos: a new process semantics for fair abstraction. M. WIRSING (ed.). *Proc. IFIP Conf. on Formal Description of Programming Concepts - III,* Ebberup 1986, North-Holland, Amsterdam, 77-103.
14. R.J. VAN GLABBEEK (1987). Bounded nondeterminism and the approximation induction principle in process algebra. F.J. BRANDENBURG, G. VIDAL-NAQUET, M. WIRSING (eds.). *Proc. STACS 87,* LNCS 247, Springer-Verlag, 336-347.
15. C.A.R. HOARE (1984). *Notes on Communicating Sequential Processes,* International Summer School in Marktoberdorf: Control Flow and Data Flow, Munich.
16. C.A.R. HOARE (1985). *Communicating Sequential Processes,* Prentice Hall.
17. E. KRANAKIS (1986). *Approximating the Projective Model,* CWI Report CS-R8607, Centre for Mathematics and Computer Science, Amsterdam.

To appear in: *Proc. of Conf. on Math. Logic and Applications,* Druzhba, Plenum Publ. Corp., New York, 273-282.

18. R. MILNER (1980). *A Calculus of Communicating Systems,* LNCS 92, Springer-Verlag.
19. R. MILNER (1984). A complete inference system for a class of regular behaviours. *Journal of Computer and System Sciences 28 (3),* 439-466.
20. D.M.R. PARK (1981). Concurrency and automata on infinite sequences. *Proc. 5th GI Conference,* LNCS 104, Springer-Verlag.
21. F.W. VAANDRAGER (1986). *Verification of Two Communication Protocols by means of Process Algebra,* CWI Report CS-R8608, Centre for Mathematics and Computer Science, Amsterdam.

Two Simple Protocols

Frits W. Vaandrager
Centre for Mathematics and Computer Science
P.O. Box 4079, 1009 AB Amsterdam, The Netherlands

After some introductory remarks about the specification and verification of distributed systems in the framework of process algebra, simple versions of the Alternating Bit Protocol and the Positive Acknowledgement with Retransmission protocol are discussed.

1. General introduction

In the ACP formalism we can define (specify) networks of processes which cooperate in an *asynchronous* way. We can do this by looking at the communication channels in the network as processes which communicate in a *synchronous* way with the processors to which they are connected. Almost always, this synchronous communication will take place according to the *handshaking paradigm*: exactly two processes participate in every communication. When we specify communications of this type we will employ a *read/send* communication function: Let $\mathbb{D}$ be a finite set of *data* which can be communicated between processes, and let $\mathbb{P}$ be a finite set of *locations* (or *ports*) where synchronous communication can take place. The alphabet of atomic actions now consists of *read actions* $rp(d)$, *send actions* $sp(d)$ and *communication actions* $cp(d)$ for $p \in \mathbb{P}$ and $d \in \mathbb{D}$. As the only communications we have: $\gamma(rp(d), sp(d)) = cp(d)$.

A typical system that can be specified in this way in ACP is depicted in Figure 1. This graphical representation was first used by Jan Willem Klop. The corresponding process expression is then for instance:

$$\partial_H(P_1 \| P_2 \| P_3 \| P_4 \| P_5 \| C_1 \| C_2 \| C_3 \| C_4 \| C_5).$$

Let us stand still for a moment at the issue of the physical interpretation of expressions of this type and the question about the nature of the events in reality that are modelled by the read and send actions. In general we will describe with expressions P_1, P_2,... and C_1, C_2,... the behaviour of physical

Partial support received from the European Community under ESPRIT project no. 432, An Integrated Formal Approach to Industrial Software Development (METEOR).

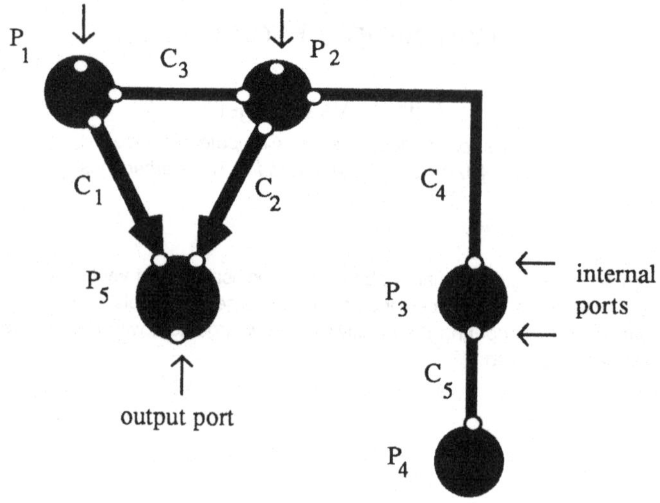

FIGURE 1

objects. P_1 and P_2 for example correspond with personal computers, P_3 and P_4 with disk drives and P_5 with a printer. C_1 up to C_5 describe cables of a network connecting all these machines together. All the components have a spatial extent. Now we associate with each port name $p \in \mathbb{P}$ a point in space on the border line between two (or more) components (see Figure 2).

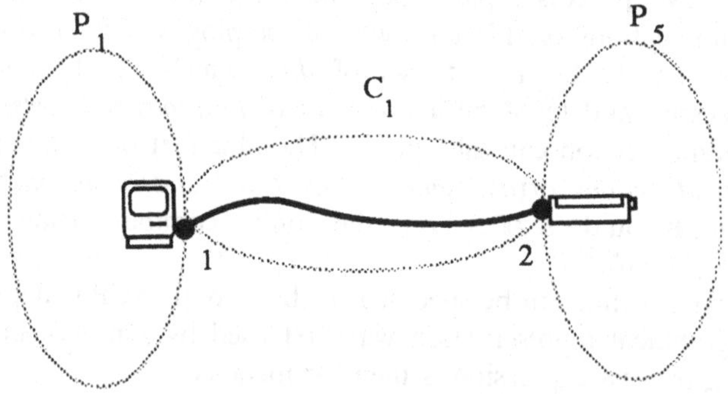

FIGURE 2

When process P_1 performs an action $s\,1(d_0)$ we relate this to the transmission of a datum d_0 by the personal computer. At the physical level this means that at the location (port 1) where cable C_1 is connected to the computer variations occur in the electric voltage during a certain amount of time. Because d_0 can have a considerable size (think of a file which is sent to the printer) the transmission can take a lot of time. The instantaneous event associated with $r\,1(d_0)$ occurs at a moment the cable 'knows' that a datum d_0 has been transmitted at port 1. Such a moment occurs when P_1 has almost finished transmission of this datum. The complementary event $s1(d_0)$ happens at the moment that the computer has made so much progress with the transmission of d_0 that the environment has enough information to 'know' that it is d_0 indeed. By defining the events in the right way we can ensure that $s1(d_0)$ and $r1(d_0)$ coincide. It is impossible that $s1(d_0)$ occurs and $r1(d_0)$ does not, or the other way around. Therefore we can consider the occurrence of $s1(d_0)$ and $r1(d_0)$ as a single event. This is precisely what we express in process algebra with the communication function and the encapsulation operator. Notice that the above interpretation of read and send actions is not in conflict with the intuition presented in [6] that the instantaneous event associated with an atomic process should be situated at the beginning of that process. Apparently a command **print**(d_0) that one can give to the computer corresponds to a process $\tau \cdot s1(d_0)$. At the moment process C_1 knows that d_0 is transmitted and the event $c1(d_0)$ occurs, the execution of processes $s1(d_0)$ and $r1(d_0)$ will not yet be finished. One possible scenario is that execution of $s1(d_0)$ finishes before the end of the execution of $r1(d_0)$.

In process theory we assume that the only thing which is interesting about a system is its external behaviour. Two systems with identical external behaviour should be identified in principle. From the point of view of process algebra there is no difference between a labourer assembling bicycle pumps, and a robot performing the same job. Unless attention is paid in the formal specification to all kind of details like fluctuations in productivity due to nocturnal excesses, the approaching weekend, depressions because of the monotony of the job, etc.

In order to realise a certain external behaviour (the *specification*), often a complex internal structure (the *implementation*) is needed. This brings us to the important issue of *abstraction*. We are interested in a technique which makes it possible to *abstract* from the internal structure of a system, so that we can derive statements about the external behaviour. Abstraction is an indispensable tool for managing the complexity of process verifications. This is because abstraction allows for a reduction of the complexity (the number of states) of subprocesses. This makes it possible to verify large processes in a *hierarchical* way. A typical verification consists of a proof that, after abstraction, an implementation *IMP* behaves like the much simpler process *SPEC* which serves as system specification:

$$ABS(IMP) = SPEC.$$

In process algebra we model abstraction by making the distinction between two types of actions, namely *external* or *observable* actions and the *internal* or *hidden* action τ, and by introducing explicit abstraction operators τ_I which transform observable actions into the hidden action (see Figure 3).

Fundamental within the ACP-formalism is the *algebraic* approach. A verification consists of a proof of a statement of the form:

$$ACP_\tau + \cdots \vdash \tau_I(IMP) = SPEC.$$

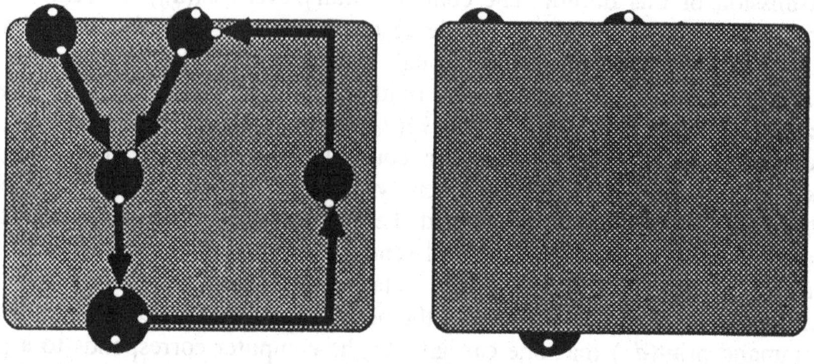

FIGURE 3

The idea is that 'users' can stay in the realm of the formal system and execute algebraic manipulations, without the need for an excursion into the semantics.

2. The Alternating Bit Protocol

The most studied communication protocol in existence is undoubtedly the Alternating Bit Protocol (ABP). Whenever somewhere in this world someone introduces a new formalism for concurrent processes, you can count on it that the practical applicability of the formalism is illustrated by means of a specification and verification of a variant of the ABP. As a first test-case for a concurrency theory the protocol is very appropriate indeed: the protocol can be described in a few words, but the formal specification and verification of it forms a non-trivial problem. However, for real practical application of a concurrency theory much more is needed. In the analysis of realistic protocols one encounters various problems of scale which cannot be observed when dealing with the ABP.

We do not want to break with the traditions concerning the ABP, and will start here with a discussion of a simple variant of the ABP in the setting of process algebra. More complex protocols are dealt with in some other contributions of this volume.

Other discussions of the Alternating Bit Protocol can be found in [2,8,10,12,15]. In the context of ACP the protocol was verified for the first time in [4]. The discussion of the ABP here is based on a streamlined version of the proof, given by the author, which can be found in [5]. Variants of the ABP are discussed in the setting of process algebra in [7,9].

2.1. Specification

The Alternating Bit Protocol can be visualised as follows:

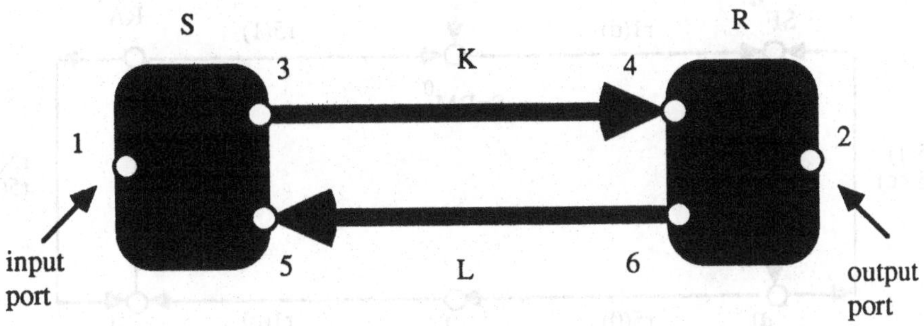

FIGURE 4

Let D be a finite set of data. Elements of D are to be transmitted by the protocol from port 1 to port 2. There are four components: a sender S, a receiver R, and two channels K and L.

2.1.1. Component S. S starts by Reading a Message (RM) at port 1. Then a *frame* consisting of the message from D and a control bit is transmitted via channel K (SF = Send Frame), until a correct acknowledgement has arrived via channel L (RA = Receive Acknowledgement). In equations we will always use the symbol d to denote elements from the set D, b denotes an element from $B = \{0,1\}$, and f finally is used for frames in $D \times B$. In Table 1 we 'declare' the recursive specification that gives the behaviour of component S. After a variable has been declared we will use it without mentioning the corresponding specification.

$$
\begin{aligned}
S &= RM^0 \\
RM^b &= \sum_{d \in D} r1(d) \cdot SF^{db} \\
SF^{db} &= s3(db) \cdot RA^{db} \\
RA^{db} &= (r5(1-b) + r5(ce)) \cdot SF^{db} + r5(b) \cdot RM^{1-b}
\end{aligned}
$$

TABLE 1. Recursive specification for component S

Graphically we can depict process S as in Figure 5. In a certain sense the figure is inaccurate: instead of a node SF^{e0} for each element e in D, there is only a single node SF^{d0}. Between each pair of nodes we draw only one edge, which however can be labelled with more than one action. Figure 5 can be considered as a 'projection' of the transition diagram belonging to S.

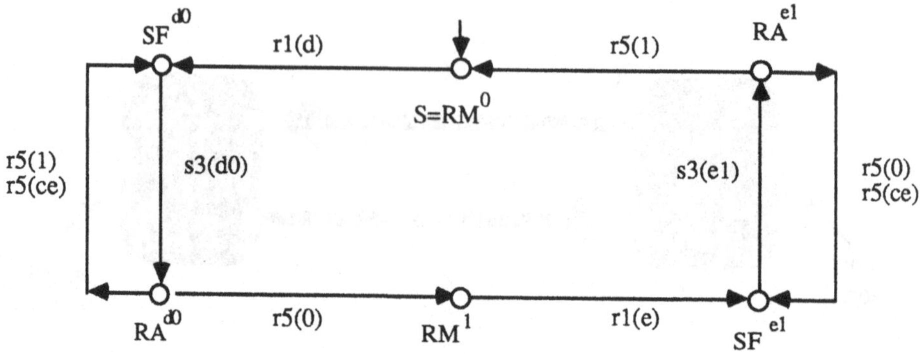

FIGURE 5

2.1.2. Component K. We assume that two things can happen if we send a frame into channel K: (1) the message is communicated correctly, (2) the message is damaged in transit. We assume that if something goes wrong with the message, the receiver hardware will detect this when it computes a *checksum* (ce = checksum error). Further the channels are supposed to be fair in the sense that they will not produce an infinite consecutive sequence of erroneous outputs. These are plausible assumptions we have to make in order to prove correctness of a protocol that is based on unreliable message passing. Data transmission channel K communicates frames in the set $D \times B$ from port 3 to 4. We give the defining equations (Table 2) and the corresponding diagram (Figure 6).

$$K = \sum_{f \in D \times B} r3(f) \cdot K^f$$

$$K^f = (\tau \cdot s4(ce) + \tau \cdot s4(f)) \cdot K$$

TABLE 2. Defining equations for channel K

The τ's in the second equation express that the choice whether or not a frame f is to be communicated correctly, is nondeterministic and cannot be influenced by one of the other components.

2.1.3. Component R. R starts by Receiving a Frame (RF) via channel K. If the control bit of the frame is correct, then the message contained in the frame is sent to port 2 (SM = Send Message). Component R Sends Acknowledgements (SA) via channel L. Figure 7 gives the transition diagram for R.

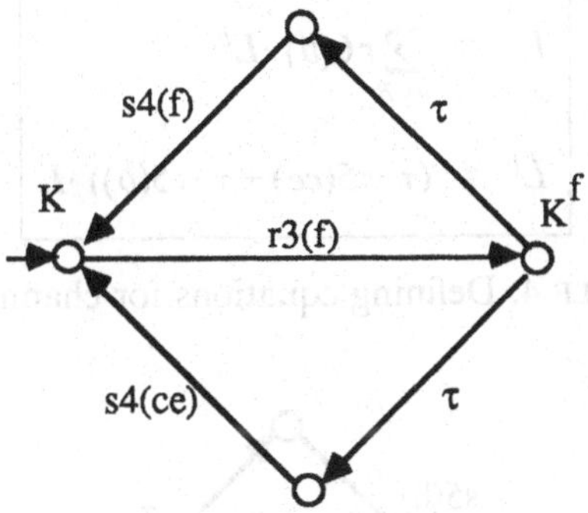

FIGURE 6

R	$= RF^0$
RF^b	$= (\sum_{d \in D} r4(d(1-b)) + r4(ce)) \cdot SA^{1-b} + \sum_{d \in D} r4(db) \cdot SM^{db}$
SA^b	$= s6(b) \cdot RF^{1-b}$
SM^{db}	$= s2(d) \cdot SA^b$

TABLE 3. Recursive specification for component R

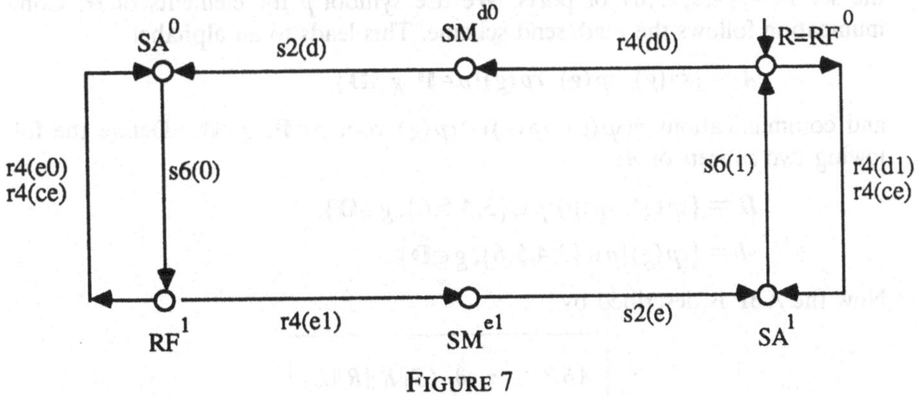

FIGURE 7

2.1.4. Component L. The task of acknowledgement transmission channel L is to communicate boolean values from R to S. The channel may yield error outputs but again we assume that this is detected, and that moreover the channel is fair. See Figure 8 for the diagram.

$$L = \sum_{b \in B} r6(b) \cdot L^b$$

$$L^b = (\tau \cdot s5(ce) + \tau \cdot s5(b)) \cdot L$$

TABLE 4. Defining equations for channel L

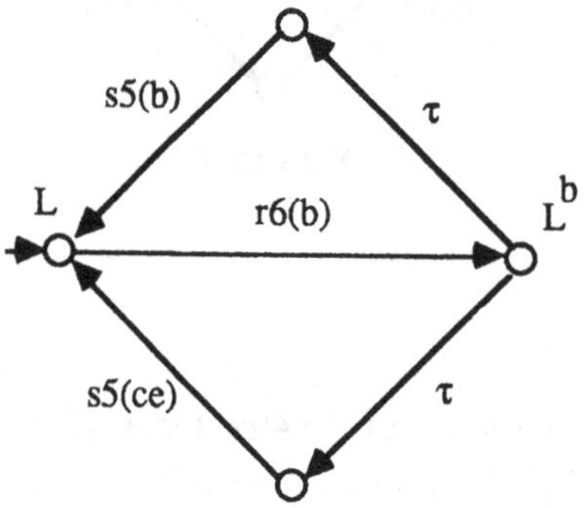

FIGURE 8

2.1.5. Sets. Define $\mathbb{D} = D \cup (D \times B) \cup B \cup \{ce\}$. $\mathbb{D}$ is the set of 'generalised' data (i.e. plain data, frames, bits, error) that occur as parameter of atomic actions. We use the notation $g \in \mathbb{D}$. The second parameter of atomic actions is the set $\mathbb{P} = \{1,2,...,6\}$ of ports. We use symbol p for elements of $\mathbb{P}$. Communication follows the read/send scheme. This leads to an alphabet

$$A = \{sp(g),\ rp(g),\ cp(g) \mid p \in \mathbb{P}, g \in \mathbb{D}\}$$

and communications $\gamma(sp(g),\ rp(g)) = cp(g)$ voor $p \in \mathbb{P}$, $g \in \mathbb{D}$. Define the following two subsets of A:

$$H = \{sp(g),\ rp(g) \mid p \in \{3,4,5,6\}, g \in \mathbb{D}\},$$

$$I = \{cp(g) \mid p \in \{3,4,5,6\}, g \in \mathbb{D}\}.$$

Now the ABP is described by

$$ABP = \tau_I \circ \partial_H(S \| K \| R \| L)$$

This is a good description in the sense that the specifications of the components S, K, R and L are guarded and consequently the specification of the ABP as a whole has a unique solution.

2.2. Verification

Verification of the ABP amounts to a proof that:

(1) the protocol will eventually send at port 2 all and only data it has read at port 1,

(2) the protocol will output data at port 2 in the same order as it has read them at port 1.

This means that, in order to verify the protocol, it is enough to prove the following theorem.

THEOREM 2.2.1. $ACP_\tau + SC + RDP + RSP + CA + CFAR \vdash$

$$ABP = \sum_{d \in D} r1(d) \cdot s2(d) \cdot ABP.$$

PROOF. Let $I' = \{cp(g) | p \in \{3,4,5\}, g \in \mathbb{D}\}$. We will use $[x]$ as a notation for $\tau_{I'} \circ \partial_H(x)$. I' is defined in such a way that we just can derive a guarded system of equations for $[x]$. Consider the following system of recursion equations in Table 5.

(0) X	$=$	X_1^0
(1) X_1^b	$=$	$\sum_{d \in D} r1(d) \cdot X_2^{db}$
(2) X_2^{db}	$=$	$\tau \cdot X_3^{db} + \tau \cdot X_4^{db}$
(3) X_3^{db}	$=$	$c6(1-b) \cdot X_2^{db}$
(4) X_4^{db}	$=$	$s2(d) \cdot X_5^{db}$
(5) X_5^{db}	$=$	$c6(b) \cdot X_6^{db}$
(6) X_6^{db}	$=$	$\tau \cdot X_5^{db} + \tau \cdot X_1^{1-b}$

TABLE 5. Recursion equations for X

The transition diagram of X is displayed in Figure 9. We claim that with the above mentioned axioms one can prove that $X = [S \| K \| R \| L]$. We prove this by showing that $[S \| K \| R \| L]$ satisfies the same recursion equations (0)-(6) as X does. In the computations below, the bold-face part denotes the part of the expression currently being 'rewritten'.

$$[S \| K \| R \| L] = [RM^0 \| K \| RF^0 \| L] \tag{0}$$

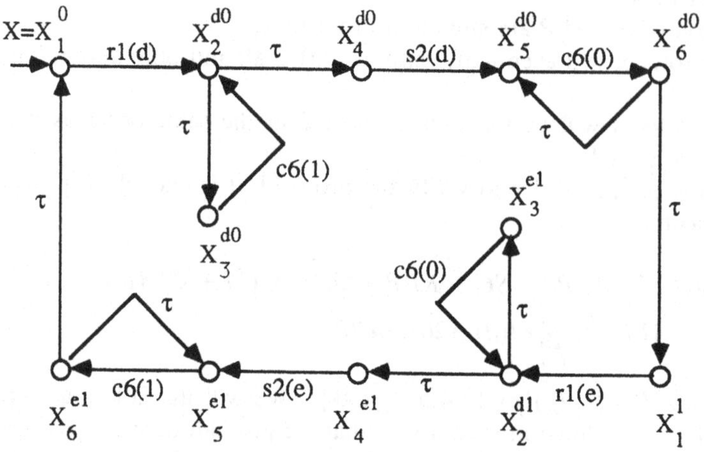

FIGURE 9

$$\begin{aligned}
[\mathbf{RM^b}\|K\|RF^b\|L] &= \sum_{d\in D} r1(d)\cdot[\mathbf{SF^{db}}\|\mathbf{K}\|RF^b\|L] && (1)\\
&= \sum_{d\in D} r1(d)\cdot\tau\cdot[RA^{db}\|K^{db}\|RF^b\|L]\\
&= \sum_{d\in D} r1(d)\cdot[RA^{db}\|K^{db}\|RF^b\|L]\\
[RA^{db}\|\mathbf{K^{db}}\|RF^b\|L] &= \tau\cdot[RA^{db}\|\mathbf{s4(ce)\cdot K}\|\mathbf{RF^b}\|L]\ + && (2)\\
&\quad +\ \tau\cdot[RA^{db}\|\mathbf{s4(db)\cdot K}\|\mathbf{RF^b}\|L]\\
&= \tau\cdot[RA^{db}\|K\|SA^{1-b}\|L]+\tau\cdot[RA^{db}\|K\|SM^{db}\|L]\\
[RA^{db}\|K\|\mathbf{SA^{1-b}}\|\mathbf{L}] &= c6(1-b)\cdot[RA^{db}\|K\|RF^b\|\mathbf{L^{1-b}}] && (3)\\
&= c6(1-b)\cdot(\tau\cdot[\mathbf{RA^{db}}\|K\|RF^b\|\mathbf{s5(ce)\cdot L}]\ +\\
&\quad +\ \tau\cdot[\mathbf{RA^{db}}\|K\|RF^b\|\mathbf{s5(1-b)\cdot L}])\\
&= c6(1-b)\cdot\tau\cdot\tau\cdot[\mathbf{SF^{db}}\|\mathbf{K}\|RF^b\|L]\\
&= c6(1-b)\cdot\tau\cdot\tau\cdot\tau\cdot[RA^{db}\|K^{db}\|RF^b\|L]\\
&= c6(1-b)\cdot[RA^{db}\|K^{db}\|RF^b\|L]\\
[RA^{db}\|K\|\mathbf{SM^{db}}\|L] &= s2(d)\cdot[RA^{db}\|K\|SA^b\|L] && (4)\\
[RA^{db}\|K\|\mathbf{SA^b}\|\mathbf{L}] &= c6(b)\cdot[RA^{db}\|K\|RF^{1-b}\|\mathbf{L^b}] && (5)\\
[RA^{db}\|K\|RF^{1-b}\|\mathbf{L^b}] &= \tau\cdot[\mathbf{RA^{db}}\|K\|RF^{1-b}\|\mathbf{s5(ce)\cdot L}]\ + && (6)\\
&\quad +\ \tau\cdot[\mathbf{RA^{db}}\|K\|RF^{1-b}\|\mathbf{s5(b)\cdot L}]\\
&= \tau\cdot[SF^{db}\|K\|RF^{1-b}\|L]+\tau\cdot[RM^{1-b}\|K\|RF^{1-b}\|L]
\end{aligned}$$

$$[\mathbf{SF^{db}} \| \mathbf{K} \| RF^{1-b} \| L] = \tau \cdot [RA^{db} \| \mathbf{K^{db}} \| RF^{1-b} \| L] \tag{7}$$
$$= \tau \cdot (\tau \cdot [RA^{db} \| \mathbf{s4(ce)} \cdot \mathbf{K} \| \mathbf{RF^{1-b}} \| L] +$$
$$+ \tau \cdot [RA^{db} \| \mathbf{s4(db)} \cdot \mathbf{K} \| \mathbf{RF^{1-b}} \| L])$$
$$= \tau \cdot [RA^{db} \| K \| SA^{b} \| L]$$

Now substitute (7) in (6) and apply RSP. Using conditional axiom CA6 we have $ABP = \tau_I([S \| K \| R \| L]) = \tau_I(X) = \tau_I(X_1^0)$. Further, an application of CFAR gives $\tau_I(X_2^{db}) = \tau \cdot \tau_I(X_4^{db})$ and $\tau_I(X_5^{db}) = \tau \cdot \tau_I(X_1^{1-b})$. Hence,

$$\tau_I(X_1^b) = \sum_{d \in D} r1(d) \cdot \tau_I(X_2^{db}) = \sum_{d \in D} r1(d) \cdot \tau_I(X_4^{db})$$
$$= \sum_{d \in D} r1(d) \cdot s2(d) \cdot \tau_I(X_5^{db}) = \sum_{d \in D} r1(d) \cdot s2(d) \cdot \tau_I(X_1^{1-b})$$

and thus

$$\tau_I(X_1^0) = \sum_{d \in D} r1(d) \cdot s2(d) \cdot \sum_{e \in D} r1(e) \cdot s2(e) \cdot \tau_I(X_1^0) \quad \text{and}$$
$$\tau_I(X_1^1) = \sum_{d \in D} r1(d) \cdot s2(d) \cdot \sum_{e \in D} r1(e) \cdot s2(e) \cdot \tau_I(X_1^1).$$

Applying RSP again yields $\tau_I(X_1^0) = \tau_I(X_1^1)$ and therefore

$$\tau_I(X_1^0) = \sum_{d \in D} r1(d) \cdot s2(d) \cdot \tau_I(X_1^0).$$

This finishes the proof of the theorem. □

REMARK. Channels K and L can contain only one datum at a time. Now one can say that this is no problem because S and R will never send a message into a channel when the previous one is still there. If S and R would do this then our process algebra modelling would be incorrect. Because they don't, there is no problem. This argument is correct for the ABP, but one should be careful in more complex situations: if one *implicitly* uses assumptions about the behaviour of a system in the specification of that system, then there is a danger that a verification shows that the system has a lot of 'wonderful' properties which in reality it has not. We give an example. Consider the situation where a process S first sends three threatening letters into channel K followed by an violent attempt to eliminate process R. Suppose K is a 1-datum-buffer. The system starts and S sends the first threatening letter into the channel. Now receiver R at the other side of the channel is very busy doing other things, and has no time to read messages from K. Only after a long, long time R looks if there is mail in K. Of course R is really shocked by the contents of the letter, and immediately tries to eliminate S. Only after this has succeeded, it reads from K again. Because S becomes dangerous only after the third message has been sent, process R will not get into trouble. The crucial point is now that this would have been different if K were a FIFO-queue.

3. THE PAR PROTOCOL (PART 1)

In this section we will describe a protocol that is very similar to the ABP, although there is a fundamental difference. The protocol, that is described in [13], is called PAR, which stands for *Positive Acknowledgement with Retransmission.* In the protocol the sender waits for an acknowledgement before a new datum is transmitted. Instead of two different acknowledgements, like in the ABP, the PAR protocol only uses one type of acknowledgement (hence the word 'Positive'). This discussion of the PAR protocol is a revised version of Sections 3 and 4 of [14].

3.1. Specification

The diagram that describes the architecture of the PAR protocol is identical to the diagram for the ABP, with as only difference that on one side of the sender a small *timer process* has been added.

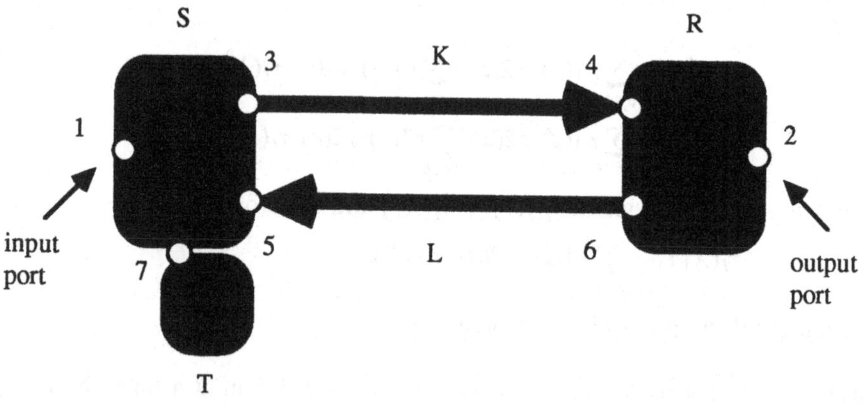

FIGURE 10

Thus, there are five components:

S: Sender
T: Timer
K: Data transmission channel
R: Receiver
L: Acknowledgement transmission channel

3.1.1. Sets. Let D be a finite set of data. Elements of D are to be transmitted by the PAR protocol from port 1 to port 2. Let $B=\{0,1\}$. Frames in $D\times B$ are transmitted by channel K. Define $\mathbb{D} = D\cup(D\times B)\cup\{ac,ce,st,to\}$ (ac = acknowledgement, ce = checksum error, st = start timer, to = time out). For the interaction with their environment, the components use ports from a set $\mathbb{P} = \{1,2,...,6,7\}$. $\mathbb{P}$ and $\mathbb{D}$ occur as parameters of atomic actions. Alphabet A and communication function γ are defined using the read/send scheme. In addition, A contains two other actions i and j which do not communicate.

3.1.2. The channels. If a message is sent into channel K or L, three things can happen:
(1) the message is communicated correctly,
(2) the message is damaged in transit,
(3) the message gets lost in the channel.

Channels K and L are described by the equations in Table 6.

$K = \sum_{f \in D \times B} r3(f) \cdot K^f$
$K^f = (i \cdot s4(f) + i \cdot s4(ce) + i) \cdot K$
$L = r6(ac) \cdot L^{ac}$
$L^{ac} = (j \cdot s5(ac) + j \cdot s5(ce) + j) \cdot L$

TABLE 6. Definition for channels K and L

The reason why we use actions i and j, instead of the τ as is done in the specification of the ABP, will become clear further on.

3.1.3. The sender. In the specification of the sender process S (Table 7) we use formal variables RH^n, SF^{dn}, ST^{dn}, WS^{dn} ($d \in D$, $n \in B$):

RH = Read a message from the Host at port 1. The host process, which is not specified here, furnishes the sender with data.
SF = Send a Frame in channel K at port 3.
ST = Start the Timer.
WS = Wait for Something to happen. Here there are three possibilities: (1) an acknowledgement frame arrives undamaged, (2) something damaged comes in, or (3) the timer goes off. If a valid acknowledgement comes in, the sender fetches the next message, and changes the control bit, otherwise a duplicate of the old frame is sent.

3.1.4. The timer. The timer process T is very simple (see Table 8). There are two states: the initial (stop-) state and the (run-) state in which the timer is running. In both states the timer can be started, but only in the running state a time out can be generated.

$$S = RH^0$$

$$RH^n = \sum_{d \in D} r1(d) \cdot SF^{dn}$$

$$SF^{dn} = s3(dn) \cdot ST^{dn}$$

$$ST^{dn} = s7(st) \cdot WS^{dn}$$

$$WS^{dn} = r5(ac) \cdot RH^{1-n} + (r5(ce) + r7(to)) \cdot SF^{dn}$$

TABLE 7. Specification of the sender process S

$$T = r7(st) \cdot T^r$$

$$T^r = r7(st) \cdot T^r + s7(to) \cdot T$$

TABLE 8. Specification of the timer process T

3.1.5. The receiver. For the specification of the receiver process R (see Table 9) we use formal variables WF^n, SA^n, SH^{dn} ($d \in D$, $n \in B$):

$WF =$ Wait for the arrival of a Frame at port 4.
$SA =$ Send an Acknowledgement at port 6.
$SH =$ Send a message to the Host at port 2. In general the host of the receiver will of course be different than the host of the sender.

$$R = WF^0$$

$$WF^n = r4(ce) \cdot WF^n + \sum_{d \in D} r4(d(1-n)) \cdot SA^n + \sum_{d \in D} r4(dn) \cdot SH^{dn}$$

$$SA^n = s6(ac) \cdot WF^n$$

$$SH^{dn} = s2(d) \cdot SA^{1-n}$$

TABLE 9. Specification of the receiver process R

When a valid frame arrives at the receiver, its control bit is checked to see if it is a duplicate. If not, it is accepted, the message contained in it is written at port 2, and an acknowledgement is generated. Duplicates and damaged frames are not written at port 2.

3.1.6. Premature time outs. We define

$$H = \{sp(g), rp(g) | p \in \{3,4,5,6,7\}, g \in \mathbb{D}\}$$

and consider the expression

$$\partial_H(S \| T \| K \| R \| L).$$

Each time after a frame is sent, the sender S starts the timer. An unpleasant property of the PAR protocol is that a premature time out can disturb the functioning of the protocol. If the sender times out too early, while the acknowledgement is still on the way, it will send a duplicate. When the previous acknowledgement finally arrives, the sender will mistakenly think that the just sent frame is the one being acknowledged and will not realise that there is potentially another acknowledgement somewhere in the channel. If the next frame sent is lost completely, but the extra acknowledgement arrives correctly, the sender will not attempt to retransmit the lost frame, and the protocol will fail.

An important observation is that in our modelling 'too early' corresponds exactly to the availability of an alternative action. Thus we can express the desired behaviour of the timer by giving the action $c7(to)$ a *lower priority* then every other atomic action. In the next section we will elaborate on this idea.

4. Priorities

The axiom system ACP_θ, introduced in [1], consists of the operators and axioms of ACP, extended with a unary *priority* operator θ, an auxiliary binary operator $\lhd$ (*unless*) and some defining axioms for these operators. We use θ to model priorities. Parameter of θ is a partial order $<$ on the atomic actions. So for $a,b,c \in A$ we have

1. $\neg(a<a)$
2. $a<b \,\&\, b<c \Rightarrow a<c.$

The constant δ can be incorporated in this ordering as a minimal element. We then have $\delta < a$ for all $a \in A$. Consider, as an example, the following partial order on atomic actions a,b and c:

$$b<a \text{ and } c<a.$$

Relative to this ordering the operator θ will forbid in a sum-context all actions that are majorated by one of the other actions in that sum-context. So we have for instance:
(i) $\theta(a+b)=a$, $\theta(a+c)=a$ but
(ii) $\theta(b+c)=b+c$.
Operator θ is axiomatized in the system ACP_θ (see Table 10).

Example. Let $b<a$ and $c<a$. Then:
(i) $\theta(a+b)=\theta(a)\lhd b+\theta(b)\lhd a = a\lhd b + b\lhd a = a+\delta = a,$
(ii) $\theta(b+c)=\theta(b)\lhd c+\theta(c)\lhd b = b\lhd c + c\lhd b = b+c,$

(iii) $\theta(b(a+c)) = \theta(b)\cdot\theta(a+c) = b\cdot(\theta(a)\lhd c + \theta(c)\lhd a) = b(a\lhd c + c\lhd a)$
$= b(a+\delta) = ba.$

ACP$_\theta$			
$x+y = y+x$	A1	$a\lhd b = a$ if $\neg(a<b)$	P1
$x+(y+z) = (x+y)+z$	A2	$a\lhd b = \delta$ if $a<b$	P2
$x+x = x$	A3	$x\lhd yz = x\lhd y$	P3
$(x+y)z = xz+yz$	A4	$x\lhd(y+z) = (x\lhd y)\lhd z$	P4
$(xy)z = x(yz)$	A5	$xy\lhd z = (x\lhd z)y$	P5
$x+\delta = x$	A6	$(x+y)\lhd z = x\lhd z+y\lhd z$	P6
$\delta x = \delta$	A7		
$a\mid b = \gamma(a,b)$	CF		
$x\Vert y = x⌊\!⌊ y+y⌊\!⌊ x+x\mid y$	CM1	$\theta(a) = a$	TH1
$a⌊\!⌊ x = ax$	CM2	$\theta(xy) = \theta(x)\cdot\theta(y)$	TH2
$ax⌊\!⌊ y = a(x\Vert y)$	CM3	$\theta(x+y) = \theta(x)\lhd y+\theta(y)\lhd x$	TH3
$(x+y)⌊\!⌊ z = x⌊\!⌊ z+y⌊\!⌊ z$	CM4		
$(ax)\mid b = (a\mid b)x$	CM5		
$a\mid(bx) = (a\mid b)x$	CM6		
$(ax)\mid(by) = (a\mid b)(x\Vert y)$	CM7		
$(x+y)\mid z = x\mid z+y\mid z$	CM8		
$x\mid(y+z) = x\mid y+x\mid z$	CM9		
$\partial_H(a) = a$ if $a\notin H$	D1		
$\partial_H(a) = \delta$ if $a\in H$	D2		
$\partial_H(x+y) = \partial_H(x)+\partial_H(y)$	D3		
$\partial_H(xy) = \partial_H(x)\cdot\partial_H(y)$	D4		

TABLE 10

In [1] the proof can be found of the following theorem:

THEOREM 4.1.
i) *For each recursion-free closed ACP_θ-term s there is a basic term t such that $ACP_\theta \vdash s = t$.*
ii) *ACP_θ is a conservative extension of ACP, i.e. for all recursion-free ACP-terms s,t we have: $ACP_\theta \vdash s=t \Rightarrow ACP \vdash s=t$.*

At present it is not altogether clear how ACP$_\theta$ and ACP$_\tau$ should be combined into ACP$_{\tau\theta}$. As a consequence of Theorem 4.1 however we can give meaning to a term like $\tau_I(s)$, where s is a recursion-free closed ACP$_\theta$-term. Expression s is related to exactly one ACP process, and ACP$_\tau$ is a conservative extension of

ACP. For infinite processes the situation is a bit more complicated. Without proof we mention that for the theory of regular process expressions (expressions that generate a finite transition diagram) we also have conservativity.

5. THE PAR PROTOCOL (PART 2)

Returning to the specification of the PAR protocol we define operator θ on the basis of the following partial ordering $<$ on A:

(1) $a < c7(st)$ for $a \in A - \{c7(st)\}$

(2) $c7(to) < a$ for $a \in A - \{c7(to)\}$.

The reason for giving action $c7(to)$ a lower priority than the other actions has already been given in Section 3.1.6. In addition we have given action $c7(st)$ a higher priority than the other actions in order to express that immediately after sending a message the timer is started. This assumption is not essential for the correctness of the protocol. The system as a whole is now described by

$$\theta \circ \partial_H(S \| T \| K \| R \| L).$$

The fact that in the scope of a priority operator no τ's are allowed explains the use of i and j actions in the specification of components K and L. We are only interested in the actions taking place at ports 1 and 2. The other actions cannot be observed.

$$I = \{cp(g) \mid p \in \{3,4,5,6,7\},\ g \in \mathbb{D}\} \cup \{i,j\}$$

The PAR protocol can now be specified by:

$$\boxed{PAR = \tau_I \circ \theta \circ \partial_H(S \| T \| K \| R \| L)}$$

For a verification of the protocol it is enough to prove the following theorem.

THEOREM 5.1. $ACP_\tau + ACP_\theta + SC + RDP + RSP + CA + CFAR \vdash$

$$PAR = \sum_{d \in D} r1(d) \cdot s2(d) \cdot PAR$$

PROOF. Let $I' = \{cp(g) \mid p \in \{4,5,7\}, g \in \mathbb{D}\} \cup \{i,j\}$. We use $[x]$ as notation for $\tau_{I'} \circ \theta \circ \partial_H(x)$. Since $I' \subseteq I$ we can apply axiom CA6:

$$PAR = \tau_I([S \| T \| K \| R \| L]).$$

In the first part of the proof we will derive a guarded system of recursion equations for the process expression $[S \| T \| K \| R \| L]$ in which only the operators $+$ and $\cdot$ occur. Thereafter, in the second part, we will abstract from the other internal actions using CFAR. Throughout the proof d ranges over D and n ranges over B. The transition diagram of $[S \| T \| K \| R \| L]$ is depicted in Figure 11.

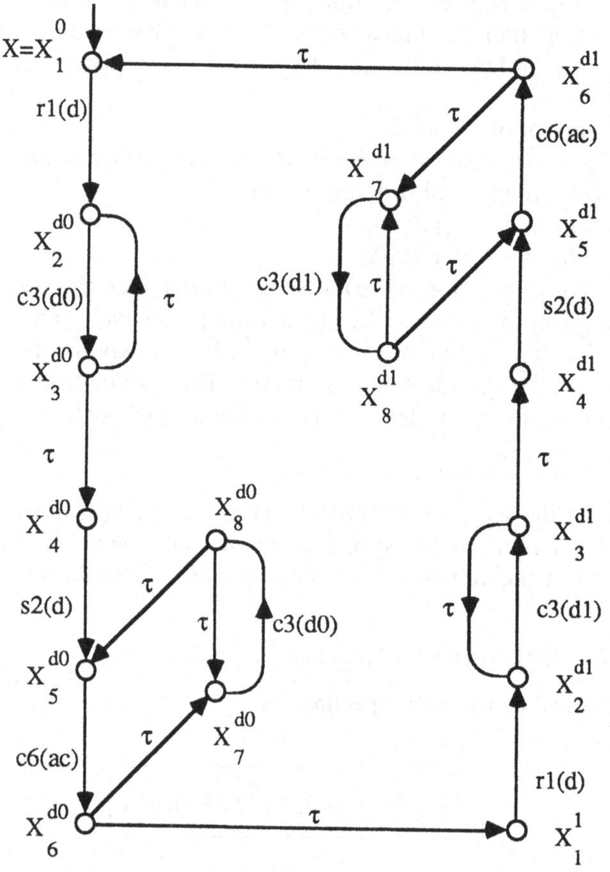

FIGURE 11

$$[S\|T\|K\|R\|L] = [RH^0\|T\|K\|WF^0\|L] \tag{0}$$

$$[RH^n\|T\|K\|WF^n\|L] = \sum_{d\in D} r1(d)\cdot[SF^{dn}\|T\|K\|WF^n\|L] \tag{1}$$

$$\begin{aligned}[SF^{dn}\|T\|K\|WF^n\|L] &= c3(dn)\cdot[ST^{dn}\|T\|K^{dn}\|WF^n\|L] \\ &= c3(dn)\cdot[WS^{dn}\|T^r\|K^{dn}\|WF^n\|L]\end{aligned} \tag{2}$$

(Here we used that the action $c7(st)$ has higher priority than the other actions.)

$$\begin{aligned}[WS^{dn}\|T^r\|K^{dn}\|WF^n\|L] = \tau_{I'}\circ\theta(&c7(to)\cdot\partial_H(SF^{dn}\|T\|K^{dn}\|WF^n\|L) + \\ &+ i\cdot\partial_H(WS^{dn}\|T^r\|s4(dn)\cdot K\|WF^n\|L) + \\ &+ i\cdot\partial_H(WS^{dn}\|T^r\|s4(ce)\cdot K\|WF^n\|L) + \\ &+ i\cdot\partial_H(WS^{dn}\|T^r\|K\|WF^n\|L)\ )\end{aligned} \tag{3}$$

(Action $c\,7(to)$ has lower priority than the other actions.)

$$= \tau \cdot [WS^{dn} \| T^r \| K \| SH^{dn} \| L] + $$
$$+ \tau \cdot [SF^{dn} \| T \| K \| WF^n \| L]$$

(If the message is damaged, the resulting state is the same as in the case in which the message gets lost. In both cases a time out event occurs.)

$$[WS^{dn} \| T^r \| K \| SH^{dn} \| L] = s\,2(d) \cdot [WS^{dn} \| T^r \| K \| SA^{1-n} \| L] \tag{4}$$

$$[WS^{dn} \| T^r \| K \| SA^{1-n} \| L] = c\,6(ac) \cdot [WS^{dn} \| T^r \| K \| WF^{1-n} \| L^{ac}] \tag{5}$$

$$[WS^{dn} \| T^r \| K \| WF^{1-n} \| L^{ac}] = \tau \cdot [RH^{1-n} \| T^r \| K \| WF^{1-n} \| L] + \tag{6}$$
$$+ \tau \cdot [SF^{dn} \| T^r \| K \| WF^{1-n} \| L] +$$
$$+ \tau \cdot [SF^{dn} \| T \| K \| WF^{1-n} \| L]$$

$$[RH^n \| T^r \| K \| WF^n \| L] = \sum_{d \in D} r\,1(d) \cdot [SF^{dn} \| T^r \| K \| WF^n \| L] \tag{1a}$$

$$[SF^{dn} \| T^r \| K \| WF^n \| L] = c\,3(dn) \cdot [WS^{dn} \| T^r \| K^{dn} \| WF^n \| L] \tag{2a}$$

$$[SF^{dn} \| T^r \| K \| WF^{1-n} \| L] = c\,3(dn) \cdot [WS^{dn} \| T^r \| K^{dn} \| WF^{1-n} \| L] \tag{7}$$

$$[SF^{dn} \| T \| K \| WF^{1-n} \| L] = c\,3(dn) \cdot [WS^{dn} \| T^r \| K^{dn} \| WF^{1-n} \| L] \tag{7a}$$

$$[WS^{dn} \| T^r \| K^{dn} \| WF^{1-n} \| L] = \tau \cdot [SF^{dn} \| T^r \| K \| WF^{1-n} \| L] + \tag{8}$$
$$+ \tau \cdot [WS^{dn} \| T^r \| K \| SA^{1-n} \| L]$$

Now observe that the processes of equations 1 and 1a, 2 and 2a, and 7 and 7a are identical. This means we have derived that X ($= [S \| T \| K \| R \| L]$) satisfies the system of recursion equations in Table 11.

(0)	$X = X_1^0$		
(1)	$X_1^n = \sum_{d \in D} r\,1(d) \cdot X_2^{dn}$	(5)	$X_5^{dn} = c\,6(ac) \cdot X_6^{dn}$
(2)	$X_2^{dn} = c\,3(dn) \cdot X_3^{dn}$	(6)	$X_6^{dn} = \tau \cdot X_1^{1-n} + \tau \cdot X_7^{dn}$
(3)	$X_3^{dn} = \tau \cdot X_2^{dn} + \tau \cdot X_4^{dn}$	(7)	$X_7^{dn} = c\,3(dn) \cdot X_8^{dn}$
(4)	$X_4^{dn} = s\,2(d) \cdot X_5^{dn}$	(8)	$X_8^{dn} = \tau \cdot X_5^{dn} + \tau \cdot X_7^{dn}$

TABLE 11. Recursion equations for X

This finishes the first part of the proof. In the second part we will abstract from the communications at ports 3 and 6. Because $PAR = \tau_I(X) = \tau_I(X_1^0)$, it is enough to show that

$$\tau_I(X_1^0) = \sum_{d \in D} r1(d) \cdot s2(d) \cdot \tau_I(X_1^0).$$

For d and n fixed, variables X_2^{dn} and X_3^{dn} form a conservative cluster from I. Hence we can apply CFAR:

$$\tau_I(X_2^{dn}) = \tau \cdot \tau_I(X_4^{dn}).$$

Variables X_5^{dn}, X_6^{dn}, X_7^{dn} and X_8^{dn} (d and n fixed) also form a conservative cluster from I. CFAR gives:

$$\tau_I(X_5^{dn}) = \tau \cdot \tau_I(X_1^{1-n}).$$

We use these two results in the following derivation:

$$\begin{aligned}
\tau_I(X_1^n) &= \sum_{d \in D} r1(d) \cdot \tau_I(X_2^{dn}) \\
&= \sum_{d \in D} r1(d) \cdot \tau \cdot \tau_I(X_4^{dn}) \\
&= \sum_{d \in D} r1(d) \cdot s2(d) \cdot \tau_I(X_5^{dn}) \\
&= \sum_{d \in D} r1(d) \cdot s2(d) \cdot \tau_I(X_1^{1-n}).
\end{aligned}$$

Substituting this equation in itself gives:

$$\tau_I(X_1^0) = \sum_{d \in D} r1(d) \cdot s2(d) \cdot \sum_{e \in D} r1(e) \cdot s2(e) \cdot \tau_I(X_1^0) \quad \text{and}$$

$$\tau_I(X_1^1) = \sum_{d \in D} r1(d) \cdot s2(d) \cdot \sum_{e \in D} r1(e) \cdot s2(e) \cdot \tau_I(X_1^1).$$

Due to the Recursive Specification Principle we have:

$$\tau_I(X_1^0) = \tau_I(X_1^1).$$

Hence

$$\tau_I(X_1^0) = \sum_{d \in D} r1(d) \cdot s2(d) \cdot \tau_I(X_1^0),$$

which is the desired result. □

Remark. For the modelling of time outs in the PAR protocol the use of the priority operator is not essential. We sketch an alternative. If a frame gets lost in one of the channels then one can say that this event in a sense *causes* a time out. This causal relationship can be expressed in process algebra by means of a communication between the channel and the pair sender/timer. For channels K and L the specifications then become as shown in Table 12.

$\overline{K} = \sum_{f \in D \times B} r3(f) \cdot \overline{K}^f$
$\overline{K}^f = (i \cdot s4(f) + i \cdot s4(ce) + i \cdot s7(to)) \cdot \overline{K}$
$\overline{L} = r6(ac) \cdot \overline{L}^{ac}$
$\overline{L}^{ac} = (j \cdot s5(ac) + j \cdot s5(ce) + j \cdot s7(to)) \cdot \overline{L}$

TABLE 12. Specification for channels $\overline{K}$ and $\overline{L}$

In a time out event *three* processes participate: the timer, the sender and a channel. This means that when dealing with time outs we have ternary communication at port 7.

$$\gamma(s7(to), s7(to)) = ss7(to) \quad \gamma(s7(to), r7(to)) = sr7(to)$$

$$\gamma(s7(to), sr7(to)) = c7(to) \quad \gamma(r7(to), ss7(to)) = c7(to)$$

This leads to a slightly bigger set of unsuccessful communications:

$$\overline{H} = H \cup \{ss7(to), sr7(to)\}.$$

The alternative specification of the PAR protocol now becomes.

$$\overline{PAR} = \tau_I \circ \partial_{\overline{H}}(S \| \overline{K} \| R \| \overline{L})$$

One can prove that $PAR = \overline{PAR}$. In [11], essentially the above idea is used to specify a simple version of the PAR protocol.

5.2. Asymmetric communication

Consider the situation where channel K contains a frame and the receiver is doing some other things and reads the datum from K only after a long time. Now one can consider it to be unnatural that during this whole period the datum keeps 'floating' in K and does not disappear. In a more realistic approach we would assume that if a datum is contained in channel K, either this is read by process R, or it gets lost if R is not willing to receive. Formally we can model this in process algebra by not encapsulating $s4(d)$ actions, but give them a lower priority than the corresponding $c4(d)$ actions. This mechanism is called *put mechanism* in [3]. One can prove that the ABP and the PAR protocol are invariant under the use of the put mechanism.

REFERENCES

1. J.C.M. BAETEN, J.A. BERGSTRA, J.W. KLOP (1986). Syntax and defining equations for an interrupt mechanism in process algebra. *Fundamenta Informaticae IX(2),* 127-168.
2. K.A. BARTLETT, R.A. SCANTLEBURY, P.T. WILKINSON (1969). A note on reliable full-duplex transmission over half-duplex links. *Communications of the ACM 12,* 260-261.
3. J.A. BERGSTRA (1985). *Put and Get, Primitives for Synchronous Unreliable Message Passing,* Logic Group Preprint Series Nr. 3, CIF, State University of Utrecht.
4. J.A. BERGSTRA, J.W. KLOP (1986). Verification of an Alternating Bit Protocol by means of process algebra. W. BIBEL, K.P. JANTKE (eds.). *Math. Methods of Spec. and Synthesis of Software Systems '85, Math. Research 31,* Akademie-Verlag, Berlin, 9-23. Also appeared as CWI Report CS-R8404, Centre for Mathematics and Computer Science, Amsterdam, 1984.
5. J.A. BERGSTRA, J.W. KLOP (1986). Process algebra: specification and verification in bisimulation semantics. M. HAZEWINKEL, J.K. LENSTRA, L.G.L.T. MEERTENS (eds.). *Mathematics and Computer Science II,* CWI Monograph 4, North-Holland, Amsterdam, 61-94.
6. R.J. VAN GLABBEEK (1987). Bounded nondeterminism and the approximation induction principle in process algebra. F.J. BRANDENBURG, G. VIDAL-NAQUET, M. WIRSING (eds.). *Proc. STACS 87,* LNCS 247, Springer-Verlag, 336-347.
7. R.J. VAN GLABBEEK, F.W. VAANDRAGER (1988). *Modular Specifications in Process Algebra - With Curious Queues,* CWI Report CS-R8821, Centre for Mathematics and Computer Science, Amsterdam. Extended abstract to appear in *Proceedings of the METEOR Workshop on Algebraic Methods: Theory, Tools and Applications,* LNCS, Springer-Verlag.
8. J.Y. HALPERN, L.D. ZUCK (1987). *A Little Knowledge Goes a Long Way: Simple Knowledge-based Derivations and Correctness Proofs for a Family of Protocols* (extended abstract), IBM Almaden Research Center.
9. C.P.J. KOYMANS, J.C. MULDER (1989). *A Modular Approach to Protocol Verification using Process Algebra.* This volume.
10. K.G. LARSEN, R. MILNER (1987). A complete protocol verification using relativized bisimulation. TH. OTTMANN (ed.). *Proceedings 14th ICALP, Karlsruhe,* LNCS 267, Springer-Verlag, 126-135.
11. J. PARROW (1985). *Fairness Properties in Process Algebra - with Applications in Communication Protocol Verification,* DoCS 85/03, Ph.D. Thesis, Department of Computer Systems, Uppsala University.
12. T. STREICHER (1987). *A Verification Method for Finite Dataflow Networks with Constraints Applied to the Verification of the Alternating Bit Protocol,* Report MIP-8706, Fakultät für Mathematik und Informatik, Universität Passau.
13. A.S. TANENBAUM (1981). *Computer Networks,* Prentice-Hall International.
14. F.W. VAANDRAGER (1986). *Verification of Two Communication Protocols by means of Process Algebra,* CWI Report CS-R8608, Centre for Mathematics and Computer Science, Amsterdam.
15. D. VERGAMINI (1986). *Verification by means of Observational Equivalence on Automata,* Report 501, INRIA, Centre Sophia-Antipolis, Valbonne Cedex.

Proving Mutual Exclusion with Process Algebra

Eric R. Nieuwland
Computer Science Department, University of Amsterdam
P.O. Box 41882, 1009 DB Amsterdam, The Netherlands

This paper provides a new method to prove mutual exclusion of concurrent processes via process algebra.

1. INTRODUCTION

1.1. Mutual exclusion

When many processes are sharing or using common computer resources it is imperative that Mutual Exclusion is taken into account. There are resources, indeed, that can be used by only one process at a time (e.g. it is not possible to have two processes printing on one printer at the same time).

The section in which a process uses such a resource is called its *critical section.* So the problem is to find a protocol that makes sure that at most one process is in its critical section for a certain resource.

In addition, it is necessary that a process will stop only in its *non-critical section* (i.e. outside its critical section and protocol section), and that all processes will have equal possibility to proceed (this is known as fair-scheduling). Under these assumptions such a protocol must have the following properties:

- ME (Mutual Exclusion) : Given a resource, no more than one process may enter its critical part in which it uses that resource.
- LC (Loosely Connected) : If a process stops within its non-critical part, the other processes must be able to proceed.
- Li (Liveness) : At least one process is able to proceed.

The reader is refered to [1] for a more complete discussion on the topic of

Partial support received from the European Community under ESPRIT project no. 432, An Integrated Approach to Industrial Software Development (METEOR).

mutual exclusion and related problems in concurrency. Consider, for example, a crossing. The properties are then as follows :

- ME : No more than one vehicle may cross at a time.
- LC : If a vehicle stops outside the crossing, the other vehicles are not affected in their movements and are able to pass the crossing.
- Li : At least one vehicle is able to move.

1.2. Mutual exclusion and process algebra

The problem of Mutual Exclusion has been studied for over two decades, which has resulted in a number of protocols. The proof of correctness of these protocols is sometimes hard and cumbersome. All kinds of tools and logics have been developed to provide these proofs. Since process algebra is designed to describe processes, it is only natural to expect that it also provides means to prove the correctness of protocols.

2. Tools in process algebra

2.1. Global variables

A global variable v, used by any number of processes, can be defined as a communicating process:

$$V_d = s(v=d)\cdot V_d + \sum_{e\in D} r(v:=e)\cdot V_e$$

where D is the set of values for v, '$v=d$' signals that v has the value d and '$v:=e$' means that the value of v becomes e. A process wishing to test the value of such a variable tries to receive it:

$$r(v=d).$$

To use its value in a calculation:

$$\sum_{d\in D} r(v=d)\cdot \text{use}(d).$$

This could also be written as '$r(v=V)\cdot\text{use}(V)$' for better readability. To assign a value to it:

$$s(v:=d).$$

2.2. Stopping a process

When n processes are running concurrently, the system is written as:

$$\mathop{\Big\|}_{1\leqslant i\leqslant n} p_i.$$

To stop one of the processes, simply delete it from the merge. The effect is that the values of global variables that are controlled by this process cannot change.

2.3. The model

The machine in which a process algebra specification is executed is depicted in Figure 1.

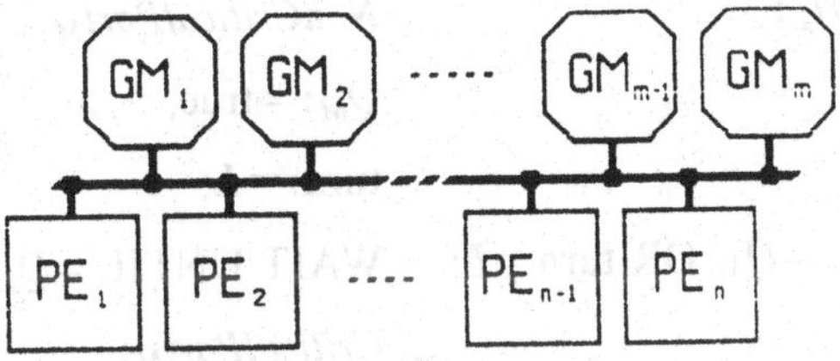

FIGURE 1. Executing machine

Here, every PE_i is an autonomous process and each GM_j one of the global variables. This machine is not only convenient for making calculations, it also exists in practice and is known as a common-bus system.

3. THE BASIC METHOD

The method of proving the properties ME, LC and Li with process algebra is founded in a simple set of descriptions that restate the definitions of these properties in terms of process algebra.

In the descriptions $\partial_H(P)$, with H the set of sends and receives used to control the global variables and P the merge of all processes and global variables, denotes any legal state of the system, while $\partial_H(P_i)$ stands for the system obtained by removing process p_i from P.

ME : For all processes p_i the following must be true: When more than one process is in its protocol section, at least one will be able to enter its critical section. And when p_i is in its critical section then $\partial_H(P_i)$ will lead to a deadlock (i.e. will equal a sequence of atomic actions followed by δ).

LC : For all processes p_i the following must be true: When p_i is in its non-critical section then $\partial_H(P_i)$ will never lead to a deadlock and process $p_k(k \neq i)$ is able to enter and leave its critical section.

Li : In any valid configuration, $\partial_H(P) \neq \delta$.

4. AN EXAMPLE: PROVING THE CORRECTNESS OF PETERSON'S PROTOCOL

Peterson's protocol [3] is one of the simplest and most elegant protocols to establish mutual exclusion of two processes:

Process L	Process M
LOOP	LOOP
NonCriticalPart$_L$;	*NonCriticalPart*$_M$;
Q_L := true;	Q_M := true;
turn := M;	turn := L;
WAIT UNTIL $\neg Q_M$ OR turn = L;	WAIT UNTIL $\neg Q_L$ OR turn = M;
CriticalPart$_L$;	*CriticalPart*$_M$;
Q_L := false;	Q_M := false;
FOREVER	FOREVER

Initial conditions: $Q_L = Q_M =$ false, turn $= L$ (or M, makes no difference)

FIGURE 2. Peterson's protocol represented as a program

To get a better notion of what happens one can use a directed graph. Each node in this graph represents a state of a process. Each arc has a label of the form [Condition $\Rightarrow$ Action], meaning that this arc may be passed only when the condition is met and that on passing the arc the action is taken. A condition *true* is always met and an action *NoAction* does nothing.

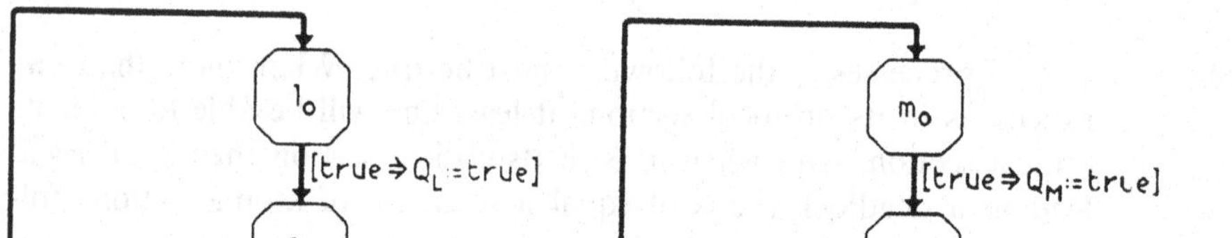

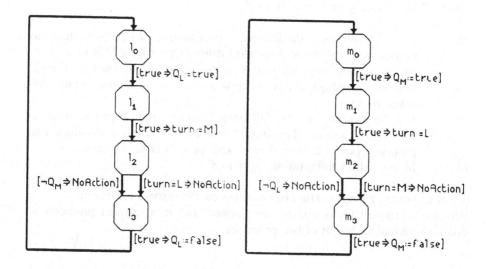

FIGURE 3. Peterson's protocol represented as a graph

Each node can now be interpreted as a variable in a set of process algebra equations. A label is translated to a test on the condition followed by an action. Obviously, a test on a condition *true* and an action *NoAction* may be discarded.

Process L:

$$
\begin{aligned}
l_0 &= s(Q_L := \text{true})l_1 \\
l_1 &= s(\text{turn} := M)l_2 \\
l_2 &= (r(\text{turn}=L)+r(Q_M=\text{false}))l_3 \\
l_3 &= s(Q_L := \text{false})l_0
\end{aligned}
$$

Process M:

$$
\begin{aligned}
m_0 &= s(Q_M := \text{true})m_1 \\
m_1 &= s(\text{turn} := L)m_2 \\
m_2 &= (r(\text{turn}=M)+r(Q_L=\text{false}))m_3 \\
m_3 &= s(Q_M := \text{false})m_0
\end{aligned}
$$

Variable Q_L:

$$
\begin{aligned}
Q_{Ltrue} &= (s(Q_L=\text{true}) \\
&\quad +r(Q_L := \text{true}))Q_{Ltrue} \\
&\quad +r(Q_L := \text{false})Q_{Lfalse} \\
Q_{Lfalse} &= (s(Q_L=\text{false}) \\
&\quad +r(Q_L := \text{false}))Q_{Lfalse} \\
&\quad +r(Q_L := \text{true})Q_{Ltrue}
\end{aligned}
$$

Variable Q_M:

$$
\begin{aligned}
Q_{Mtrue} &= (s(Q_M=\text{true}) \\
&\quad +r(Q_M := \text{true}))Q_{Mtrue} \\
&\quad +r(Q_M := \text{false})Q_{Mfalse} \\
Q_{Mfalse} &= (s(Q_M=\text{false}) \\
&\quad +r(Q_M := \text{false}))Q_{Mfalse} \\
&\quad +r(Q_M := \text{true})Q_{Mtrue}
\end{aligned}
$$

Variable turn:

$$
\begin{aligned}
\text{turn}_L &= (s(\text{turn}=L)+r(\text{turn} := L))\text{turn}_L+r(\text{turn} := M)\text{turn}_M \\
\text{turn}_M &= (s(\text{turn}=M)+r(\text{turn} := M))\text{turn}_M+r(\text{turn} := L)\text{turn}_L
\end{aligned}
$$

$$
\begin{aligned}
H = \{&s(Q_L{:=}\text{true}),\ s(Q_L{:=}\text{false}),\ s(Q_M{:=}\text{true}),\ s(Q_M{:=}\text{false}),\ s(\text{turn}{:=}M), \\
&s(\text{turn}{:=}L),\ r(Q_L{:=}\text{true}),\ r(Q_L{:=}\text{false}),\ r(Q_M{:=}\text{true}),\ r(Q_M{:=}\text{false}), \\
&r(\text{turn}{:=}M),\ r(\text{turn}{:=}L), s(Q_L=\text{true}),\ s(Q_L=\text{false}),\ s(Q_M=\text{true}), \\
&s(Q_M=\text{false}),\ s(\text{turn}=M),\ s(\text{turn}=L),\ r(Q_L=\text{true}),\ r(Q_L=\text{false}), \\
&r(Q_M=\text{true}),\ r(Q_M=\text{false}),\ r(\text{turn}=M),\ r(\text{turn}=L)\}
\end{aligned}
$$

$$P = (L \| M \| Q_L \| Q_M \| \text{turn})$$

4.1. Mutual Exclusion

The fact that process L is in state i and M is in j, will be denoted as (l_i, m_j). When both processes are in the first state of their protocol sections this gives (l_1, m_1), $Q_L = Q_M = \text{true}$ and turn is either L or M:

$$
\begin{aligned}
&\partial_H(l_1 \| m_1 \| Q_{Ltrue} \| Q_{Mtrue} \| \text{turn}_L) + \partial_H(l_1 \| m_1 \| Q_{Ltrue} \| Q_{Mtrue} \| \text{turn}_M) = \\
&\qquad = c(\text{turn}{:=}L)\partial_H(l_1 \| m_2 \| Q_{Ltrue} \| Q_{Mtrue} \| \text{turn}_L) \\
&\qquad\quad + c(\text{turn}{:=}M)\partial_H(l_2 \| m_1 \| Q_{Ltrue} \| Q_{Mtrue} \| \text{turn}_M).
\end{aligned}
$$

Since this is $(l_1, m_2)+(l_2, m_1)$, it is, by symmetry, sufficient to prove (l_1, m_2).

$$\partial_H(l_1 \| m_2 \| Q_{Ltrue} \| Q_{Mtrue} \| \text{turn}_L)$$

$$= c(\text{turn:} = M)\partial_H(l_2 \| m_2 \| Q_{Ltrue} \| Q_{Mtrue} \| \text{turn}_M) \quad (1)$$

$$= c(\text{turn:} = M)c(\text{turn} = M)\partial_H(l_2 \| m_3 \| Q_{Ltrue} \| Q_{Mtrue} \| \text{turn}_M). \quad (2)$$

This is the first requirement; (1) is (l_2, m_2), (2) is (l_2, m_3). So process M entered its critical section. Now, let M be the process held. Let L start in its Critical Part. (A situation which should not appear, but makes the proof easier.) So L is in state l_3 and M is in state m_3. Clearly $Q_L = Q_M = \text{true}$. The value of turn is either L or M. This gives:

$$\partial_H(l_3 \| Q_{Ltrue} \| Q_{Mtrue} \| \text{turn}_L) + \partial_H(l_3 \| Q_{Ltrue} \| Q_{Mtrue} \| \text{turn}_M) =$$

$$= c(Q_L := \text{false})\ \partial_H(l_0 \| Q_{Lfalse} \| Q_{Mtrue} \| \text{turn}_L) + \quad (3)$$

$$+ c(Q_L := \text{false})\ \partial_H(l_0 \| Q_{Lfalse} \| Q_{Mtrue} \| \text{turn}_M)$$

$$= c(Q_L := \text{false})\ c(Q_L := \text{true})\ \partial_H(l_1 \| Q_{Ltrue} \| Q_{Mtrue} \| \text{turn}_L)$$

$$+ c(Q_L := \text{false})\ c(Q_L := \text{true})\ \partial_H(l_1 \| Q_{Ltrue} \| Q_{Mtrue} \| \text{turn}_M) \quad (4)$$

$$= c(Q_L := \text{false})\ c(Q_L := \text{true})\ c(\text{turn:} = M)\ \partial_H(l_2 \| Q_{Ltrue} \| Q_{Mtrue} \| \text{turn}_M) +$$

$$+ c(Q_L := \text{false})c(Q_L := \text{true})c(\text{turn:} = M)\ \partial_H(l_2 \| Q_{Ltrue} \| Q_{Mtrue} \| \text{turn}_M)$$

$$= c(Q_L := \text{false})\ c(Q_L := \text{true})\ c(\text{turn:} = M)\ \partial_H(l_2 \| Q_{Ltrue} \| Q_{Mtrue} \| \text{turn}_M) \quad (5)$$

$$= c(Q_L := \text{false})\ c(Q_L := \text{true})\ c(\text{turn:} = M)\delta.$$

Since (3), (4) and (5) are the situations in which L is at l_0, l_1 and l_2 respectively, it is shown that, no matter where L starts, a deadlock occurs and thus - because of symmetry - ME is guaranteed.

4.2. Loosely Connected

This is almost the same as ME except that the process that is held is in its Non-Critical Part. So this problem is tackled in a similar way. M will be held in m_0 and L will be in l_0. So $Q_L = Q_M = \text{false}$. The value of turn is either L or M.

$$\partial_H(l_0 \| Q_{Lfalse} \| Q_{Mfalse} \| \text{turn}_L) + \partial_H(l_0 \| Q_{Lfalse} \| Q_{Mfalse} \| \text{turn}_M) = \quad (6)$$

$$= c(Q_L := \text{true})\ \partial_H(l_1 \| Q_{Ltrue} \| Q_{Mfalse} \| \text{turn}_L) +$$

$$+ c(Q_L := \text{true})\ \partial_H(l_1 \| Q_{Ltrue} \| Q_{Mfalse} \| \text{turn}_M)$$

$$= c(Q_L := \text{true})\ c(\text{turn:} = M)\ \partial_H(l_2 \| Q_{Ltrue} \| Q_{Mfalse} \| \text{turn}_M)$$

$$= c(Q_L := \text{true})\ c(\text{turn:} = M)\ c(Q_M = \text{false})\ \partial_H(l_3 \| Q_{Ltrue} \| Q_{Mfalse} \| \text{turn}_M)$$

$$= c(Q_L := \text{true})\ c(\text{turn:} = M)\ c(Q_M = \text{false})\ c(Q_L := \text{false})$$

$$\partial_H(l_0 \| Q_{Lfalse} \| Q_{Mfalse} \| \text{turn}_M) \quad (7)$$

This last term (7) is one of the summands in (6). This proves that L can always continue when M is held in its Non-Critical Part. So, by symmetry again, LC is guaranteed.

4.3. Liveness

To prove Li one has to consider all possible combinations of the states of L and M. A list of the possibilities:

$$\begin{array}{llll} (l_0, m_0) & (l_0, m_1) & (l_0, m_2) & (l_0, m_3) \\ (l_1, m_0) & (l_1, m_1) & (l_1, m_2) & (l_1, m_3) \\ (l_2, m_0) & (l_2, m_1) & (l_2, m_2) & (l_2, m_3) \\ (l_3, m_0) & (l_3, m_1) & (l_3, m_2) & (l_3, m_3) \end{array}$$

From ME it is known that (l_0, m_3), (l_1, m_1), (l_1, m_2), (l_2, m_2), (l_1, m_3), (l_2, m_3) and (l_3, m_3) have a successor. The same is known from LC for (l_0, m_0), (l_1, m_0), (l_2, m_0) and (l_3, m_0). Because of symmetry all configurations have a successor. So Li is guaranteed.

5. Conclusions

This paper provides a simple method based on process algebra to verify the desired features of a Mutual Exclusion protocol. The method is truly easy to apply. Also important is that process algebra provides a tool to verify the cooperation of hardware components (assuming that these components operate correct). This was the key idea that lead to this paper: modelling a (part of a) global memory as a process. It should be noted that in this paper ACP is used to prove properties. The standard process algebra techniques use abstraction from ACP_τ [2] to prove the correctness of external behaviour of a process. The properties considered here result from the cooperation of the processes involved, so abstraction was not used, as cooperation is internal to the processes.

Acknowledgements

I would like to thank Jos Baeten; he taught me process algebra and encouraged me to write this paper. Evangelos Kranakis should also be mentioned here; various discussions with him inspired me to try to apply process algebra to the problem of Mutual Exclusion. Maarten Heijblok and Gert Veltink were in charge of moral support.

References

1. M. Ben-Ari (1982). *Principles of Concurrent Programming,* Prentice Hall.
2. J.A. Bergstra, J.W. Klop (1984). Process algebra for synchronous communication. *Information and Control 60 (1/3),* 109-137.
3. G.L. Peterson (1981). Myths about the Mutual Exclusion Problem. *Information Processing Letters 12(3),* 115-116.

Process Algebra as a Tool for the Specification and Verification of CIM-architectures

S. Mauw
Programming Research Group, University of Amsterdam
P.O. Box 41882, 1009 DB Amsterdam, The Netherlands

Flexibility of a manufacturing system implies that it must be possible to reorganize the configuration of the system's components efficiently and correctly. To avoid costly redesign, we have the need for a formal description technique for specifying the (co)operation of the components. Process algebra - a theory for concurrency - will be shown to be expressive enough to specify, and even verify, the correct functioning of such a system. This will be demonstrated by formally specifying and verifying two workcells, which can be viewed as units of a small number of cooperating machines.

1. Introduction

One can speak of *Computer Integrated Manufacturing* (CIM) if the computer is used in all phases of the production of some industrial product. In this paper we will focus on the design of the product-flow and the information-flow, which occurs when products are actually produced. Topics like product-development, marketing and management are beyond the scope of this paper. The technique used in this paper is based on a theory for concurrency, called *process algebra* (see [4] or [5]). It can be used to describe the total phase of manufacturing, from the ordering of raw materials up to the shipping of the products which are made from this materials. During this process many machines are used, which can operate independently, but often depend on the correct operation of each other. Providing a correct functioning of the total of all machines, computers and transport-services is not a trivial exercise. Before actually building such a system (a *CIM-architecture*) there must be some design. Such a specification, when validated, describes a properly functioning system. The current trend towards *Flexible Manufacturing Systems* (FMS) introduces the need for a tool, able to validate a new design of a plant, before implementing it. The possibilities to use methods developed in process algebra for *specification* and *verification* of concurrent systems are described in this paper.

From a high level of view, a plant can be seen as constructed from several

Partial support received from the European Community under ESPRIT project no. 432, An Integrated Formal Approach to Industrial Software Development (METEOR).

concurrently operating *workcells* (W1-W5 in Figure 1). Every workcell is responsible for some well-defined part of the manufacturing process, e.g. filling and capping a number of milk bottles. The various workcells are connected to each other via some transport-service, which manages input and output of goods for the workcells (the *logistics*). Of course some supervisor (control) must keep track of the (co)operation of all workcells. This control has connections to all other components of the plant, along which commands and status-reports are transmitted. The components labeled *supply* and *shipping* are used to store raw materials and processed goods.

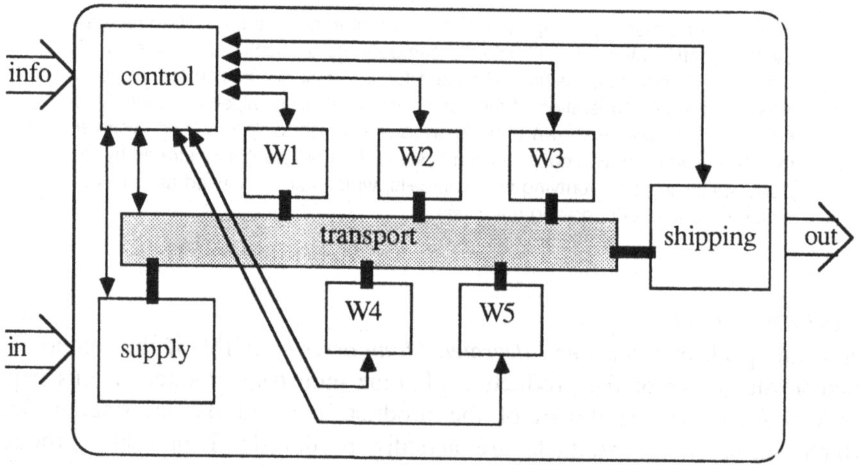

FIGURE 1. A sample architecture of a plant

Seen from a lower level, each workcell is constructed from a number of basic components which can perform one function, e.g. drilling a hole or assembling two parts. For controlling the communication with the outside and to instruct the various components of the workcell, each workcell has a *workcell-controller*. Also some simple transport-system must be present to transport the products within the workcell (see Figure 2).

The description of the components of some workcell can be given using process algebra. When abstracting from the internal actions of that workcell, it is possible to determine its external behaviour. At the high level view on the flow of products, we are only interested in the products which enter the workcell and the products leaving it. Also at the high level view on the flow of information, we only look at the commands we give a workcell to produce or process a number of products and the status-reports sent back.

The simple two level view on a manufacturing process expressed above, can be refined into a multi layered model, as is done in e.g. [7].

As an illustration of the technique we specify and verify two workcells in the theory ACP_τ (see [5]). The first one is a very simple one, able to produce and process one kind of product. The second one is more involved. It has the possibility to process some input product either correctly or faultily. Part of the workcell is a quality-check tool, which decides upon rejecting the product or not.

One should notice that in process algebra no real-time aspects are captured. So the important notions of *efficiency* (maximal productivity of the machines) and *tuning* (synchronization of the speed of the machines) cannot be modeled.

NOTE. This paper is partially based on discussions with F. Biemans, and inspired by his article [8], who used the specification language LOTOS (see [9]) to describe CIM-architectures. Other applications of theories for concurrency to CIM can be found in [10] and [11].

2. A SIMPLE WORKCELL

2.1. Specification

2.1.1. General description. In this section a simple workcell will be specified and verified, which consists of four components (see Figure 2). This workcell is identical to the one described in Biemans and Blonk [8]. Workstation A (*WA*) produces a product (product1) and offers this to the Transport service (*T*). Then the product is transported to Workstation B (*WB*), which processes the product and outputs it to the environment. The Workcell Controller (*WC*) receives a command from the environment to produce a number of products, then controls the operating of the other components and reports a ready-status back to the environment. So the total of the four components can be viewed as one workcell, producing and processing a number of products. The aim is to specify the components in such a way that the workcell behaves as desired.

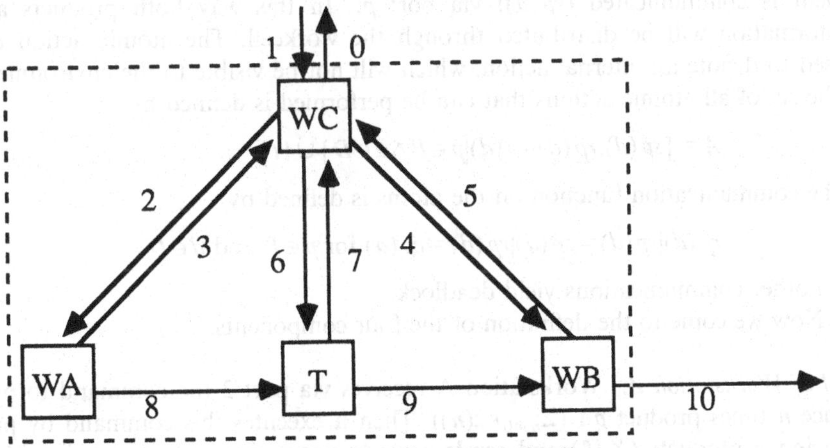

FIGURE 2. A simple workcell

2.1.2. Definitions. The four components are connected by 11 ports. Some ports are used to transmit data (the ports 0 through 7), while others are used to exchange products (the ports 8 through 10). Three ports are connected to the environment (the ports 0, 1 and 10). The set P of Ports is defined by

$$P = \{0, 1, ..., 10\}.$$

The set *PROD* contains all products that are produced and processed within the workstation (or the complete factory). It contains the products product1 ($p1$) and the processed product1 ($proc(p1)$), but could contain other products as well.

$$PROD \supseteq \{p1, proc(p1)\}$$

Different kinds of data have to be transmitted. Via the ports 1, 2 and 4 a non-negative integer (n) can be sent to indicate that the receiver has to produce (or process) n products. We assume that this number has some upper bound N, which determines the maximum number of products the workcell can deal with in one drive. One can consider this number as a parameter of the specification. A ready message (r) is sent back over the ports 0, 3 and 5 to indicate that the component has fulfilled its task. Over port 6 the Workcell Controller can send a Transport Command (tc) to the Transport service, indicating that one product has to be transported from WA to WB. If this is done, an arrival-message (ar) is sent back via port 7. The ports 8 and 9 are used to transmit product1 ($p1$) and port 10 is used to transmit the processed product1 ($proc(p1)$). So the set of items that can be transmitted (D) is defined as

$$D = \{n \mid 0 \leqslant n \leqslant N\} \cup \{r, tc, ar\} \cup PROD.$$

A component can offer some element d of D at some port p by executing a send action ($sp(d)$). If simultaneously another component is able to execute a read action ($rp(d)$) at the same port and with the same element of D, this element is communicated ($cp(d)$) via port p. In this way both products and information will be distributed through the workcell. The atomic action t is used to denote an internal action, which will not be visible to the environment. The set of all atomic actions that can be performed is defined by

$$A = \{sp(d), rp(d), cp(d) \mid p \in P \wedge d \in D\} \cup \{t\}.$$

The communication function on the atoms is defined by

$$rp(d) | sp(d) = sp(d) | rp(d) = cp(d) \text{ for } p \in P \text{ and } d \in D.$$

All other communications yield deadlock.

Now we come to the definition of the four components.

2.1.3. Workstation A. Workstation A receives via port 2 the command to produce n times product $p1$ ($\Sigma_{n \geqslant 0} r2(n)$). Then it executes this command by producing n products (XA^n) and sends a ready-status message at port 3 ($s3(r)$). Then WA starts all over. If WA was commanded to produce zero products, XA^0 just ends after doing some internal action t. If a positive number of products has to be produced (XA^{n+1}), this is done by producing one product, followed by the production of n products (XA^n).

$$WA = \sum_{n \geq 0} (r2(n) \cdot XA^n \cdot s3(r) \cdot WA)$$

$$XA^0 = t$$

$$XA^{n+1} = s8(p1) \cdot XA^n$$

2.1.4. Workstation B. Workstation B has almost the same definition as Workstation A. It accepts the command to process n products via port 4 ($\Sigma_{n \geq 0} r4(n)$), processes n products (XB^n), sends a ready-status message ($s5(r)$) and starts all over. The processing of n products is achieved by repeatedly receiving an arbitrary product p at port 9 ($\Sigma_{p \in PROD} r9(p)$) and sending the processed version of this product to port 10 ($s10(proc(p))$).

$$WB = \sum_{n \geq 0} (r4(n) \cdot XB^n \cdot s5(r) \cdot WB)$$

$$XB^0 = t$$

$$XB^{n+1} = \sum_{p \in PROD} (r9(p) \cdot s10(proc(p)) \cdot XB^n)$$

2.1.5. Transport service. The Transport service (T) can be seen as a FIFO-queue. It is indexed with its contents. Adding an element p to the queue with contents σ, yields the queue with as its contents the concatenation $p * \sigma$. The empty queue is denoted by λ. The transport system either has an empty queue, or contains elements. If the queue is empty, T can receive a transport-command via port 6 ($r6(tc)$) and then it receives some product via port 8 ($\Sigma_{p \in PROD} r8(p)$). Next the transport service behaves as the transport service with one element in its queue (T^p). It is also possible to receive the product first and then receive the transport-command. If the queue was not empty, the Transport service has both options as mentioned for the empty queue, but it also has the option to send an element out of the queue at port 9 ($s9(q)$). Then the arrival of this element is reported to the Workcell Controller ($s7(ar)$) and the element is deleted from the queue.

$$T^{\lambda} = r6(tc) \cdot \sum_{p \in PROD} (r8(p) \cdot T^p) + \sum_{p \in PROD} (r8(p) \cdot r6(tc) \cdot T^p)$$

$$T^{\sigma * q} = r6(tc) \cdot \sum_{p \in PROD} (r8(p) \cdot T^{p * \sigma * q}) +$$

$$+ \sum_{p \in PROD} (r8(p) \cdot r6(tc) \cdot T^{p * \sigma * q}) + s9(q) \cdot s7(ar) \cdot T^{\sigma}$$

2.1.6. Workcell Controller. The Workcell Controller (WC) controls the communication with the environment and the interaction of the other components. It receives via port 1 the command to produce and process n products ($\Sigma_{n\geq 0} r1(n)$). Then it commands Workstation B to process n products ($s4(n)$) and goes into state D^n were n times product1 is produced and transported. Then finally it receives a ready-status message from WB via port 5 ($r5(r)$) and sends *ready* to the environment ($s0(r)$), returning to its initial state. The production and transport of n products is done in D^n. It repeatedly commands via port 2 Workstation A to produce one single product ($s2(1)$). If this is done a ready message is received at port 3 ($r3(r)$) and a transport command is sent at port 6 ($s6(tc)$). If the product has arrived at Workstation B, an arrival message is received at port 7 ($r7(ar)$).

$$WC = \sum_{n\geq 0} (r1(n)\cdot s4(n)\cdot D^n \cdot r5(r)\cdot s0(r)\cdot WC)$$

$$D^0 = t$$

$$D^{n+1} = s2(1)\cdot r3(r)\cdot s6(tc)\cdot r7(ar)\cdot D^n$$

2.1.7. The workcell. The concurrent operation of these four components can be considered as the specification of the whole workcell:

$$WC \| T^{\lambda} \| WA \| WB.$$

Notice that the Transport service has to start with an empty queue.

Of course all unsuccessful communications must be encapsulated, so define the encapsulation set H to contain all internal send and receive actions:

$$H = \{rp(d),\ sp(d) | 2\leq p\leq 9 \wedge d\in D\}.$$

Furthermore we are only interested in the external behaviour of the system, so define

$$I = \{cp(d) | 2\leq p\leq 9 \wedge d\in D\} \cup \{t\}.$$

Now the complete definition of the Workcell (W) is

$$\boxed{W = \tau_I \partial_H (WC \| T^{\lambda} \| WA \| WB)}$$

SPECIFICATION 2.1

2.2. Correctness

When designing the workcell, we had in mind some idea about its external behaviour. It receives a command at port 1, which indicates the number of products that has to be produced, then these products are produced and offered at port 10 and finally a ready message is offered at port 0 and we return to the starting state. This intended behaviour can easily be specified:

$$V = \sum_{n \geq 0}(r1(n) \cdot E^n \cdot V)$$

$$E^0 = s0(r)$$

$$E^{n+1} = s10(proc(p1)) \cdot E^n$$

SPECIFICATION 2.2

Now, using RDP, let v and w be solutions of the two given specifications, 2.1 and 2.2. A proof that the processes v and w are equal can be seen as a verification that the specification of W is correct with respect to its intended external behaviour.

THEOREM 2.3. *The specification of the workcell is correct.*

$$ACP_\tau + RDP + RSP + ET \vdash v = w$$

PROOF. The proof consists of a series of successive expansions. All atoms that do not communicate yield deadlock, because they are encapsulated. The atoms that do communicate are underlined. All actions that are not abstracted from are boldfaced.

$$\begin{aligned}
W &= \tau_I \partial_H(WC \| T^\lambda \| WA \| WB) \\
&= \tau_I \partial_H((\sum r1(n) \cdot \underline{s4(n)} \cdot D^n \cdot r5(r) \cdot s0(r) \cdot WC) \| \\
&\qquad (r6(tc) \cdot \sum(r8(p) \cdot T^p) + \sum(r8(p) \cdot r6(tc) \cdot T^p)) \| \\
&\qquad (\sum r2(n) \cdot XA^n \cdot s3(r) \cdot WA) \| \\
&\qquad (\sum \underline{r4(n)} \cdot XB^n \cdot s5(r) \cdot WB)) \\
&= \sum \mathbf{r1(n)} \cdot \tau_I \partial_H((\underline{s4(n)} \cdot D^n \cdot r5(r) \cdot s0(r) \cdot WC) \| \\
&\qquad (r6(tc) \cdot \sum(r8(p) \cdot T^p) + \sum(r8(p) \cdot r6(tc) \cdot T^p)) \| \\
&\qquad (\sum r2(n) \cdot XA^n \cdot s3(r) \cdot WA) \| \\
&\qquad (\sum \underline{r4(n)} \cdot XB^n \cdot s5(r) \cdot WB)) \\
&= \sum \mathbf{r1(n)} \cdot \tau_I(c4(n) \cdot \partial_H((D^n \cdot r5(r) \cdot s0(r) \cdot WC) \| \\
&\qquad (r6(tc) \cdot \sum(r8(p) \cdot T^p) + \sum(r8(p) \cdot r6(tc) \cdot T^p)) \| \\
&\qquad (\sum r2(n) \cdot XA^n \cdot s3(r) \cdot WA) \| \\
&\qquad (XB^n \cdot s5(r) \cdot WB)))
\end{aligned}$$

Now let

$$
\begin{aligned}
K^n \;=\; & \tau_I \partial_H((D^n \cdot r5(r) \cdot s0(r) \cdot WC) \| \\
& \quad (r6(tc) \cdot \sum(r8(p) \cdot T^p) + \sum(r8(p) \cdot r6(tc) \cdot T^p)) \| \\
& \quad (\sum r2(n) \cdot XA^n \cdot s3(r) \cdot WA) \| \\
& \quad (XB^n \cdot s5(r) \cdot WB)), \text{ then}
\end{aligned}
$$

$$
\begin{aligned}
K^0 = & \tau_I \partial_H((t \cdot r5(r) \cdot s0(r) \cdot WC) \| \\
& \quad (r6(tc) \cdot \sum(r8(p) \cdot T^p) + \sum(r8(p) \cdot r6(tc) \cdot T^p)) \| \\
& \quad (\sum r2(n) \cdot XA^n \cdot s3(r) \cdot WA) \| \\
& \quad (t \cdot s5(r) \cdot WB)) \\
= \; & \tau \cdot \tau_I \partial_H((s0(r) \cdot WC) \| \\
& \quad (r6(tc) \cdot \sum(r8(p) \cdot T^p) + \sum(r8(p) \cdot r6(tc) \cdot T^p)) \| \\
& \quad (\sum r2(n) \cdot XA^n \cdot s3(r) \cdot WA) \| \\
& \quad (WB)) \\
= \; & \tau \cdot \mathbf{s0(r)} \cdot W
\end{aligned}
$$

$$
\begin{aligned}
K^{n+1} \;=\; & \tau_I \partial_H((s2(1) \cdot r3(r) \cdot s6(tc) \cdot r7(ar) \cdot D^n \cdot r5(r) \cdot s0(r) \cdot WC) \| \\
& \quad (r6(tc) \cdot \sum(r8(p) \cdot T^p) + \sum(r8(p) \cdot r6(tc) \cdot T^p)) \| \\
& \quad (\sum r2(n) \cdot XA^{n+1} \cdot s3(r) \cdot WA) \| \\
& \quad (\sum r9(p) \cdot s10(proc(p)) \cdot XB^n \cdot s5(r) \cdot WB)) \\
= \; & \tau_I(c2(1) \cdot \partial_H((r3(r) \cdot s6(tc) \cdot r7(ar) \cdot D^n \cdot r5(r) \cdot s0(r) \cdot WC) \| \\
& \quad (r6(tc) \cdot \sum(r8(p) \cdot T^p) + \sum(r8(p) \cdot r6(tc) \cdot T^p)) \| \\
& \quad (s8(p1) \cdot XA^0 \cdot s3(r) \cdot WA) \| \\
& \quad (\sum r9(p) \cdot s10(proc(p)) \cdot XB^n \cdot s5(r) \cdot WB))) \\
= \; & \tau \cdot \tau_I(c8(p1) \cdot \partial_H((r3(r) \cdot s6(tc) \cdot r7(ar) \cdot D^n \cdot r5(r) \cdot s0(r) \cdot WC) \| \\
& \quad (r6(tc) \cdot T^{p1}) \| \\
& \quad (t \cdot s3(r) \cdot WA) \| \\
& \quad (\sum r9(p) \cdot s10(proc(p)) \cdot XB^n \cdot s5(r) \cdot WB))) \\
= \; & \tau \cdot \tau_I(c3(r) \cdot \partial_H((s6(tc) \cdot r7(ar) \cdot D^n \cdot r5(r) \cdot s0(r) \cdot WC) \| \\
& \quad (r6(tc) \cdot T^{p1}) \| \\
& \quad (WA) \| \\
& \quad (\sum r9(p) \cdot s10(proc(p)) \cdot XB^n \cdot s5(r) \cdot WB)))
\end{aligned}
$$

$$
\begin{aligned}
(**) &= \tau\cdot\tau_I(c\,6(tc)\cdot\partial_H((r\,7(ar)\cdot D^n\cdot r\,5(r)\cdot s\,0(r)\cdot WC)\|\\
&\qquad (r\,6(tc)\cdot\textstyle\sum(r\,8(p)\cdot T^{p*p\,1})+\sum(r\,8(p)\cdot r\,6(tc)\cdot T^{p*p\,1})+s\,9(p\,1)\cdot s\,7(ar)\cdot T^{\lambda})\|\\
&\qquad (WA)\|\\
&\qquad (\textstyle\sum r\,9(p)\cdot s\,10(proc\,(p))\cdot XB^n\cdot s\,5(r)\cdot WB)))\\
&= \tau\cdot\tau_I(c\,9(p\,1)\cdot\partial_H((r\,7(ar)\cdot D^n\cdot r\,5(r)\cdot s\,0(r)\cdot WC)\|\\
&\qquad (s\,7(ar)\cdot T^{\lambda})\|\\
&\qquad (WA)\|\\
&\qquad (s\,10(proc\,(p\,1))\cdot XB^n\cdot s\,5(r)\cdot WB)))\\
&= \tau((\tau_I(c\,7(ar)\cdot\partial_H((D^n\cdot r\,5(r)\cdot s\,0(r)\cdot WC)\|\\
&\qquad (T^{\lambda})\|\\
&\qquad (WA)\|\\
&\qquad (s\,10(proc\,(p\,1))\cdot XB^n\cdot s\,5(r)\cdot WB)))+\\
&\qquad +\mathbf{s10(proc(p1))}\cdot K^n)
\end{aligned}
$$

Now let

$$
\begin{aligned}
L^n &= \tau_I\partial_H((D^n\cdot r\,5(r)\cdot s\,0(r)\cdot WC)\|\\
&\qquad (T^{\lambda})\|\\
&\qquad (WA)\|\\
&\qquad (s\,10(proc\,(p\,1))\cdot XB^n\cdot s\,5(r)\cdot WB)), \text{ then}\\
L^0 &= \tau_I\partial_H((t\cdot r\,5(r)\cdot s\,0(r)\cdot WC)\|\\
&\qquad (T^{\lambda})\|\\
&\qquad (WA)\|\\
&\qquad (s\,10(proc\,(p\,1))\cdot t\cdot s\,5(r)\cdot WB))\\
&= \mathbf{s10(proc(p1))}\cdot\tau_I\partial_H((t\cdot r\,5(r)\cdot s\,0(r)\cdot WC)\|\\
&\qquad (T^{\lambda})\|\\
&\qquad (WA)\|\\
&\qquad (\tau\cdot s\,5(r)\cdot WB))+\\
&\quad \tau\cdot\mathbf{s10(proc(p1))}\cdot\tau_I\partial_H((r\,5(r)\cdot s\,0(r)\cdot WC)\|\\
&\qquad (T^{\lambda})\|\\
&\qquad (WA)\|\\
&\qquad (t\cdot s\,5(r)\cdot WB))
\end{aligned}
$$

$$
\begin{aligned}
&= \tau{\cdot}\mathbf{s10(proc(p1))}{\cdot}\tau_I(c\,5(r){\cdot}\partial_H((\mathbf{s0(r)}{\cdot}WC)\| \qquad \text{[using T2]}\\
&\qquad (T^{\lambda})\|\\
&\qquad (WA)\|\\
&\qquad (WB)))\\
&= \tau{\cdot}\mathbf{s10(proc(p1))}{\cdot}\mathbf{s0(r)}{\cdot}W\\
L^{n+1} &= \tau_I\partial_H((\underline{s\,2(1)}{\cdot}r\,3(r){\cdot}s\,6(tc){\cdot}r\,7(ar){\cdot}D^n{\cdot}r\,5(r){\cdot}s\,0(r){\cdot}WC)\|\\
&\qquad (r\,6(tc){\cdot}\textstyle\sum(r\,8(p){\cdot}T^p)+\sum(r\,8(p){\cdot}r\,6(tc){\cdot}T^p))\|\\
&\qquad (\textstyle\sum \underline{r\,2(n)}{\cdot}XA^n{\cdot}s\,3(r){\cdot}WA)\|\\
&\qquad (\underline{s\,10(proc\,(p\,1))}{\cdot}XB^{n+1}{\cdot}s\,5(r){\cdot}WB))\\
&= \tau_I(c\,2(1){\cdot}\partial_H((r\,3(r){\cdot}s\,6(tc){\cdot}r\,7(ar){\cdot}D^n{\cdot}r\,5(r){\cdot}s\,0(r){\cdot}WC)\|\\
&\qquad (r\,6(tc){\cdot}\textstyle\sum(r\,8(p){\cdot}T^p)+\sum(\underline{r\,8(p)}{\cdot}r\,6(tc){\cdot}T^p))\|\\
&\qquad (\underline{s\,8(p\,1)}{\cdot}XA^0{\cdot}s\,3(r){\cdot}WA)\|\\
&\qquad (\underline{s\,10(proc\,(p\,1))}{\cdot}XB^{n+1}{\cdot}s\,5(r){\cdot}WB)))+\\
&\quad \mathbf{s10(proc(p1))}{\cdot}\tau_I\partial_H((\underline{s\,2(1)}{\cdot}r\,3(r){\cdot}s\,6(tc){\cdot}r\,7(ar){\cdot}D^n{\cdot}r\,5(r){\cdot}s\,0(r){\cdot}WC)\|\\
&\qquad (r\,6(tc){\cdot}\textstyle\sum(r\,8(p){\cdot}T^p)+\sum(r\,8(p){\cdot}r\,6(tc){\cdot}T^p))\|\\
&\qquad (\textstyle\sum \underline{r\,2(n)}{\cdot}XA^n{\cdot}s\,3(r){\cdot}WA)\|\\
&\qquad (XB^{n+1}{\cdot}s\,5(r){\cdot}WB))\\
&= \tau{\cdot}\tau_I(c\,8(p\,1){\cdot}\partial_H((r\,3(r){\cdot}s\,6(tc){\cdot}r\,7(ar){\cdot}D^n{\cdot}r\,5(r){\cdot}s\,0(r){\cdot}WC)\|\\
&\qquad (r\,6(tc){\cdot}T^{p\,1})\|\\
&\qquad (XA^0{\cdot}s\,3(r){\cdot}WA)\|\\
&\qquad (\underline{s\,10(proc\,(p\,1))}{\cdot}XB^{n+1}{\cdot}s\,5(r){\cdot}WB)))+\\
&\quad \tau{\cdot}\mathbf{s10(proc(p1))}{\cdot}\tau_I\partial_H((r\,3(r){\cdot}s\,6(tc){\cdot}r\,7(ar){\cdot}D^n{\cdot}r\,5(r){\cdot}s\,0(r){\cdot}WC)\|\\
&\qquad (r\,6(tc){\cdot}\textstyle\sum(r\,8(p){\cdot}T^p)+\sum(\underline{r\,8(p)}{\cdot}r\,6(tc){\cdot}T^p))\|\\
&\qquad (\underline{s\,8(p\,1)}{\cdot}XA^0{\cdot}s\,3(r){\cdot}WA)\|\\
&\qquad (XB^{n+1}{\cdot}s\,5(r){\cdot}WB))+\\
&\quad \mathbf{s10(proc(p1))}{\cdot}\tau_I(c\,2(1){\cdot}\partial_H((r\,3(r){\cdot}s\,6(tc){\cdot}r\,7(ar){\cdot}D^n{\cdot}r\,5(r){\cdot}s\,0(r){\cdot}WC)\|\\
&\qquad (r\,6(tc){\cdot}\textstyle\sum(r\,8(p){\cdot}T^p)+\sum(\underline{r\,8(p)}{\cdot}r\,6(tc){\cdot}T^p))\|\\
&\qquad (\underline{s\,8(p\,1)}{\cdot}XA^0{\cdot}s\,3(r){\cdot}WA)\|\\
&\qquad (XB^{n+1}{\cdot}s\,5(r){\cdot}WB)))
\end{aligned}
$$

(The first two summands in this expression come from the first summand in the previous expression. Axiom T2 states that the summation of the second and third summand equals the second summand.)

$$= \tau{\cdot}\tau_I(c8(p1){\cdot}\partial_H((r3(r){\cdot}s6(tc){\cdot}r7(ar){\cdot}D^n{\cdot}r5(r){\cdot}s0(r){\cdot}WC)\|$$
$$(r6(tc){\cdot}T^{p1})\|$$
$$(t{\cdot}s3(r){\cdot}WA)\|$$
$$(s10(proc(p1)){\cdot}XB^{n+1}{\cdot}s5(r){\cdot}WB)))+$$
$$\tau{\cdot}\mathbf{s10(proc(p1))}{\cdot}\tau_I\partial_H((r3(r){\cdot}s6(tc){\cdot}r7(ar){\cdot}D^n{\cdot}r5(r){\cdot}s0(r){\cdot}WC)\|$$
$$(r6(tc){\cdot}\sum(r8(p){\cdot}T^p)+\sum(r8(p){\cdot}r6(tc){\cdot}T^p))\|$$
$$(s8(p1){\cdot}XA^0{\cdot}s3(r){\cdot}WA)\|$$
$$(XB^{n+1}{\cdot}s5(r){\cdot}WB))$$

$$= \tau{\cdot}\tau_I(c3(r){\cdot}\partial_H((s6(tc){\cdot}r7(ar){\cdot}D^n{\cdot}r5(r){\cdot}s0(r){\cdot}WC)\|$$
$$(r6(tc){\cdot}T^{p1})\|$$
$$(WA)\|$$
$$(s10(proc(p1)){\cdot}XB^{n+1}{\cdot}s5(r){\cdot}WB)))+$$
$$\tau{\cdot}\mathbf{s10(proc(p1))}{\cdot}\tau_I(c8(p1){\cdot}\partial_H(r3(r){\cdot}s6(tc){\cdot}r7(ar){\cdot}D^n{\cdot}r5(r){\cdot}s0(r){\cdot}WC)\|$$
$$(r6(tc){\cdot}T^{p1})\|$$
$$(t{\cdot}s3(r){\cdot}WA)\|$$
$$(XB^{n+1}{\cdot}s5(r){\cdot}WB)))$$

$$= \tau{\cdot}\tau_I(c6(tc){\cdot}\partial_H((r7(ar){\cdot}D^n{\cdot}r5(r){\cdot}s0(r){\cdot}WC)\|$$
$$(T^{p1})\|$$
$$(WA)\|$$
$$(s10(proc(p1)){\cdot}XB^{n+1}{\cdot}s5(r){\cdot}WB)))+$$
$$\tau{\cdot}\mathbf{s10(proc(p1))}{\cdot}\tau_I(c3(r){\cdot}\partial_H((s6(tc){\cdot}r7(ar){\cdot}D^n{\cdot}r5(r){\cdot}s0(r){\cdot}WC)\|$$
$$(r6(tc){\cdot}T^{p1})\|$$
$$(WA)\|$$
$$(XB^{n+1}{\cdot}s5(r){\cdot}WB)))$$

$$= \tau{\cdot}\mathbf{s10(proc(p1))}{\cdot}\tau_I\partial_H((r7(ar){\cdot}D^n{\cdot}r5(r){\cdot}s0(r){\cdot}WC)\|$$
$$(T^{p1})\|$$
$$(WA)\|$$
$$(\sum r9(p){\cdot}s10(proc(p)){\cdot}XB^n{\cdot}s5(r){\cdot}WB))$$

$$= \tau{\cdot}\mathbf{s10(proc(p1))}{\cdot}K^{n+1} \qquad \text{[see(**)]}$$

So the process w is a solution of the following system:

$$W = \sum r1(n) \cdot K^n$$
$$K^0 = \tau \cdot s0(r) \cdot W$$
$$K^{n+1} = \tau(\tau \cdot L^n + s10(proc(p1)) \cdot K^n)$$
$$L^0 = \tau \cdot s10(proc(p1)) \cdot s0(r) \cdot W$$
$$L^{n+1} = \tau \cdot s10(proc(p1)) \cdot K^{n+1}$$

SPECIFICATION 2.3

Now look at the specification of the process V, which specifies the intended behaviour. From RDP it follows that a solution (v, e^n) exists. Now, if v is also a solution of the specification for W, RSP can be used to infer that v equals w.

Define k^n and l^n by:

$$k^n = \tau \cdot e^n \cdot v$$
$$l^n = \tau \cdot e^{n+1} \cdot v, \text{ then}$$
$$v = \sum r1(n) \cdot e^n \cdot v = \sum r1(n) \cdot k^n$$
$$k^0 = \tau \cdot e^0 \cdot v = \tau \cdot s0(r) \cdot v$$
$$k^{n+1} = \tau \cdot e^{n+1} \cdot v = \tau(\tau \cdot e^{n+1} \cdot v + e^{n+1} \cdot v) = \tau(\tau \cdot l^n + s10(proc(p1) \cdot e^n \cdot v)$$
$$= \tau \cdot (\tau \cdot l^n + s10(proc(p1)) \cdot k^n)$$
$$l^0 = \tau \cdot e^1 \cdot v = \tau \cdot s10(proc(p1)) \cdot e^0 \cdot v = \tau \cdot s10(proc(p1)) \cdot s0(r) \cdot v$$
$$l^{n+1} = \tau \cdot e^{n+2} \cdot v = \tau \cdot s10(proc(p1)) \cdot e^{n+1} \cdot v = \tau \cdot s10(proc(p1)) \cdot l^n$$

So (v, k^n, l^n) is a solution of specification 2.3.

2.4. Redundancy

Note that the specification of the workcell contains some redundancy. Although the transport service has the capability to store any number of products in the queue, this feature is not used in the workcell. At any moment not more than one product is stored in the buffer. So a one-item buffer would have functioned in the same way. Also, the option of receiving first a transport command and then a product is not used.

The capability of workstation A to receive a command to produce more than one product is also not used.

3. A Workcell with quality check

3.1. *Specification*

3.1.1. Global description. In this section a more complex workcell will be defined, having the possibility of checking the quality of the produced goods. Again we assume that some upper bound N is given which is the maximum number of products the workcell can produce in one drive. The workcell consists of four components. (1) Workstation A (WA) accepts a product, processes it and returns either a good product or a faulty product. (2) The Transport service (T) is a queue, at the one end accepting and at the other end sending products. After receiving a product, the (3) Quality check (Q) determines whether it is a good product or not. A good product will be passed along, while a rejected product will be removed. The latter occurrence is signaled to the (4) Workcell Controller (WC). This part controls the workcell. It receives the number of products that have to be processed, and instructs the workcell to do so. While the processing is going on, it will count the number of rejected products. At the end the workcell is instructed to process again an amount of products, equal to the number of rejections.

The workcell is graphically depicted in Figure 3.

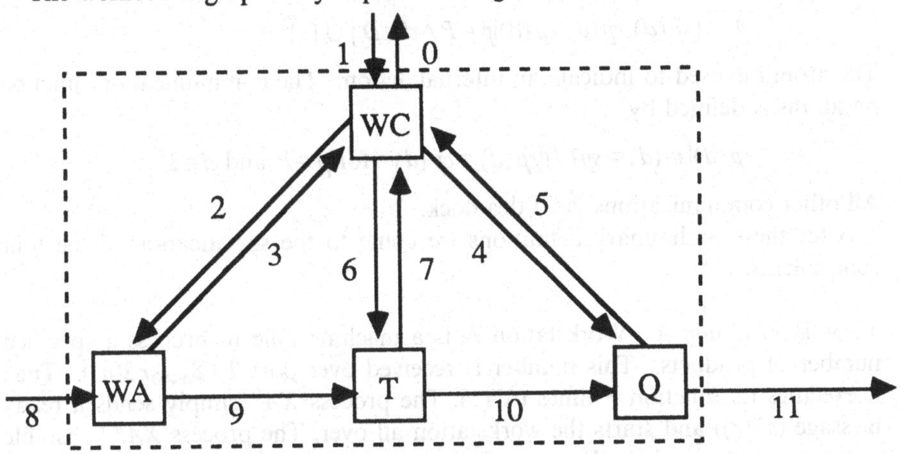

FIGURE 3. A workcell with quality check

3.1.2. Definitions. The four components are connected to each other by 12 ports. The ports 0 through 7 are used to transmit data and the ports 8 through 11 are used to exchange products. The ports 0, 1, 8 and 11 are connected to the environment. The set P of Ports is defined by

$$P = \{0, 1, ..., 11\}.$$

The set $PROD$ contains all products that are produced and processed within the workstation. It contains product1 ($p1$) and the product $p1$ after either good or faulty processing ($proc(p1, ok)$ and $proc(p1, fault)$).

$$PROD \supseteq \{p1, proc(p1,ok), proc(p1,fault)\}$$

A partial function *qual* can determine whether the processing of a product has been good or faulty.

$$qual(proc(p1,ok))=ok$$

$$qual(proc(p1,fault))=fault$$

Note that the information about the quality of a processed product is attached to the product itself, and one can only become aware of it by explicitly using the *qual* function. As an example consider drilling a hole in some product. After drilling, the hole is in the right position or not, but one can only become aware of this after applying some measuring tool, which reveals the quality. Along ports 1, 2, 4 and 6 a non-negative integer (n) can be sent to indicate that the receiver has to cope with n products. A ready message (r) is sent back over the ports 0, 3, 5 and 7 to indicate that the component has fulfilled its task. Port 5 is also used to indicate that a product has been rejected (rej). So the set D, of items that can be transmitted is defined as

$$D=\{n|0 \leqslant n \leqslant N\} \cup \{r,rej\} \cup PROD.$$

Thus the set of atomic actions can be defined by:

$$A=\{sp(d),rp(d),cp(d)|p \in P \wedge d \in D\} \cup \{i\}.$$

The atom i is used to indicate an internal action. The communication function on atoms is defined by

$$rp(d)|sp(d)=sp(d)|rp(d)=cp(d) \quad \text{for } p \in P \text{ and } d \in D.$$

All other communications yield deadlock.

After these preliminary definitions we come to the specification of the four components.

3.1.3. Workstation A. Workstation A is a machine able to process a specified number of products. This number is received over port 2 ($\Sigma_{n \geqslant 0} r2(n)$). Then it executes its function n times (XA^n). The process XA^0 simply sends a ready message ($s3(r)$) and starts the workstation all over. The process XA^{n+1} is able to receive some product ($\Sigma_{p \in PROD} r8(p)$), which has to be processed. The possibility of either doing a good job or making an error while processing, is modeled by using the nondeterministic choice operator. By prefixing the actions with the internal atom i, a choice is made which cannot be influenced by the environment.

$$WA=\sum_{n \geqslant 0} r2(n) \cdot XA^n$$

$$XA^0=s3(r) \cdot WA$$

$$XA^{n+1}=\sum_{p \in PROD} (r8(p) \cdot (i \cdot s9(proc(p,ok))+i \cdot s9(proc(p,fault)))) \cdot XA^n$$

3.1.4. Transport service. The transport service can best be seen as a bounded FIFO-queue. First it receives the number of products that have to be transported ($\Sigma_{n\geq 0} r6(n)$). Then it behaves like the empty queue with bound n (T_n^λ). After transporting n products (T_0^λ) a ready message is sent to the controller ($s7(r)$) and it starts all over. The process T_n^σ is intended to model a queue with contents σ, where n denotes the number of products that still have to be read in to the queue. T_{n+1}^λ has an empty buffer, so it can only read in products ($\Sigma_{p\in PROD} r9(p)$). $T_0^{\sigma*q}$ can only output the contents of its buffer. The process $T_{n+1}^{\sigma*q}$ can either accept some product ($\Sigma_{p\in PROD} r9(p)$) or it can send a queued item ($s10(q)$). This transport service differs from the one defined in the previous section in the sense that it needs less external control and that the capability of buffering more than one product is being used. Also, its specification has less redundancy.

$$T = \sum_{n\geq 0} r6(n)\cdot T_n^\lambda$$

$$T_0^\lambda = s7(r)\cdot T$$

$$T_{n+1}^\lambda = \sum_{p\in PROD} (r9(p)\cdot T_n^p)$$

$$T_0^{\sigma*q} = s10(q)\cdot T_0^\sigma$$

$$T_{n+1}^{\sigma*q} = \sum_{p\in PROD} (r9(p)\cdot T_n^{p*\sigma*q}) + s10(q)\cdot T_{n+1}^\sigma$$

3.1.5. Quality check. The quality of the processed product is tested by the process Q. It receives the command to test n products ($\Sigma_{n\geq 0} r4(n)$). Then the n tests are performed (XQ^n). If there are no tests left to do (XQ^0) a ready message is sent back ($s5(r)$) and the quality check returns to its initial state. The checks are done by accepting some product ($\Sigma_{p\in PROD} r10(p)$) and determining the quality of that product ($XQ^n_{p,qual(p)}$). If the quality is *ok* then the product can continue on its way ($s11(p)$). If the quality is *fault* then a rejection message is sent to the workcell controller ($s5(rej)$) and the product is rejected (i.e. discarded).

$$Q = \sum_{n\geq 0} r4(n)\cdot XQ^n$$

$$XQ^0 = s5(r)\cdot Q$$

$$XQ^{n+1} = \sum_{p\in PROD} r10(p)\cdot XQ^n_{p,qual(p)}$$

$$XQ^n_{p,ok} = s11(p)\cdot XQ^n$$

$$XQ^n_{p,fault} = s5(rej)\cdot XQ^n$$

3.1.6. Workcell Controller. The workcell is controlled by the Workcell Controller. It receives the message to process n products ($\Sigma_{n \geq 0} r1(n)$). When this is done (D^0), a ready message is reported ($s0(r)$) and the controller starts all over. The process D^{n+1} handles the processing of $n+1$ products. It sends the number of products that have to be processed to Workstation A ($s2(n+1)$), the Transport service ($s6(n+1)$) and the Quality check ($s4(n+1)$). Then it starts to count the number of rejections, starting with 0 (RC_0). The Rejection Counter will be incremented when it receives a rejection message ($r5(rej)$). When the Quality check, the Transport service and Workstation A respectively send their ready messages ($r5(r) \cdot r7(r) \cdot r3(r)$), the controller again commands the workcell to process some number of products (D^n). This new number of products is equal to the number of rejections encountered up to that moment.

$$WC = \sum_{n \geq 0} r1(n) \cdot D^n$$

$$D^0 = s0(r) \cdot WC$$

$$D^{n+1} = s4(n+1) \cdot s6(n+1) \cdot s2(n+1) \cdot RC_0$$

$$RC_n = r5(r) \cdot r7(r) \cdot r3(r) \cdot D^n + r5(rej) \cdot RC_{n+1}$$

Note that the order in which the ready messages are received is of importance. If e.g. the ready message of WA can be received first, it is still possible for Q to contain faulty products. But then, since WC is not able to receive any rejection messages from Q, a deadlock would occur.

3.1.7. The workcell. Now we are interested in the parallel operation of the four components as described above:

$$WC \| T \| WA \| Q.$$

To filter out all unsuccessful communications we use the encapsulation operator. All unsuccessful communications are gathered in the set H:

$$H = \{rp(d), sp(d) | (p \in \{2,3,4,5,6,7,9,10\} \wedge d \in D\}.$$

Because we are only interested in the external behaviour of the system, we abstract from the internal actions and communications, and define

$$I = \{cp(d) \| p \in \{2,3,4,5,6,7,9,10\} \wedge d \in D\} \cup \{i\}.$$

Thus the final definition of the workcell W becomes

$$\boxed{W = \tau_I \partial_H (WC \| T \| WA \| Q)}$$

SPECIFICATION 3.1

3.2. Correctness

Now we have to define some criterion for correctness of the specification. It is not enough to require that for any command n along port 1 the workcell processes n products correctly and reports a ready message. The problem is that if there is not enough supply of products along port 8, the workcell can reach a deadlock situation, waiting for more products. So we will only consider the behaviour of the workcell in an environment, supplying an unlimited number of products. The supplier is repeatedly sending product $p\,1$ along port 8, and is defined by

$$S \quad = s\,8(p\,1)\cdot S.$$

Of course we have to encapsulate unsuccessful communications over port 8 and abstract from successful communications over this port.

$$H' = \{rp(d), sp(d) | p = 8 \wedge d \in D\}$$

$$I' = \{cp(d) | p = 8 \wedge d \in D\}$$

So we will consider the behaviour of the following specification (See also Figure 4).

$$W' = \tau_{I'} \partial_{H'}(S \| W)$$

SPECIFICATION 3.2.1

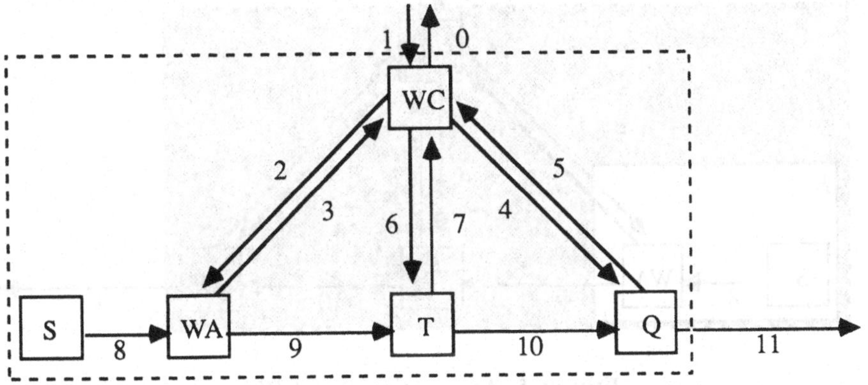

FIGURE 4. Adding a supplier to the workcell

The intended behaviour can be specified by the following specification 3.2.2. A command to process n products correctly will be received, then the n processed products will be delivered and a ready message will be reported.

$$V = \sum_{n \geq 0} (r1(n) \cdot E^n \cdot V)$$

$$E^0 = s0(r)$$

$$E^{n+1} = s11(proc(p1, ok)) \cdot E^n$$

SPECIFICATION 3.2.2

Now a verification of the correctness of the specification of the workcell will consist of a proof that specification 3.2.1. and specification 3.2.2. define the same process. So if w' and v are solutions of the two specifications, we have to prove $v = w'$.

THEOREM 3.3. *The specification of the workcell is correct.*

$$ACP_\tau + RDP + RSP + ET + CFAR + CA \vdash v = w'$$

PROOF

3.3.1. Step 1. First we reduce the number of components by aggregating the supplier S and workstation A. The resulting process (K) can be seen as being a supplier of either good or bad products (Figure 5).

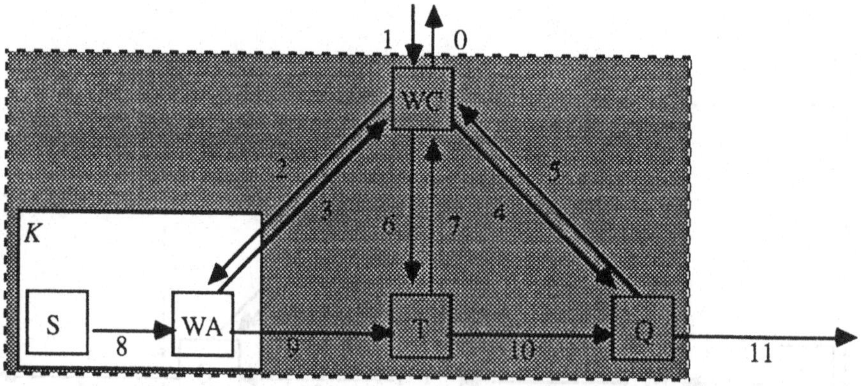

FIGURE 5. Aggregating S and WA

Let the process K be specified by

$$K = \sum r2(n) \cdot XK^n$$

$$XK^0 = s3(r) \cdot K$$

$$XK^{n+1} = (\tau \cdot s9(proc(p, ok)) + \tau \cdot s9(proc(p, fault))) \cdot XK^n.$$

And let the encapsulation set and the abstraction set be defined by

$$H1 = \{rp(d), sp(d) \mid p = 8 \wedge d \in D\},$$
$$I1 = \{cp(d) \mid p = 8 \wedge d \in D\} \cup \{i\},$$

then the following proposition holds:

PROPOSITION 3.3.1.1. $K = \tau_{I1}\partial_{H1}(S \| WA)$.

PROOF. Let the process L be defined by

$$L = \tau_{I1}\partial_{H1}(S \| WA)$$
$$= \tau_{I1}\partial_{H1}(S \| \textstyle\sum_{n \geq 0} r2(n) \cdot XA^n)$$
$$= \textstyle\sum_{n \geq 0} r2(n) \cdot \tau_{I1}\partial_{H1}(S \| XA^n)$$

Let L^n be defined by

$L^n = \tau_{I1}\partial_{H1}(S \| XA^n)$, then

$$L^0 = \tau_{I1}\partial_{H1}(S \| s3(r) \cdot WA)$$
$$= s3(r) \cdot L$$
$$L^{n+1} = \tau_{I1}\partial_{H1}(s8(p1) \cdot S \| \textstyle\sum_{p \in PROD}(r8(p) \cdot (i \cdot s9(proc(p, ok)) + i \cdot s9(proc(p, fault)))) \cdot XA^n)$$
$$= \tau_{I1}(c8(p1) \cdot \partial_{H1}(S \| (i \cdot s9(proc(p1, ok)) + i \cdot s9(proc(p1, fault)))) \cdot XA^n)$$
$$= \tau \cdot (\tau \cdot s9(proc(p1, ok)) + \tau \cdot s9(proc(p1, fault))) \cdot L^n$$

Thus we have

$$L = \sum_{n \geq 0} r2(n) \cdot L^n$$
$$L^0 = s3(r) \cdot L$$
$$L^{n+1} = \tau \cdot (\tau \cdot s9(proc(p1, ok)) + \tau \cdot s9(proc(p1, fault))) \cdot L^n$$

Now it is easy to see that K and L define the same process. Use RSP to prove that a solution of K is also a solution of system L.

As a consequence of this proposition we can replace the two components S and WA by one simpler component K. This technique is called local replacement and was introduced in [12]. In order to actually replace the two components in the specification of the workcell, we need the conditional axioms (see [1]).

$$W' = \tau_{I'}\partial_{H'}(S \| W)$$
$$= \tau_{I'}\partial_{H'}(S \| \tau_I\partial_H(WA \| T \| Q \| WC))$$

$$=\tau_{I'\cup I}\partial_{H'\cup H}(S\|WA\|T\|Q\|WC)$$
$$=\tau_{I'\cup I}\partial_{H'\cup H}(\tau_{I1}\partial_{H1}(S\|WA)\|T\|Q\|WC)$$
$$=\tau_{I'\cup I}\partial_{H'\cup H}(K\|T\|Q\|WC)$$
$$=\tau_I\partial_H(K\|T\|Q\|WC)$$

3.3.2. Step 2. In the second step we will remove the parallelism in the specification by expanding the merges. This will result in a complex process, which describes all states that the workcell has.

First we define a new abstraction set, $I2$, obtained by deleting the communication of the rejection message from the old one. This will be useful when applying CFAR in step 3.

$$I2=I\setminus\{c5(rej)\}$$

If we define

$$U=\tau_{I2}\partial_H(K\|T\|Q\|WC)\text{, then we have}$$
$$W'=\tau_{\{c5(rej)\}}(U).$$

For U we can derive

$$U=\tau_{I2}\partial_H(K\|T\|Q\|WC)=\sum_{n\geq 0} r1(n)\cdot\tau_{I2}\partial_H(K\|T\|Q\|D^n)$$

Let U^n be defined by $\tau_{I2}\partial_H(K\|T\|Q\|D^n)$, then

$$U^0=\tau_{I2}\partial_H(K\|T\|Q\|D^0)=s0(r)\cdot U$$
$$U^{n+1}=\tau_{I2}\partial_H(K\|T\|Q\|D^{n+1})$$
$$=\tau_{I2}(c4(n+1)\cdot c6(n+1)\cdot c2(n+1)\cdot\partial_H(XK^{n+1}\|T^{\lambda}_{n+1}\|XQ^{n+1}\|RC^{\prime}))$$

The process U^n denotes the total workcell, which has just received a command to produce a certain number of products. After distributing this command, the workcell enters the state in which the products will be produced. In the process of producing the products, there are several intermediate states. These states are determined by e.g. the number of products that still have to be produced, and the contents of the buffer of the transport service. The quality-check can also contain some product, i.e. the product which is read in and will be checked. All values that determine the actual state the workcell is in, are listed below:

choice The choice made in K about processing correctly or faulty. The choice can be *ok* or *fault*. If no choice has been made yet, the value of this variable is $\times$.

count The number of products that still have to be produced (not considering the number of rejected products).

buffer The contents of the buffer in the transport service. The value is λ if the buffer is empty.

Qcont The contents of the quality-check part. The value is λ if Q contains no product.

rc The rejection counter, counting the number of rejected products.

All states can be described using these five variables. Now it is possible to define the process U, indexed by these five variables, which describes the behaviour of the workcell during the production of the products.

Define

$$U^{\text{choice, count, buffer, Qcont,rc}}$$

as the composition of the four components K, T, Q and WC, where the superscripts determine the state of the four components as follows:

If $choice = \times$ then K is in state XK^{count}, otherwise K is in state $s9(proc(p1,choice))\cdot XK^{\text{count}-1}$. T is in state $T^{\text{buffer}}_{\text{count}}$.

If $Qcont = \lambda$ then Q is in state $XQ^{\text{count}+|\text{buffer}|}$, otherwise Q is in state

$$XQ^{\text{count}+|\text{buffer}|}_{\text{Qcont,qual(Qcont)}}.$$

WC is in state RC_{count}.

For every combination of values we can calculate the behaviour of the system. Note that the choice can only be unequal to $\times$ if the count is positive. Let *ch* be some quality (i.e. either *ok* or *fault*), let n and rc be natural numbers, let σ be a series of processed products and let q be a processed product.

$$U^{ch,n+1,\sigma,proc(p1,ok),rc}$$

$$\begin{aligned}
&= \tau_I \partial_H(s9(proc(p1,ch))\cdot XK^n \| T^\sigma_{n+1} \| XQ^{n+1+|\sigma|}_{p,ok} \| RC_{rc}) \\
&= \tau_I(c9(proc(p1,ch))\cdot\partial_H(XK^n \| T^{proc(p1,ch)*\sigma}_n \| XQ^{n+1+|\sigma|}_{p,ok} \| RC_{rc}) + \\
&\quad s11(p)\cdot\partial_H(s9(proc(p1,ch))\cdot XK^n \| T^\sigma_{n+1} \| XQ^{n+1+|\sigma|} \| RC_{rc})) \\
&= \tau\cdot U^{\times,n,proc(p1,ch)*\sigma,proc(p1,ok),rc} + s11(proc(p1,ok))\cdot U^{ch,n+1,\sigma,\lambda,rc}
\end{aligned}$$

$$U^{ch,n+1,\sigma,proc(p1,fault),rc}$$

$$\begin{aligned}
&= \tau_I \partial_H(s9(proc(p1,ch))\cdot XK^n \| T^\sigma_{n+1} \| XQ^{n+1+|\sigma|}_{p,fault} \| RC_{rc}) \\
&= \tau_I(c9(proc(p1,ch))\cdot\partial_H(XK^n \| T^{proc(p1,ch)*\sigma}_n \| XQ^{n+1+|\sigma|}_{p,fault} \| RC_{rc}) + \\
&\quad c5(rej)\cdot\partial_H(s9(proc(p1,ch))\cdot XK^n \| T^\sigma_{n+1} \| XQ^{n+1+|\sigma|} \| RC_{rc+1})) \\
&= \tau\cdot U^{\times,n,proc(p1,ch)*\sigma,proc(p1,fault),rc} + c5(rej)\cdot U^{ch,n+1,\sigma,\lambda,rc+1}
\end{aligned}$$

$$U^{ch,n+1,\sigma*q,\lambda,rc}$$

$$\begin{aligned}
&= \tau_I \partial_H(s9(proc(p1,ch))\cdot XK^n \| T^{\sigma*q}_{n+1} \| XQ^{n+2+|\sigma|} \| RC_{rc}) \\
&= \tau_I(c9(proc(p1,ch))\cdot\partial_H(XK^n \| T^{proc(p1,ch)*\sigma*q}_n \| XQ^{n+2+|\sigma|} \| RC_{rc}) + \\
&\quad c10(q)\cdot\partial_H(s9(proc(p1,ch))\cdot XK^n \| T^\sigma_{n+1} \| XQ^{n+1+|\sigma|}_{q,qual(q)} RC_{rc})) \\
&= \tau\cdot U^{\times,n,proc(p1,ch)*\sigma*q,\lambda,rc} + \tau\cdot U^{ch,n+1,\sigma,q,rc}
\end{aligned}$$

$U^{ch,n+1,\lambda,\lambda,rc}$

$$=\tau_I\partial_H(s9(proc(p1,ch))\cdot XK^n \| T^{\lambda}_{n+1} \| XQ^{n+1} \| RC_{rc})$$
$$=\tau_I(c9(proc(p1,ch))\cdot\partial_H(XK^n \| T^{proc(p1,ch)}_n \| XQ^{n+1} \| RC_{rc}))$$
$$=\tau\cdot U^{\times,n,proc(p1,ch),\lambda,rc}$$

$U^{\times,n+1,\sigma,proc(p1,ok),rc}$

$$=\tau_I\partial_H(XK^{n+1} \| T^{\sigma}_{n+1} \| XQ^{n+1+|\sigma|}_{p,ok} \| RC_{rc})$$
$$=\tau_I(\tau\cdot\partial_H(s9(proc(p1,ok))XK^n \| T^{\sigma}_{n+1} \| XQ^{n+1+|\sigma|}_{p,ok} \| RC_{rc})+$$
$$\tau\cdot\partial_H(s9(proc(p1,fault))XK^n \| T^{\sigma}_{n+1} \| XQ^{n+1+|\sigma|}_{p,ok} \| RC_{rc})+$$
$$s11(p)\cdot\partial_H(XK^{n+1} \| T^{\sigma}_{n+1} \| XQ^{n+1+|\sigma|} \| RC_{rc}))$$
$$=\tau\cdot U^{ok,n+1,\sigma,proc(p1,ok),rc}+\tau\cdot U^{fault,n+1,\sigma,proc(p1,ok),rc}+$$
$$s11(proc(p1,ok))\cdot U^{\times,n+1,\sigma,\lambda,rc}$$

$U^{\times,n+1,\sigma,proc(p1,fault),rc}$

$$=\tau_I\partial_H(XK^{n+1} \| T^{\sigma}_{n+1} \| XQ^{n+1+|\sigma|}_{p,fault} \| RC_{rc})$$
$$=\tau_I(\tau\cdot\partial_H(s9(proc(p1,ok))XK^n \| T^{\sigma}_{n+1} \| XQ^{n+1+|\sigma|}_{p,fault} \| RC_{rc})+$$
$$\tau\cdot\partial_H(s9(proc(p1,fault))XK^n \| T^{\sigma}_{n+1} \| XQ^{n+1+|\sigma|}_{p,fault} \| RC_{rc})+$$
$$c5(rej)\cdot\partial_H(XK^{n+1} \| T^{\sigma}_{n+1} \| XQ^{n+1+|\sigma|} \| RC_{rc+1}))$$
$$=\tau\cdot U^{ok,n+1,\sigma,proc(p1,fault),rc}+\tau\cdot U^{fault,n+1,\sigma,proc(p1,fault),rc}+$$
$$c5(rej)\cdot U^{\times,n+1,\sigma,\lambda,rc+1}$$

$U^{\times,n+1,\sigma*q,\lambda,rc}$

$$=\tau_I\partial_H(XK^{n+1} \| T^{\sigma*q}_{n+1} \| XQ^{n+2+|\sigma|} \| RC_{rc})$$
$$=\tau_I(\tau\cdot\partial_H(s9(proc(p1,ok))XK^n \| T^{\sigma*q}_{n+1} \| XQ^{n+2+|\sigma|} \| RC_{rc})+$$
$$\tau\cdot\partial_H(s9(proc(p1,fault))XK^n \| T^{\sigma*q}_{n+1} \| XQ^{n+2+|\sigma|} \| RC_{rc})+$$
$$c10(q)\cdot\partial_H(XK^{n+1} \| T^{\sigma}_{n+1} \| XQ^{n+1+|\sigma|}_{q,qual(q)} \| RC_{rc}))$$
$$=\tau\cdot U^{ok,n+1,\sigma*q,\lambda,rc}+\tau\cdot U^{fault,n+1,\sigma*q,\lambda,rc}+\tau\cdot U^{\times,n+1,\sigma,q,rc}$$

$U^{\times,n+1,\lambda,\lambda,rc}$

$$=\tau_I\partial_H(XK^{n+1} \| T^{\lambda}_{n+1} \| XQ^{n+1} \| RC_{rc})$$
$$=\tau_I(\tau\cdot\partial_H(s9(proc(p1,ok))XK^n \| T^{\lambda}_{n+1} \| XQ^{n+1} \| RC_{rc})+$$
$$\tau\cdot\partial_H(s9(proc(p1,fault))XK^n \| T^{\lambda}_{n+1} \| XQ^{n+1} \| RC_{rc}))$$
$$=\tau\cdot U^{ok,n+1,\lambda,\lambda,rc}+\tau\cdot U^{fault,n+1,\lambda,\lambda,rc}$$

$U^{\times,0,\sigma,proc(p1,ok),rc}$

$$=\tau_I\partial_H(XK^0 \| T_0^\sigma \| XQ_{p,ok}^{|\sigma|} \| RC_{rc})$$
$$=\tau_I(s11(p)\cdot\partial_H(XK^0 \| T_0^\sigma \| XQ^{|\sigma|} \| RC_{rc}))$$
$$=s11(proc(p1,ok))\cdot U^{\times,0,\sigma,\lambda,rc}$$

$U^{\times,0,\sigma,proc(p1,fault),rc}$

$$=\tau_I\partial_H(XK^0 \| T_0^\sigma \| XQ_{p,fault}^{|\sigma|} \| RC_{rc})$$
$$=\tau_I(c5(rej)\cdot\partial_H(XK^0 \| T_0^\sigma \| XQ^{|\sigma|} \| RC_{rc+1}))$$
$$=c5(rej)\cdot U^{\times,0,\sigma,\lambda,rc+1}$$

$U^{\times,0,\sigma*q,\lambda,rc}$

$$=\tau_I\partial_H(XK^0 \| T_0^{\sigma*q} \| XQ^{|\sigma|+1} \| RC_{rc})$$
$$=\tau_I(c10(q)\cdot\partial_H(XK^0 \| T_0^\sigma \| XQ_{q,qual(q)}^{|\sigma|} \| RC_{rc}))$$
$$=\tau\cdot U^{\times,0,\sigma,q,rc}$$

$U^{\times,0,\lambda,\lambda,rc}$

$$=\tau_I\partial_H(XK^0 \| T_0^\lambda \| XQ^0 \| RC_{rc})$$
$$=\tau_I(c5(r)\cdot c7(r)\cdot c3(r)\cdot\partial_H(K \| T \| Q \| D^{rc}))$$
$$=\tau\cdot U^{rc}$$

Thus we have the following system:

1)	$U = \sum_{n \geqslant 0} r1(n) \cdot U^n$
2)	$U^0 = s0(r) \cdot U$
3)	$U^{n+1} = \tau \cdot U^{\times, n+1, \lambda, \lambda, 0}$
4)	$U^{ch, n+1, \sigma, proc(p1, ok), rc} =$ $= \tau \cdot U^{\times, n, proc(p1, ch)*\sigma, proc(p1, ok), rc} + s11(proc(p1, ok)) \cdot U^{uch, n+1, \sigma \lambda, rc}$
5)	$U^{ch, n+1, \sigma, proc(p1, fault), rc} =$ $= \tau \cdot U^{\times, n, proc(p1, ch)*\sigma, proc(p1, fault), rc} + c5(rej) \cdot U^{ch, n+1, \sigma, \lambda, rc+1}$
6)	$U^{ch, n+1, \sigma * q, \lambda, rc} = \tau \cdot U^{\times, n, proc(p1, ch)*\sigma * q, \lambda, rc} + \tau \cdot U^{ch, n+1, \sigma, q, rc}$
7)	$U^{ch, n+1, \lambda, \lambda, rc} = \tau \cdot U^{\times, n, proc(p1, ch), \lambda, rc}$
8)	$U^{\times, n+1, \sigma, proc(p1, ok), rc} =$ $= \tau \cdot U^{ok, n+1, \sigma, proc(p1, ok), rc} + \tau \cdot U^{fault, n+1, \sigma, proc(p1, ok), rc} +$ $s11(proc(p1, ok)) \cdot U^{\times, n+1, \sigma, \lambda, rc}$
9)	$U^{\times, n+1, \sigma, proc(p1, fault), rc} =$ $= \tau \cdot U^{ok, n+1, \sigma, proc(p1, fault), rc} + \tau \cdot U^{fault, n+1, \sigma, proc(p1, fault), rc} +$ $c5(rej) \cdot U^{\times, n+1, \sigma, \lambda, rc+1}$
10)	$U^{\times, n+1, \sigma * q, \lambda, rc} =$ $= \tau \cdot U^{ok, n+1, \sigma * q, \lambda, rc} + \tau \cdot U^{fault, n+1, \sigma * q, \lambda, rc} + \tau \cdot U^{\times, n+1, \sigma, q, rc}$
11)	$U^{\times, n+1, \lambda, \lambda, rc} = \tau \cdot U^{ok, n+1, \lambda, \lambda, rc} + \tau \cdot U^{fault, n+1, \lambda, \lambda, rc}$
12)	$U^{\times, 0, \sigma, proc(p1, ok), rc} = s11(proc(p1, ok)) \cdot U^{\times, 0, \sigma, \lambda, rc}$
13)	$U^{\times, 0, \sigma, proc(p1, fault), rc} = c5(rej) \cdot U^{\times, 0, \sigma, \lambda, rc+1}$
14)	$U^{\times, 0, \sigma * q, \lambda, rc} = \tau \cdot U^{\times, 0, \sigma, q, rc}$
15)	$U^{\times, 0, \lambda, \lambda, rc} = \tau \cdot U^{rc}$

SPECIFICATION 3.3.2

3.3.3. Step 3. In the final part of the proof we use CFAR (see [12]) and RSP (see [2]) to prove that the system derived in step 2 (specification 3.3.2) can be reduced to the desired specification V (specification 3.2.2).

Some observations about the specification above can be made. The number of products that still have to be produced correctly (m) can be determined from the values of the superscripts of the process:

$$\text{count} + |\text{buffer}| + |\text{Qcont}| + rc.$$

So we must prove the equality

$$\tau \cdot E^m = \tau \cdot \tau_{\{c5(rej)\}}(U^{\text{choice}, \text{count}, \text{buffer}, \text{Qcont}, \text{rc}})$$

for $m = count + |\text{buffer}| + |\text{Qcont}| + rc$. We must also prove

$$\tau \cdot E^m = \tau \cdot \tau_{\{c5(rej)\}}(U^m).$$

Comparing the two processes one easily notes that U^m has the possibility to produce only faulty products, hence it can loop forever, sending rejection messages. The process E^m however does not have this possibility. Thus we must make the assumption that workstation *WA* is not completely broken. It now and then must process some product correctly. This fairness assumption can be modeled in process algebra with the Cluster Fair Abstraction Rule.

The only cases in which it is possible to never process a product correctly are the processes which are indexed such that (i) choice$\neq$*ok*, (ii) the buffer contains no correctly processed products and (iii) Qcont$\neq$*proc*$(p1, ok)$. This observation leads us to consider clusters of processes which satisfy these conditions and have to produce the same number of products. Thus cluster m (for $m > 0$) is defined by:

$$CL(m) = \{U^m\} \cup \{U^{\text{choice,count,buffer,Qcont},rc} \mid$$

$$choice \neq ok \wedge proc(p1, ok) \notin buffer \wedge \text{Qcont} \neq proc(p1, ok) \wedge$$

$$count + |buffer| + |Qcont| + rc = m\}.$$

This defines a conservative cluster from $\{c5(rej)\}$ in specification 3.3.2 (using terminology of [12]). The workcell can choose to loop forever in such a cluster, or it can choose to process some product correctly. This will be indicated by setting the *choice*-index to *ok*. After some time, this choice leads to a correctly processed product leaving the workcell. In the meantime the workcell has to make new choices. If they are all negative, we again enter a cluster that permits infinite loops. If a choice was made to produce one or more correct products, we are still in a state in which progress can be made.

Now we can determine the exits of such a cluster. These are all states which can be reached from the cluster, but are no member of it. Thus there are no correctly processed products in the buffers and the choice has been made to process the next product correctly.

$$EXITS(m) = \{U^{ok, n+1, \sigma, proc(p1, fault), rc} \mid n + 1 + |\sigma| + 1 + rc = m \wedge proc(p1, ok) \notin \sigma\} \cup$$

$$\{U^{ok, n+1, \sigma * q, \lambda, rc} \mid n + 1 + |\sigma| + 1 + rc = m \wedge proc(p1, ok) \notin \sigma * q\} \cup$$

$$\{U^{ok, n+1, \lambda, \lambda, rc} \mid n + 1 + rc = m\}$$

Applying CFAR to the specification derived in step 2 leads to a new specification. This specification is equal to the old one for states which contain some correctly processed products and is modified for states which only contain faulty products.

Now set

$$W' = \tau_{\{c5(rej)\}}(U)$$

$$W^n = \tau_{\{c5(rej)\}}(U^n)$$

$$W^{\text{choice,count,buffer,Qcont},rc} = \tau_{\{c5(rej)\}}(U^{\text{choice,count,buffer,Qcont},rc})$$

In the first part of the following specification we assume that there are correctly processed products in the buffer σ, or in $Qcont$, or $ch = ok$. The numbers correspond to the numbers in the specification of U.

1) $W' = \Sigma_{n \geqslant 0} r1(n) \cdot W^{n}$

2) $W^{0} = s0(r) \cdot W'$

4) $W^{ch, n+1, \sigma, proc(p1, ok), rc} =$
$= \tau \cdot W^{\times, n, proc(p1, ch)^{*}\sigma, proc(p1, ok), rc} + s11(proc(p1, ok)) \cdot W^{ch, n+1, \sigma\, \lambda, rc}$

5) $W^{ch, n+1, \sigma, proc(p1, fault), rc} =$
$= \tau \cdot W^{\times, n, proc(p1, ch)^{*}\sigma, proc(p1, fault), rc} + \tau \cdot W^{ch, n+1, \sigma, \lambda, rc+1}$

6) $W^{ch, n+1, \sigma^{*}q, \lambda, rc} = \tau \cdot W^{\times, n, proc(p1, ch)^{*}\sigma^{*}q, \lambda, rc} + \tau \cdot W^{ch, n+1, \sigma, q, rc}$

7) $W^{ch, n+1, \lambda, \lambda, rc} = \tau \cdot W^{\times, n, proc(p1, ch), \lambda, rc}$

8) $W^{\times, n+1, \sigma, proc(p1, ok), rc} =$
$= \tau \cdot W^{ok, n+1, \sigma, proc(p1, ok), rc} + \tau \cdot W^{fault, n+1, \sigma, proc(p1, ok), rc} +$
$s11(proc(p1, ok)) \cdot W^{\times, n+1, \sigma, \lambda, rc}$

9) $W^{\times, n+1, \sigma, proc(p1, fault), rc} =$
$= \tau \cdot W^{ok, n+1, \sigma, proc(p1, fault), rc} + \tau \cdot W^{fault, n+1, \sigma, proc(p1, fault), rc} +$
$\tau \cdot W^{\times, n+1, \sigma, \lambda, rc+1}$

10) $W^{\times, n+1, \sigma^{*}q, \lambda, rc} =$
$= \tau \cdot W^{ok, n+1, \sigma^{*}q, \lambda, rc} + \tau \cdot W^{fault, n+1, \sigma^{*}q, \lambda, rc} + \tau \cdot W^{\times, n+1, \sigma, q, rc}$

12) $W^{\times, 0, \sigma, proc(p1, ok), rc} = s11(proc(p1, ok)) \cdot W \times, 0, \sigma, \lambda, rc$

13) $W^{\times, 0, \sigma, proc(p1, fault), rc} = \tau \cdot W^{\times, 0, \sigma, \lambda, rc+1}$

14) $W^{\times, 0, \sigma^{*}q, \lambda, rc} = \tau \cdot W^{\times, 0, \sigma, q, rc}$

SPECIFICATION 3.4.3, PART 1

In the second part we assume that there are no correct products in the workcell, so we are in a cluster. The expression $\sum EXITS(m)$ is shorthand for $\sum_{p \in EXITS(m)} \tau_{\{c5(rej)\}}(p)$.

3)	$W^{n+1} = \tau \cdot \sum EXITS(n+1)$
5a)	$W^{ch,n+1,\sigma,proc(p1,fault),rc} = \tau \cdot \sum EXITS(n+1+\vert\sigma\vert+1+rc)$
6a)	$W^{ch,n+1,\sigma*q,\lambda,rc} = \tau \cdot \sum EXITS(n+1+\vert\sigma\vert+1+rc)$
7a)	$W^{ch,n+1,\lambda,\lambda,rc} = \tau \cdot \sum EXITS(n+1+rc)$
9a)	$W^{\times,n+1,\sigma,proc(p1,fault),rc} = \tau \cdot \sum EXITS(n+1+\vert\sigma\vert+1+rc)$
10a)	$W^{\times,n+1,\sigma*q,\lambda,rc} = \tau \cdot \sum EXITS(n+1+\vert\sigma\vert+1+rc)$
11)	$W^{\times,n+1,\lambda,\lambda,rc} = \tau \cdot \sum EXITS(n+1+rc)$
13a)	$W^{\times,0,\sigma,proc(p1,fault),rc} = \tau \cdot \sum EXITS(\vert\sigma\vert+1+rc)$
14a)	$W^{\times,0,\sigma*q,\lambda,rc} = \tau \cdot \sum EXITS(\vert\sigma\vert+1+rc)$
15)	$W^{\times,0,\lambda,\lambda,rc} = \tau \cdot \sum EXITS(rc)$

SPECIFICATION 3.4.3, PART 2

This specification now describes exactly the same process as specification 3.2.2. This can be easily verified by substituting V for W', E^0 for W^0, $\tau \cdot E^{n+1}$ for W^{n+1} and $\tau \cdot E^{count+|buffer|+|Qcont|+rc}$ for $W^{ch,count,buffer,Qcont,rc}$. Note that the only equation not starting with a τ is equation 12. So we must substitute $E^{|\sigma|+1}$ for $W^{\times,0,\sigma,proc(p1,ok)}$. So we see that V is a solution of the system defining W', and thus we can use RSP to conclude that V equals W'.

Note that RSP is only applicable if the specifications are guarded. A proof of the guardedness of specification 3.4.3 is straightforward.

4. FINAL REMARKS

The techniques introduced in this paper seem to be powerful enough to aid in the specification and verification of CIM-architectures. Although two workcells were considered of low complexity, the basic concepts of the technique are well illustrated. Now, due to the compositionality of the specifications, one can build a large plant consisting of a number of workcells which are already proved to function correctly. Thus, increasing the scale of the system will be possible.

It is also possible to add new features to the workcell and model them in process algebra. Possible features are: interrupts (modeled by the priority-operator, see [3]), detailed reports on the functioning of a machine, changing the tools of a machine, etc. Most of these features are not more complex than adding quality checks to a workcell.

Since a wide range of proof-rules and proof-techniques are developed in process algebra, the specification of a CIM-architecture in process algebra has advantages over specification in e.g. LOTOS. To name one, in LOTOS there is no equivalent of the fairness assumption.

ACKNOWLEDGEMENTS
I would like to express my thanks to Frank Biemans and Pieter Blonk of the Philips CAM centre for the fruitful discussions on this subject. I would also like to thank Jos Baeten, Jan Bergstra, Frits Vaandrager and Freek Wiedijk for proof reading and commenting on this paper.

REFERENCES

1. J.C.M. BAETEN, J.A. BERGSTRA, J.W. KLOP (1987). Conditional axioms and α/β calculus in process algebra. M. WIRSING (ed.). *Proc. IFIP Conf. on Formal Description of Programming Concepts - III,* Ebberup 1986, North-Holland, Amsterdam, 53-75.
2. J.C.M. BAETEN, J.A. BERGSTRA, J.W. KLOP (1987). On the consistency of Koomen's Fair Abstraction Rule. *Theoretical Computer Science 51 (1/2),* 129-176.
3. J.C.M. BAETEN, J.A. BERGSTRA, J.W. KLOP (1986). Syntax and defining equations for an interrupt mechanism in process algebra. *Fundamenta Informaticae IX(2),* 127-168.
4. J.A. BERGSTRA, J.W. KLOP (1986). Algebra of communicating processes. J.W. DE BAKKER, M. HAZEWINKEL, J.K. LENSTRA (eds.). *Mathematics and Computer Science,* CWI Monograph 1, North-Holland, Amsterdam, 89-138.
5. J.A. BERGSTRA, J.W. KLOP (1985). Algebra of communicating processes with abstraction. *Theoretical Computer Science 37(1),* 77-121.
6. J.A. BERGSTRA, J.W. KLOP (1984). Process algebra for synchronous communication. *Information and Control 60(1/3),* 109-137.
7. F. BIEMANS (1986). Reference model of production control systems. *Proc. of the IECON 86,* Milwaukee.
8. F. BIEMANS, P. BLONK (1986). On the formal specification and verification of CIM architectures using LOTOS. *Computers in Industry 7(6),* 491-504.
9. E. BRINKSMA (ed.) (1987). *LOTOS - A Formal Description Technique Based on the Temporal Ordering of Observational Behaviour,* Report ISO DIS 8807.
10. H. KODATE, K. FUJII, K. YAMANOI (1987). Representation of FMS with petrinet graph and its application to simulation of system operation. *Robotics and Computer-Integrated Manufacturing 3(3),* 275-283.
11. N. KOMODA, K. KERA, T. KUBO (1984). An autonomous, decentralized control system for factory automation. *IEEE Trans. Comput 17(12),* 73-83.
12. F.W. VAANDRAGER (1984). *Verification of Two Communication Protocols by means of Process Algebra,* CWI Report CS-R8608, Centre for Mathematics and Computer Science, Amsterdam.

A Process Creation Mechanism in Process Algebra

J.A. Bergstra
Programming Research Group, University of Amsterdam
P.O.Box 41882, 1009 DB Amsterdam, The Netherlands
Department of Philosophy, State University of Utrecht
Heidelberglaan 2, 3584 CS Utrecht, The Netherlands

We introduce an encapsulation operator E_φ that provides process algebra with a process creation mechanism. Several simple examples are considered. It is shown that E_φ does not extend the defining power of the system 'ACP with guarded recursion'.

1. Introduction

1.1. Extension of process algebra

In this paper we extend process algebra with a new operator that will be helpful to describe process creation. From a methodological point of view the extension of process algebra with new operators is just the right way to incorporate new features. Only in a very rich calculus with many operators one may hope to be able to perform significant algebraic calculations on systems. In many cases a new feature requires new (additional) syntax and more equations, only in very rare circumstances the addition of equations alone suffices to obtain an appropriate model of some new system aspect. The core system ACP, see [4,5,6], describes asynchronous cooperation with synchronous communication.

On top of ACP various features can be added, for instance: *asynchronous communication* [7], cooperation in the presence of *shared data* [1], *broadcasting* [3], *interrupts* [2]. This note adds *process creation* to the features that are compatible with process algebra.

For historical remarks and relations with previous literature we refer to [4].

1.2. Process creation

We start on basis of the axiom system ACP which is supposed to be known to the reader. We assume the presence of a finite set of data D and introduce for each $d \in D$ an action $cr(d)$. The action $cr(d)$ stands for: create a process on basis of initial information d. Let $cr(D)$ denote the set $\{cr(d) | d \in D\}$.

Let φ be a mapping that assigns to each $d \in D$ a process $\varphi(d)$. Then the operator E_φ (process creation encapsulation w.r.t. φ) is defined by the following equations. We assume that always $cr(d)|a = \delta$ and never $a|b = cr(d)$.

$$E_\varphi(\delta) = \delta$$
$$E_\varphi(a) = a\cdot\delta \text{ if } a\notin cr(D)$$
$$E_\varphi(a\cdot X) = a\cdot E_\varphi(X) \text{ if } a\notin cr(D)$$
$$E_\varphi(cr(d)) = \overline{cr}(d)\cdot E_\varphi(\varphi(d))$$
$$E_\varphi(cr(d)\cdot X) = \overline{cr}(d)\cdot E_\varphi(\varphi(d)\| X)$$
$$E_\varphi(x+y) = E_\varphi(x) + E_\varphi(y)$$

TABLE 1. Definition of E_φ

Here $\overline{cr}(d)$ is a new atom which indicates that process creation has taken place ($\varphi(d)$ is 'born').

As usual it is the case that on all finite terms E_φ can be eliminated (provided $\varphi(d)$ contains no $cr(d)$ actions). In any case one can compute for each n the n-th projection $\pi_n(t)$ of a term with E_φ as a term without E_φ by applying the equations as rewrite rules from left to right.

2. VERY SMALL EXAMPLES

In this section we provide several examples that should support the claim that E_φ properly describes process creation on top of ACP. It should be noted that in terms of [1] we are dealing with concrete process algebra, i.e. there is no abstraction present.

EXAMPLE 2.1. $D=\{d\}$, $\varphi(d)=cr(d)$.
Let $P=E_\varphi(cr(d))$, then $P=\overline{cr}(d)\cdot E_\varphi(\varphi(d))=\overline{cr}(d)\cdot E_\varphi(cr(d))= \overline{cr}(d)\cdot P$. It follows that E_φ involves recursion already under the simplest conditions.

We assume that we will always use guarded recursive specifications, and have a semantics in the standard model of graphs modulo bisimulation. Then one may use the approximation induction principle AIP (see [1]):

$$\frac{\text{for all } n, \pi_n(X) = \pi_n(Y)}{X = Y}.$$

Using AIP one can prove that in the absence of communication ($a|b=\delta$ for all a,b) the following holds:

$$E_\varphi(X\| Y) = E_\varphi(X)\| E_\varphi(Y) \qquad (*)$$

This leads to the second example.

EXAMPLE 2.2. Let $D=\{d\}$, $\varphi(d)=a\cdot cr(d)\| b\cdot cr(d)$, $a|b=\delta$ and $p=E_\varphi(cr(d))$. Then

$$p=\overline{cr}(d)\cdot E_\varphi(a\cdot cr(d)\| b\cdot cr(d)) \qquad \text{(using (*))}$$

$$=\overline{cr}(d)\cdot(E_\varphi(a\cdot cr(d))\|E_\varphi(b\cdot cr(d)))$$

$$=\overline{cr}(d)\cdot(a\cdot E_\varphi(cr(d))\|b\cdot E_\varphi(cr(d)))=\overline{cr}(d)\cdot(ap\|bp).$$

EXAMPLE 2.3. Let $D=\{d\}$, $\varphi(d)=a\cdot(cr(d)\|cr(d))+b$, let $a|b=\delta$ and put $p=E_\varphi(cr(d))$. Now

$$p=E_\varphi(\overline{cr}(d))=\overline{cr}(d)\cdot E_\varphi(a\cdot(cr(d)\|cr(d))+b)$$

$$=\overline{cr}(d)\cdot(a\cdot E_\varphi(cr(d)\|cr(d))+b\delta)=cr(d)\cdot(a\cdot(p\|p)+b\cdot\delta)$$

(again using (*)).

3. SMALL BUT GENUINE EXAMPLES

3.1. A population of animals

Let D be a finite set of genetic codes provided with a mixing operation $*$: $D\times D\rightarrow D$ and a predicate F (female) on D. Moreover there is a predicate V on D that indicates which genetic codes are vital and which are not. A vital genetic code will lead to living offspring whereas a non-vital code will not. Let for $a\in D$:

$$p^a = (\text{hunt}(a) + \text{sleep}(a) + \text{eat}(a) + \text{idle}(a))\cdot p^a + \text{end}(a).$$

Further for $a\in F$ we define the process q^a as follows:

$$q^a = \sum_{b\notin F}\text{pair}(a,b)\cdot(cr(a*b)\cdot q^a+\text{end}(a))+\text{end}(a).$$

On the other hand if $a\notin F$ then we define

$$q^a=\sum_{b\in F}\text{pair}(b,a)\cdot q^a+\text{end}(a).$$

Take the following communication function:

$$\text{end}(d)|\text{end}(d) = \overline{\text{end}}(d)$$

$$\text{pair}(a,b)|\text{pair}(a,b) = \overline{\text{pair}}(a,b)$$

(all other communications δ). Let

$$H_0 = \{\text{end}(d)|d\in D\}$$

$$H_1 = \{\text{pair}(a,b)|a,b\in D\}.$$

Then define

$$\varphi(a) = \partial_{H_0}(p^a\|q^a)$$

if a is vital (i.e. an element of V), otherwise take

$$\varphi(a) = \delta.$$

Now define the system S as follows:

$$S = \partial_{H_1}(E_\varphi(\varphi(a)\|\varphi(b))).$$

S describes a population of animals starting with two individuals. Each animal can hunt, sleep, eat, idle, pair, create (when female) and end (its life).

The population can develop in many different ways, in particular it can die out. Very simple observations can be made on this system. For instance if both a and b are male (i.e. $\notin F$) then no create action will take place.

3.2. The bag

Let $B = \Sigma_{d\in D}\text{read}(d)\cdot cr(d)\cdot B$ and $\varphi(d) = \text{write}(d)$. Consider $B^* = E_\varphi(B)$ then

$$\begin{aligned}
B^* &= E_\varphi(\sum_{d\in D}\text{read}(d)\cdot cr(d)\cdot B)\\
&= \sum_{d\in D}\text{read}(d)\cdot\overline{cr}(d)\cdot E_\varphi(\varphi(d)\|B)\\
&= \sum_{d\in D}\text{read}(d)\cdot\overline{cr}(d)\cdot E_\varphi(\text{write}(d)\|B)\\
&= \sum_{d\in D}\text{read}(d)\cdot\overline{cr}(\text{write}(d)\cdot\delta\|E_\varphi(B))\\
&= \sum_{d\in D}\text{read}(d)\cdot\overline{cr}(d)\cdot(\text{write}(d)\|E_\varphi(B)\cdot\delta)\\
&= \sum_{d\in D}\text{read}\cdot\overline{cr}(d)\cdot(\text{write}(d)\|B^*)
\end{aligned}$$

Here we use the fact that B has no finite traces which implies that $E_\varphi(B)$ has no finite traces from which it follows that $E_\varphi(B)\cdot\delta$ equals $E_\varphi(B)$. Moreover we use the fact that in the absence of communication E_φ distributes over $\|$, as well as the identity $X\|(Y\cdot\delta)=(X\cdot\delta)\|Y$.

If we now use abstraction and substitute τ for $\overline{cr}(d)$ then we obtain (with $I=\{\overline{cr}(d)|d\in D\}$ and τ_I as in [5]) that $\tau_I(B^*)$ satisfies the equation for a bag over D:

$$\tau_I(B^*) = \sum_{d\in D}\text{read}(d)\cdot(\text{write}(d)\|\tau_I(B^*)).$$

This equation was discussed in several earlier papers, for instance [6].

The above calculation shows the intuition behind the equation for $\tau_I(B^*)$: the read(d) action creates the option to write(d).

3.3. A sieve of Eratosthenes

We will write a program that generates all prime numbers in $\overline{N}=[1\,...,N]$ in increasing order. The program is called SIEVE, all its internal steps and communications will be represented by the action t, and it is claimed (but not proved) that $\tau_{\{t\}}(\text{SIEVE}) \underline{=} \text{write}(2)\cdot\text{write}(3)\cdot\ldots\cdot\text{write}(q)\cdot S$ where $2,3,\ldots,q$ enumerates the primes in $\overline{N}$ in increasing order.

3.3.1. Alphabet of actions A. δ: deadlock

t: internal step

for all $i, j \in \overline{N}$

write (i):	output i
send $i(j)$:	send j through port i
read $i(j)$:	read j through port i
cr(i):	create a new process from data i, we write $\overline{cr}(i)=t$

Then there is a family of atomic actions parametrized by pairs of elements of $\overline{N}$ as follows:

$$t(i=0 \bmod j)=\begin{cases} t & \text{if} \quad i=0 \bmod j \\ \delta & \text{otherwise} \end{cases}$$

$$t(i\neq 0 \bmod j)=\begin{cases} t & \text{if} \quad i\neq 0 \bmod j \\ \delta & \text{otherwise} \end{cases}$$

The communication function is taken as follows: send $i(j)|$read $i(j)=t$, all other communications are δ. Counting the actions we find $\#(A)=5N^2+N+2$.

3.3.2. Construction of the SIEVE. We have SIEVE $=\partial_H E_\varphi(S_1)$ where H, φ and S_1 are given below.

$$H=\{\text{send } i(j), \text{ read } i(j)|i,j\in\overline{N}\}$$

$$S_1=cr(2)\cdot \text{ send } 2(3)\ldots\text{send } 2(N)$$

thus S_1 creates a process for the (first) prime 2 and then sends all numbers in [3, N] in increasing order through port 2. (These messages are going to be received by $\varphi(2)$.)

$$\varphi(p)=S_p \text{with}$$

$$S_p=\text{write}(p).$$

$$\sum_{z\in\overline{N}} \text{read}p(z)\left[t(z=0 \bmod p)\cdot S_p+t(z\neq 0 \bmod p)\cdot cr(z)\cdot R_p^z\right]$$

$$R_p^i=\sum_{z\in\overline{N}}\text{read}p(z)\left[t(z=0 \bmod p)\cdot R_p^i+t(z\neq 0 \bmod p)\cdot\text{send } i(z)\cdot R_p^i\right]$$

The explanation of S_p is as follows: S_p will be created as soon as a new prime p is found by S_q (with q the prime preceding p). The first task of S_p is to output p, then it receives a sequence of larger numbers and checks all of these on being 0 mod p. The first $z\neq 0 \bmod p$ must be a prime since it has survived the entire pipeline from S_1 to S_2 to S_3 to S_5... till S_q. For this z a new process S_z is created. Thereafter S_p restricts itself to filtering out all numbers in the pipeline that are a multiple of p and transmitting the others to S_z.

4. E_φ CAN ALREADY BE DEFINED IN ACP

We assume a situation where the E_φ operator is not explicitly mentioned in the definition of φ. All foregoing examples are of that nature.

We will then show how to eliminate E_φ in favour of synchronous communication. For each $d \in D$ an action $cr^*(d)$ is introduced and communication works as follows:

$$cr(d)|cr^*(d) = \overline{cr}(d)$$

(the create-actions are not involved in any other proper communications). Now define K_φ as follows:

$$K_\varphi = \sum_{d \in D} cr^*(d) \cdot (K_\varphi \| \varphi(d)).$$

Let $H = \{cr(d), cr^*(d) | d \in D\}$. Suppose that p does not contain E_φ. Then

$$\boxed{E_\varphi(p) = \partial_H(K_\varphi \| p)}$$

Note that K_φ does not involve E_φ any more. We support this identity by showing that the operator $p \rightarrow \partial_H(K_\varphi \| p)$ satisfies the defining equations of E_φ. On appropriate models, like the standard graph model modulo bisimulation it can be shown that this type of functional recursion has a unique solution indeed. We have to distinguish several cases

$\boxed{p = \delta}$ $\quad E_\varphi(p) = \delta$

$$\partial_H(K_\varphi \| p) = \partial_H(K_\varphi \cdot \delta) = \delta = E_\varphi(p)$$

$\boxed{p = X + Y}$ $\quad E_\varphi(p) = E_\varphi(X) + E_\varphi(Y)$

$$\begin{aligned}\partial_H(K_\varphi \| p) &= \partial_H(K_\varphi \mathbin{\lfloor\!\lfloor} p) + \partial_H(K_\varphi | p) + \partial_H(p \mathbin{\lfloor\!\lfloor} K_\varphi) \\ &= \delta + \partial_H(K_\varphi | X) + \partial_H(K_\varphi | Y) + \partial_H(X \mathbin{\lfloor\!\lfloor} K_\varphi) + \partial_H(Y \mathbin{\lfloor\!\lfloor} K_\varphi) \\ &= \partial_H(K_\varphi \mathbin{\lfloor\!\lfloor} X) + \partial_H(K_\varphi | X) + \partial_H(X \mathbin{\lfloor\!\lfloor} K_\varphi) + \cdots \\ &= \partial_H(K_\varphi \| X) + \partial_H(K_\varphi \| Y) \\ &= E_\varphi(X) + E_\varphi(Y) = p\end{aligned}$$

Then there are the following cases for p involving the execution of an atomic action:

$$\left.\begin{array}{l} p = a \\ p = a \cdot X \end{array}\right\} \text{ } a \text{ not of the form } cr(d)$$

$cr(d)$

$cr(d) \cdot X$

We consider the last case only, the others being similar or simpler.

$$\boxed{p = cr(d) \cdot X}$$

$$E_\varphi(p) = \overline{cr}\ (d) \cdot E_\varphi(X \| \varphi(d))$$

$$\partial_H(K_\varphi \| p) = \partial_H(\sum_{a \in D} cr^*(a) \cdot (K_\varphi \| \varphi(a)) \| cr(d) \cdot X)$$

$$= \overline{cr}(d) \cdot \partial_H((K_\varphi \| \varphi(d)) \| X)$$

$$= \overline{cr}(d) \cdot \partial_H(K_\varphi \| (\varphi(d) \| X)) = \overline{cr}(d) \cdot E_\varphi(\varphi(d) \| X)$$

5. Concluding remarks

The message of this note is that process creation is a feature not too distant from process algebra. It should be stated that this introduction of process creation can equally well be applied within related formalisms like CCS [9], CSP [8], or trace theory [10] provided sufficiently many recursion equations can be solved. In CCS it would be natural to write τ for create (d).

References

1. J.C.M. Baeten, J.A. Bergstra (1988). Global renamings in concrete process algebra. *Information and Computation 78(3),* 205-245.
2. J.C.M. Baeten, J.A. Bergstra, J.W. Klop (1986). Syntax and defining equations for an interrupt mechanism in process algebra. *Fundamenta Informaticae IX (2),* 127-168.
3. J.A. Bergstra (1985). *Put and Get, Primitives for Synchronous Unreliable Message Passing,* Logic Group Preprint Series Nr. 3, CIF, State University of Utrecht.
4. J.A. Bergstra, J.W. Klop (1984). Process algebra for synchronous communication. *Information and Control 60 (1/3),* 109-137.
5. J.A. Bergstra, J.W. Klop (1985). Algebra of communicating processes with abstraction. *Theoretical Computer Science 37(1),* 77-121.
6. J.A. Bergstra, J.W. Klop (1984). The algebra of recursively defined processes and the algebra of regular processes. J. Paredaens (ed.). *Proc.*

11th Colloq. Automat. Lang. and Programming, Antwerpen, LNCS 172, Springer-Verlag, 82-94.

7. J.A. BERGSTRA, J.W. KLOP, J.V. TUCKER (1984). Process algebra with asynchronous communicating mechanisms. S.D. BROOKES, A.W. ROSCOE, G. WYNSKEL (eds.). *Proc. Seminar on Concurrency,* LNCS 197, Springer-Verlag, 76-95.
8. S.D. BROOKS, C.A.R. HOARE, A.W. ROSCOE (1981). A theory of communicating sequential processes. *J. Assoc. Comp. Mach. 31 (3),* 560-599.
9. R. MILNER (1980). *A Calculus of Communicating Systems,* LNCS 92, Springer-Verlag.
10. M. REM (1983). Partially ordered computations with applications to VLSI design. J.W. DE BAKKER, J. VAN LEEUWEN (eds.). *Proc. Found. of Comp. Sci. IV.2,* MC Tract 159, Centre for Mathematics and Computer Science, Amsterdam, 1-44.

Correctness Proofs for Systolic Algorithms: Palindromes and Sorting

L. Kossen

W.P. Weijland

Centre for Mathematics and Computer Science
P.O. Box 4079, 1009 AB Amsterdam, The Netherlands

In designing VLSI-circuits it is very useful, if not necessary, to construct the specific circuit by placing simple components in regular configurations. Systolic systems are circuits built up from arrays of cells and therefore very suitable for formal analysis and induction methods. In two examples correctness proofs are given using bisimulation semantics with asynchronous cooperation. These examples also have been worked out by Hennessy in a setting of failure semantics with synchronous cooperation. Finally the notion of process creation is introduced and used to construct machines with unbounded capacity.

1. Introduction

In this article we will present simple descriptions of so-called *systolic systems.* Such systems can be looked at as a large integration of identical cells in such a way that the behaviour of the total system strongly resembles the behaviour of the individual cells. In fact the total system behaves like one of its individual cells 'on a larger scale'.

For example one can think of a machine sorting arrays of numbers with a certain maximum length. Suppose we need a machine handling arrays that are much longer. A typical 'systolic approach' to this problem would be to try to *interconnect* the smaller machines such that the total circuit sorts arrays of a greater length. As a matter of fact this specific example will be worked out in the following sections. In designing VLSI-circuits (short for *very large scale integrated* circuits) it is very useful, if not necessary, to construct the specific circuit by placing simple components in regular configurations ([9]). Otherwise one looses all intuition about the behaviour of the circuit that is eventually constructed. For this reason one may see systolic systems as a sort of regular subclass of VLSI-circuits which is very suitable for formal analysis. As we will see from two typical examples from Kung [8] these regular circuits can easily be analyzed as to their correct behaviour.

In designing a systolic system, finding a correct definition of the individual cells turns out to be the main problem. Apparently we already have in mind what we want the total network to do and hence we may assume there is some general *specification* of the desired behaviour. Indeed this specification may be *general* in the sense that it only needs to describe the 'outside behaviour' of the machine without specifying in detail the internal actions.

On the other hand looking for a correct definition of the individual cells we are working with a much more detailed description, since all relevant actions need to be described. This means we are looking for a certain *implementation* that satisfies the general specification we had in mind.

In this article we will add an extra element to ACP_τ denoting chaos (see Brookes, Hoare and Roscoe [4] and Bergstra, Klop and Olderog [3]). One can look at this element, written as Ω, as a process which runs totally out of order without any restriction as to its behaviour. We assume that Ω does not (successfully) terminate.

There is a specific reason for introducing Ω in ACP_τ. In fact, in a specification Ω will stand for a process that is of no theoretical interest to us at the moment. Think for example of the behaviour of a computer just after memory-overflow occurs: in reasoning about the correct behaviour of the machine we do not *specify* what the machine should do after having announced its memory- overflow; the machine even may cause a deadlock instead of announcing its memory-overflow at all, since the announcement itself is already a diverging step from its specified behaviour.

So, not having specified part of its behaviour, we could say that the same specification can be implemented by many different machines. This notion '...is implemented by...' will be denoted by $\models$ in the sequel.

We will define a new relation $\models$ on processes in an algebraical setting as is shown below in Table 1. By *definition* we assume $\models$ to be reflexive, transitive and closed under contexts. Moreover we assume all general laws holding for atoms to hold for Ω as well.

In Koymans and Mulder [7] this notion has already been worked out in a semantical setting of process graphs. So far it has not been verified whether this leads to the same interpretation.

$\Omega \cdot x = \Omega$	CH1
$\Omega + x = \Omega$	CH2
$\Omega \models x$	IM1
$a \cdot \Omega \models \delta$	IM2

TABLE 1. The axioms of chaos and of implementation

Within the semantical setting of Process Algebra (see Bergstra and Klop [2]), in two specific examples we will be able to prove *correctness* of certain implementations of systolic systems with respect to these specifications. These proofs already were presented by Hennessy [6] using *synchronous* ('clocked') cooperation between cells. In the following, however, we will specify *asynchronous* versions of these examples. We therefore construct *delay-insensitive* circuits (see Ebergen [5]), which says that the system can 'wait' for communication at its channels without starting to malfunction.

Other authors working with formal specifications to describe the behaviour of VLSI-circuits are for instance Milne [10] and Rem [11].

It turns out that ACP_τ provides us with a convenient proof system in which correctness proofs can be presented in a fairly standard way.

At this place we especially want to thank Jos Baeten who took the trouble to check this article several times and who gave so much of his support in developing its content.

2. A PALINDROME-RECOGNISER

In the following we will describe a machine which is able to recognise palindromes from strings of input symbols i.e. a machine that answers 'true' if and only if a given string of input symbols is equal to its reverse.

Suppose S is a finite set of symbols from which the input strings are built up.

The actions of sending and receiving a symbol d along a certain channel are written as $s(d)$ and $r(d)$ respectively. Moreover we have a predicate *ispal* with strings of symbols as its domain which is true if and only if its argument is a palindrome. Finally we write $|w|$ for the length of the string w.

Now we can easily write down the specification of the palindrome-recogniser PAL as is done in Table 2.

$$\mathrm{PAL}(\epsilon)=s(\mathrm{true})\cdot\mathrm{PAL}(\epsilon)+\sum_{x\in S} r(x)\cdot s(\mathrm{true})\cdot\mathrm{PAL}(x)$$

$$\mathrm{PAL}(w)=\sum_{x\in S} r(x)\cdot s(\mathrm{ispal}(x\cdot w))\cdot\mathrm{PAL}(x\cdot w) \qquad (|w|>0)$$

TABLE 2. A specification of the palindrome-recogniser PAL

The specification in Table 2 describes precisely our intuition about what a palindrome-recogniser should do.

Note that the machine PAL only receives input symbols. Since it is clear that a palindrome-recogniser should not throw away any of its received information the machine described in Table 2 needs to be able to contain arbitrarily long strings of symbols. In practice, however, machines are of a finite size. So from a more practical point of view we should first give a specification of a machine that only works on input strings with a limited length.

In Table 3 a machine PAL_k is specified working exactly like the previous palindrome-recogniser but now with a limit to the length of its input strings. For reasons to be explained later this limit is put $2k$ instead of k.

We assume our machine PAL_k has an in/output channel numbered $k+1$. So $s_{k+1}(d)$ and $r_{k+1}(d)$ will denote the actions of sending and receiving a symbol d.

$$\mathrm{PAL}_0(w) = s_1(\mathrm{true}) \cdot \mathrm{PAL}_0(w) + \sum_{x \in S} r_1(x) \cdot \Omega \qquad (0 \leq |w|)$$

$$\mathrm{PAL}_{k+1}(\epsilon) = s_{k+2}(\mathrm{true}) \cdot \mathrm{PAL}_{k+1}(\epsilon) + \sum_{x \in S} r_{k+2}(x) \cdot s_{k+2}(\mathrm{true}) \cdot \mathrm{PAL}_{k+1}(x)$$

$$\mathrm{PAL}_{k+1}(w) = \sum_{x \in S} r_{k+2}(x) \cdot s_{k+2}(\mathrm{ispal}(x \cdot w)) \cdot \mathrm{PAL}_{k+1}(x \cdot w) \qquad (0 < |w| < 2(k+1))$$

$$\mathrm{PAL}_{k+1}(w) = \sum_{x \in S} r_{k+2}(x) \cdot \Omega \qquad (2(k+1) \leq |w|)$$

TABLE 3. A specification of PAL_k for arbitrary natural number k

The fourth equation tells us that if PAL_k has reached its maximum capacity it will turn into chaos, i.e. it will not be restricted any more as to its behaviour. Indeed if the machine has thrown away any of its input it can never react like a palindrome-recogniser with respect to this input.

We will now introduce an implementation of a palindrome-recogniser of some given size k. This means we will construct a machine implementing the specification given above.

As mentioned in the introduction this particular implementation has the look of a large integration of identical cells. As a matter of fact each cell itself is again a palindrome-recogniser of size 2. We will prove that a merge of k such cells gives us exactly a palindrome-recogniser of size $2k$.

Consider the cell pictured in Figure 1. The i-th cell C_i has two communication channels i and $i+1$. Internally C_i has three storage locations, one for boolean values and two for symbols.

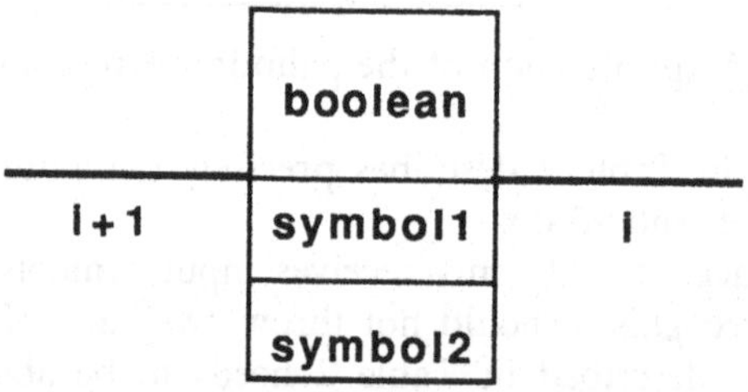

FIGURE 1. An individual cell, C_i, of the palindrome-recogniser

The cell C_i has three distinct states.

(0) In the initial state the cell carries no symbols, i.e.: carries the empty word, and since the empty word is a palindrome it can always output the boolean value true to the left. If a symbol is input from the left it is stored in the location **symbol2**, then the boolean value true is output to the left

since a word consisting of a single symbol always is a palindrome. The cell now is in state one.

(1) In state one a symbol is input from the left and a boolean from the right (in any order), and stored in the remaining locations **symbol1** and **boolean.** The cell is now in state two.

(2) In state two the cell contains two symbols **symbol1** and **symbol2** forming a word that is a palindrome iff **symbol1 = symbol2.** Now a boolean value b is output to the left, which is calculated according to the formula

$$b = \textbf{boolean} \wedge (\textbf{symbol1} = \textbf{symbol2}).$$

Hence before deciding about its output the cell C_i *consults* messages received from the outside world. Together with this boolean output the symbol in location **symbol1** is output to the right (in any order interleaved) making room for new input symbols. The cell is now in state one once more.

In the language of ACP_τ the behaviour of the cell C_i described above can be expressed by the equations shown in Table 4. The fourth equation defines a machine called TC which stands for *terminal cell.* This terminal cell has a fairly destructive behaviour with respect to its input data since they are simply thrown away. Since TC never 'contains' any symbol (or always contains the empty string) it can always output a boolean value true and thus behaves like a palindrome-recogniser of size zero (note that the empty string is a palindrome). In the sequel we write B for the set of booleans {true, false}.

$$C_i = s_{i+1}(\text{true}) \cdot C_i + \sum_{x \in S} r_{i+1}(x) \cdot s_{i+1}(\text{true}) \cdot C'_i(x)$$

$$C'_i(x) = (\sum_{y \in S} r_{i+1}(y) \| \sum_{v \in B} r_i(v)) \cdot C''_i(x, y, v)$$

$$C''_i(x, y, v) = (s_{i+1}(|x = y| \wedge v) \| s_i(y)) \cdot C'_i(x)$$

$$TC = s_1(\text{true}) \cdot TC + \sum_{x \in S} r_1(x) \cdot TC$$

TABLE 4. Formal definition of the behaviour of an individual cell

Note that the second equation violates the scope rules of $\sum$ since y and v are bounded variables in the first term. We will nevertheless use this notation as a shorthand for the correct but much more complex term

$$\sum_{y \in S} r_{i+1}(y) \cdot (\sum_{v \in B} r_i(v) \cdot C''_i(x,y,v)) + \sum_{v \in B} r_i(v) \cdot (\sum_{y \in S} r_{i+1}(y) \cdot C''_i(x, y, v)).$$

We prefer not to introduce a formal notion here.

From the cells described above we now construct a stronger machine by putting the cells in a chain and defining communications between connected cells.

Consider the configuration as pictured in Figure 2 below. Since now the cells are connected by their channels it is easy to see how we should define an appropriate communication function. Through channel i the cells C_{i-1} and C_i communicate by the communication action $s_i(x)|r_i(x)$. Any separate action $s_i(x)$ or $r_i(x)$ means something like 'waiting to communicate' and since we do not want our machine to wait eternally for communication we have to encapsulate them. The only exceptions are $s_{k+1}(x)$ and $r_{k+1}(x)$ since there is no cell C_{k+1} to communicate with them. Hence these two actions can communicate with the outside world.

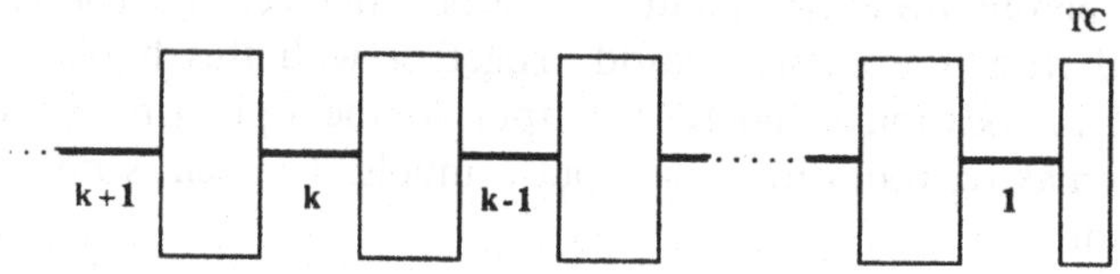

FIGURE 2. A chain configuration of k cells

From now we assume k to be fixed.

We have in general the following *communication function* defined on atomic actions:

$$s_i(x)|r_i(x) = c_i(x) \quad \text{for all } x \in S \cup B \text{ and } i < k+1$$

$$a|b = \delta \quad \text{for all other pairs of actions } a,b \in A.$$

The *encapsulation set* H_k of actions resulting in a deadlock is defined as

$$H_k = \{s_i(x), r_i(x): x \in S \cup B \text{ and } i < k+1\}.$$

The *abstraction set* I of invisible machine actions is defined as

$$I = \{c_i(x): x \in S \cup B \text{ and } i < \omega\}.$$

Note that by definition machine actions are *invisible* if and only if they do not occur in the specification of the particular machine. One can also look at them as *internal actions* that can not be influenced from the outside.

The machine pictured in Figure 2 can algebraically be described as a communication merge $M(k)$ of k individual cells i.e:

$$M(k) = \tau_I \partial_{H_k}(C_k \| \cdots \| C_1 \| \mathrm{TC}).$$

In the following we will formally prove that $M(k)$ indeed is an implementation of the palindrome-recogniser given in Table 3.

3. A FORMAL PROOF OF CORRECTNESS

Before turning to the formal proof itself let us first try an example to see how the machine works. Indeed this gives us some intuition about the practical behaviour of $M(k)$ which will be helpful later in this section. The specific example given below was found in [8].

In Figure 3 four connected cells are pictured and we can look at the machine until the string *baabaaba* is input. As we see, immediately after receiving a new input symbol the machine returns a boolean value at the left-most channel to state whether the string in the machine is a palindrome or not.

In Figure 4 we connect the *terminal cell* TC to our previous machine and assume *aababba* has already been input. When in addition *abb* is input we get as output, true, although *abbaababba* is not a palindrome. So we see that the behaviour of the machine depends on the length of the input.

If the input gets too long TC will destruct input symbols loosing all relevant information about them.

We will now get to the main fact in this paragraph which will be proved by means of the equations of ACP_τ together with RSP, the Recursive Specification Principle which says that if two processes satisfy the same guarded recursive specification then they are equal.

To do this we first need to give a more detailed specification of the machine we have constructed so far. As a matter of fact we will prove our machine to be equal to the process DP_k specified below in Table 5.

$$DP_0(w) = TC \qquad (0 \leqslant |w|)$$

$$DP_{k+1}(\epsilon) = s_{k+2}(\text{true})\cdot DP_{k+1}(\epsilon) + \sum_{x \in S} r_{k+2}(x)\cdot s_{k+2}(\text{true})\cdot DP_{k+1}(x)$$

$$DP_{k+1}(w) = \sum_{x \in S} r_{k+2}(x)\cdot s_{k+2}(\text{ispal}(x\cdot w))\cdot DP_{k+1}(x\cdot w) \qquad (0 < |w| < 2(k+1))$$

$$DP_{k+1}(w) = \sum_{x \in S} r_{k+2}(x)\cdot s_{k+2}(\text{ispal}(x\cdot f(k+1, w)))\cdot DP_{k+1}(x\cdot w) \qquad (2(k+1) \leqslant |w|)$$

$$TC = s_1(\text{true})\cdot TC + \sum_{x \in S} r_1(x)\cdot TC$$

where a function $f(k,w)$ is defined as

$$f(k,w) = \begin{cases} w & \text{if } |w| < 2k \\ \text{first}(k-1,w)\cdot\text{last}(k,w) & \text{otherwise} \end{cases}$$

with the obvious extra functions

$$\text{first}(k, x_1 \cdots x_n) = (x_1 \cdots x_k)$$

$$\text{last}(k, x_1 \cdots x_n) = (x_{n-k+1} \cdots x_n).$$

TABLE 5. A specification of DP_k for arbitrary natural number k

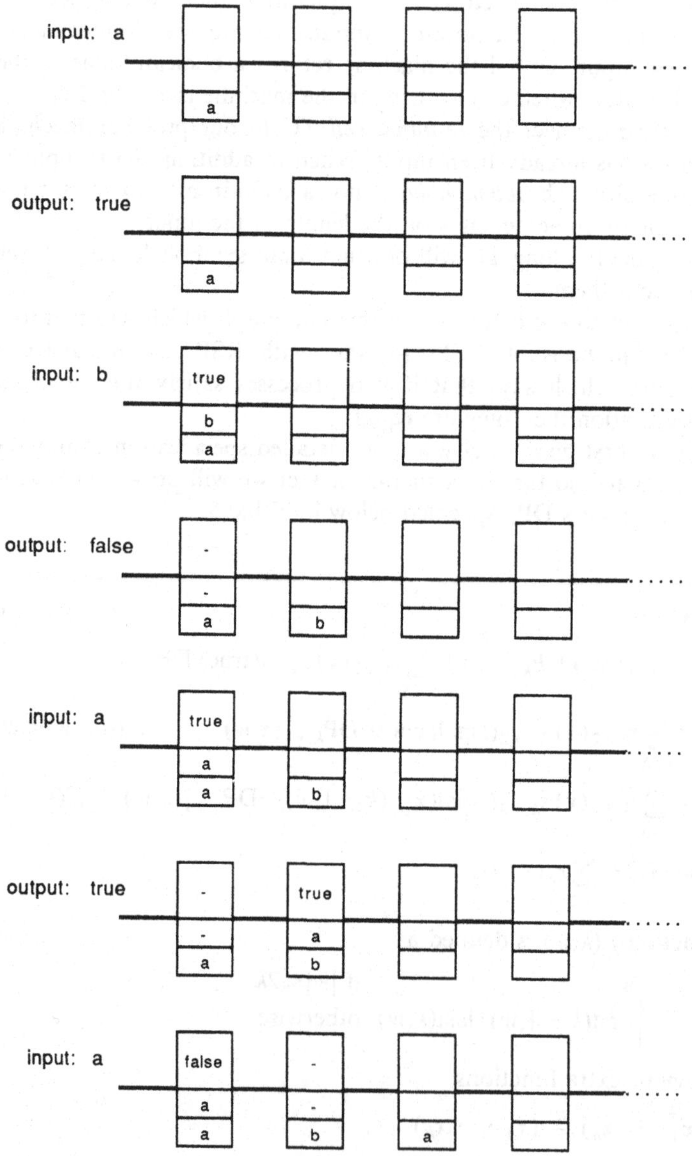

FIGURE 3. An example to give an idea of how the machine works (to be continued)

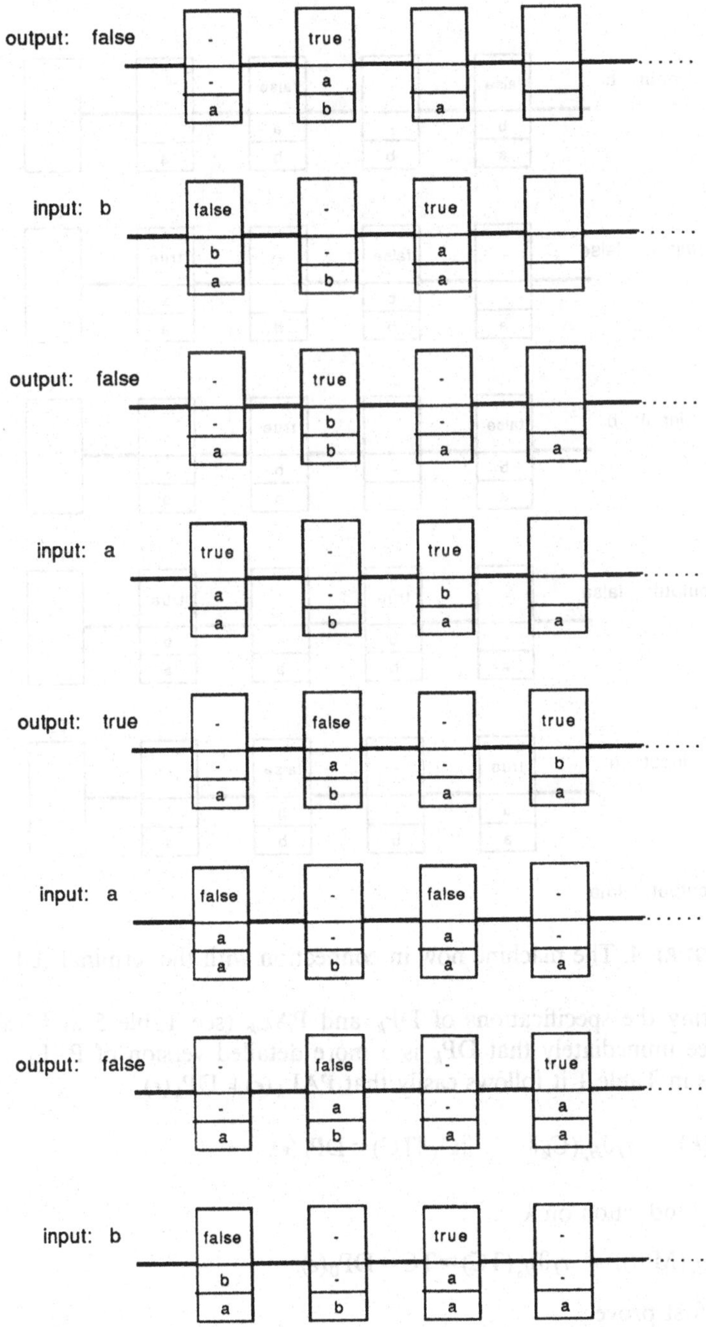

FIGURE 3. (continued)

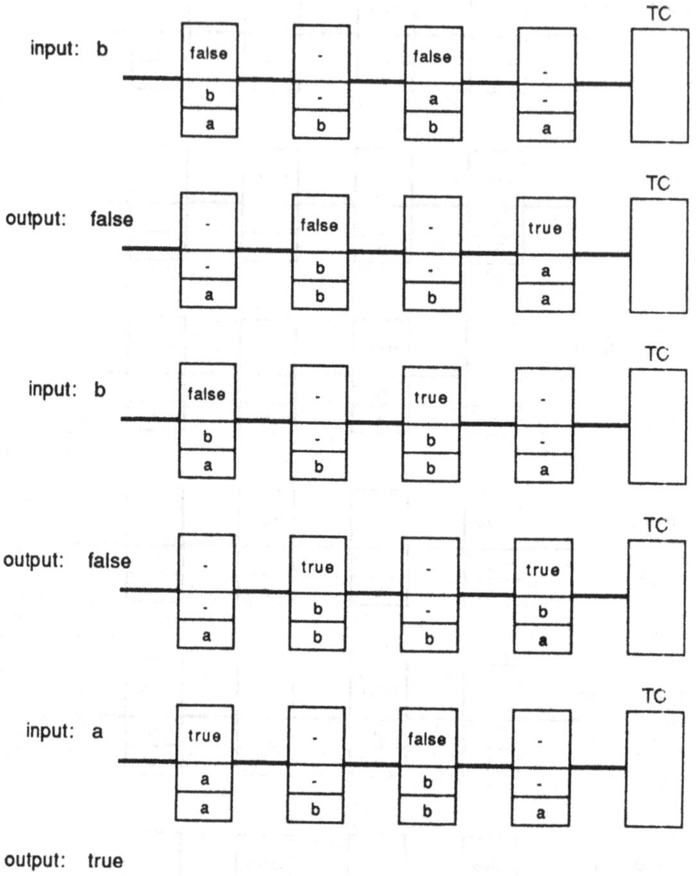

FIGURE 4. The machine now in connection with the terminal cell

Comparing the specifications of DP_k and PAL_k (see Table 5 and Table 3) one can see immediately that DP_k is a more detailed version of PAL_k. From the axioms in Table 1 it follows easily that $PAL_k(\epsilon) \models DP_k(\epsilon)$.

FACT. $M(k) = \tau_I \partial_{H_k}(C_k \| \cdots \| C_1 \| TC) = DP_k(\epsilon)$.

PROOF. By induction on k.

$k=0$: $\tau_I \partial_{H_0}(M(0)) = \tau_I \partial_{H_0}(TC) = TC = DP_0(\epsilon)$.

$k+1$: we first prove

$$\tau_I \partial_{H_{k+1}}(C_{k+1} \| DP_k(\epsilon)) = DP_{k+1}(\epsilon).$$

Then the result can easily be proved by use of the conditional axioms. It is easily checked that the following two equations hold:

$$\tau_I\partial_{H_{k+1}}(C_{k+1}\|DP_k(\epsilon)) = s_{k+2}(\text{true})\cdot\tau_I\partial_{H_{k+1}}(C_{k+1}\|DP_k(\epsilon))+$$
$$+\sum_{x\in S} r_{k+2}(x)\cdot s_{k+2}(\text{true})\cdot\tau_I\partial_{H_{k+1}}(C'_{k+1}(x)\|DP_k(\epsilon)). \quad (1)$$

$$\tau_I\partial_{H_{k+1}}(C'_{k+1}(x)\|DP_k(\epsilon)) =$$
$$= \tau\cdot\sum_{y\in S} r_{k+2}(y)\cdot\tau_I\partial_{H_{k+1}}(C''_{k+1}(x,y,\text{true})\|DP_k(\epsilon)). \quad (2)$$

To continue we need a definition.

DEFINITION. $g(k,v) = \begin{cases} v & \text{if } |v|\leqslant 2k \\ \text{first}(k,v)\cdot\text{last}(k,v) & \text{otherwise} \end{cases}$

Now we can formulate what is in fact the crucial induction hypothesis:

LEMMA. *For all symbols $x,y\in S$ and strings $v\in S^*$ we have*

(i) $\tau_I\partial_{H_{k+1}}(C'_{k+1}(x)\|(s_{k+1}(\text{ispal}(g(k,v)))\cdot DP_k(v))) = \tau\cdot DP_{k+1}(v\cdot x)$

(ii) $\tau_I\partial_{H_{k+1}}(C''_{k+1}(x, y, \text{ispal}(g(k,v)))\|DP_k(v))$

$$= \tau\cdot s_{k+1}(\text{ispal}(y\cdot f(k+1, v\cdot x)))\cdot DP_{k+1}(y\cdot v\cdot x).$$

PROOF. Let

$$Q(x, v) = \tau_I\partial_{H_{k+1}}(C'_{k+1}(x)\|(s_{k+1}(\text{ispal}(g(k, v)))\cdot DP_k(v))).$$

Now we prove that we have

$$Q(x, v) = \tau\cdot\sum_{y\in S} r_{k+2}(y)\cdot s_{k+2}(\text{ispal}(y\cdot f(k+1, v\cdot x)))\cdot Q(x, y\cdot v)$$

which gives us precisely $\tau\cdot DP_{k+1}(v\cdot x)$ given in Table 5, and hence Lemma (i) by RSP. We have

$Q(x,v) =$

$$= \tau_I\partial_{H_{k+1}}(((\sum_{y\in S} r_{k+2}(y)\|\sum_{b\in B} r_{k+1}(b))\cdot C''_{k+1}(x, y, b))\|$$
$$\|(s_{k+1}(\text{ispal}(g(k,v)))\cdot DP_k(v)))$$

$$= \sum_{y\in S} r_{k+2}(y)\cdot\tau_I\partial_{H_{k+1}}((\sum_{b\in B} r_{k+1}(b)\cdot C''_{k+1}(x, y, b))\|(s_{k+1}(\text{ispal}(g(k,v)))\cdot DP_k(v)))+$$
$$+\tau\cdot\tau_I\partial_{H_{k+1}}((\sum_{y\in S} r_{k+2}(y)\cdot C''_{k+1}(x, y, \text{ispal}(g(k,v))))\|DP_k(v))$$

$$= \tau\cdot\sum_{y\in S} r_{k+2}(y)\cdot\tau_I\partial_{H_{k+1}}(C''_{k+1}(x, y, \text{ispal}(g(k,v)))\|DP_k(v)) \quad \text{(using axiom T2).}$$

Furthermore we have

$$\tau_I \partial_{H_{k+1}}(\mathrm{C}''_{k+1}(x, y, \mathrm{ispal}(g(k,v)))\|\mathrm{DP}_k(v)) =$$

$$= s_{k+2}(|x=y|\wedge \mathrm{ispal}(g(k,v)))\cdot \tau_I \partial_{H_{k+1}}((s_{k+1}(y)\cdot \mathrm{C}'_{k+1}(x))\|$$
$$\|(\sum_{z\in S} r_{k+1}(z)\cdot s_{k+1}(\mathrm{ispal}(z\cdot f(k, v)))\cdot \mathrm{DP}_k(z\cdot v)))+$$
$$+\tau\cdot\tau_I \partial_{H_{k+1}}((s_{k+1}(|x=y|\wedge \mathrm{ispal}(g(k,v)))\cdot \mathrm{C}'_{k+1}(x))\|$$
$$\|(s_{k+1}(\mathrm{ispal}(y\cdot f(k, v)))\cdot \mathrm{DP}_k(y\cdot v)))$$

$$= \tau\cdot s_{k+2}(|x=y|\wedge \mathrm{ispal}(g(k,v)))\cdot$$
$$\cdot\tau_I \partial_{H_{k+1}}(\mathrm{C}'_{k+1}(x)\|(s_{k+1}(\mathrm{ispal}(y\cdot f(k, v)))\cdot \mathrm{DP}_k(y\cdot v)))$$

and since

$$|x=y|\wedge \mathrm{ispal}(g(k,v)) = \mathrm{ispal}(y\cdot f(k, v\cdot x))$$
$$y\cdot f(k,v) = g(k, y\cdot v)$$

we have

$$=\tau\cdot s_{k+2}(\mathrm{ispal}(y\cdot f(k+1, v\cdot x)))\cdot$$
$$\cdot\tau_I \partial_{H_{k+1}}(\mathrm{C}'_{k+1}(x)\|(s_{k+1}(\mathrm{ispal}(g(k, y\cdot v)))\cdot \mathrm{DP}_k(y\cdot v)))$$
$$=\tau\cdot s_{k+2}(\mathrm{ispal}(y\cdot f(k+1, v\cdot x)))\cdot Q(x, y\cdot v).$$

After substitution we find

$$Q(x, v) = \tau\cdot \sum_{y\in S} r_{k+2}(y)\cdot s_{k+2}(\mathrm{ispal}(y\cdot f(k+1, v\cdot x)))\cdot Q(x, y\cdot v)$$

which is precisely what we wanted.
By RSP we have Lemma (i). Note that we implicitly proved (ii). □ (Lemma)

The rest of the proof is straightforward:
With Lemma (ii) and (2) we have

$$\tau_I \partial_{H_{k+1}}(\mathrm{C}'_{k+1}(x)\|\mathrm{DP}_k(\epsilon)) =$$
$$= \tau\cdot \sum_{y\in S} r_{k+2}(y)\cdot s_{k+2}(\mathrm{ispal}(y\cdot f(k+1, x)))\cdot \mathrm{DP}_{k+1}(y\cdot x)$$
$$= \tau\cdot \mathrm{DP}_{k+1}(x).$$

Finally with (1) we have

$$\tau_I\partial_{H_{k+1}}(C_{k+1}\|DP_k(\epsilon)) =$$
$$= s_{k+2}(\text{true})\cdot\tau_I\partial_{H_{k+1}}(C_{k+1}\|DP_k(\epsilon)) + \sum_{x\in S} r_{k+2}(x)\cdot s_{k+2}(\text{true})\cdot\tau\cdot DP_{k+1}(x)$$
$$= DP_{k+1}(\epsilon)$$

using RSP again.

Note that we have proved

$$\tau_I\partial_{H_{k+1}}(C_{k+1}\|\tau_I\partial_{H_k}(C_k\| \cdots \tau_I\partial_{H_1}(C_1\|TC)\cdots)) = DP_{k+1}(\epsilon).$$

It is easy to prove by induction, however, that

$$\alpha(C_{k+1})|(\alpha(C_k\|M(k-1))\cap H_k)\subseteq H_k$$

for all k (in fact $\alpha(C_{k+1})|(\alpha(C_k\|M(k-1))\cap H_k)=\varnothing$, and

$$\alpha(C_{k+1})|(\alpha(C_k\|M(k-1))\cap I) = \varnothing).$$

So because $H_{k+1}\supseteq H_k$ we find with the use of the conditional axioms CA1, CA2 and CA5:

$$\tau_I\partial_{H_{k+1}}(C_{k+1}\|\tau_I\partial_{H_k}(C_k\| \cdots \tau_I\partial_{H_1}(C_1\|TC)\cdots))=$$
$$= \tau_I\partial_{H_{k+1}}(\tau_I\partial_{H_k}(\cdots \tau_I\partial_{H_1}(C_{k+1}\|C_k\| \cdots \|C_1\|TC)\cdots)).$$

Since

$$H\cap I = \varnothing$$

we have

$$\tau_I\partial_{H_{k+1}}(\tau_I\partial_{H_k}(\cdots \tau_I\partial_{H_1}(C_{k+1}\|C_k\| \cdots \|C_1\|TC)\cdots)) =$$
$$= \tau_I \cdots \tau_I\partial_{H_{k+1}} \cdots \partial_{H_1}(C_{k+1}\|C_k\| \cdots \|C_1\|TC)$$

by axiom CA7 and finally with axioms CA5 and CA6 we find

$$\tau_I \cdots \tau_I\partial_{H_{k+1}} \cdots \partial_{H_1}(C_{k+1}\|C_k\| \cdots \|C_1\|TC) =$$
$$=\tau_I\partial_{H_{k+1}}(C_{k+1}\|C_k\| \cdots \|C_1\|TC)$$

which is exactly $M(k+1)$.

Therefore, we have $M(k)=DP_k(\epsilon)$, for all k. This finishes the induction. □

Finally we find

$$PAL_k(\epsilon) \models DP_k(\epsilon)=M(k)=\tau_I\partial_{H_k}(C_k\| \cdots \|C_1\|TC)$$

so we have

$$PAL_k(\epsilon) \models \tau_I\partial_{H_k}(C_k\| \cdots \|C_1\|TC)$$

which is the formal way to express that $\tau_I\partial_{H_k}(C_k\| \cdots \|C_1\|TC)$ indeed is a palindrome-recogniser.

4. A SORTING MACHINE

A second example of a machine implemented by a 'systolic system' is a sorting machine. A sorting machine can input a sequence of numbers and output them in increasing order. First we will discuss a restricted sorting machine which is a sorting machine with a restricted capacity. For a good performance of such a restricted sorting machine with capacity n it is necessary that the machine does not contain more than n numbers. If the absolute value of the difference of the number of input and output actions is greater than n, the behaviour of the restricted sorting machine is undefined. Later on, a sorting machine which can contain an arbitrary amount of numbers will be discussed.

Before we discuss in what way the restricted sorting machine is constructed we first state its expected external behaviour. This is done in Table 6.

$\text{SORT}_k(\varnothing)=s_k(\text{empty})\cdot\text{SORT}_k(\varnothing)+\sum_{d\in D} r_k(d)\cdot\text{SORT}_k(\{d\})$	
$\text{SORT}_k(B)=s_k(\mu B)\cdot\text{SORT}_k(B-\{\mu B\})+\sum_{d\in D} r_k(d)\cdot\text{SORT}_k(B\cup\{d\})$	$0<\|B\|<k$
$\text{SORT}_k(B)=s_k(\mu B)\cdot\text{SORT}_k(B-\{\mu B\})+\sum_{d\in D} r_k(d)\cdot\Omega$	$\|B\|=k$

TABLE 6. Specification of a restricted sorting machine with capacity $k\,(k>0)$

Some explanation is useful here. B is a bag or multiset with $|B|$ elements. $\varnothing$ is the empty bag. If bag B is not empty the minimal element of B is denoted by μB. On bags the operations $\cup$ and $-$ are defined in the standard way. $\text{SORT}_k(B)$ is the restricted sorting machine of capacity k with contents B. SORT_k has a communication channel k. Through this channel the restricted sorting machine can output (s_k) and input (r_k) data to and from the outside. A datum can be a number or a special symbol called 'empty'. The relevance of sending an empty signal is made clear in the implementation part later on. There it turns out to be an inevitable action as a result of that implementation. The Ω stands for the process chaos discussed in Section 2. Ω is encountered when the content of the restricted sorting machine gets greater than its capacity. The behaviour of the machine then becomes irrelevant.

Now we will describe the implementation of a restricted sorting machine of a certain capacity by connecting a number of identical cells. It shall be proved that k connected cells plus one special cell is an implementation of the restricted sorting machine SORT_{2k}. The notion of implementation, denoted by $\models$ is described in Section 2. Before we discuss a chain of cells we first turn to an individual cell.

An individual cell has two storage locations called MIN and MAX and two communication channels. The channels of cell C_i ($i>0$) are called i and $i-1$.

Elements of a number set D can be stored in MIN and MAX. Elements of D and 'empty' can be transmitted through the communication channels. An individual cell C_i is pictured in Figure 5.

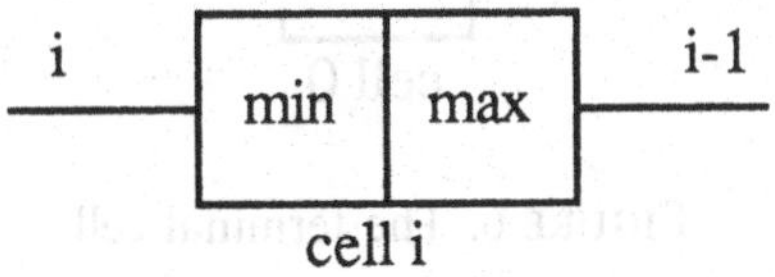

FIGURE 5. An individual cell C_i

Each cell can be in three states.

(0) In this state both storage locations MIN and MAX are empty. The cell C_i can receive a number from the left. This number is stored in MIN and the cell enters state (1). Another possible action is sending an 'empty' to the left. In this case the cell remains in state (0). State (0) is also the initial state for each cell C_i ($i>0$).

(1) In state (1), MIN is filled and MAX is empty (really empty). A number from the left can be received. The minimum of the content of MIN and the received number is stored in MIN. The other number is stored in MAX. State (2) is entered. The second possibility is sending the content of MIN to the left and entering state (0) again.

(2) Now MIN and MAX are both filled and the content of MIN is less than or equal to the content of MAX. The cell C_i can receive a number from the left and send the content of MAX to the right. MIN becomes the minimum of the content of MIN and the received number. The other number is stored in MAX. The cell remains in state (2). The other action the cell can perform is sending the content of MIN to the left. Now two possibilities arise: the cell receives an empty signal from the right, MIN gets the content of MAX and the cell enters state (1). The second possibility is receiving a number from the right. MIN becomes the minimum of MAX and the received number and MAX becomes the maximum of the two. The cell C_i remains in state (2).

Because we are building a restricted sorting machine an extra cell is needed. This cell is called C_0. It is pictured in Figure 6. This cell has one communication channel called 0 and contains no storage locations. C_0 remains always in the same state. In this state C_0 is able to send an 'empty' to the left or receive a number from the left. The number received disappears completely. C_0 can be considered as a cell crushing the incoming numbers.

The specification of the cell C_i ($i \geq 0$) is given in Table 7.

All parts needed for building a restricted sorting machine have been discussed. A restricted sorting machine with capacity $2k$ can be built by interconnecting $k+1$ cells C_i ($0 \leq i \leq k$). C_i and C_{i-1}($1 \leq i \leq k$) communicate through channel $i-1$. Channel k is the external input/output channel for the machine.

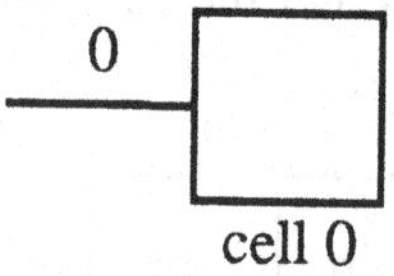

FIGURE 6. The terminal cell

$$i=0: \quad C_0=\sum_{d\in D} r_0(d)\cdot C_0+s_0(\text{empty})\cdot C_0$$

$$i>0: \quad C_i=\sum_{d\in D} r_i(d)\cdot C'_i(d)+s_i(\text{empty})\cdot C_i$$

$$C'_i(d)=\sum_{e\in D} r_i(e)\cdot C''_i(sw(d,e))+s_i(d)\cdot C_i$$

$$C''_i(d,e)=\sum_{f\in D} r_i(f)\cdot s_{i-1}(e)\cdot C_i''(sw(d,f))$$
$$+s_i(d)\cdot(r_{i-1}(\text{empty})\cdot C'_i(e)+\sum_{f\in D} r_{i-1}(f)\cdot C''_i(sw(e,f)))$$

Here sw stands for swap: $sw(d,e)=(\min(d,e),\max(d,e))$

TABLE 7. Specification of an individual cell C_i for $i\geqslant 0$

When an internal cell i (that is a cell which is not the first cell in the chain) performs an action $s_i(d)$, $r_i(d)$, $s_{i-1}(d)$ or $r_{i-1}(d)$, $d\in D\cup\{\text{empty}\}$, this action must be matched by a complementary action of a neighbouring cell. For cell C_k only actions $s_{k-1}(d)$ and $r_{k-1}(d)$ must be answered by complementary actions of cell $k-1$. This is achieved in Process Algebra by defining communications $c_i(d)$ as the result of $s_i(d)$ and $r_i(d)$ and encapsulating the individual actions $s_i(d)$ and $r_i(d)$. Of course the actions $r_k(d)$ and $s_k(d)$ are not encapsulated because these actions are the communications with the outside world. To illustrate that this chain of k cells plus one special cell really gives a restricted sorting machine of capacity $2k$ an example is worked out in Figure 7 In this case $k=3$.

A formal description of the machine discussed before and pictured in Figure 7 is given in Table 8. We call the empty restricted sorting machine built from k normal cells plus the terminal cell SORT*$_{2k}(\epsilon)$. H_k is the encapsulation set and contains the actions that should not be performed without a partner. To describe the external behaviour of the restricted sorting machine we abstract from the internal actions that still can be performed after encapsulation. Symbols to be abstracted from are in I. The resulting sorting machine is called SORT*$_{2k}(\epsilon)$. Now it will be proved that this restricted sorting machine is an implementation of the restricted sorting machine defined by the specification in Table 6.

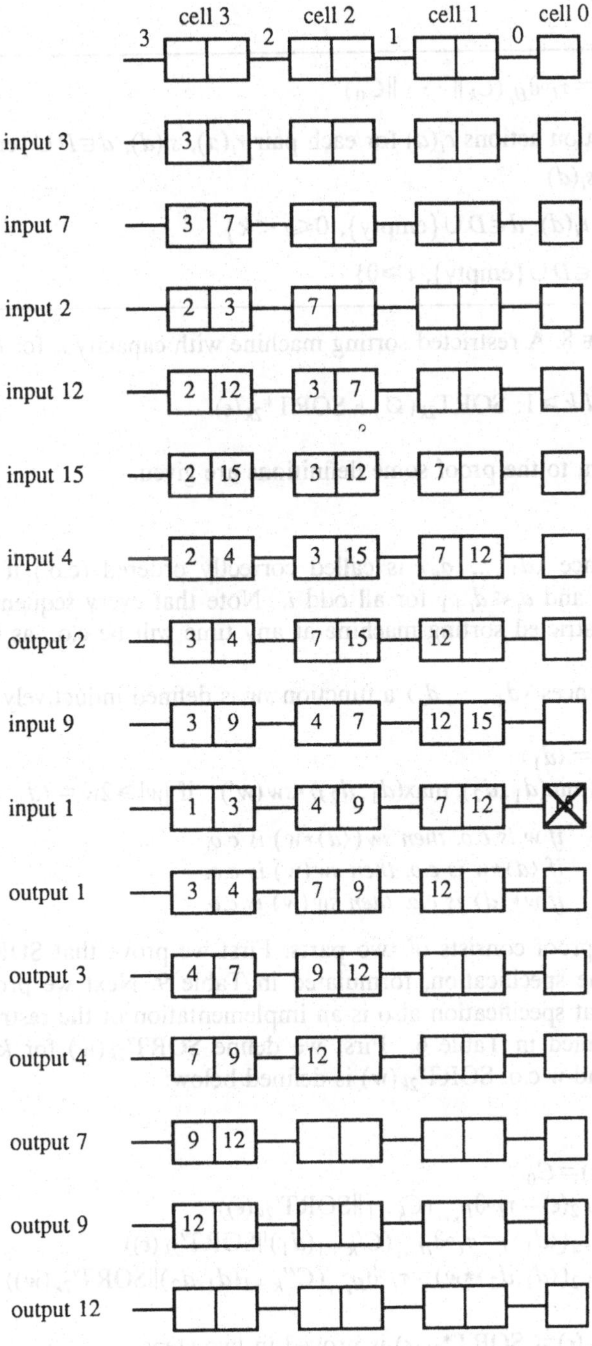

FIGURE 7. Example of restricted sorting machine

$\mathrm{SORT}^*_{2k}(\epsilon)=\tau_I \circ \partial_{H_k}(C_k \| \cdots \| C_0)$
Communication actions $c_i(d)$ for each pair $r_i(d)$, $s_i(d)$, $d \in D \cup \{\text{empty}\}$, $i<k$: $c_i(d)=r_i(d) \| s_i(d)$
$H_k=\{s_i(d), r_i(d): d \in D \cup \{\text{empty}\}, 0 \leqslant i<k\}$
$I=\{c_i(d): d \in D \cup \{\text{empty}\}, i \geqslant 0\}$

TABLE 8. A restricted sorting machine with capacity k for $k>0$

FACT. *For all* $k \geqslant 1$: $\mathrm{SORT}_{2k}(\varnothing) \models \mathrm{SORT}^*_{2k}(\epsilon)$.

Before we turn to the proof some definitions are given.

DEFINITION.
(i) A sequence $\langle d_1, \ldots, d_n \rangle$ is called correctly ordered (c.o.) if and only if $d_i \leqslant d_{i+2}$ and $d_i \leqslant d_{i+1}$ for all odd i. Note that every sequence contained in the restricted sorting machine at any time will be c.o., as illustrated in Figure 7.
(ii) On sequences $\langle d_1, \ldots, d_n \rangle$ a function sw is defined inductively as follows:
$sw(\epsilon)=\epsilon$
$sw(\langle d_1 \rangle)=\langle d_1 \rangle$
$sw(w)=\langle \min(d_1, d_2), \max(d_1, d_2) \rangle * sw(w')$ if $|w| \geqslant 2 w=\langle d_1, d_2 \rangle * w'$

FACT. (i) *if* w *is c.o. then* $sw(\langle d \rangle * w)$ *is c.o.*
(ii) *if* $\langle d \rangle * w$ *is c.o. then* $sw(w)$ *is c.o.*
(iii) *if* $w * \langle d \rangle$ *is c.o. then* $sw(w)$ *is c.o.*

PROOF. The proof consists of two parts. First we prove that $\mathrm{SORT}^*_{2k}(\epsilon)$ is a solution of the specification, formulated in Table 9. Next we prove that any solution of that specification also is an implementation of the restricted sorting machine specified in Table 6. First we define $\mathrm{SORT}'_{2k}(w)$ for $k \geqslant 0$, $w \in S^*$, $0 \leqslant |w| \leqslant 2k$ and w c.o. $\mathrm{SORT}'_{2k}(w)$ is defined below:

DEFINITION.
(i) $\mathrm{SORT}'_0(\epsilon)=C_0$
(ii) $\mathrm{SORT}'_{2k+2}(\epsilon)=\tau_I \circ \partial_{H_{k+1}}(C_{k+1} \| \mathrm{SORT}'_{2k}(\epsilon))$
(iii) $\mathrm{SORT}'_{2k+2}(\langle d_1 \rangle)=\tau_I \circ \partial_{H_{k+1}}(C'_{k+1}(d_1) \| \mathrm{SORT}'_{2k}(\epsilon))$
(iv) $\mathrm{SORT}'_{2k+2}(\langle d_1, d_2 \rangle * w)=\tau_I \circ \partial_{H_{k+1}}(C''_{k+1}(d_1, d_2) \| \mathrm{SORT}'_{2k}(w))$

Now $\mathrm{SORT}''_{2k}(\epsilon)= \mathrm{SORT}^*_{2k}(\epsilon)$ is proved in two steps:

$\mathrm{SORT}''_{2k}(\epsilon)=s_k(\mathrm{empty})\cdot\mathrm{SORT}''_{2k}(\epsilon)+\sum_{d\in D} r_k(d)\cdot\mathrm{SORT}''_{2k}(\langle d\rangle)$
for all w with $\lvert\langle d_1\rangle\star w\rvert<2k$ and $\langle d_1\rangle\star w$ c.o.:
$\mathrm{SORT}''_{2k}(\langle d_1\rangle\star w)=\sum_{d\in D} r_k(d)\cdot\mathrm{SORT}''_{2k}(sw(\langle d\rangle\star\langle d_1\rangle\star w))$ $+s_k(d_1)\cdot\mathrm{SORT}''_{2k}(sw(w))$
for all w with $\lvert\langle d_1\rangle\star w\star\langle d_{2k}\rangle\rvert=2k$ and $\langle d_1\rangle\star w\star\langle d_{2k}\rangle$ c.o.:
$\mathrm{SORT}''_{2k}(\langle d_1\rangle\star w\star\langle d_{2k}\rangle)=\sum_{d\in D} r_k(d)\cdot\mathrm{SORT}''_{2k}(sw(\langle d\rangle\star\langle d_1\rangle\star w))$ $+s_k(d_1)\cdot\mathrm{SORT}''_{2k}(sw(w\star\langle d_{2k}\rangle))$

TABLE 9. Intermediate specification of a restricted sorting machine with capacity $2k$

first step: for all $k\geq 1$, w c.o. and $0\leq w\leq 2k$:

$$\mathrm{SORT}''_{2k}(w)=\mathrm{SORT}'_{2k}(w) \qquad (\star)$$

second step: for all $k\geq 1$: $\mathrm{SORT}'_{2k}(\epsilon)=\mathrm{SORT}^*_{2k}(\epsilon)$ $(\star\star)$

PROOF $(\star)$. The first step will be proved by induction on k and the length of the content. $k=1$: three subcases have to be considered:

$w=\epsilon$ (i)

$$\mathrm{SORT}'_2(\epsilon) = \tau_I\circ\partial_{H_1}(C_1\|C_0) =$$
$$=\tau_I\circ\partial_{H_1}(\sum_{d\in D} r_1(d)\cdot C'_1(d)+s_1(\mathrm{empty})\cdot C_1\|C_0)$$
$$=\sum_{d\in D} r_1(d)\cdot\tau_I\circ\partial_{H_1}(C'_1(d)\|C_0)+s_1(\mathrm{empty})\cdot\tau_I\circ\partial_{H_1}(C_1\|C_0)$$

Using the definition of $\mathrm{SORT}'_{2k}(w)$ the intended result is obtained:

$$\mathrm{SORT}'_2(\epsilon)=\sum_{d\in D} r_1(d)\cdot\mathrm{SORT}'_2(\langle d\rangle)+s_1(\mathrm{empty})\cdot\mathrm{SORT}'_2(\epsilon)$$

$w = \langle d_1\rangle$ (ii)

$$\mathrm{SORT}'_2(\langle d_1\rangle)=\tau_I\circ\partial_{H_1}(C'_1(d_1)\|C_0)$$
$$=\tau_I\circ\partial_{H_1}(\sum_{d\in D} r_1(d)\cdot C''_1(sw(d, d_1))+s_1(d_1)\cdot C_1\|C_0)$$

$$= \sum_{d \in D} r_1(d) \cdot \tau_I \circ \partial_{H_1}(C''_1(sw(d,d_1)) \| \mathrm{SORT}'_0(\epsilon)) +$$

$$+ s_1(d_1) \cdot \tau_I \circ \partial_{H_1}(C_1 \| \mathrm{SORT}'_0(\epsilon))$$

Using again the definition of $\mathrm{SORT}'_{2k}(w)$:

$$\mathrm{SORT}'_2(\langle d_1 \rangle) = \sum_{d \in D} r_1(d) \cdot \mathrm{SORT}'_2(sw(\langle d, d_1 \rangle)) + s_1(d) \cdot \mathrm{SORT}_2(\epsilon)$$

$w = \langle d_1, d_2 \rangle$, w is c.o. (iii)

$$\mathrm{SORT}'_2(\langle d_1, d_2 \rangle) = \tau_I \circ \partial_{H_1}(C''_1(d_1, d_2) \| C_0)$$

$$= \sum_{d \in D} r_1(d) \cdot \tau_I \circ \partial_{H_1}((s_0(d_2) \cdot C''_1(sw(d, d_1))) \| C_0) +$$

$$+ s_1(d_1) \cdot \tau_I \circ \partial_{H_1}((r_0(\mathrm{empty}) \cdot C'_1(d_2) + \sum_{e \in D} r_0(e) \cdot C''_1(sw(d_2, e))) \| C_0)$$

$$= \sum_{d \in D} r_1(d) \cdot \tau \cdot \tau_I \circ \partial_{H_1}(C''_1(sw(d, d_1)) \| C_0) + s_1(d_1) \cdot \tau \cdot \tau_I \circ \partial_{H_1}(C'_1(d_2) \| C_0)$$

so we have

$$\mathrm{SORT}'_2(\langle d_1, d_2 \rangle) = \sum_{d \in D} r_1(d) \cdot \mathrm{SORT}'_2(sw(\langle d, d_1 \rangle)) + s_1(d_1) \cdot \mathrm{SORT}'_2(\langle d_2 \rangle)$$

$k = n+1$ where $n > 0$. Five cases have to be considered:

$w = \epsilon$ (i)

$$\mathrm{SORT}'_{2(n+1)}(\epsilon) = \tau_I \circ \partial_{H_{n+1}}(C_{n+1} \| \mathrm{SORT}'_{2n}(\epsilon)) =$$

$$= \tau_I \circ \partial_{H_{n+1}}(\sum_{d \in D} r_{n+1}(d) \cdot C'_{n+1}(d) + s_{n+1}(\mathrm{empty}) \cdot C_{n+1} \| \mathrm{SORT}'_{2n}(\epsilon))$$

$$= \sum_{d \in D} r_{n+1}(d) \cdot \tau_I \circ \partial_{H_{n+1}}(C'_{n+1}(d) \| \mathrm{SORT}'_{2n}(\epsilon)) +$$

$$+ s_{n+1}(\mathrm{empty}) \cdot \tau_I \circ \partial_{H_{n+1}}(C_{n+1} \| \mathrm{SORT}'_{2n}(\epsilon))$$

$$= \sum_{d \in D} r_{n+1}(d) \cdot \mathrm{SORT}'_{2(n+1)}(\langle d \rangle) + s_{n+1}(\mathrm{empty}) \cdot \mathrm{SORT}'_{2(n+1)}(\epsilon)$$

This expression is in the form of the specification of Table 9.

$w=\langle d_1\rangle$ (ii)

$$\mathrm{SORT}'_{2(n+1)}(\langle d_1\rangle)=\tau_I\circ\partial_{H_{n+1}}(C'_{n+1}(d_1)\|\mathrm{SORT}'_{2n}(\epsilon))$$

$$=\tau_I\circ\partial_{H_{n+1}}(\sum_{d\in D} r_{n+1}(d)\cdot C''_{n+1}(sw(d,d_1))+s_{n+1}(d_1)\cdot C_{n+1}\|\mathrm{SORT}'_{2n}(\epsilon))$$

$$=\sum_{d\in D} r_{n+1}(d)\cdot\tau_I\circ\partial_{H_{n+1}}(C''_{n+1}(sw(d,d_1))\|\mathrm{SORT}'_{2n}(\epsilon))+$$

$$+s_{n+1}(d_1)\cdot\tau_I\circ\partial_{H_{n+1}}(C_{n+1}\|\mathrm{SORT}'_{2n}(\epsilon)) =$$

$$=\sum_{d\in D} r_{n+1}(d)\cdot\mathrm{SORT}'_{2(n+1)}(sw(\langle d,d_1\rangle))+s_{n+1}(d_1)\cdot\mathrm{SORT}'_{2(n+1)}(\epsilon)$$

Again in the form of the specification of Table 9.

$|w|=2,\ w=\langle d_1,d_2\rangle,\ w$ c.o. (iii)

$$\mathrm{SORT}'_{2(n+1)}(\langle d_1,d_2\rangle)=\tau_I\circ\partial_{H_{n+1}}(C''_{n+1}(d_1,d_2)\|\mathrm{SORT}'_{2n}(\epsilon))$$

$$=\sum_{d\in D} r_{n+1}(d)\cdot\tau_I\circ\partial_{H_{n+1}}(s_n(d_2)\cdot C''_{n+1}(sw(d,d_1))\|\mathrm{SORT}'_{2n}(\epsilon))+$$

$$+s_{n+1}(d)\cdot\tau_I\circ\partial_{H_{n+1}}((r_n(\mathrm{empty})\cdot C'_{n+1}(d_2)+$$

$$+\sum_{e\in D} r_n(e)\cdot C_{n+1}(sw(d_2,e)))\|\mathrm{SORT}'_{2n}(\epsilon))$$

(induction hypothesis)

$$=\sum_{d\in D} r_{n+1}(d)\cdot\tau\cdot\tau_I\circ\partial_{H_{n+1}}(C''_{n+1}(sw(d,d_1))\|\mathrm{SORT}'_{2n}(\langle d_2\rangle))+$$

$$+s_{n+1}(d_1)\cdot\tau\cdot\tau_I\circ\partial_{H_{n+1}}(C'_{n+1}(d_2)\|\mathrm{SORT}'_{2n}(\epsilon))$$

$$=\sum_{d\in D} r_{n+1}(d)\cdot\mathrm{SORT}'_{2(n+1)}(sw(\langle d,d_1,d_2\rangle))+s_{n+1}(d)\cdot\mathrm{SORT}'_{2(n+1)}(\langle d_2\rangle)$$

which is the intended form.

$3\leqslant|w|<2k,\ w=\langle d_1,d_2\rangle * w',\ w'=\langle d_3\rangle * w'',\ w$ c.o. (iv)

$$\mathrm{SORT}'_{2(n+1)}(w)=\tau_I\circ\partial_{H_{n+1}}(C''_{n+1}(d_1,d_2)\|\mathrm{SORT}'_{2n}(w')) =$$

$$= \sum_{d \in D} r_{n+1}(d) \cdot \tau_I \circ \partial_{H_{n+1}}(s_n(d_2) \cdot C''_{n+1}(sw(d, d_1)) \| \mathrm{SORT}'_{2n}(w')) +$$

$$+ s_{n+1}(d_1) \cdot \tau_I \circ \partial_{H_{n+1}}((r_n(\mathrm{empty}) \cdot C'_{n+1}(d_2) +$$

$$+ \sum_{e \in D} r_n(e) \cdot C''_{n+1}(sw(d_2, e))) \| \mathrm{SORT}'_{2n}(w'))$$

(induction hypothesis)

$$= \sum_{d \in D} r_{n+1}(d) \cdot \tau \cdot \tau_I \circ \partial_{H_{n+1}}(s_n(d_2) \cdot C''_{n+1}(sw(d, d_1)) \|$$

$$\| \mathrm{SORT}'_{2n}(sw(\langle d_2 \rangle * \langle d_3 \rangle * w'))) +$$

$$+ s_{n+1}(d_1) \cdot \tau \cdot \tau_I \circ \partial_{H_{n+1}}(C''_{n+1}(sw(d_2, d_3)) \| \mathrm{SORT}'_{2n}(sw(w'')))$$

$$= \sum_{d \in D} r_{n+1}(d) \cdot \mathrm{SORT}'_{2(n+1)}(sw(\langle d \rangle * w)) + s_{n+1}(d_1) \cdot \mathrm{SORT}'_{2(n+1)}(sw(\langle d_2 \rangle * w'))$$

again the intended form.

$$\boxed{|w| = 2k, \ w = \langle d_1, d_2 \rangle * w', \ w' = \langle d_3 \rangle * w', \ w'' = w''' * \langle d_k \rangle} \qquad \text{(v)}$$

$$\mathrm{SORT}'_{2(n+1)}(w) = \tau_I \circ \partial_{H_{n+1}}(C''_{n+1}(d_1, d_2) \| \mathrm{SORT}'_{2n}(w'))$$

$$= \sum_{d \in D} r_{n+1}(d) \cdot \tau_I \circ \partial_{H_{n+1}}(s_n(d_2) \cdot C''_{n+1}(sw(d, d_1)) \| \mathrm{SORT}'_{2n}(w')) +$$

$$+ s_{n+1}(d_1) \cdot \tau_I \circ \partial_{H_{n+1}}\{(r_n(\mathrm{empty}) \cdot C'_{n+1}(d_2) +$$

$$+ \sum_{f \in D} r_n(f) \cdot C''_{n+1}(sw(d_2, f))) \| \mathrm{SORT}'_{2n}(w')\}$$

(induction hypothesis)

$$= \sum_{d \in D} r_{n+1}(d) \cdot \tau \cdot \tau_I \circ \partial_{H_{n+1}}(C''_{n+1}(sw(d, d_1)) \| \mathrm{SORT}_{2n}(sw(\langle d_2 \rangle * w'''))) +$$

$$+ s_{n+1}(d_1) \cdot \tau \cdot \tau_I \circ \partial_{H_{n+1}}(C''_{n+1}(sw(d_2, d_3)) \| \mathrm{SORT}'_{2n}(sw(w'')))$$

$$= \sum_{d \in D} r_{n+1}(d) \cdot \mathrm{SORT}'_{2(n+1)}(sw(\langle d \rangle * w)) +$$

$$+ s_{n+1}(d_1) \cdot \mathrm{SORT}'_{2(n+1)}(sw(\langle d_2 \rangle * w'))$$

which is the intended form.

From this we can conclude $\mathrm{SORT}'(w)$ satisfies the specification in Table 9. Using RSP we get for all $k \geq 1$, w c.o. and $0 \leq |w| \leq 2k$:

$$\mathrm{SORT}'_{2k}(w) = \mathrm{SORT}''_{2k}(w).$$

This ends the proof of (*). □

PROOF (**). $SORT'_{2k}(\epsilon)=SORT^*_{2k}(\epsilon)$, is proved by induction on k.

$k=1$ $SORT'_2(\epsilon)=\tau_I \circ \partial_{H_1}(C_1 \| C_0)=SORT^*_2(\epsilon)$

$k>1$ $SORT'_{2k}(\epsilon)=\tau \circ \partial_{H_k}(C_k \| SORT'_{2k-2}(\epsilon))$

$=\tau_I \circ \partial_{H_k}(C_k \| \tau_I \circ \partial_{H_{k-1}}(C_{k-1} \| \cdots \| C_0))$

Because $H_k \cap I = \varnothing$ one can rewrite this to

$$=\tau_I \circ \partial_{H_k} \circ \tau_I(C_k \| \partial_{H_{k-1}}(C_{k-1} \| \cdots \| C_0))$$

Because $\alpha(C_k)|\alpha(\partial_{H_{k-1}}(C_{k-1} \| \cdots \| C_0)) \cap I = \varnothing$ axiom CA2 can be applied

$$=\tau_I \circ \partial_{H_k}(C_k \| \partial_{H_{k-1}}(C_{k-1} \| \cdots \| C_0))$$

Because $\alpha(C_k)|\alpha(C_{k-1} \| \cdots \| C_0) \cap H_{k-1} \subseteq H_{k-1}$ axiom CA1 can be applied

$$=\tau_I \circ \partial_{H_k} \circ \partial_{H_{k-1}}(C_k \| C_{k-1} \| \cdots \| C_0)$$

Using axiom CA5 the induction step is completed

$$=\tau_I \circ \partial_{H_k}(C_k \| C_{k-1} \| \cdots \| C_0)=SORT^*_{2k}(\epsilon)$$

This ends the proof of (**). □

Comparing the specification of Table 9 to the one in Table 10 we directly conclude that $SORT'''_{2k}(\epsilon) \models SORT''_{2k}(\epsilon)$ follows from the definition of $\models$.

Because of the transitivity of $\models$ and since $x=y \Rightarrow x \models y$ we only need to prove the equation $SORT'''_{2k}(\epsilon)=SORT_{2k}(\varnothing)$ to prove $SORT_{2k}(\varnothing) \models SORT^*_{2k}(\epsilon)$. Consider the specification in Table 10 then it follows that $SORT_{2k}(B_w)$ (B_w denotes the bag containing the elements of w, w c.o., $0 \leq |w| \leq 2k$) satisfies this specification, substituting it for $SORT'''_{2k}(w)$. It is crucial here that of any correctly ordered sequence the first element also is the minimal element of that sequence. Using RSP we can conclude $SORT'''_{2k}(\epsilon)=SORT_{2k}(\varnothing)$. So, $SORT_{2k}(\varnothing) \models SORT^*_{2k}(\epsilon)$. □

$$SORT'''_{2k}(\epsilon)=s_k(\text{empty}) \cdot SORT'''_{2k}(\epsilon)+\sum_{d \in D} r_k(d) \cdot SORT'''_{2k}(\langle d \rangle)$$

$$SORT'''_{2k}(\langle d_1 \rangle * w)=\sum_{d \in D} r_k(d) \cdot SORT'''_{2k}(sw(\langle d \rangle * \langle d_1 \rangle * w))+$$

$$+s_k(d_1) \cdot SORT'''_{2k}(sw(w')) \quad \text{for } |\langle d_1 \rangle * w| < 2k-1,\ \langle d_1 \rangle * w \text{ c.o.}$$

$$SORT'''_{2k}(\langle d_1 \rangle * w * \langle d_{2k} \rangle)=\sum_{d \in D} r_k(d) \cdot \Omega + s_k(d_1) \cdot SORT'''_{2k}(sw(\langle d_1 \rangle * w * \langle d_{2k} \rangle))$$

$$\text{for } |\langle d_1 \rangle * w * \langle d_{2k} \rangle| = 2k,\ w \text{ c.o.}$$

TABLE 10. Intermediate specification of restricted sorting machine using Ω

5. A palindrome-recogniser with unrestricted capacity

In this section we will remove the restriction on the length of the input string of Section 3. Thus no terminal cell is present. The specification of this machine is given in Table 11 (compare with Table 2). k is the name of the input/output channel. Note that the subscript k in $PAL_k(w)$ has nothing to do with its capacity. It just indicates the name of the input/output channel.

$$PAL_k(\epsilon) = \sum_{x \in S} r_k(x) \cdot s_k(\text{true}) \cdot PAL_k(x) + s_k(\text{true}) \cdot PAL_k(\epsilon)$$

$$PAL_k(w) = \sum_{x \in S} r_k(x) \cdot s_k(\text{ispal}(xw)) \cdot PAL_k(xw) \quad (|w| > 0)$$

TABLE 11. Specification of palindrome recogniser with unbounded capacity

When more capacity is needed, a new cell is created. A cell can be in two major states: it is a cell left from the last cell or the last cell in the chain. The last cell is always empty. When the last cell is filled it creates a new cell on the right.

As an extension of ACP the mechanism of process creation is described in [3]. With this mechanism it is possible to create a new process concurrent with the present one. To make process creation possible a creation atom and a special operator E_ϕ are introduced. We assume that a creation atom is neither a result of a communication nor communicates with another atom. For all $d \in D$, where D is a set of data, creation atoms $cr(d)$ are introduced. This in combination with the special operator E_ϕ gives a mechanism to create a process $\phi(d)$. When E_ϕ is applied to a process all the atoms which are not creation atoms will be executed without any problem. Whenever a creation atom is detected a new process will be started. The axioms for process creation are formulated in Table 12.

$E_\phi(a) = a$	
$E_\phi(\tau) = \tau$	
$E_\phi(cr(d)) = \overline{cr}(d) \cdot E_\phi(\phi(d))$	
$E_\phi(\tau x) = \tau \cdot E_\phi(x)$	
$E_\phi(ax) = a \cdot E_\phi(x)$	$a \notin cr(D)$, $a \in A \cup \{\delta\}$
$E_\phi(cr(d) \cdot x) = \overline{cr}(d) \cdot E_\phi(\phi(d) \| x)$	$d \in D$
$E_\phi(x+y) = E_\phi(x) + E_\phi(y)$	

TABLE 12. Axioms for process creation

The atom $\overline{cr}(d)$ indicates that the process $\phi(d)$ has been created.

Since a creation atom neither communicates nor is the result of a communication, the following propositions hold.

PROPOSITION 1. *For all closed terms* x: $E_\phi \circ E_\phi(x) = E_\phi(x)$.

PROPOSITION 2. *For all closed terms* x, y: $E_\phi(x \| y) = E_\phi(x) \| E_\phi(y)$.

We assume these propositions to hold for all recursively defined processes. An example of process creation is given below. This example can be found in [3].

EXAMPLE. $D = \{d\}$, $\phi(d) = a \cdot cr(d) \| b \cdot cr(d)$, $a | b = \delta$. When $P = E_\phi(cr(d))$ then using proposition 2 we have $P = \overline{cr}(d) \cdot (aP \| bP)$.

Now let's return to our palindrome-recogniser and see how, in this specific example, process creation works. We will first discuss an individual cell C_i which is pictured in Figure 8.

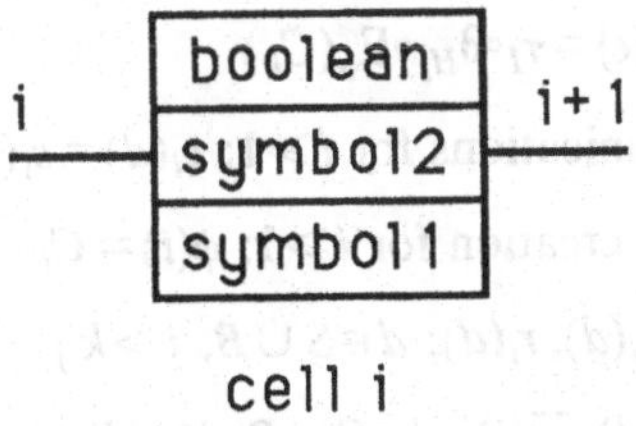

FIGURE 8. An individual cell C_i

Note that the names of the channels are reversed in comparison with Section 2.

A cell C_i can be in three states.

(0) The cell is the last cell and it is empty. When a symbol is received from the left a new cell is created. The symbol is stored in symbol1 and the cell enters state (1). The second possibility is that a true signal can be sent to the left. In this case, the cell remains in the same state.

(1) The cell contains one symbol. It can receive a symbol from the left and a boolean value from the right in either order. These are stored in locations symbol2 and boolean respectively. The cell enters state (2).

(2) The cell contains two symbols. We need the boolean value b to be calculated in the following way:

$$b = \mathbf{boolean} \wedge (\mathbf{symbol1} = \mathbf{symbol2})$$

The cell sends value b to the left and symbol2 to the right. The cell enters state (1) again.

A formal description of an individual cell is given in Table 13. C_i, C'_i, and

C''_i correspond to the states (0), (1) and (2) respectively.

$C_i = \sum_{x \in S} r_i(x) \cdot cr(i+1) \cdot s_i(\text{true}) \cdot C'_i(x) + s_i(\text{true}) \cdot C_i$
$C'_i(x) = (\{\sum_{y \in S} r_i(y)\} \parallel \{\sum_{v \in B} r_{i+1}(v)\}) \cdot C''_i(x, y, v)$
$C''_i(x, y, v) = (s_i(\lvert x = y \rvert \text{ and } v) \parallel s_{i+1}(y)) \cdot C_i(x)$
$\phi(i+1) = C_{i+1}$

TABLE 13. Specification of an individual cell

An example (the same example as pictured in Section 4) is written out in Figure 9 on the next page. A formal definition of the palindrome-recogniser with input/output channel k is given in Table 14.

$\text{PAL}^*_k(\epsilon) = \tau_I \circ \partial_{H_k} \circ \text{E}_\phi(C_k)$
Communications for $i \geqslant 1$: $c_i(d) = s_i(d) \mid r_i(d)$
Process creation for $i \geqslant 1$: $\phi(i) = C_i$
$H_k = \{s_i(d), r_i(d): d \in S \cup B, i > k\}$
$I = \{c_i(d), \overline{cr}(i): d \in S \cup B, i \geqslant 1\}$

TABLE 14. Formal definition of implementation of palindrome-recogniser

This definition is extended in the following Table 15.

$\text{IPAL}_k(\epsilon) = \tau_I \circ \partial_{H_k} \circ \text{E}_\phi(C_k)$
$\text{IPAL}_k(x) = \tau_I \circ \partial_{H_k} \circ \text{E}_\phi(C'_k(x) \parallel \text{IPAL}_{k+1}(\epsilon))$
$\text{IPAL}_k(yx) = \tau_I \circ \partial_{H_k} \circ \text{E}_\phi(C'_k(x) \parallel \text{IPAL}_{k+1}(y))$
$\text{IPALH}_k(ywx) = \tau_I \circ \partial_{H_k} \circ \text{E}_\phi(C''_k(x, y, \text{ispal}(w)) \parallel \text{IPAL}_{k+1}(w))$
$\text{IPAL}_k(wx) = \tau_I \circ \partial_{H_k} \circ \text{E}_\phi(C'_k(x) \parallel \text{IPALH}_{k+1}(w)) \quad \lvert w \rvert \geqslant 2$
H_k, I, communications, ϕ: see Table 14.

TABLE 15. Alternative implementation of the palindrome-recogniser $k \geqslant 1$

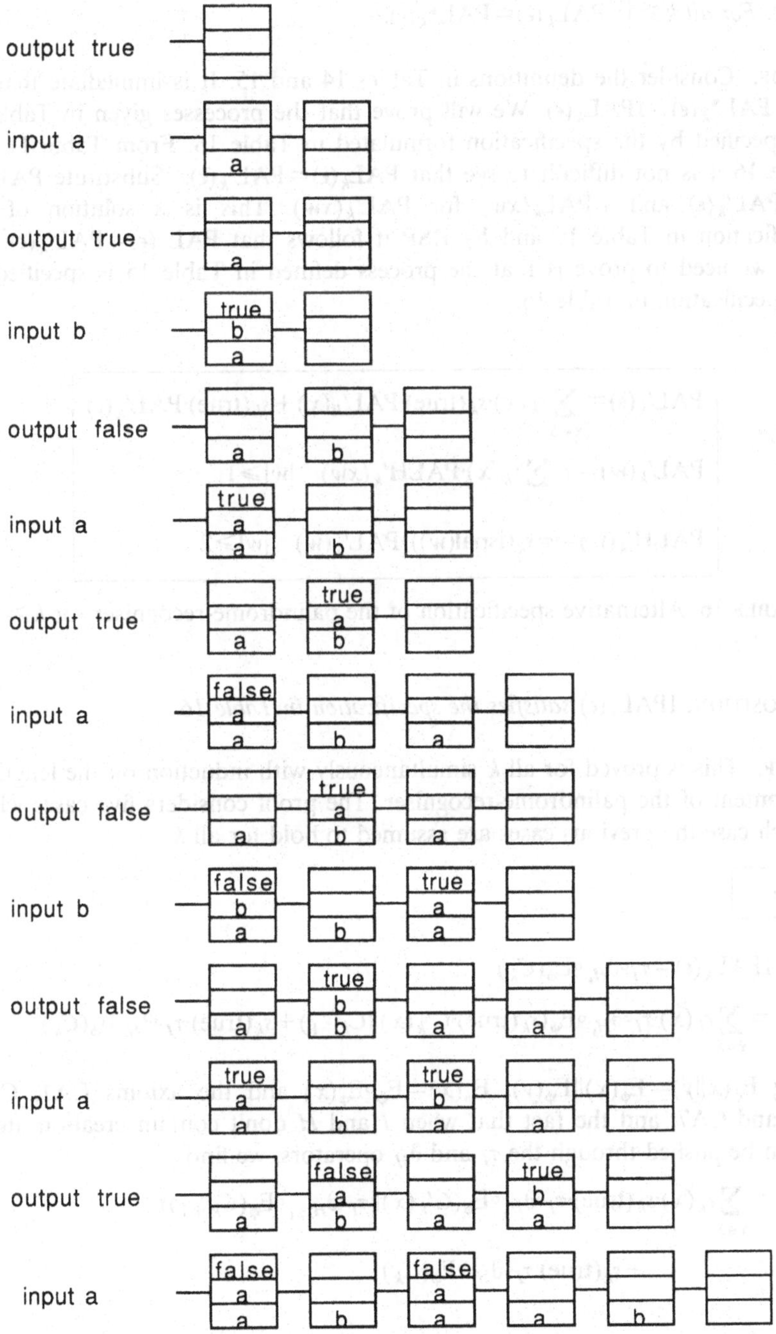

FIGURE 9. Example of unrestricted palindrome-recogniser

FACT. *For all* $k \geqslant 1$: $PAL_k(\epsilon) = PAL^*_k(\epsilon)$.

PROOF. Consider the definitions in Tables 14 and 15. It is immediate that for all k $PAL^*_k(\epsilon) = IPAL_k(\epsilon)$. We will prove that the processes given in Table 15 are specified by the specification formulated in Table 16. From Table 11 and Table 16 it is not difficult to see that $PAL_k(\epsilon) = PAL'_k(\epsilon)$. Substitute $PAL_k(\epsilon)$ for $PAL'_k(\epsilon)$ and $\tau \cdot PAL_k(xw)$ for $PAL'_k(xw)$. This is a solution of the specification in Table 16 and by RSP it follows that $PAL_k(\epsilon) = PAL'_k(\epsilon)$. So what we need to prove is that the process defined in Table 15 is specified by the specification in Table 16.

$$PAL'_k(\epsilon) = \sum_{x \in S} r_k(x) \cdot s_k(\text{true}) \cdot PAL'_k(x) + s_k(\text{true}) \cdot PAL'_k(\epsilon)$$

$$PAL'_k(w) = \tau \cdot \sum_{x \in S} r_k(x) \cdot PALH'_k(xw) \quad |w| \geqslant 1$$

$$PALH'_k(w) = \tau \cdot s_k(\text{ispal}(w)) \cdot PAL'_k(w) \quad |w| \geqslant 2$$

TABLE 16. Alternative specification of the palindrome-recogniser for $k \geqslant 1$

PROPOSITION. $IPAL_k(\epsilon)$ *satisfies the specification in Table 16.*

PROOF. This is proved for all k simultaneously with induction on the length of the content of the palindrome-recogniser. The proof considers five cases where in each case the previous cases are assumed to hold for all k.

$w = \epsilon$ (i)

$$IPAL_k(\epsilon) = \tau_I \circ \partial_{H_k} \circ E_\phi(C_k)$$

$$= \sum_{x \in S} r_k(x) \cdot \tau_I \circ \partial_{H_k} \circ E_\phi(s_k(\text{true}) \cdot C'_k(x) \| C_{k+1}) + s_k(\text{true}) \cdot \tau_I \circ \partial_{H_k} E_\phi(C_k)$$

Using $E_\phi(x \| y) = E_\phi(x) \| E_\phi(y)$, $E_\phi(x) = E_\phi \circ E_\phi(x)$ and the axioms CA1, CA2, CA5 and CA7, and the fact that when I and H don't contain creation atoms E_ϕ can be pushed through the τ_I and ∂_H operators, we find

$$= \sum_{x \in S} r_k(x) \cdot s_k(\text{true}) \cdot \tau_I \circ \partial_{H_k} \circ E_\phi(C'_k(x) \| \tau_I \circ \partial_{H_{k+1}} \circ E_\phi(C_{k+1}))$$

$$+ s_k(\text{true}) \cdot \tau_I \circ \partial_{H_k} \circ E_\phi(C_k)$$

$$= \sum_{x \in S} r_k(x) \cdot s_k(\text{true}) \cdot \tau_I \circ \partial_{H_k} \circ E_\phi(C'_k(x) \| \text{IPAL}_{k+1}(\epsilon)) +$$
$$+ s_k(\text{true}) \cdot \tau_I \circ \partial_{H_k} \circ E_\phi(C_k)$$

So for all $k \geqslant 1$:

$$\text{IPAL}_k(\epsilon) = \sum_{x \in S} r_k(x) \cdot s_k(\text{true}) \cdot \text{IPAL}_k(x) + s_k(\text{true}) \cdot \text{IPAL}_k(\epsilon).$$

| $w = x$ | (ii)

$$\text{IPAL}_k(x) = \tau_I \circ \partial_{H_k} \circ E_\phi(C'_k(x) \| \text{IPAL}_{k+1}(\epsilon))$$

using step (i) we get

$$= \tau_I((\sum_{y \in S} r_k(y) \cdot c_{k+1}(\text{true}) +$$
$$+ c_{k+1}(\text{true}) \cdot \sum_{y \in S} r_k(y)) \cdot \partial_{H_k} \circ E_\phi(C''_k(x, y, \text{true}) \| \text{IPAL}_{k+1}(\epsilon)))$$

$$= \tau \cdot \sum_{y \in S} r_k(y) \cdot \tau_I \circ \partial_{H_k} \circ E_\phi(C''_k(x, y, \text{true}) \| \text{IPAL}_{k+1}(\epsilon))$$

(using step (i) and T2).
So for all $k \geqslant 1$:

$$\text{IPAL}_k(x) = \tau \cdot \sum_{y \in S} r_k(y) \cdot \text{IPAL}_k(yx).$$

| $w = yx$ | (iii)

$$\text{IPAL}_k(yx) = \tau_I \circ \partial_{H_k} \circ E_\phi(C'_k(x) \| \text{IPAL}_{k+1}(y))$$

Using (ii) and T2,

$$= \tau \cdot \sum_{z \in S} r_k(z) \cdot \tau_I \circ \partial_{H_k} \circ E_\phi(C''_k(x, z, \text{true}) \| \text{IPAL}_{k+1}(y)))$$

So for all $k \geqslant 1$:

$$\text{IPAL}_k(yx) = \tau \cdot \sum_{z \in S} r_k(z) \cdot \text{IPALH}_k(zyx).$$

| $w = yvx, |v| \geqslant 0$ | (iv)

$$\text{IPALH}_k(yvx) = \tau_I \circ \partial_{H_k} \circ E_\phi(C''_k(x, y, \text{ ispal}(v)) \| IPAL_{k+1}(v))$$

Using the induction hypothesis we obtain:

$$=\tau_I(s_k(|x=y|\wedge \text{ispal}(v))\cdot c_{k+1}(y)+$$
$$+c_{k+1}(y)\cdot s_k(|x=y|\wedge \text{ispal}(v))\cdot \partial_{H_k}\circ \text{E}_\phi(C'_k(x)\|\text{IPALH}_{k+1}(yv)))$$

$$=\tau\cdot s_k(|x=y|\wedge \text{ispal}(v))\cdot \tau_I\circ\partial_{H_k}\circ \text{E}_\phi(C'_k(x)\|\text{IPALH}_{k+1}(yv)) \qquad \text{(using T2)}$$

So for all $k \geq 1$:

$$\text{IPALH}_k(yvx)=\tau\cdot s_k(\text{ispal}(yvx))\cdot \text{IPAL}_k(yvx).$$

$w=vx, |v|\geq 2$ (v)

$$\text{IPAL}_k(vx)=\tau_I\circ\partial_{H_k}\circ \text{E}_\phi(C'_k(x)\|\text{IPALH}_{k+1}(v))$$

Using the induction hypothesis and T2 we obtain:

$$=\tau\cdot \sum_{y\in S} r_k(y)\cdot \tau_I\circ\partial_{H_k}\circ \text{E}_\phi(C''_k(x,y,\text{ispal}(v))\|\text{IPAL}_{k+1}(v)))$$

So for all $k \geq 1$:

$$\text{IPAL}_k(vx)=\tau\cdot \sum_{y\in S} r_k(y)\cdot \text{IPALH}_k(yvx).$$

This ends the proof of the proposition. Then, using RSP as described above we obtain the desired equality $\text{PAL*}_k(\epsilon)=\text{PAL}_k(\epsilon)$. □

6. The sorting machine with unrestricted capacity

After handling the restricted sorting machine in Section 5 we now come to the sorting machine with unrestricted capacity. The specification of a sorting machine with infinite capacity, which we call sorting machine from now on, is given in Table 17. Note that the subscript in $\text{SORT}_k(B)$ indicates the name of the input/output channel.

The implementation of the sorting machine is different from the implementation of the restricted sorting machine. The number of cells of the restricted sorting machine was fixed but the sorting machine is built by using a variable number of cells. The last cell is always empty. When this last cell receives a number from the left it creates a new cell. When a stop signal is received the cell stops working and disappears.

$$\text{SORT}_k(\emptyset)= \sum_{d\in D} r_k(d)\cdot \text{SORT}_k(\{d\})+s_k(\text{empty})\cdot \text{SORT}_k(\emptyset)$$

$$\text{SORT}_k(B)= \sum_{d\in D} r_k(d)\cdot \text{SORT}_k(B\cup\{d\})+s_k(\mu B)\cdot \text{SORT}_k(B-\{\mu B\}) \qquad |B|>0$$

Table 17. Specification of a sorting machine with infinite capacity for $k\geq 1$

Just like the cells of the restricted sorting machine these cells can contain two numbers in MIN and MAX. The content of MIN is less than or equal to the content of MAX. The last cell can create a new cell when needed. A cell C_i is pictured in Figure 10. Note that the names of the channels are reversed in comparison with Section 5.

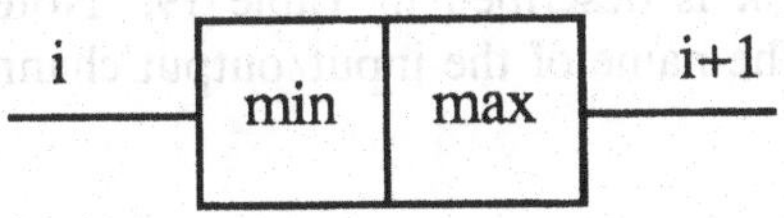

cell i

FIGURE 10. An individual cell

A cell can be in three states.

(0) The cell is empty. From the left the cell can receive a number or the stop signal. When the cell receives a number from the left a new cell on the right is created. The number is stored in MIN. The cell enters state (1). When the cell receives the stop signal the cell stops working and disappears.

(1) The cell contains one number, stored in MIN. (a) The cell can receive a number from the left. The minimum of the content of MIN and the received number is stored in MIN. The larger of the two numbers is stored in MAX. State (2) is entered. (b) The cell can send the content of MIN to the left. Because the cell has become empty a stop signal is send to the right. The cell enters state (0).

(2) The cell contains two numbers, stored in MIN and MAX. (a) When a number is received from the left, the content of MAX is send to the right. The minimum of the content of MIN and the received number is stored in MIN. The other number is stored in MAX. The cell remains in the same state. (b) When a number is sent to the left two possibilities arise. If an empty signal is received from the right, then the content of MAX is stored in MIN, MAX becomes empty and the cell changes to state (1). Receiving a number from the right doesn't change the state of the cell. The minimum of the content of MAX and the received number is stored in MIN. The other number is stored in MAX.

A formal description of an individual cell is given in Table 18.

$$C_i = \sum_{d \in D} r_i(d) \cdot cr(i+1) \cdot C'_i(d) + r_i(\text{stop}) + s_i(\text{empty}) \cdot C_i$$

$$C'_i(d) = \sum_{e \in D} r_i(e) \cdot C''_i(sw(d, e)) + s_i(d) \cdot s_{i+1}(\text{stop}) \cdot C_i$$

$$C''_i(d,e) = \sum_{f \in D} r_i(f) \cdot s_{i+1}(e) \cdot C''_i(sw(d, f)) +$$

$$+ s_i(d) \cdot (\sum_{f \in D} r_{i+1}(f) \cdot C''_i(sw(f, e)) + r_{i+1}(\text{empty}) C'_i(e))$$

$$sw(d,e) = (\min(d, e), \max(d,e))$$

TABLE 18. Specification of cell i, $i \geqslant 0$

In Figure 11 below a chain configuration of cells is pictured to illustrate how the unbounded sorting machine works. Note how cells are created and killed. These cells are connected in the same way as is done in the restricted sorting machine implementation. The behaviour of the sorting machine with input/output channel k is described in Table 19. Note that the subscript of $\text{SORT}^*_k(\epsilon)$ indicates the name of the input/output channel, and has nothing to do with its capacity.

$\text{SORT}^*_k(\epsilon) = \tau_I \circ \partial_{H_k} E_\phi(C_k), \quad k \geqslant 1$
Communication: $c_i(d = r_i(d) \vert s_i(d),\ d \in D \cup \{\text{empty, stop}\}),\ i \geqslant 1$
Process creation: $\phi(i) = C_i, \quad i \geqslant 2$
$H_k = \{r_i(d), s_i(d)\colon d \in D \cup \{\text{empty, stop}\},\ i \geqslant k+1\} \cup \{r_k(\text{stop})\}$
$I = \{c_i(d), \overline{cr}(i+1)\colon d \in D \cup \{\text{empty, stop}\},\ i \geqslant 1\}$

TABLE 19. Formal description of a sorting machine with input/output channel k

FACT. *For all* $k \geqslant 1$ $\text{SORT}^*_k(\epsilon) = \text{SORT}_k(\varnothing)$.

PROOF. The definitions of c.o. and *sw* (see Section 5) will be used in this proof. Similarly to the restricted sorting machine section an intermediate specification is given in Table 20. This specification includes the possibility to stop the sorting machine. An extended definition for the chain of cells is given in Table 21.

$\text{SORT}'_k(\epsilon) = \sum_{d \in D} r_k(d) \cdot \text{SORT}''_k(\langle d \rangle) + r_k(\text{stop}) + s_k(\text{empty}) \cdot \text{SORT}''_k(\epsilon)$
$\text{SORT}''_k(\langle d_1 \rangle * w) = \sum_{d \in D} r_k(d) \cdot \text{SORT}''_k(sw(\langle d \rangle * \langle d_1 \rangle * w)) +$
$+ s_k(d_1) \cdot \text{SORT}'_k(sw(w)) \quad \langle d_1 \rangle * w$ c.o.

TABLE 20. Intermediate specification of unrestricted sorting machine

By putting $r_k(\text{stop})$ in H_k the machine described above is obtained. This step is necessary to make a proof by induction possible. However, the desired equation is obtained after abstraction from $r_k(\text{stop})$ in $\text{SORT}'_k(\epsilon)$.

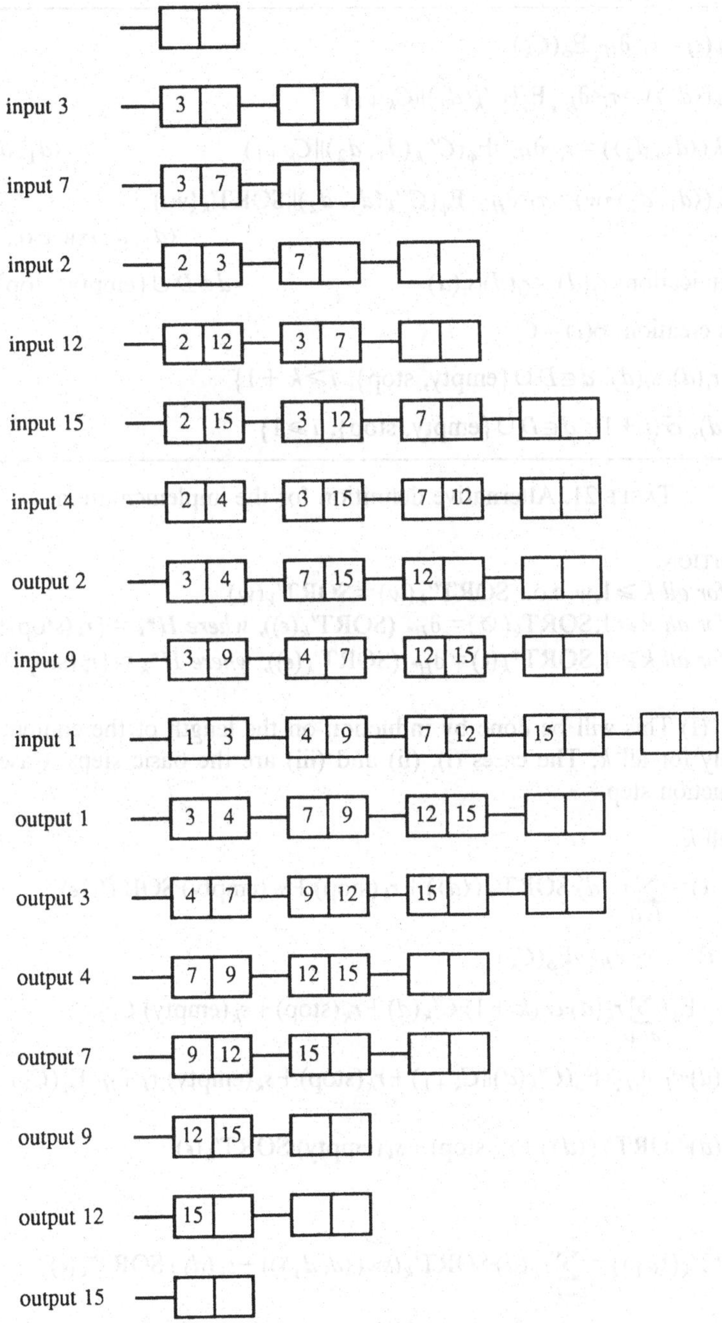

FIGURE 11. Example of unrestricted sorting machine

$\text{SORT}'_k(\epsilon)=\tau_I\circ\partial_{H'_k}\text{E}_\phi(C_k)$	
$\text{SORT}'_k(\langle d_1\rangle)=\tau_I\circ\partial_{H'_k}\text{E}_\phi(C'_k(d_1)\|C_{k+1})$	
$\text{SORT}'k(\langle d_1,d_2\rangle)=\tau_I\circ\partial_{H'_k}\circ\text{E}_\phi(C''_k(d_1,d_2)\|C_{k+1})$	$\langle d_1,d_2\rangle$ c.o.
$\text{SORT}'_k(\langle d_1,d_2\rangle\ast w)=\tau_I\circ\partial_{H'_k}\circ\text{E}_\phi(C''_k(d_1,d_2)\|\text{SORT}'_k(w))$	$\langle d_1,d_2\rangle\ast w$ c.o., $\|w\|>0$
Communication: $c_i(d)=r_i(d)\|s_i(d)$	$d\in D\cup\{\text{empty, stop}\},\ i\geqslant 1$
Process creation: $\phi(i)=C_i$	$i\geqslant 2$
$H'_k=\{r_i(d),s_i(d)\text{: } d\in D\cup\{\text{empty, stop}\},\ i\geqslant k+1\}$	
$I=\{c_i(d),\ \overline{cr}(i+1)\text{: } d\in D\cup\{\text{empty, stop}\},\ i\geqslant 1\}$	

TABLE 21. Alternative definition for the implementation

PROPOSITION.
(I) *for all* $k\geqslant 1, w$ c.o.: $\text{SORT}''_k(w)=\text{SORT}'_k(w)$
(II) *for all* $k\geqslant 1, \text{SORT}_k(\varnothing)=\partial_{H^*_k}(\text{SORT}'_k(\epsilon))$, *where* $H^*_k=\{r_k(\text{stop})\}$
(III) *for all* $k\geqslant 1, \text{SORT}^*_k(\epsilon)=\partial_{H^*_k}(\text{SORT}'_k(\epsilon))$, *where* $H^*_k=\{r_k(\text{stop})\}$

PROOF. (I) This will be done by induction on the length of the content simultaneously for all k. The cases (i), (ii) and (iii) are the basic steps. Case (iv) is the induction step.

(i) for all k

$$\text{SORT}'_k(\epsilon)=\sum_{d\in D} r_k(d)\cdot\text{SORT}'_k(\langle d\rangle)+r_k(\text{stop})+s_k(\text{empty})\cdot\text{SORT}'_k(\epsilon)$$

$$\text{SORT}_k(\epsilon)=\tau_I\circ\partial_{H'_k}\circ\text{E}_\phi(C_k)$$

$$=\tau_I\circ\partial_{H'_k}\circ\text{E}_\phi(\sum_{d\in D} r_k(d)\cdot cr(k+1)\cdot C'_k(d)+r_k(\text{stop})+s_k(\text{empty})\cdot C_k)$$

$$=\sum_{d\in D} r_k(d)\cdot\tau_I\circ\partial_{H'_k}\circ\text{E}_\phi(C'_k(d)\|C_{k+1})+r_k(\text{stop})+s_k(\text{empty})\cdot\tau_I\circ\partial_{H'_k}\text{E}_\phi(C_k)$$

$$=\sum_{d\in D} r_k(d)\cdot\text{SORT}'_k(\langle d\rangle)+r_k(\text{stop})+s_k(\text{empty})\cdot\text{SORT}'_k(\epsilon)$$

(ii) $\text{SORT}'_k(\langle d_1\rangle)=\sum_{d\in D} r_k(d)\cdot\text{SORT}'_k(sw(\langle d,d_1\rangle))+s_k(d_1)\cdot\text{SORT}'_k(\epsilon)$

$$\text{SORT}'_k(\langle d_1\rangle)=\tau_I\circ\partial_{H'_k}\circ\text{E}_\phi(C'_k(d_1)\|C_{k+1})=$$

$$=\sum_{d\in D} r_k(d)\cdot\tau_I\circ\partial_{H'_k}\circ\text{E}_\phi(C''_k(sw(d,d_1))\|C_{k+1})+s_k(d_1)\cdot\tau_I\circ\partial_{H'_k}\circ\text{E}_\phi(C_k)$$

$$= \sum_{d \in D} r_k(d) \cdot \mathrm{SORT'}_k(sw(\langle d, d_1 \rangle)) + s_k(d_1) \cdot \mathrm{SORT'}_k(\epsilon)$$

(iii) $\mathrm{SORT'}_k(\langle d_1, d_2 \rangle) =$

$$= \sum_{d \in D} r_k(d) \cdot \mathrm{SORT'}_k(sw(\langle d, d_1, d_2 \rangle)) + s_k(d_1) \cdot \mathrm{SORT'}_k(\langle d_2 \rangle) \qquad \langle d_1, d_2 \rangle \text{ c.o.}$$

$$\mathrm{SORT'}_k(\langle d_1, d_2 \rangle) = \sum_{d \in D} r_k(d) \cdot \tau_I \circ \partial_{H'_k} \circ \mathrm{E}_\phi(C''_k(d_1, d_2) \| C_{k+1})$$

$$= \sum_{d \in D} r_k(d) \cdot \tau_I \circ \partial_{H'_k} \circ \mathrm{E}_\phi(C''_k(sw(d, d_1)) \| C'_{k+1}(d_2) \| C_{k+2}) +$$

$$+ s_k(d_1) \cdot \tau_I \circ \partial_{H'_k} \circ \mathrm{E}_\phi(C'_k(d_2) \| C_{k+1}).$$

Using the standard concurrency axioms and $\mathrm{E}_\phi(x \| y) = \mathrm{E}_\phi(x) \| \mathrm{E}_\phi(y)$ we obtain:

$$\tau_I \circ \partial_{H'_k} \circ \mathrm{E}_\phi(C''_k(sw(d, d_1)) \| C'_{k+1}(d_2) \| C_{k+2}) =$$

$$= \tau_I \circ \partial_{H'_k} (\mathrm{E}_\phi(C''_k(sw(d, d_1))) \| \mathrm{E}_\phi(C'_{k+1}(d_2) \| C_{k+2})).$$

Applying conditional axioms CA, $\mathrm{E}_\phi \circ \mathrm{E}_\phi(x) = \mathrm{E}_\phi(x)$ and using the fact that when I and H don't contain creation atoms E_ϕ can be pushed through the τ_I and ∂_H operators this last expression becomes

$$= \tau_I \circ \partial_{H'_k} \circ \mathrm{E}_\phi(C''_k(sw(d, d_1)) \| \tau_I \circ \partial_{H'_{k+1}} \circ \mathrm{E}_\phi(C'_{k+1}(d_2) \| C_{k+2})).$$

Using the definitions in Table 21:

$$= \tau_I \circ \partial_{H'_k} \circ \mathrm{E}_\phi(C''_k(sw(d, d_1)) \| \mathrm{SORT'}_{k+1}(\langle d_2 \rangle)) = \mathrm{SORT'}_k(sw(\langle d, d_1, d_2 \rangle)).$$

Making this observation the desired result is obtained:

$\mathrm{SORT'}_k(\langle d_1, d_2 \rangle) =$

$$= \sum_{d \in D} r_k(d) \cdot \mathrm{SORT'}_k(sw(\langle d, d_1, d_2 \rangle)) + s_k(d_1) \cdot \mathrm{SORT'}_k(\langle d_2 \rangle).$$

(iv) This case is the induction step. The proposition will be proved for all k and w, $|w| \geqslant 3$, assuming it has already been proved for all $k \geqslant 1$ and w', $|w'| < |w|$. In this proof $w = \langle d_1, d_2 \rangle * v$ is c.o., $|v| \geqslant 1$ and $v = \langle d_3 \rangle * v'$.

$$\mathrm{SORT'}_k(w) = \sum_{d \in D} r_k(d) \cdot \mathrm{SORT'}_k(sw(\langle d \rangle * w)) + s_k(d_1) \cdot \mathrm{SORT'}_k(sw(\langle d_2 \rangle * v))$$

$$\mathrm{SORT'}_k(\langle d_1, d_2 \rangle * v) = \tau_I \circ \partial_{H'_k} \circ \mathrm{E}_\phi(C''_k(d_1, d_2) \| \mathrm{SORT'}_{k+1}(v))$$

Using the induction hypothesis on $\mathrm{SORT'}_{k+1}(v)$, $|v| \geqslant 1$, we obtain:

$$= \sum_{d \in D} r_k(d) \cdot \tau_I \circ \partial_{H'_k} \circ \mathrm{E}_\phi(C''_k(sw(d, d_1)) \| \mathrm{SORT''}_{k+1}(sw(\langle d_2 \rangle * v)))$$

$$+ s_k(d_1) \cdot \tau_I \circ \partial_{H'_k} \mathrm{E}_\phi(C''_k(sw(d_2, d_3)) \| \mathrm{SORT'}_{k+1}(v')).$$

Considering the definition of sw we obtain:

$$= \sum_{d \in D} r_k(d) \cdot \mathrm{SORT}'_k(sw(\langle d \rangle \star w)) + s_k(d_1) \cdot \mathrm{SORT}'_k(sw(\langle d_2 \rangle \star v))$$

Using RSP we have the desired result. This ends the proof of proposition I.

Proof. (II) For w c.o. $\mathrm{SORT}'_k(w)$ satisfies the specification in Table 20. Then it is easy to deduce that $\partial_{H^*_k}(\mathrm{SORT}'_k(\epsilon))$ is specified by the specification in the following Table 22.

$$\partial_{H^*_k}(\mathrm{SORT}'_k(\epsilon)) = \sum_{d \in D} r_k(d) \cdot \partial_{H^*_k}(\mathrm{SORT}'_k(\langle d \rangle)) + s_k(\mathrm{empty}) \cdot \partial_{H^*_k}(\mathrm{SORT}'_k(\epsilon))$$

$$\partial_{H^*_k}(\mathrm{SORT}_k(\langle d_1 \rangle \star w)) = \sum_{d \in D} r_k(d) \cdot \partial_{H^*_k}(\mathrm{SORT}'_k(sw(\langle d, d_1 \rangle \star w)))$$

$$+ s_k(d_1) \cdot \partial_{H^*_k}(\mathrm{SORT}'_k(sw(w))) \qquad \langle d_1 \rangle \star w \text{ c.o.}$$

Table 22. Specification of $\partial_{H^*_k}(\mathrm{SORT}'_k(\epsilon))$

To prove proposition II substitute for all c.o. w $\mathrm{SORT}_k(B_w)$ for $\partial_{H^*_k}(\mathrm{SORT}'_k(w))$ where B_w is the bag containing the elements in the sequence w. Because the first element of a c.o. w is the minimal element of the sequence it is easy to see that $\mathrm{SORT}_k(\varnothing)$ satisfies the specification in Table 22. Then, with RSP the equation in proposition II is proved.

Proof. (III) This is proved using the conditional axioms CA5 and CA7.
We find:
for all $k \geqslant 1$:

$$\partial_{H^*_k}(\mathrm{SORT}'_k(\epsilon)) = \partial_{H^*_k} \circ \tau_I \circ \partial_{H'_k} \circ \mathrm{E}_\phi(C_k) = \tau_I \circ \partial_{H^*_k \cup H'_k} \circ \mathrm{E}_\phi(C_k) = \mathrm{SORT}^*_k(\epsilon)$$

so we can conclude for all k $\mathrm{SORT}^*_k(\epsilon) = \mathrm{SORT}_k(\varnothing)$. □

References

1. J.A. Bergstra (1989). *A Process Creation Mechanism in Process Algebra.* This volume.
2. J.A. Bergstra, J.W. Klop (1986). Algebra of communicating processes. J.W. de Bakker, M. Hazewinkel, J.K. Lenstra (eds.). *Mathematics and Computer Science,* CWI Monograph 1, North-Holland, Amsterdam, 89-138.
3. J.A. Bergstra, J.W. Klop, E.-R. Olderog (1987). Failures without chaos: a new process semantics for fair abstraction. M. Wirsing (ed.). *Proc. IFIP Conf. on Formal Description of Programming Concepts - III,* Ebberup 1986, North-Holland, 77-103.

4. S.D. Brookes, C.A.R. Hoare, A.W. Roscoe (1984). A theory of communicating sequential processes. *J. ACM 31,* 560-599.
5. J.C. Ebergen (1986). *A Technique to Design Delay-Insensitive VLSI Circuits,* CWI Report CS-R8622, Centre for Mathematics and Computer Science, Amsterdam.
6. M. Hennessy (1986). Proving systolic systems correct. *TOPLAS 8(3),* 344-387.
7. C.P.J. Koymans, J.C. Mulder (1989). *A Modular approach to Protocol Verification using Process Algebra.* This volume.
8. K.T. Kung (1979). Let's design algorithms for VLSI systems. *Proceedings of the Conference on VLSI: Architecture, Design, Fabrication,* California Institute of Technology.
9. C.A. Mead, L.A Conway (1980). *Introduction to VLSI-systems,* Addison-Wesley Publ. Comp., Reading, Massachusetts.
10. G.J. Milne (1983). CIRCAL: a calculus for circuit description. *Integration 1,* 121-160.
11. M. Rem (1983). Partially ordered computations with applications to VLSI-design. J. de Bakker, J. van Leeuwen (eds.). *Proc. Found. of Comp. Sci. IV.2,* MC Tract 159, Centre for Mathematics and Computer Science, Amsterdam, 1-44.

Verification of an Algorithm for Log-time Sorting by Square Comparison

J.C. Mulder
Programming Research Group, University of Amsterdam
P.O. Box 41882, 1009 DB Amsterdam, The Netherlands

W.P. Weijland
Centre for Mathematics and Computer Science
P.O. Box 4079, 1009 AB Amsterdam, The Netherlands

In this paper a concurrent sorting algorithm called RANKSORT is presented, able to sort an input sequence of length n in $\log n$ time, using n^2 processors. The algorithm is formally specified as a *delay-insensitive* circuit. Then, a formal correctness proof is given, using bisimulation semantics in the language ACP_τ. The algorithm has area-time$^2 = O(n^2 \log^4 n)$ complexity which is slightly sub-optimal with respect to the lower bound of $AT^2 = \Omega(n^2 \log n)$.

1. INTRODUCTION

Many authors have studied the concurrency aspects of sorting, and indeed the n-time *bubblesort* algorithm (using n processors) is rather thoroughly analyzed already (e.g. see: Hennessy [3], Kossen and Weijland [4]). However, *bubblesort* is not the most efficient sorting algorithm in sequential programming, since it is n^2-time and for instance *heapsort* and *mergesort* are $n \log n$-time sorting algorithms. So, the natural question arises whether it would be possible to design an algorithm using even less than n-time.

In this paper we discuss a concurrent algorithm, capable of sorting n numbers in $O(\log n)$ time. This algorithm is based on the idea of *square comparison*: putting all numbers to be sorted in a square matrix, all comparisons can be made in $O(1)$ time, using n^2 processors (one for each cell of the matrix). Then, the algorithm only needs to evaluate the result of this operation.

The algorithm presented here, which is called RANKSORT, is not the only concurrent time-efficient sorting algorithm. Several *sub* n-time algorithms have been developed by others (see: Thompson [5]). For instance algorithms were presented of time-complexity $\sqrt{n}$, $\log^3 n$, $\log^2 n$ and $\log n$. Indeed, the square

Partial support received from the European Community under ESPRIT project no. 432, An Integrated Formal Approach to Industrial Software Development (METEOR).

comparison algorithm presented here, appeared in [5] as well. Its network has been given various names, like *mesh of trees* or *orthogonal tree network.*

In this paper we will show how a $\log n$-sorter can be constructed. Moreover we will present a formal specification of the algorithm and prove it correct using bisimulation semantics with asynchronous cooperation.

At this place we want to thank Niek van Diepen (University of Nijmegen) and Karl Meinke (University of Leeds) for their contributions to this paper. Moreover we thank Jaap Jan de Bruin for his assistance concerning the illustrations which were made on an Apple Macintosh. Finally, we thank Jos Baeten for his remarks on the early drafts of this paper.

2. Sorting by square comparison

Suppose we have a sequence $\langle a_0, a_1, a_2, \ldots, a_{n-1} \rangle$ of distinct numbers, for some $n > 0$, and consider the problem of computing a non-decreasing permutation of this sequence. Note that, in fact, we can start from an arbitrary set of symbols and any linear ordering $>$, defined on this finite set. Now restrict this ordering to the n elements that are considered, then we obtain a finite ordering, which can be represented in a matrix as pictured in Figures 1 and 2.

$>$:1 $\leqslant$:0	a_0	a_1	a_2	a_3	a_4	a_5	a_6	a_7
a_0								
a_1								
a_2								
a_3								
a_4								
a_5								
a_6								
a_7								

FIGURE 1. Defining $\geqslant$ by laying out a full matrix

In every cell (i,j) of the matrix in Figure 1 we write 1 if $a_i > a_j$, and 0 otherwise. Note that now the matrix has only 0's on its diagonal. Moreover it is antisymmetric, i.e.: if $i \neq j$ we have 1 in (i,j) if and only if we have 0 in (j,i). So in fact we only need one 'half' of the matrix.

The idea of square comparison now simply reads as follows: suppose we have a finite sequence of numbers to be sorted, then all the information relevant to the ordering problem can be computed in unit time, starting from the matrix above. Indeed, in one blow all n^2 individual cells (i,j) can do one comparison (between a_i and a_j), and next all information about $>$ is available. Note that we can set up this matrix in $O(\log n)$ time, starting from n processors containing the values to be sorted. Thus all ordering information can be computed in $O(\log n)$ time.

After $O(\log n)$ time we have computed a matrix which is full of 0's and 1's.

Note, that on the i-th row, we have a 1 for every a_j which is smaller than a_i. Hence the number of 1's in the i-th row is precisely the number of elements a_j out of $\langle a_0, a_1, a_2, \ldots, a_{n-1} \rangle$, satisfying $a_j < a_i$. However, the number of elements less than a_i is exactly the index of a_i in the *sorted* sequence, i.e. represents the *place* of the number a_i in the sorted array.

Finally note that the number of 1's can simply be found, by computing the sum of all matrix values on the row considered. This computation can be done in $O(\log n)$ time, since we can repeatedly add pairs of numbers concurrently, until there is only one single value left. Thus we conclude that, for all input values, we can compute the 'sorted index' in $O(\log n)$ time.

In fact we have computed a *permutation* of the index values $\langle 0, 1, 2, \ldots, n-1 \rangle$. From this permutation one can compute the sorted array in $O(1)$ time, since all cells consider the computed index value, as an address to send the value to, they actually contain. Having enough wires to interconnect all cells, this can be done in one single computation step. (By putting the processors in a tree configuration once again, we can do this in $O(\log n)$ time, with many wires less.)

So, indeed, we can sort a sequence of numbers in $\log n$ time using n^2 processors. An example of this square comparison method is presented in Figure 2.

$>$ / $\geqslant$	2	7	1	-5	11	2	3	8	
2	0	0	1	1	0	0	0	0	$+ \rightarrow 2$
7	1	0	1	1	0	1	1	0	$+ \rightarrow 5$
1	0	0	0	1	0	0	0	0	$+ \rightarrow 1$
-5	0	0	0	0	0	0	0	0	$+ \rightarrow 0$
11	1	1	1	1	0	1	1	1	$+ \rightarrow 7$
2	1	0	1	1	0	0	0	0	$+ \rightarrow 3$
3	1	0	1	1	0	1	0	0	$+ \rightarrow 4$
8	1	1	1	1	0	1	1	0	$+ \rightarrow 6$

FIGURE 2. An example of the square comparison method on the sequence $\langle 2, 7, 1, -5, 11, 2, 3, 8 \rangle$

Here we have a small problem: suppose two numbers in the array are equal (the numbers are no longer distinct), then the matrix values, computed in Figure 1, would be equal for both numbers. Thus the problem is that the computed array of index values no longer is a permutation of $\langle 0, 1, 2, \ldots, n-1 \rangle$, since some of the computed indices might be equal.

In Figure 2, this problem is solved by slightly changing the former procedure. Now, the 'lower' cells, i.e. the cells below the main diagonal of the matrix, do not compare two values via '$>$' but via '$\geqslant$'. It turns out that the computed indices indeed are a permutation of $\langle 0, 1, 2, \ldots, n-1 \rangle$ and that the 'original order' of equal numbers is preserved in the sorted array.

In Figure 2 the sequence $\langle 2, 7, 1, -5, 11, 2, 3, 8 \rangle$ is considered. Note that here, the computed index values ⟨2,5,1,0,7,3,4,6⟩ indeed form a permutation of ⟨0,1,2,3,4,5,6,7⟩. To be specific: note that the number 2 has two different computed indices (namely 2 and 3); without the adaptation mentioned above, both occurrences of the value 2 would yield the index value 2.

The sorting machine considered in this paper is pictured in Figure 3, for $n=4$. Note that on the upper side we have n trees, one for every input value. Each input value is broadcast to n leaves in a row of the matrix, which is in the middle part of the machine. Then, the cells on the main diagonal will send the value received from the upper tree downwards to the bottom of the connected lower tree; this value is broadcast upwards again to n matrix cells, belonging to a column of the matrix. So, every matrix cell now contains two values, precisely in the way as in Figure 1. Then the n^2 comparisons are made and each cell sends a 1 or a 0 to its upper tree. In every node the addition of two input values is computed, and the result is sent upwards again. Finally, the computed index permutation can be read from the roots of the upper trees.

3. A FORMAL SPECIFICATION OF THE SORTING MACHINE

In this section we will present a formal specification of RANKSORT, using the language ACP. First, we have to name the channels of the machine (Figures 3-5) in order to be able to give a precise definition of the behaviour of the individual cells. For reasons of simplicity, in the following we will assume $n=2^k$ for some given $k>0$, n being the length of the array to be sorted.

In Figure 4 we present the names of the processes, corresponding to the vertices in the trees and the cells of the matrix. The upper trees are called $U_i\,(0 \leqslant i<n)$ and the cells in these trees are numbered $U_{i,j}\,(0<j<n)$. Likewise, the lower trees are called L_j, with cells $L_{i,j}\,(0<i<n)$, and the matrix cells are called $M_{i,j}\,(0 \leqslant i,j<n)$. The bottom cells will be called $B_j\,(0 \leqslant j<n)$.

Note that for all i, U_i has depth ${}^2\log n=k$ and has $2^k-1=n-1$ cells. Further, the cells and channels in the trees are numbered 'left first/breadth first', as one can see in the Figures 4 and 5.

Now, let us present a more detailed description of the behaviour of the individual processes.

- A cell $U_{i,j}$ will receive a value from its upper neighbour. Next, it will send this value to both of its lower neighbours, and from both of them it will receive another value in return. Since both lower neighbours are independent processes, these send and receive actions are fully interleaved. Finally, having received two values from below, $U_{i,j}$ will send its sum up again.
- A matrix cell $M_{i,j}$ in the middle of the sorter will first receive a value from the upper neighbour. Then, if it is a *diagonal* cell, it will send this value downwards to its lower neighbour. For sake of simplicity, we will make *non-diagonal* cells send a value **nil** downwards as well. Next, the cell will receive a new value from below, and send up a 0 or a 1, depending on its position (see Figure 2) and the two input values.
- A cell $L_{i,j}$ from one of the lower trees, will first receive two values from above (in any order). Note that in any lower tree only one leaf, the one in

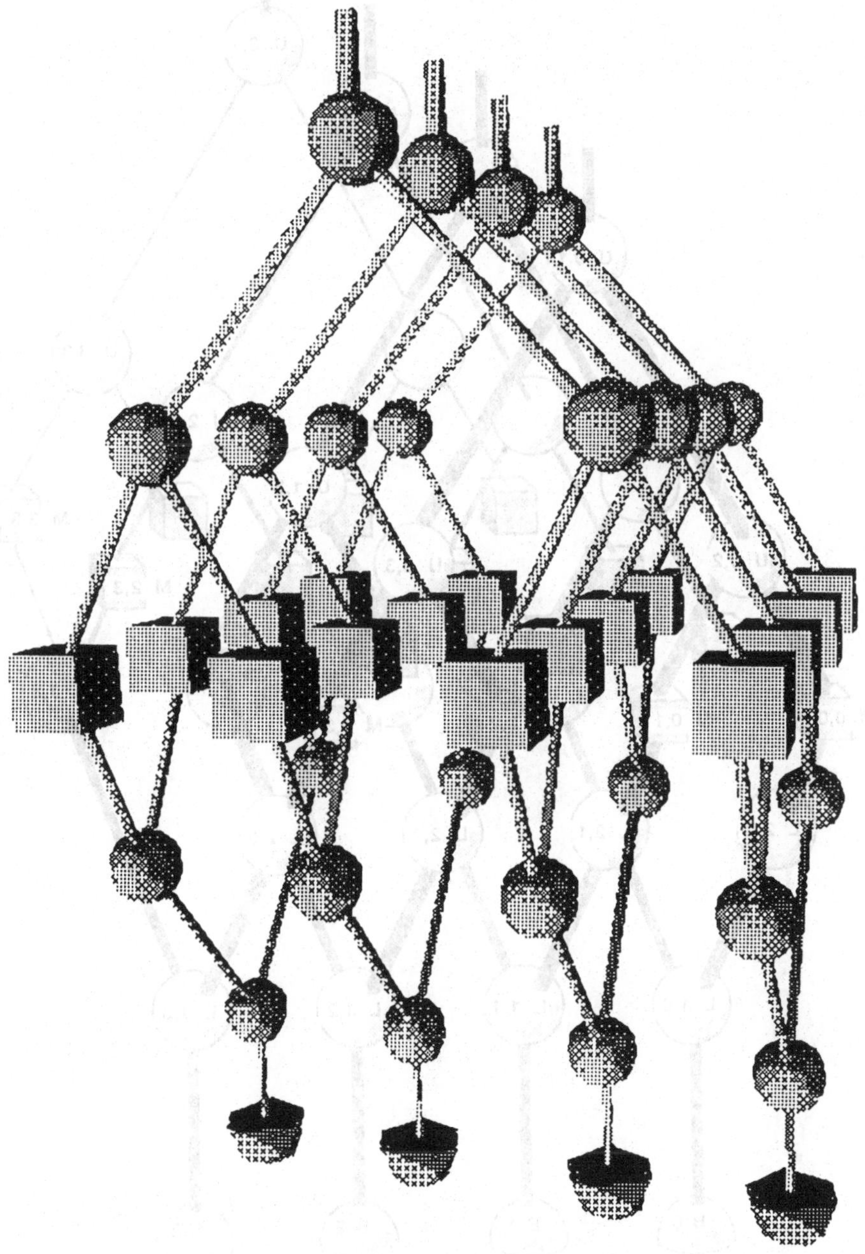

FIGURE 3. A 'mesh of trees'; the circuit configuration of RANKSORT

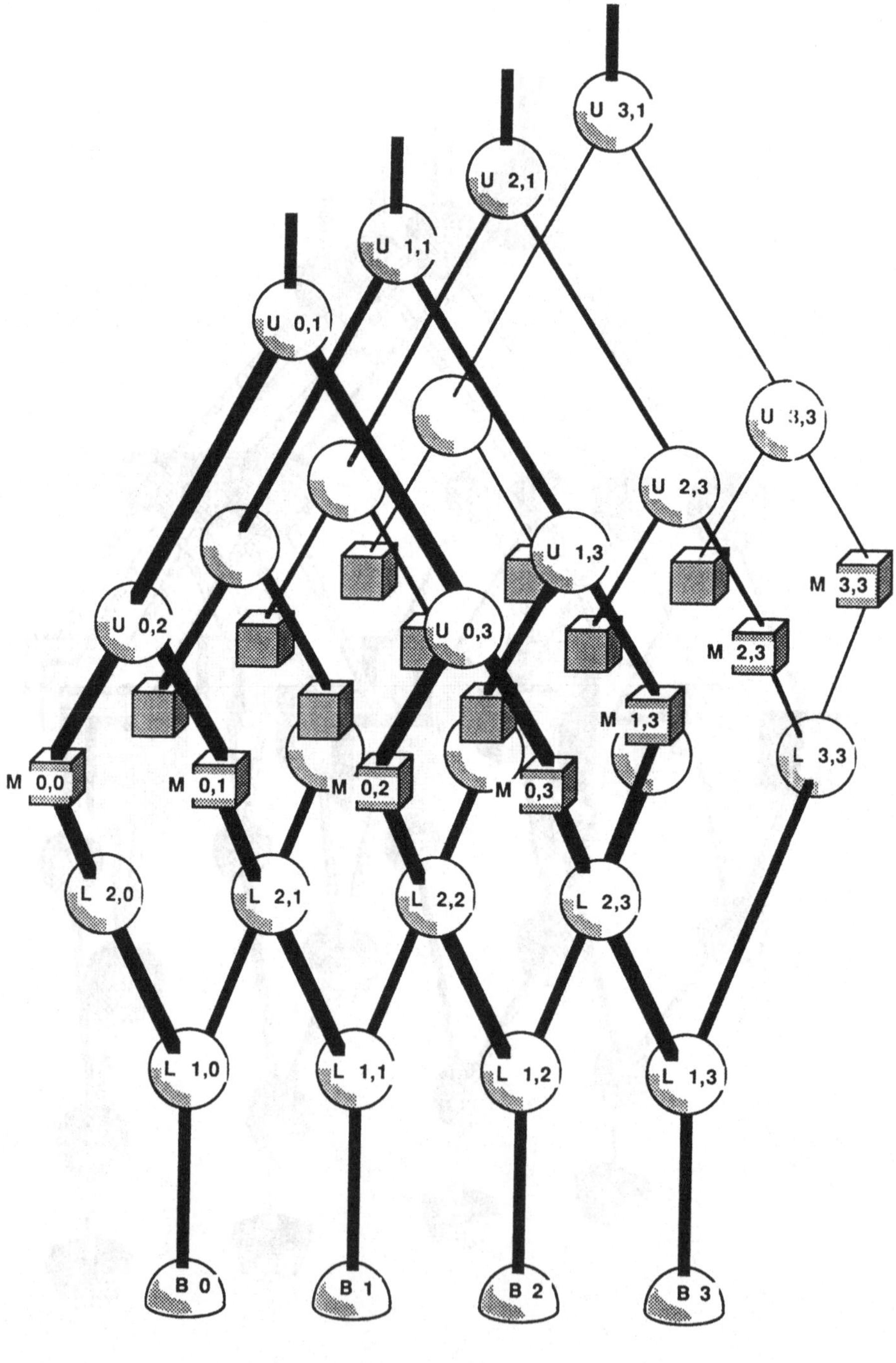

FIGURE 4. The names of the individual cells in the sorter

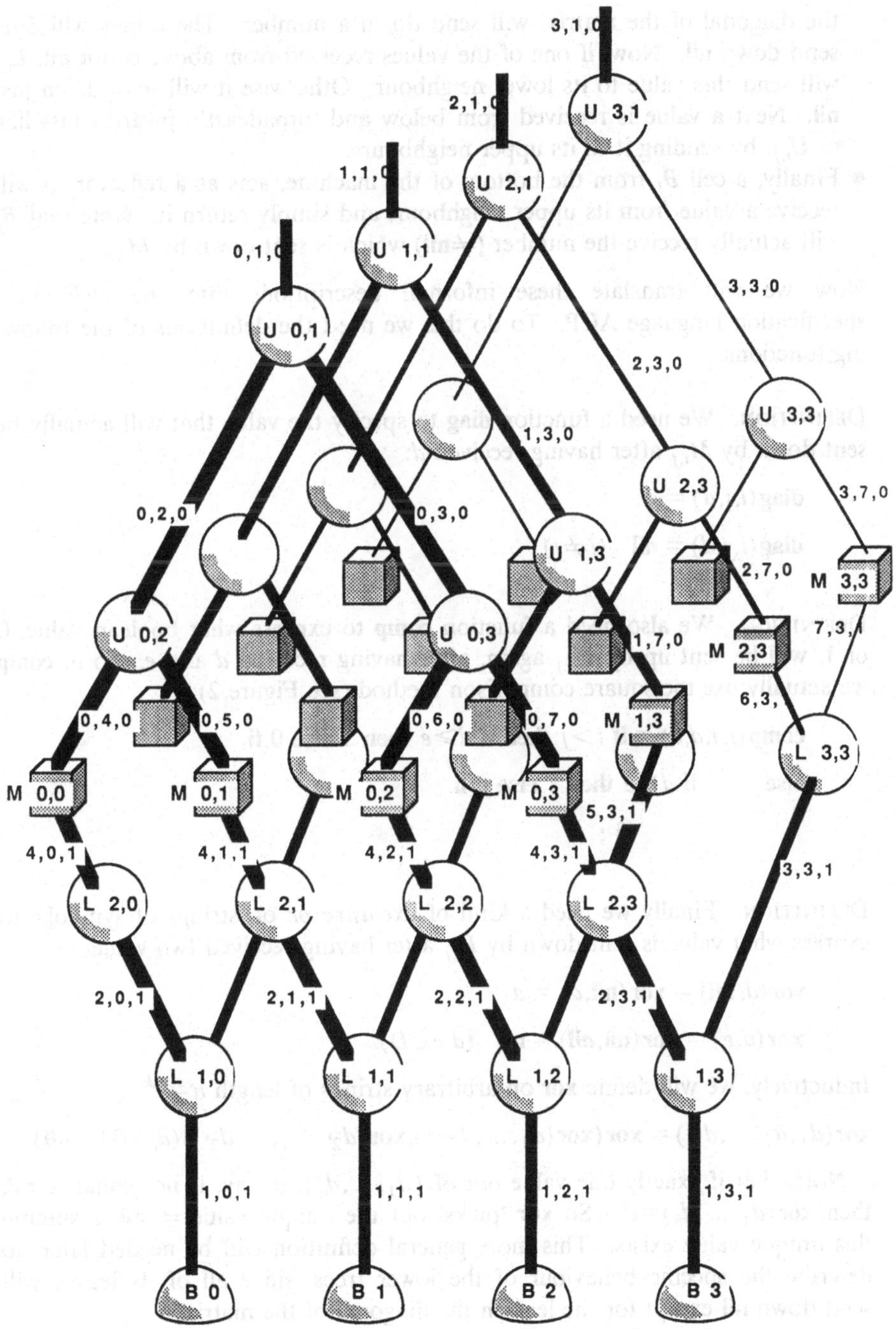

FIGURE 5. The channel numbers are in 'left first/breadth first' order

the diagonal of the matrix, will send down a number. The others will only send down **nil**. Now, if one of the values received from above is not **nil**, $L_{i,j}$ will send this value to its lower neighbour. Otherwise it will send down just **nil**. Next a value is received from below and 'broadcast' upwards, just like in $U_{i,j}$, by sending it to its upper neighbours.

- Finally, a cell B_j from the bottom of the machine, acts as a reflector: it will receive a value from its upper neighbour, and simply return it. Note that B_j will actually receive the number ($\neq$**nil**) which is sent down by $M_{j,j}$.

Now we will translate these informal descriptions into the algebraical specification language ACP. To do this we need the definitions of the following functions.

DEFINITION. We need a function **diag** to specify the value that will actually be sent down by $M_{i,j}$ after having received d:

$$\mathbf{diag}(i,i,d) = d$$

$$\mathbf{diag}(i,j,d) = \mathbf{nil} \quad (i \neq j).$$

DEFINITION. We also need a function **comp** to express what boolean value, 0 or 1, will be sent up by $M_{i,j}$ again, after having received d and e. So in **comp** we actually use the square comparison method (see Figure 2):

$$\mathbf{comp}(i,j,d,e) = \mathbf{if}\ i>j\ \mathbf{then\ if}\ d \geqslant e\ \mathbf{then}\ 1\ \mathbf{else}\ 0\ \mathbf{fi}$$

$$\mathbf{else} \qquad \mathbf{if}\ d>e\ \mathbf{then}\ 1\ \mathbf{else}\ 0\ \mathbf{fi}$$

$$\mathbf{fi}\ ;$$

DEFINITION. Finally we need a kind of *exclusive or* on strings of symbols, to express what value is sent down by $L_{i,j}$ after having received two values:

$$\mathbf{xor}(d, \mathbf{nil}) = \mathbf{xor}(\mathbf{nil}, d) = d$$

$$\mathbf{xor}(d,e) = \mathbf{xor}(\mathbf{nil},\mathbf{nil}) = \mathbf{nil} \quad (d,e \in D).$$

Inductively, we will define **xor** on arbitrary strings of length $n=2^k$:

$$\mathbf{xor}(d_1,d_2,\ldots,d_{2^k}) = \mathbf{xor}(\mathbf{xor}(d_1,\ldots,d_{2^{k-1}}),\mathbf{xor}(d_{2^{k-1}+1},\ldots,d_{2^k}))\,(d_i \in D \cup \{\mathbf{nil}\}).$$

Note, that if exactly one value out of $\{d_1,\ldots,d_n\}$, d_i say, is not equal to **nil**, then $\mathbf{xor}(d_1,\ldots,d_n)=d_i$. So **xor** 'picks' out the unique value $\neq$ **nil**, assuming this unique value exists. This more general definition will be needed later, to describe the specific behaviour of the lower trees, since all of its leaves will send down **nil** except for the leaf on the diagonal of the matrix.

Now we will turn to the formal specification of the cells (see Table 1). In this specification we have atomic actions $r_{i,j,m}(d)$ and $s_{i,j,m}(d)$ for *receiving* and *sending* a datum d from and to the channel $[i,j,m]$. Note that receive and send actions do not have a fixed 'direction' in the channel. We assume D to be a (finite) set of numbers. All (bound) variables are written in italics.

$$U_{i,j} = \sum_{d \in D} r_{i,j,0}(d) \cdot \left[\left\{ s_{i,2j,0}(d) \cdot \sum_{n \in \mathbb{N}} r_{i,2j,0}(n) \right\} \| \right.$$

$$\left. \| \left\{ s_{i,2j+1,0}(d) \cdot \sum_{m \in \mathbb{N}} r_{i,2j+1,0}(m) \right\} \right] \cdot s_{i,j,0}(n+m)$$

$$M_{i,j} = \sum_{d \in D} r_{i,j+n,0}(d) \cdot s_{i+n,j,1}(\mathbf{diag}(i,j,d)) \cdot$$

$$\cdot \sum_{e \in D} r_{i+n,j,1}(e) \cdot s_{i,j+n,0}(\mathbf{comp}(i,j,d,e))$$

$$L_{i,j} = \left[\sum_{d \in D \cup \{\mathbf{nil}\}} r_{2i,j,1}(d) \| \sum_{e \in D \cup \{\mathbf{nil}\}} r_{2i+1,j,1}(e) \right] \cdot s_{i,j,1}(\mathbf{xor}(d,e)) \cdot$$

$$\cdot \sum_{f \in D} r_{i,j,1}(f) \cdot \left[s_{2i,j,1}(f) \| s_{2i+1,j,1}(f) \right]$$

$$B_j = \sum_{d \in D} r_{1,j,1}(d) \cdot s_{1,j,1}(d)$$

TABLE 1. Specification of the cells in the sorter

As a shorthand, the scope rules of Σ are violated in the first equation. Writing out $\|$ using the axioms CM1-4 of [1], $U_{i,j}$ can easily be specified correctly (see also [4] and [6]). It takes some effort to check all the indices, corresponding to the names of the channels. However, making use of the regular configuration of the circuit, and comparing the specification with Figures 3 and 4, one can find out that they are presented correctly here. Furthermore, in the next section we will concentrate on a formal proof of correctness of the sorter, and from any such proof it follows immediately that the channel numbers in the specification above are correct.

Now we present the final specification of the sorting machine as a whole by simply interconnecting all cells (see Table 2).

$$\text{RANKSORT}(n) = \mathop{\|}_{i,j<n} \left\{ U_{i,j} \| M_{i,j} \| L_{i,j} \right\} \| \mathop{\|}_{i<n} B_i$$

TABLE 2. Specification of RANKSORT

So this is the specification, in detail, of RANKSORT. Indeed, it is not clear at all why such a complex machine would be a sorting machine. In the next section we will hide almost all of the internal actions of the machine (only actions via channels $[i,1,0]$ are of interest to the user). Then we will prove the result to be a sorting machine, and hence prove RANKSORT correct.

4. FORMULATING A CORRECTNESS THEOREM

In this section we will present a formal theorem of correctness for RANKSORT, i.e.: abstracting from internal actions, we will state that RANKSORT indeed behaves like a sorting machine. To do this, we first have to specify what actually *is* a sorting machine.

DEFINITION. In the following we define the *sorted indices* of a given sequence of numbers. Suppose $a = \langle a_0, a_1, a_2, \ldots, a_{n-1} \rangle$ is such a sequence of numbers, then we have:
(i) $\langle p_0(a), \ldots, p_{n-1}(a) \rangle \in PERM(\langle 0, \ldots, n-1 \rangle)$,
(ii) $p_i(a) < p_j(a)$ implies $a_i \leq a_j$,
(iii) $p_i(a) < p_j(a)$ & $a_i = a_j$ implies $i < j$.

Because of part (iii) of the definition the permutation $p_i(a)_{0 \leq i < n}$ satisfying all three conditions, is uniquely determined.

Note that from the sorted indices $p_i(a)_{0 \leq i < n}$ we can immediately compute the sorted sequence itself: assume we have n processors $P_0, \ldots, P_{n-1}$, containing the values $p_0(a), \ldots, p_{n-1}(a)$ and $a_0, \ldots, a_{n-1}$ respectively, and suppose all processors are interconnected by channels (wires) then in one step every process P_i can send the number a_i to the 'address' given by $p_i(a)$, i.e.: to $P_{p_i(a)}$.

Next we will formulate a crucial proposition, stating a criterion for correctness of the square comparison method. A proof of this proposition is omitted.

PROPOSITION. *For all sequences $a = \langle a_0, \ldots, a_{n-1} \rangle$ and all $0 \leq i < n$ we have:*

$$\sum_{j=0}^{n-1} \mathbf{comp}(i,j,a_i,a_j) = p_i(a).$$

Clearly, the proposition states that the square comparison method provides us with the sorted indices of the input sequence. Using this proposition we will be able to prove RANKSORT correct, in the sense that RANKSORT turns out to calculate precisely $\Sigma_{0 \leq j < n} \mathbf{comp}(i,j,a_i,a_j)$ for all sequences $\langle a_0, \ldots, a_{n-1} \rangle$

DEFINITION. Suppose a process SORT(n) satisfies the equation

$$\mathrm{SORT}(n) = \left[\Big\|_{0 \leq i < n} \left[\sum_{x_i} r_{i,1,0}(x_i) \right] \right] \cdot \left[\Big\|_{0 \leq i < n} s_{i,1,0}(p_i(x)) \right],$$

and $x = \langle x_0, \ldots, x_{n-1} \rangle$, then SORT($n$) is called a *sorting machine* of size n.

So we agree that any machine that receives a sequence of n numbers, and consequently outputs all sorted indices of this input sequence, may be called a sorting machine. Now we will return to RANKSORT again.

Let D be a (finite) set of numbers. Suppose $n=2^k$, $k \geqslant 0$. The *communication function* $|$ is defined by

$$(r_{i,j,m}(d)|s_{i,j,m}(d)) = (s_{i,j,m}(d)|r_{i,j,m}(d)) = c_{i,j,m}(d) \quad \text{for all } i,j,m,$$

all other communication actions result in deadlock, δ.

The *encapsulation sets* M_n, B_n, H_n and E_n are defined by

$$M_n = \{s_{i,j+n,0}(d), r_{i,j+n,0}(d) : d \in D \cup \mathbb{N},\ i,j<n\} \cup$$
$$\{s_{i+n,j,1}(d), r_{i+n,j,1}(d) : d \in D \cup \{\mathbf{nil}\},\ i,j<n\}$$

corresponding to all channels connected with the matrix cells $M_{i,j}$,

$$B_n = \{s_{1,j,1}(d), r_{1,j,1}(d) : d \in D \cup \{\mathbf{nil}\},\ j<n\}$$

corresponding to the channels connected with the bottom cells B_j,

$$H_n = \{s_{i,j,m}(d), r_{i,j,m}(d) : d \in D \cup \mathbb{N} \cup \{\mathbf{nil}\};\ \text{for all } i,j,m, \text{ such that:}$$
$$(j,m) \neq (1,0) \text{ and } (i,m) \neq (1,1) \text{ and } i,j<n\}$$

which is the set of all communicating actions, except for actions from M_n or B_n or the ones corresponding to the input/output channels $[i,1,0]$ $(i<n)$,

$$E_n = H_n \cup M_n \cup B_n.$$

Finally, the *abstraction set* I is defined by

$$I = \{c_{i,j,m}(d) : d \in D \cup \{\mathbf{nil}\};\ \text{for all appropriate } i,j,m\}.$$

The definition of the communication function says, that receive and send actions only result in a communication $c_{i,j,m}(d)$ if they correspond to the same channel $[i,j,m]$ and the same datum d. If not, a deadlock occurs, e.g. if $d_1 \neq d_2$ then $(r_{2,7,0}(d)|s_{5,2,1}(d)) = (r_{i,j,m}(d_1)|s_{i,j,m}(d_2)) = (r_{i,j,m}(d)|r_{i,j,m}(d)) = \delta$. The choice of the encapsulation sets M_n, B_n and H_n is quite standard: we want no single receive or send actions to happen without direct communication with their 'partner', since otherwise data would be sent to a channel but never read from it. Except for the receive and send actions on the channels $[i,1,0]$ $(0 \leqslant i<n)$: they are the input and output channels of the machine, and are ready for communication with the outside world. The encapsulation sets, M_n and B_n, are defined separately from H_n, to simplify the proofs that will be presented later. At the end of the proof, however, we will encapsulate all actions from $E_n = H_n \cup M_n \cup B_n$.

The abstraction set I has no index n since it contains *all* communication actions $c_{i,j,m}(d)$. By renaming all actions from I into τ we can *hide* internal communication actions from the outside world. Note that any user of RANKSORT will indeed not be interested in the internal communications of the machine; only the outside behaviour will be observed, i.e.: $\tau_I\partial_{E_n}(\text{RANKSORT}(n))$.

Now a correctness theorem can easily be formulated as follows:

THEOREM (CORRECTNESS OF RANKSORT). *For all $k \geq 0$ and $n = 2^k$, we have*

$$\text{ACP}_\tau \vdash \tau_I\partial_{E_n}(\text{RANKSORT}(n)) = \text{SORT}(n)$$

where SORT(n) *is specified earlier.*

This theorem states that $\tau_I\partial_{E_n}(\text{RANKSORT}(n))$ is indeed a sorting machine in the sense of the definition of SORT(n). The proof will be presented in the next section.

5. A FORMAL PROOF OF CORRECTNESS

In this section we will present the final proof of the correctness theorem. First we will simplify the problem by stating and proving two lemmas. Combining both of them we can easily find the proof we are looking for.

First we will formulate what we expect the i-th upper tree $U_{i,1} \| \cdots \| U_{i,n-1}$ to behave like. This is done in Lemma 1 below.

LEMMA 1. *Assume $n = 2^k$, for some given $k > 0$. Then in the theory* ACP_τ *we can prove*

$$\tau_I\partial_{H_n}(U_{i,1} \| \cdots \| U_{i,n-1}) = \sum_{x_i} r_{i,1,0}(x_i) \cdot \mathop{\|}_{0 \leq j < n} \left[s_{i,j+n,0}(x_i) \cdot \sum_{y_{i,j}} r_{i,j+n,0}(y_{i,j}) \right] \cdot s_{i,1,0}\left(\sum_{j=0}^{n-1} y_{i,j}\right)$$

PROOF. By induction on k.

$k = 1$: Now $n = 2$, so $\tau_I\partial_{H_n}(U_{i,1} \| \cdots \| U_{i,n-1}) = \tau_I\partial_{H_2}(U_{i,1}) = U_{i,1}$, and the lemma directly follows from the definition of $U_{i,1}$.

$k+1$: Suppose the lemma holds for $n = 2^k$. Now we prove it to hold for $2n = 2^{k+1}$ as well:

$$\tau_I\partial_{H_{2n}}(U_{i,1} \| \cdots \| U_{i,2n-1}) =$$

$$= \tau_I\partial_{H_{2n}}(\tau_I\partial_{H_n}(U_{i,1} \| \cdots \| U_{i,n-1}) \| U_{i,n} \| \cdots \| U_{i,2n-1})$$

$$= \tau_I\partial_{H_{2n}}\left(\left\{\sum_{x_i} r_{i,1,0}(x_i) \cdot \mathop{\|}_{0 \leq j < n} \left[s_{i,j+n,0}(x_i) \cdot \sum_{y_{i,j}} r_{i,j+n,0}(y_{i,j}) \right] \cdot s_{i,1,0}\left(\sum_{j=0}^{n-1} y_{i,j}\right)\right\} \| \mathop{\|}_{0 \leq j < n} U_{i,j+n}\right)$$

Note, that we needed the conditional axioms to prove the first step. Using the definition of $U_{i,j+n}$ we immediately find

$$= \tau_I \partial_{H_{2n}} \left[\left\{ \sum_{x_i} r_{i,1,0}(x_i) \cdot \underset{0 \leq j < n}{\|} \left[s_{i,j+n,0}(x_i) \cdot \sum_{y_{i,j}} r_{i,j+n,0}(y_{i,j}) \right] \cdot s_{i,1,0}\left[\sum_{j=0}^{n-1} y_{i,j} \right] \right\} \| \right.$$

$$\left. \underset{0 \leq j < n}{\|} \sum_{d_j \in D} r_{i,j+n,0}(d_j) \cdot \left[\left\{ s_{i,2(j+n),0}(d_j) \cdot \sum_{n_{i,j} \in \mathbf{N}} r_{i,2(j+n),0}(n_{i,j}) \right\} \| \right. \right.$$

$$\left. \left. \| \left\{ s_{i,2(j+n)+1,0}(d_j) \cdot \sum_{m_{i,j} \in \mathbf{N}} r_{i,2(j+n)+1,0}(m_{i,j}) \right\} \right] \cdot s_{i,j+n,0}(n_{i,j}+m_{i,j}) \right]$$

Note that for every $0 \leq j < n$ we have two communications: the first one binding the variable d_j and the value x_i, and the second one binding $y_{i,j}$ and $n_{i,j}+m_{i,j}$. So we find:

$$= \tau_I \partial_{H_{2n}} \left(\sum_{x_i} r_{i,1,0}(x_i) \cdot \underset{0 \leq j < n}{\|} \left\{ c_{i,j+n,0}(x_i) \cdot \right. \right.$$

$$\cdot \left[\left\{ s_{i,2(j+n),0}(x_i) \cdot \sum_{n_{i,j} \in \mathbf{N}} r_{i,2(j+n),0}(n_{i,j}) \right\} \| \right.$$

$$\left. \left. \| \left\{ s_{i,2(j+n)+1,0}(x_i) \cdot \sum_{m_{i,j} \in \mathbf{N}} r_{i,2(j+n)+1,0}(m_{i,j}) \right\} \right] \cdot c_{i,j+n,0}(n_{i,j}+m_{i,j}) \right\} \cdot$$

$$\left. \cdot s_{i,1,0} \left[\sum_{j=0}^{n-1} (n_{i,j}+m_{i,j}) \right] \right)$$

$$= \sum_{x_i} r_{i,1,0}(x_i) \cdot \underset{0 \leq j < n}{\|} \left[\left\{ s_{i,2(j+n),0}(x_i) \cdot \sum_{n_{i,j} \in \mathbf{N}} r_{i,2(j+n),0}(n_{i,j}) \right\} \| \right.$$

$$\left. \| \left\{ s_{i,2(j+n)+1,0}(x_i) \cdot \sum_{m_{i,j} \in \mathbf{N}} r_{i,2(j+n)+1,0}(m_{i,j}) \right\} \right] \cdot s_{i,1,0} \left[\sum_{j=0}^{n-1} (n_{i,j}+m_{i,j}) \right]$$

using the equation $(\tau x \| y) = \tau(x \| y)$, which can be derived directly from the axioms of ACP_τ. Thus we have

$$= \sum_{x_i} r_{i,1,0}(x_i) \cdot \underset{0 \leq j < 2n}{\|} \left[s_{i,j+2n,0}(x_i) \cdot \sum_{y_{i,j} \in \mathbf{N}} r_{i,j+2n,0}(y_{i,j}) \right] \cdot s_{i,1,0} \left(\sum_{j=0}^{2n-1} y_{i,j} \right)$$

renaming the n's and m's into y's again. □

So indeed, the i-th upper tree first will receive a number x_i from channel $[i,1,0]$, i.e.: from its own root. Next, after some time, we will see all of its leaves send this value downward to the cells in the matrix, getting some other value in return. All processes in the leaves of the tree are interleaved, precisely as we expected. Finally, after some time, we will find the sum of all values being sent up from the leaves, appears at the root channel $[i,1,0]$ again.

In the same way we can describe what the j-th lower tree acts like, as is done in Lemma 2.

LEMMA 2. *Assume $n = 2^k$, for some given $k > 0$. Then we have (for $j < n$)*

$$\tau_I \partial_{H_n}(L_{1,j} \| \cdots \| L_{n-1,j}) = \underset{0 \leq i < n}{\|} \left[\sum_{z_{i,j} \in D \cup \{\mathbf{nil}\}} r_{i+n,j,1}(z_{i,j}) \right] \cdot$$

$$\cdot s_{1,j,1}(\mathbf{xor}(z_{0,j}, \ldots, z_{n-1,j})) \cdot \sum_{u_j \in D} r_{1,j,1}(u_j) \cdot \underset{0 \leq i < n}{\|} s_{i+n,j,1}(u_j)$$

PROOF. By induction on k.

$k = 1$: Now $n = 2$, so the result directly follows from the definition of $L_{1,j}$.

$k+1$: $\tau_I \partial_{H_{2n}}(\tau_I \partial_{H_n}(L_{1,j} \| \cdots \| L_{n-1,j}) \| L_{n,j} \| \cdots \| L_{2n-1,j}) =$

$$= \tau_I \partial_{H_{2n}} \left(\underset{0 \leq i < n}{\|} \left[\sum_{z_{i,j} \in D \cup \{\mathbf{nil}\}} r_{i+n,j,1}(z_{i,j}) \right] \cdot s_{1,j,1}(\mathbf{xor}(z_{0,j}, \ldots, z_{n-1,j})) \cdot \right.$$

$$\cdot \sum_{u_j \in D} r_{1,j,1}(u_j) \cdot \underset{0 \leq i < n}{\|} s_{i+n,j,1}(u_j) \;\|$$

$$\| \underset{0 \leq i < n}{\|} \left[\sum_{d_{i,j} \in D \cup \{\mathbf{nil}\}} r_{2i+2n,j,1}(d_{i,j}) \| \sum_{e_{i,j} \in D \cup \{\mathbf{nil}\}} r_{2i+1+2n,j,1}(e_{i,j}) \right] \cdot$$

$$\cdot s_{i+n,j,1}(\mathbf{xor}(d_{i,j}, e_{i,j})) \cdot$$

$$\left. \cdot \sum_{f_{i,j} \in D} r_{i+n,j,1}(f_{i,j}) \cdot \left[s_{2i+2n,j,1}(f_{i,j}) \| s_{2i+1+2n,j,1}(f_{i,j}) \right] \right)$$

using the definition of $L_{i,j}$ and the lemma for $n = 2^k$

$$= \tau_I \partial_{H_{2n}} \left(\mathop{\|}_{0 \leq i < n} \left[\sum_{d_{i,j} \in D \cup \{\mathbf{nil}\}} r_{2i+2n,j,1}(d_{i,j}) \| \sum_{e_{i,j} \in D \cup \{\mathbf{nil}\}} r_{2i+1+2n,j,1}(e_{i,j}) \right] \cdot \right.$$

$$\cdot c_{i+n,j,1}(\mathbf{xor}(d_{i,j}, e_{i,j})) \cdot s_{1,j,1}(\mathbf{xor}(\mathbf{xor}(d_{0,j}, e_{0,j}), \ldots, \mathbf{xor}(d_{n-1,j}, e_{n-1,j}))) \cdot$$

$$\left. \cdot \sum_{u_j \in D} r_{1,j,1}(u_j) \cdot \mathop{\|}_{0 \leq i < n} \left\{ c_{i+n,j,1}(u_j) \cdot \left[s_{2i+2n,j,1}(u_j) \| s_{2i+1+2n,j,1}(u_j) \right] \right\} \right)$$

binding $\mathbf{xor}(d_{i,j}, e_{i,j})$ and $z_{i,j}$; moreover the variables u_j and $f_{i,j}$ are identified, for all i,j. Note that $\mathbf{xor}(\mathbf{xor}(d_{0,j}, e_{0,j}), \ldots, \mathbf{xor}(d_{n-1,j}, e_{n-1,j})) =$ $\mathbf{xor}(d_{0,j}, e_{0,j}, \ldots, d_{n-1,j}, e_{n-1,j})$; renaming $d_{i,j}$ and $e_{i,j}$ into $z_{2i,j}$ and $z_{2i+1,j}$ respectively, we find

$$= \mathop{\|}_{0 \leq i < 2n} \left[\sum_{z_{i,j} \in D \cup \{\mathbf{nil}\}} r_{i+2n,j,1}(z_{i,j}) \right] \cdot$$

$$\cdot s_{1,j,1}(\mathbf{xor}(z_{0,j}, \ldots, z_{2n-1,j})) \cdot \sum_{u_j \in D} r_{1,j,1}(u_j) \cdot \mathop{\|}_{0 \leq i < 2n} s_{i+2n,j,1}(u_j)$$

□

From Lemma 2 we read that the j-th lower tree first will receive n values (probably with some **nil**'s) from its leaves, say $z_{0,j}, \ldots, z_{n-1,j}$. Then it will send $\mathbf{xor}(z_{0,j}, \ldots, z_{n-1,j})$ to the bottom. Next it waits until it gets a value u_j from the bottom in return, and it will broadcast this value up to the leaves again, i.e.: after some time all leaves, in any order, will send up u_j. Using both lemmas we can now easily find the final proof of the correctness theorem.

Proof of the correctness theorem

Let $n = 2^k$ for some $k \geq 0$. Using the conditional axioms of [1], one easily verifies

$$\tau_I \partial_{H_n \cup M_n}(U_{i,1} \| \cdots \| U_{i,n-1} \| M_{i,0} \| \cdots \| M_{i,n-1}) =$$
$$= \tau_I \partial_{H_n \cup M_n}(\tau_I \partial_{H_n}(U_{i,1} \| \cdots \| U_{i,n-1}) \| M_{i,0} \| \cdots \| M_{i,n-1}).$$

Then, using Lemma 1 and the definition of $M_{i,j}$ we find

$$\tau_I \partial_{H_n}(U_{i,1} \| \cdots \| U_{i,n-1}) \| M_{i,0} \| \cdots \| M_{i,n-1} =$$

$$= \sum_{x_i} r_{i,1,0}(x_i) \cdot \mathop{\|}_{0 \leq j < n} \left[s_{i+n,j,1}(\mathbf{diag}(i,j,x_i)) \cdot \sum_{w_{i,j}} r_{i+n,j,1}(w_{i,j}) \right] \cdot$$

$$\cdot s_{i,1,0} \left(\sum_{j=0}^{n-1} \mathbf{comp}(i,j,x_i,w_{i,j}) \right).$$

Using the conditional axioms once again we have

$$\tau_I \partial_{E_n}(L_{1,j} \| \cdots \| L_{n-1,j} \| B_j) = \tau_I \partial_{E_n}(\tau_I \partial_{H_n}(L_{1,j} \| \cdots \| L_{n-1,j}) \| B_j).$$

From the definition of B_j and Lemma 2 we find directly

$$\tau_I \partial_{E_n}(\tau_I \partial_{H_n}(L_{1,j} \| \cdots \| L_{n-1,j}) \| B_j) =$$

$$= \mathop{\Big\|}_{0 \leq i < n} \left[\sum_{z_{i,j}} r_{i+n,j,1}(z_{i,j}) \right] \cdot \mathop{\Big\|}_{0 \leq i < n} s_{i+n,j,1}(\mathbf{xor}(z_{0,j}, \ldots, z_{n-1,j}))$$

so we have

$$\tau_I \partial_{E_n}(\text{RANKSORT}(n)) =$$

$$= \tau_I \partial_{E_n} \left[\mathop{\Big\|}_{0 \leq i < n} \left[\tau_I \partial_{H_n \cup M_n}(\tau_I \partial_{H_n}(U_{i,1} \| \cdots \| U_{i,n-1}) \| M_{i,0} \| \cdots \| M_{i,n-1}) \right] \right\| $$

$$\left\| \mathop{\Big\|}_{0 \leq j < n} \left[\tau_I \partial_{E_n}(L_{1,j} \| \cdots \| L_{n-1,j} \| B_j) \right] \right]$$

$$= \tau_I \partial_{E_n} \left[\mathop{\Big\|}_{0 \leq i < n} \left\{ \sum_{x_i} r_{i,1,0}(x_i) \cdot \mathop{\Big\|}_{0 \leq j < n} c_{i+n,j,1}(\mathbf{diag}(i,j,x_i)) \right\} \cdot \right.$$

$$\cdot \mathop{\Big\|}_{0 \leq i < n} \left\{ \mathop{\Big\|}_{0 \leq j < n} \left[c_{i+n,j,1}(\mathbf{xor}(\mathbf{diag}(0,j,x_0), \ldots, \mathbf{diag}(n-1,j,x_{n-1}))) \right] \cdot \right.$$

$$\left. \left. \cdot s_{i,1,0} \left[\sum_{j=0}^{n-1} \mathbf{comp}(i,j,x_i,\mathbf{xor}(\mathbf{diag}(0,j,x_0), \ldots, \mathbf{diag}(n-1,j,x_{n-1}))) \right] \right\} \right]$$

$$= \tau_I \partial_{E_n} \left[\mathop{\Big\|}_{0 \leq i < n} \left\{ \sum_{x_i} r_{i,1,0}(x_i) \cdot \mathop{\Big\|}_{0 \leq j < n} c_{i+n,j,1}(\mathbf{diag}(i,j,x_i)) \right\} \cdot \right.$$

$$\left. \cdot \mathop{\Big\|}_{0 \leq i,j < n} c_{i+n,j,1}(x_j) \cdot s_{i,1,0} \left[\sum_{j=0}^{n-1} \mathbf{comp}(i,j,x_i,x_j) \right] \right]$$

$$= \mathop{\Big\|}_{0 \leq i < n} \left[\sum_{x_i} r_{i,1,0}(x_i) \right] \cdot \mathop{\Big\|}_{0 \leq i < n} s_{i,1,0} \left[\sum_{j=0}^{n-1} \mathbf{comp}(i,j,x_i,x_j) \right]$$

$$= \mathop{\Big\|}_{0 \leq i < n} \left[\sum_{x_i} r_{i,1,0}(x_i) \right] \cdot \mathop{\Big\|}_{0 \leq i < n} s_{i,1,0}(p_i(x))$$

$$= \text{SORT}(n)$$

using the proposition of Section 4 for the last but one equality. □

6. Some remarks about the complexity of Ranksort

It is beyond the subject of this paper to study the complexity of the machine described in the former sections. Still, some obvious remarks can be made to indicate that Ranksort in fact is only slightly suboptimal with respect to other well-known algorithms. All of these remarks are from [5], in which a review over thirteen VLSI sorting algorithms is presented.

As it turns out, Ranksort works with n^2 processors and in $\log n$ time. So one could say, comparing this complexity behaviour with for instance the $n\log n$ time sequential mergesort algorithm, a factor $O(n)$ time can be 'won' by exchanging it for a large amount of space. In some well-known models of VLSI complexity this notion of 'space' is worked out in more detail (see: Bilardi & Preparata [2] and Thompson [5]). A convenient unit of *area* of a VLSI chip is the square of the minimum separation between parallel wires. Every square unit on the chip surface may contain a *wire* element, or a piece of a *gate*, i.e.: a localized set of transistors or other switching elements, which perform a simple logical function. Starting from a square tessellation of the chip surface, some restrictions on the design of the chip are made. For instance, no pieces of gates may overlap (i.e.: any square unit only contains a part of at most one gate) and only two (or perhaps three, depending on the model) wires can pass over the same point (any square unit can represent the crossing of at most two wires).

The unit of time can be taken to be the time of one clock pulse, so the time behaviour of the chip can be expressed as a number of pulses. Note, that the specification of Ranksort, as given in Section 4, can be implemented in an *unclocked* network, since we have asynchronous cooperation between individual processes. A *clocked* network, however, is a special case of the general network in which no restrictions on timing are made, so a clock can do no 'harm' to the correct behaviour of the machine.

Of course, the list of restrictions mentioned here is not complete. In [2] all restrictions are formulated in detail, as rules on the underlying graphs representing the VLSI networks.

In [2] and [5], VLSI models are used to find lower and upper bounds for the complexity behaviour of sorting algorithms. Assume a VLSI chip has area A and needs time T to do its task, then a useful complexity measure turns out to be $A \cdot T^2$ (although AT and $AT/\log A$ can be used as well). In [5] a lower bound for the complexity of any sorting algorithm is put at $AT^2 = \Omega(n^2 \log n)$. Moreover about thirteen VLSI sorting algorithms are examined, ranging from $O(n^2 \log^2 n)$ to $O(n^2 \log^5 n)$, and hence all are only slightly suboptimal in AT^2 behaviour.

Although we have $O(n^2)$ wires in the network, we need some more wire unit elements to implement the orthogonal tree network on a VLSI chip. The Ranksort algorithm turns out to be $A = O(n^2 \log^2 n)$, and thus $AT^2 = O(n^2 \log^4 n)$, which can be understood by making the following observation.

As we can see, the orthogonal tree network consists of $O(n^2)$ processors, interconnected by a number of wires. Note that every wire has width $O(1)$, not 0. Now consider the projection of the orthogonal tree network on a plane, as pictured in Figure 6. We see we have to leave at least $\log n$ units of space between two rows or columns of matrix cells, since this is the minimum area needed to construct a tree in between these cells. So, we may conclude that the width of the whole circuit is $O(n \log n)$, since the distance between two matrix processors is $O(\log n)$, and any processor is $O(\log n)$ square. So we find directly that the total area of the orthogonal tree network is $O(n^2 \log^2 n)$. Since the sorting task can be done in $O(\log n)$ time, we have $AT^2 = O(n^2 \log^4 n)$.

Indeed, RANKSORT can be said to be slightly suboptimal with respect to the lower bound $AT^2 = \Omega(n^2 \log n)$. Clearly, however, the strong time performance of the algorithm takes a large amount of area, so we may not expect the circuit to be of much interest until chip area is cheap enough.

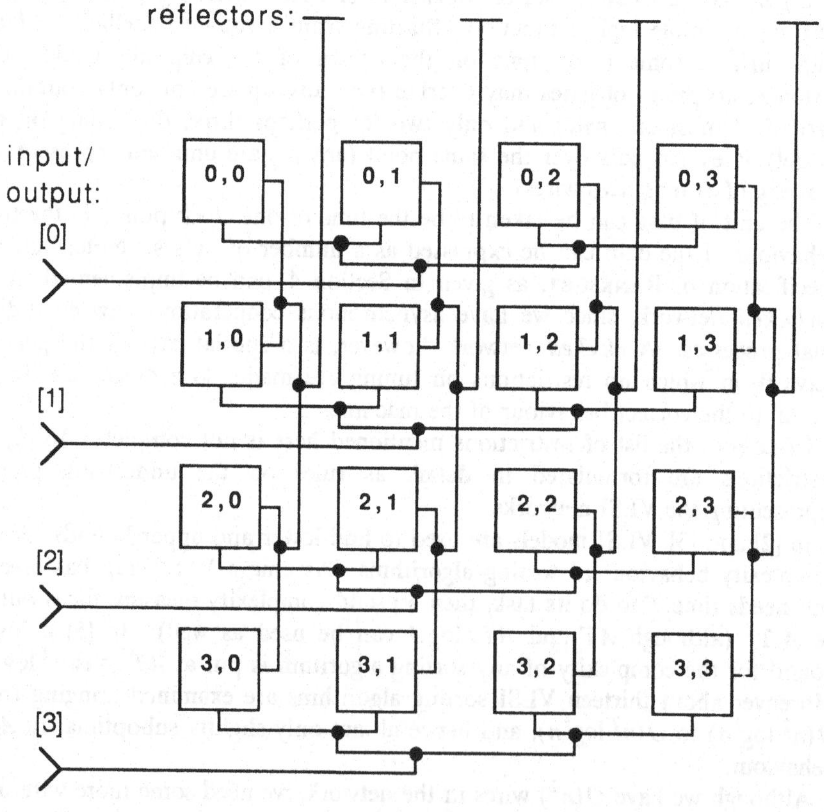

FIGURE 6. A two dimensional projection of the orthogonal tree network with $n=4$

REFERENCES

1. J.A. BERGSTRA, J.W. KLOP (1989). *An Introduction to Process Algebra.* This volume.
2. G. BILARDI, F.P. PREPARATA (1986). Area-time lower-bound techniques with applications to sorting. *Algorithmica 1,* 65-91.
3. M. HENNESSY (1986). Proving systolic systems correct. *TOPLAS 8(3),* 344-387.
4. L. KOSSEN, W.P. WEIJLAND (1989). *Correctness Proofs for Systolic Algorithms: Palindromes and Sorting.* This volume.
5. CLARK D. THOMPSON (1983). The VLSI complexity of sorting. *IEEE Transactions on Computers: Vol. C-32, 12,* December 1983.
6. W.P. WEIJLAND (1987). A systolic algorithm for matrix-vector multiplication. *Proc. SION Conference CSN 1987,* Centre for Mathematics and Computer Science, Amsterdam, 143-160.

On the *Amoeba* Protocol

J.C. Mulder

Programming Research Group, University of Amsterdam
P.O. Box 41882, 1009 DB Amsterdam, The Netherlands

The *Amoeba* distributed operating system supports the transaction as its communication primitive. The protocol that the *Amoeba* system uses to carry out sequences of transactions reliably and efficiently is analyzed in terms of process algebra. The design goals are formulated as process algebra equations and it is established that one of them is not met. This can be repaired by adding an extra transition. Subsequently it is verified that the revised version meets its specifications.

It has been observed that formal verification methods for mathematical proofs, computer programs, communication protocols and the like are usually illustrated by 'toy' examples and that such proofs tend to be discouragingly long. In order to demonstrate that it is feasible to verify a 'real-life' communication protocol by means of process algebra, we picked one from the literature.

In his Ph.D. thesis [9], Mullender investigates issues he considered while developing the *Amoeba* distributed operating system. In Section 3.2.4 of [9] a transaction protocol is described to which we will refer as the *Amoeba* protocol. In the preceding sections of [9] the design goals are described that this protocol is supposed to satisfy. He does not give a formal verification that his protocol meets this criteria. In fact, it turns out that one of them is not met. Note that this only applies to the simplified version of the protocol that appears in [9], the actual implementation uses a much more complicated version in which this mistake is not found.

Section 1 of this article gives the minimum background information necessary for understanding the rest of the article.

In Section 2 the design goals are formulated in English and in terms of process algebra.

Section 3 describes the protocol and explains what is wrong.

In Section 4 the (obvious) correction is given and it is verified that the resulting protocol meets the requirements.

The reader is supposed to be acquainted with process algebra. For an introduction we refer to e.g. [1,3,4,5].

1. Some background on the *Amoeba* distributed operating system

1.0. It should be stressed that this section is not intended to give an accurate picture of the *Amoeba* system. We will only sketch the environment in which the *Amoeba* protocol operates. For a more detailed introduction the reader is referred to [9].

1.1. The context in which *Amoeba* operates is essentially a local area network connecting several machines with (possibly) different capabilities. E.g. some network nodes may have (or be) printers, huge disks, fast floating point hardware, etc. Needless to say, when a user posts a request, the system may decide to carry it out on another network node.

1.2. The centralized approach to such a configuration would use a request dispatcher residing on a fixed node in the center of the network. All requests would be mailed to the dispatcher, who would forward it to the machine that was most suitable for carrying it out. Of course this dispatcher must have up-to-date knowledge of work load, availability of services, etc.

This method is probably optimal in a star-shaped network, i.e. one in which one central machine is connected to all others and the others are connected to this central node only. In such a configuration all messages have to travel via the center node anyway.

However, in a more general network, the overhead of diverting each and every request via the center and keeping the dispatchers picture of the system up-to-date can probably better be avoided. Moreover, the central node might crash and it would be nice if the rest of the system would continue operating without it.

1.3. *Amoeba* uses a more distributed approach: each network node does its own dispatching. The *Amoeba* system does not try to maintain at every node a complete overview of what services are available on what nodes. If a user posts a request, the local *Amoeba* kernel may have to broadcast the question 'which machines can carry out requests of type X?'. Several machines may answer 'I can' and then one of them is chosen; perhaps the first one to respond.

1.4. The *Amoeba* kernel does not carry out requests itself; it merely forwards them to a suitable server process, that may or may not live on the same machine. To the user the difference is immaterial, he is just posting requests and getting replies. In fact, a 'user' may very well be a server process handing out a subtask of the request he is resolving.

1.5. In some network protocols, e.g. in the ISO model, the basic service is the virtual stream, carrying unlimited amounts of data from *A* to *B*. This may be very efficient when large amounts of data are to be transferred, but the designers of *Amoeba* felt that this would be a rare event in an *Amoeba* system. If, for instance, a user wants to query a large database, the database will not be transferred to the user, rather the query will be transferred to the database, thereby saving huge amounts of data transfer.

If it turns out that the information to be transferred in an average request fits in a single packet, then establishing and maintaining a virtual stream is not optimal.

1.6. The other end of the spectrum is a model in which the basic communication service is passing a single message. If this is to happen reliably, then for each message sent, an acknowledgement message must be sent back.

One might even be misled to think that this acknowledgement should also be acknowledged, and so on indefinitely. Fortunately, this is not the case: if the acknowledgement message does not arrive, then the sender of the original message will have to retransmit it. So if the receiver is able to recognize this retransmitted message as one it has received before, then it can simply re-acknowledge it, and forget about it.

1.7. Nevertheless, *Amoeba* does not support the message passing primitive. The designers expect that most requests will lead to some sort of reply from the server, at the very least an indication of whether the request could be carried out. Obviously, a reply implicitly acknowledges receipt of the request. In fact, if the server has established his reply before the user feels like retransmitting his request, the original acknowledgement becomes superfluous.

To exploit the above possibility, *Amoeba* supports the *transaction* as its primitive communication service. This means that the process receiving the message (called the *server*) is obliged to send some sort of reply back to the sender (hereafter called the *client*). The client, on the other hand, is not obliged to return a follow-up query, so communication might stop after two messages.

1.8. The ISO communication standard prescribes some complicated seven-layer model. The *Amoeba* designers think that such a complicated system cannot possibly operate quickly, so they invented their own, three-layered model.

- The lowest layer is the physical layer. It consists of physical interconnections. We will not explore it any further.
- The middle layer is the port layer. The port layer transfers so-called 'datagrams' of up to 32K to specified ports. A datagram is guaranteed to arrive *at most* once; it is left to the next higher layer to resubmit the datagram if necessary.
- The upper layer is the transaction layer. This is the layer we will investigate. It implements the transaction service, using the port layer's datagram service. If a datagram does not arrive the transaction layer will have to

resubmit it. To detect such mishaps the transaction layer employs the usual devices: timers and acknowledgement datagrams.

1.9. The transaction layer software on each network node has three interfaces: on the lower side there is an interface to the port layer and on the upper side there is an interface for clients and one for server processes.

When a client files a request, he indicates the type of service required by mentioning an associated port number. The transaction layer then uses the port layer for locating a server process offering this sort of service. If more then one server process offers this service, it is up to the port layer to pick a suitable one. Once this choice has been made, only four processes are relevant to the transaction from the transaction layer's point of view: the client, the server, the transaction layer software at the client's node, and the transaction layer at the server's node. In the sequel we will denote these as *CL*, *SV*, *TLCN* and *TLSN*, respectively.

1.10. In order to simplify the picture, we will largely ignore the fact that the port layer has to choose an available server able to carry out the specified type of request and act as if only the four processes mentioned above are involved. Obviously, we will concentrate on *TLCN* and *TLSN*, who try to communicate on behalf of *CL* and *SV* respectively via an unreliable medium provided by the port layer.

1.11. There is one more aspect of *Amoeba* that we do take into account. Sometimes, one of the network nodes crashes, i.e. it stops whatever it is doing and does not respond to any attempts to communicate.

We will assume that after a while this mishap is noticed and the malfunctioning machine is restarted. When restarted, the machine does not remember what it was doing before the crash, so it won't do anything before new requests arrive.

Consequently, when the *TLCN* has successfully delivered a request, it cannot simply wait for a reply. The network node where the server is working on a reply might crash and the client would be waiting forever. Instead, the *TLCN* will regularly poll the *TLSN* to check whether it is still alive. If the *TLSN* does not seem to be responding, the *TLCN* will assume that the server's network node has crashed and reissue the request, hoping that the unfortunate node has been restarted, or that some other server of the same type exists in the network. It might also notify some trouble server.

1.12. Conversely, it is not really a problem for a server if its client has crashed. If this happens the *TLSN* will be unable to deliver the reply, but once that fact has been discovered, there is not really any problem, though the *TLSN* might notify the trouble server, just for the record. The server may have done some processing in vain, but that is tolerable, as crashes are rare events. Anyway, if the client had crashed immediately after receiving and acknowledging the reply, the result would have been the same: request carried out, result not used.

1.13. One might be tempted to think that, from a theoretical point of view, crashing machines are just another innocent feature, but this is not the case. If one wants to communicate reliably via an unreliable medium, one must be prepared to retransmit a message any number of times. If, on the other hand, one takes into consideration the possibility that one's partner has crashed, one should give up after a predetermined finite number of attempts. These options are evidently incompatible.

This does not necessarily imply that the *Amoeba* system is unreliable. In case of trouble the *TLCN* can usually restart the whole transaction. For some types of service it might be inappropriate to redo the essential processing. For example, suppose an accounting service keeps track of the usage of some services. Whenever one of the monitored servers satisfies a request, it notifies the accounting server. When the latter has updated its bookkeeping, it returns an acknowledgement. If this acknowledgement fails to be delivered, the accounting *TLSN* will assume that the other party has crashed. If this assumption is false, the *TLCN*, after a while, resubmits an account request. This glitch should not cause the user to be charged doubly, so the accounting server should be able to deduce from its files that it has satisfied this request before and react accordingly.

We will assume that this sort of safety precaution has been made and thus we will let the *TLCN* restart the whole transaction whenever it cannot be completed satisfactorily.

2. The requirements

2.0. In this section we will try to pin down the design goals that the *Amoeba* system is supposed to satisfy, both in English and in terms of process algebra.

2.1. The main problem is to distinguish the three possible reasons why a client does not get an answer from a server:

(i) the server is still busy computing,

(ii) the server is trying to transmit a response, but the communication channel is malfunctioning,

(iii) the server has crashed.

As explained in Section 1, we assume that if a server crashes, so does its interface. Consequently, case (i) can be distinguished from (iii) by periodically polling the interface. If it reacts, we will assume that the server is still alive. On the other hand, as long as we don't get a response we know that either the channel malfunctions or the server has crashed (or both). If we fail to get a response a number of times successively, we find it highly unlikely that this is due to a faulty communication channel, so we assume that the server has crashed and start afresh. After a while the server will be in its initial state again, either because it had indeed crashed and is being restarted, or because it found that is was unable to deliver a reply to our original request.

In the real *Amoeba* system, the number of successive failures it takes before the client system decides to give up is fixed. In our presentation, whenever a client process fails to receive a sign of life it decides non-deterministically whether it will give up or try again.

2.2. Perhaps surprisingly, the hardest notion to catch in process algebra is periodical polling. The point is that process algebra does not explicitly mention time. After an event has happened, the next one takes place and there is no mention of the intervening time. If at a certain stage the only possible next event is that the server comes up with a result, this will be the next step in the process term, no matter how long it takes. Algebraically, we cannot say anything about the time spent waiting, because it does not appear in our formalism.

The only way to describe in process algebra that the interfaces exchange acknowledgements while waiting for the real reply, is saying that if the server never yields a reply, then infinitely many reacknowledgements will be transferred.

2.3. A first approximation to an algebraic formulation of the above is the following. Let *ans* be the event that the server delivers an answer; let *ack* be the event that the client receives an acknowledgement message; let I be the set of all other events; then we require, at least, that:

$$\tau_I \partial_{\{ans\}}(Amoeba) = \tau \cdot ack^{\omega}.$$

2.4. The main defect of the above formula is that it describes the situation that every reply takes for ever. In particular the first request will never be answered, so there will never be a second request. This can easily be repaired. It so happens that requests and replies will be indexed by natural numbers. Consequently, we can use $\partial_{\{ans(n)\}}$ to express that the server thinks infinitely long about the n-th request. So we will require (taking I to be all actions except *ack*):

$$\forall n \in \mathbb{N}\ \tau_I \partial_{\{ans(n)\}}(Amoeba) = \tau \cdot ack^{\omega}.$$

To be quite honest, we should mention that a finite number of the acknowledgements mentioned above may have been exchanged while the server was contemplating the first $n-1$ requests.

2.5. The server network node runs (at least) two processes: the actual server process and its interface to the network. If this network node crashes, then both processes die simultaneously. This is not too hard to model. We introduce an atomic action *crash* and add to each and every term of the specification a summand *crash*. Or rather, $crash \cdot Server$, to model the fact that the server is eventually restarted by a crash server.

A minor complication is the fact that the specification is presented in the form *Server* = *Interface*||*ServerProper*. We could, of course, introduce yet another operator $x \rightarrow y$ that adds a summand y to every state of process x. In fact, in [2] such an operator is proposed under the name *mode transfer operator*. A similar operator occurs in LOTOS [7], where it is denoted $x[>y$ and called *disable operator*. But we can also use existing operators. We introduce an atomic action *crash'*, that communicates with itself: $crash' | crash' = crash$, and we (textually) add summands *crash'* to all states of the interface and server proper.

2.6. The usual fairness assumptions in process algebra imply that, if the server is given the chance to crash infinitely often, it eventually will. One might interpret this as an instance of Murphy's law, or regard it as a defect of process algebra. In any case, in this article we will not propose any alternative notion of fairness. We will limit ourselves to verifying that the protocol does not abuse crashes to escape from problematic situations. In other words, for some suitable set I of internal actions, we will require:

$$\tau_I(Amoeba) = \tau_I \partial_{\{crash\}}(Amoeba).$$

2.7. The client process crashes in much the same way the server does. A minor difference is that a client process is not restarted when it crashes. As a result, the entire system will get stuck as soon as the server tries to communicate to its client again. Here our toy system with only one client deviates from the real *Amoeba* system where there is more than one client and one naturally requires that if one client dies, the server goes on to serve other clients. Thus we are led to also considering a two-client version and requiring:

$$\tau_I \partial_H(Client_1 \| Client_2 \| Server) = \tau_I \partial_H(Client_1 \| Server)$$

where I contains at least all actions pertaining to $Client_2$.

2.8. By now we have exhausted the requirements associated with crashing processes. We proceed by describing the regular behaviour of the system.

First of all, if the client does not crash, then it submits requests and the server should answer these. The requests are indexed by natural numbers and so are their responses. This gives something like:

$$\tau_I \partial_H(Amoeba) = \tau \cdot \prod_{n \in \mathbb{N}} req(n) \cdot ans(n).$$

Here, and in the sequel, we use $\prod_{n \in \mathbb{N}} T_n$ as a notation for a solution for X_0 of the system of equations $\{X_n = T_n \cdot X_{n+1} \mid n \in \mathbb{N}\}$.

The attentive reader has noticed that the above equation disagrees with our description in 2.7 in case of a client crash. A better approximation is:

$$\tau_I \partial_H(\partial_{\{crash\}}(Client) \| Server) = \tau \cdot \prod_{n \in \mathbb{N}} req(n) \cdot ans(n).$$

This one, however fails to take into account, that a server crash may cause the request to be repeated. In fact, the easiest way out is to assume that the server never generates an answer unless it received a corresponding request and only specify that in the long run it is going to send all answers:

$$\tau_{I\cup\{req(n)\,|\,n\in\mathbb{N}\}}\partial_H(\partial_{\{crash\}}(Client)\|Server) = \tau\cdot\prod_{n\in\mathbb{N}} ans(n).$$

2.9. An important aspect we have been ignoring so far, is the communication channel connecting the *Client* and *Server* processes. In the *Amoeba* system this channel is set up and run by the port layer software. In process algebra, this channel is modelled as a separate process.

This *Channel* process is described most easily as the parallel composition of two one-way channels. Such a one-way channel would accept a datum at one end and then choose non-deterministically between three options:

- deliver the datum at the other end undisturbed
- deliver it corrupted (this is assumed to be detectable)
- do not deliver anything at all.

In process algebra, this is easily described:

$$OWC = (read(datum)\cdot(i\cdot deliver(datum)+i\cdot deliver(error)+i))\cdot OWC.$$

In this equation i is an internal step, used as a guard. In [8], we use different guards for different options, but we now feel that this only opens up such weird possibilities as cutting out the second option by applying a $\partial_{\{i_2\}}$-operator. In fact, we would prefer to use τ as a guard here, but that is impossible.

2.9.1. If the one-way channel specified above could systematically choose, say, the second alternative, it would not be usable. Therefore we will adopt the usual fairness rule, which implies that this cannot happen: if the same datum is input to the channel often enough, it will eventually be delivered correctly.

2.10. Incidentally, the *Amoeba* system does not respond at all if a corrupted message arrives. For one thing, one cannot extract the sender's name from a corrupted message. So the receiver is described in process algebra by a system of equations of the form:

$$Rec_k = accept(error)\cdot Rec_k + \sum_l a_{kl} Rec_l$$

where the a_{kl} are atomic actions distinct from *accept*(*error*).

Now, if such a receiver is connected to a simplified one-way channel that does not deliver errors, but only 'forgets' data, the result is the same as before.

Lemma. *Suppose processes OWC, OWC′ and Rec are defined by the following systems of equations:*

$$OWC \;= read(datum)\cdot OWC_2$$

$$OWC_2 = i \cdot OWC_3 + i \cdot OWC_4 + i \cdot OWC$$
$$OWC_3 = deliver(datum) \cdot OWC$$
$$OWC_4 = deliver(error) \cdot OWC$$
$$OWC' = read(datum) \cdot OWC'_2$$
$$OWC'_2 = i \cdot OWC'_3 + i \cdot OWC'$$
$$OWC'_3 = deliver(datum) \cdot OWC'$$
$$Rec_k = accept(error) \cdot Rec_k + \sum a_l Rec_l \text{ and } Rec = Rec_0$$

Let

$$deliver(error) \mid accept(error) = arrives(error)$$
$$H = \{deliver(error), accept(error)\}$$
$$I = \{arrives(error)\}$$

Then

$$\tau_I \partial_H(OWC \| Rec) = \tau_I \partial_H(OWC' \| Rec).$$

PROOF. In every state the receiver can perform an action *accept(error)*. Execution of this action never results in a state change. Hence the receiver can be described in process algebra by a system of equations of the form:

$$Rec = accept(error)^{\omega} \| Rec'$$
$$Rec'_k = \sum_l a_{kl} Rec'_l \text{ and } Rec' = Rec'_0$$

Using the CA rules we find:

$$\begin{aligned}\tau_I \partial_H(OWC \| Rec) &= \tau_I \partial_H(OWC \| Rec' \| accept(error)^{\omega}) \\ &= \tau_I \partial_H(\tau_I \partial_H(OWC \| accept(error)^{\omega}) \| Rec) \\ &= \tau_I \partial_H(OWC' \| Rec)\end{aligned}$$ □

2.11. The upshot of all this is that there is no point in mentioning the possibility of the channel producing an error-value. Consequently, we will leave it out in the sequel. Thus the one-way channel will be described as:

$$OWC = read(datum) \cdot (i \cdot deliver(datum) + i) \cdot OWC.$$

3. PROCESS ALGEBRA EQUATIONS

3.0. In this section we will present both the design criteria and the actual system in the form of process algebra equations. As it happens, the system presented in Section 3.2 does not satisfy the criteria in Section 3.3. This is easily mended and we will do so in Section 3.4.

3.1 Preliminaries

As a preliminary to the equations in 3.2, this subsection presents the alphabet, the communication function, etc.

3.1.1. The architecture. The architecture is depicted schematically in Figure 1:

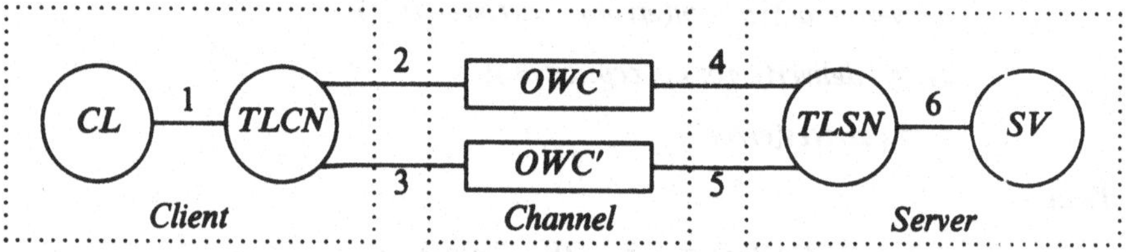

FIGURE 1

The *Amoeba* system contains a *Client* process and a *Server* process, connected by a communication channel. The *Client* process consists of a client proper and an interface. In 1.9 we have called these *CL* and *TLCN*, respectively. Likewise, the *Server* process consists of the server proper, *SV* and an interface, *TLSN*. Lastly there is the communication channel, that consists of two one-way channels.

These processes are connected by ports numbered as indicated in Figure 1.

3.1.2. Data. Four types of messages are passed around: requests, answers, enquiries and acknowledgements. They will be denoted *req*, *ans*, *enq* and *ack*, respectively. For later reference, we collect them in a set $D = \{req, ans, enq, ack\}$. It does not make things clearer if we introduce actual contents for the requests and answers and consequently we will refrain from doing so.

In order to be able to describe the two-client version, we introduce the set $C = \{1,2\}$ of client numbers.

To make messages recognizable as pertaining to the same request, they are tagged with tags drawn from $T = C \times \mathbb{N}$, i.e. pairs consisting of the client's number and a sequence number.

We will need two auxiliary functions on T: if $t = (c,n)$, then $t^+ = (c,n+1)$ is the next tag from the same client and $t^- = (c,n-1)$ is the previous one (provided $n > 0$).

The complete set of possible messages is $M = D \times T$.

3.1.3. Atomic actions. For $m \in M$ and $p \in \{1,...,6\}$ there are *read*, *send* and *communicate* actions:

$r(p,m)$: read message m at port p.
$s(p,m)$: send message m at port p.
$c(p,m)$: communicate message m at port p.

In fact $c(p,m)$ is a communication action: $c(p,m) = r(p,m) \mid s(p,m)$.

A message m is in fact an element of $D \times T$, and we will often leave out some parentheses, and write e.g. $r(p,d,c,n)$ for $r(p,(d,(c,n)))$.

In Section 2.5 we introduced the atoms *crash* and *crash'*, satisfying $crash = crash' \mid crash'$.

Finally we need an atomic action *to* denoting the timeout event and the communication channels contain an internal action *i*. The entire alphabet is then:

$$A = \{r(p,m), s(p,m), c(p,m) \mid m \in M,\ 1 \leq p \leq 6\} \cup \{crash, crash', i, to\}$$

and the communication function is:

$$a \mid b = \begin{cases} c & \text{if } \exists m \in M,\ p \in \{1,...,6\}\,[\{a,b\} = \{r(p,m), s(p,m)\} \wedge c = c(p,m)] \\ crash & \text{if } a = b = crash' \\ \delta & \text{otherwise} \end{cases}$$

Some subsets of A will be referred to in the next subsection:

For $P \subseteq \{1,...,6\}$: $H_P = \{r(p,m), s(p,m) \mid m \in M, p \in P\} \cup \{crash'\}$

$$H = H_{\{1,...,6\}}$$

$$I = A - \{c(1, ans, 1, n) \mid n \in \mathbb{N}\}$$

3.2 The specification

The *Amoeba* system consists of three component processes:

$$Amoeba = \partial_H(Client \| Channel \| Server).$$

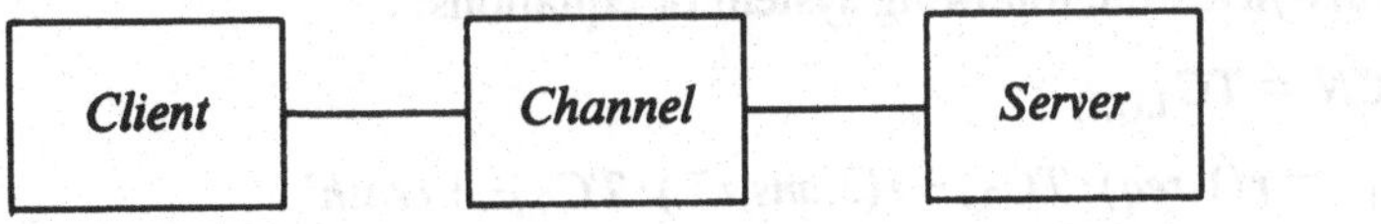

We will describe these components in detail in the next three subsections.

3.2.1. The Client process.

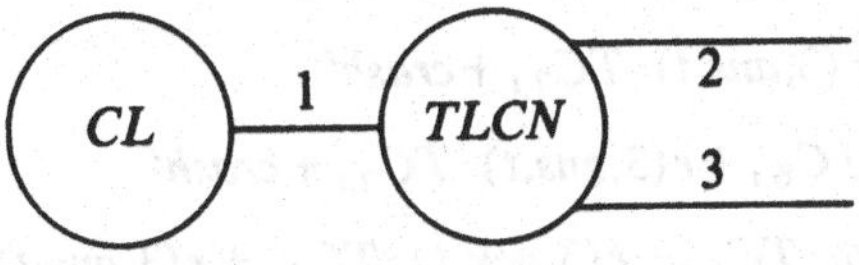

The *Client* process consists of the client proper and its interface:

$$Client = \partial_{H_{(1)}}(CL \| TLCN).$$

3.2.1.1. From our point of view, the client only generates requests and sometimes crashes:

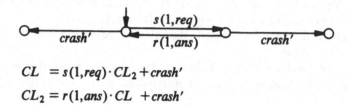

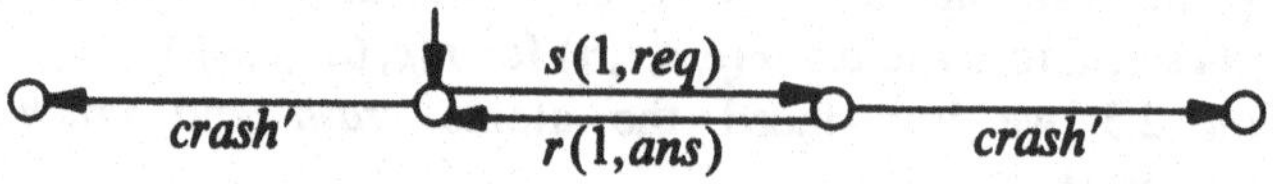

$$CL \ = s(1,req)\cdot CL_2 + crash'$$
$$CL_2 = r(1,ans)\cdot CL \ + crash'$$

3.2.1.2. The client's interface, *TLCN*, accepts a request from the client process, gives it a sequence number and sends it to the server. If no answer arrives for some time, a timeout occurs and the request is sent again. If an acknowledgement arrives, the interface moves on to the next stage, where it periodically sends an enquiry message and expects another acknowledgement. If this acknowledgement fails to arrive, the *TLSN* non-deterministically chooses between sending another enquiry and believing that the server has crashed, in which case he starts afresh sending the request.
At any time during these stages, an answer to the request may arrive. The *TLCN* then delivers this answer, stripped of its tag, to the client and starts waiting for a further request. If the next request comes quickly enough, the *TLCN* will enter the next cycle at the second stage, otherwise, it sends an acknowledgement and starts its next cycle at the beginning. In the first three states, it may happen that the answer to the previous question arrives again. The interface reacts by sending the current request, if it has one, and an acknowledgement otherwise.

The resulting process graph is shown in Figure 2, except that the incrementing of the sequence number is not shown, in order to keep the picture finite.

This yields the following system of equations:

$$TLCN = TC_{1,(1,1)}$$

$$TC_{1,t} = r(1,req)\cdot TC_{2,t} + r(3,ans,t^{-})\cdot TC_{9,t^{-}} + crash'$$

$$TC_{2,t} = s(2,req,t)\cdot TC_{3,t} + r(3,ans,t^{-})\cdot TC_{2,t} + r(3,ans,t)\cdot TC_{7,t} + crash'$$

$$TC_{3,t} = to\cdot TC_{2,t} + r(3,ack,t)\cdot TC_{4,t} + r(3,ans,t)\cdot TC_{7,t}$$
$$+ r(3,ans,t^{-})\cdot TC_{2,t} + crash'$$

$$TC_{4,t} = to\cdot TC_{5,t} + r(3,ans,t)\cdot TC_{7,t} + crash'$$

$$TC_{5,t} = s(2,enq,t)\cdot TC_{6,t} + r(3,ans,t)\cdot TC_{7,t} + crash'$$

$$TC_{6,t} = to\cdot TC_{2,t} + to\cdot TC_{5,t} + r(3,ack,t)\cdot TC_{4,t} + r(3,ans,t)\cdot TC_{7,t} + crash'$$

$TC_{7,t} = s(1,ans) \cdot TC_{8,t} + crash'$

$TC_{8,t} = r(1,req) \cdot TC_{2,t^+} + to \cdot TC_{9,t} + crash'$

$TC_{9,t} = s(2,ack,t) \cdot TC_{1,t^+} + crash'$

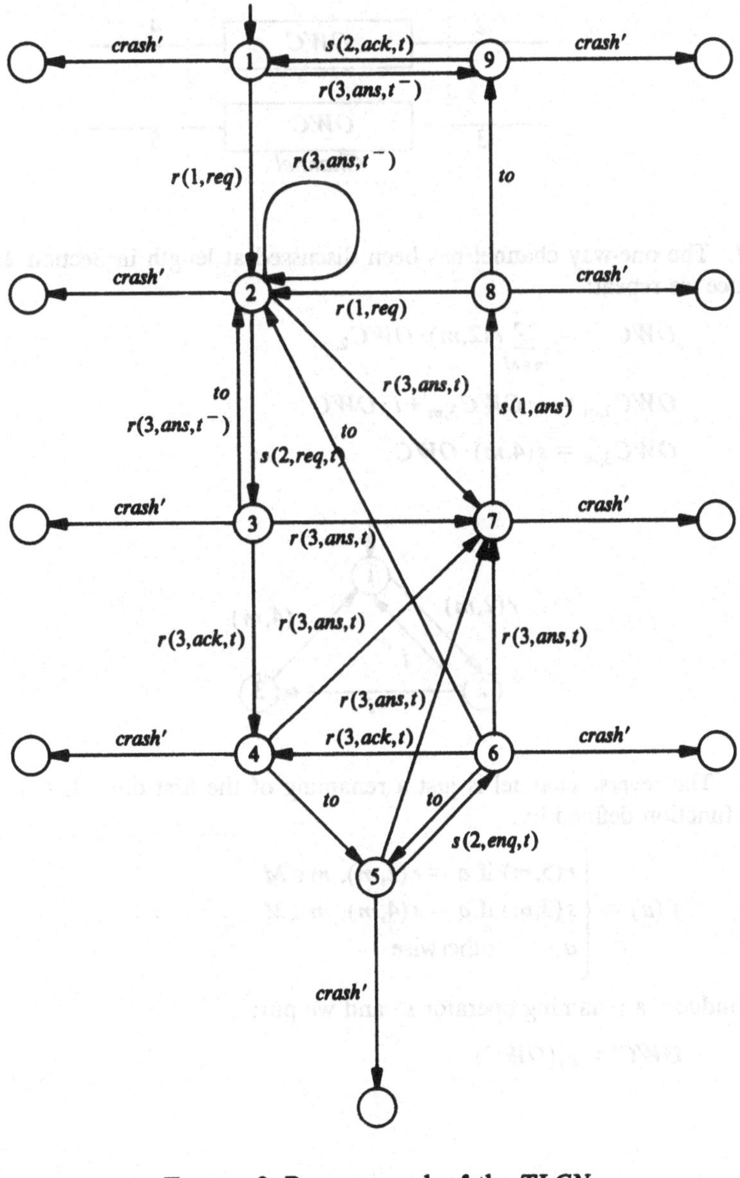

FIGURE 2. Process graph of the *TLCN*

3.2.2. The Channel process. The channel consists of two non-interacting one-way channels:

$$Channel = OWC \| OWC'.$$

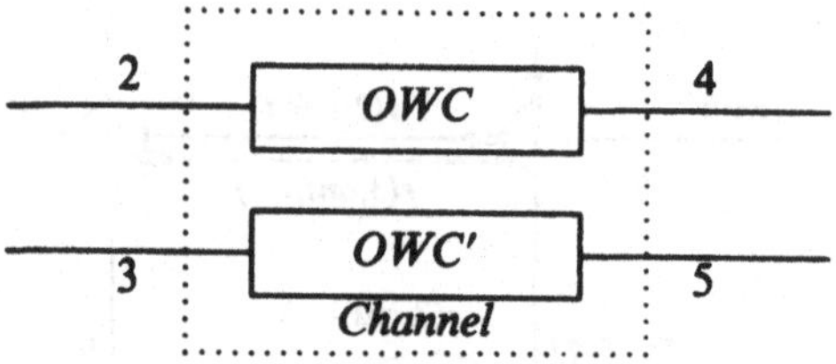

3.2.2.1. The one-way channel has been discussed at length in Section 2.9. For reference we repeat:

$$OWC = \sum_{m \in M} r(2,m) \cdot OWC_{2,m}$$

$$OWC_{2,m} = i \cdot OWC_{3,m} + i \cdot OWC$$

$$OWC_{3,m} = s(4,m) \cdot OWC$$

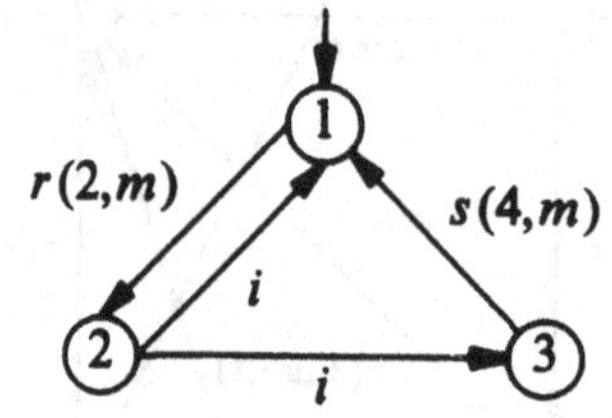

3.2.2.2. The reverse channel is just a renaming of the first one. Let $f: A \rightarrow A$ be the function defined by:

$$f(a) = \begin{cases} r(5,m) \text{ if } a = r(2,m),\ m \in M \\ s(3,m) \text{ if } a = s(4,m),\ m \in M \\ a \quad \text{otherwise} \end{cases}$$

This f induces a renaming operator ρ_f and we put:

$$OWC' = \rho_f(OWC).$$

3.2.3. The Server process. The *Server* process consists of the server proper and its interface. If it ever stops, it is restarted:

$$Server = \partial_{H_{(6)}}(TLSN \| SV) \cdot Server.$$

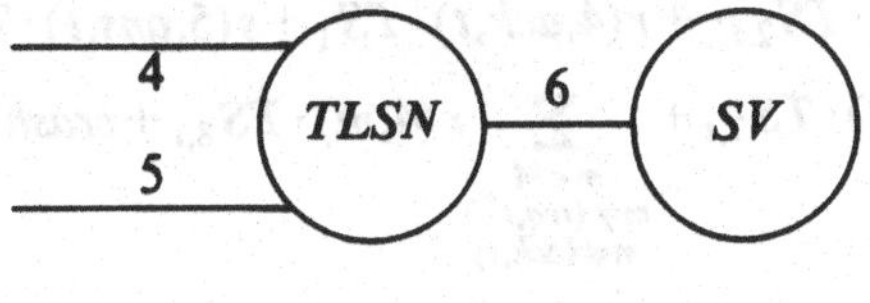

3.2.3.1. Like the client, the server is not studied in detail. It is just a sink of requests and a source of answers:

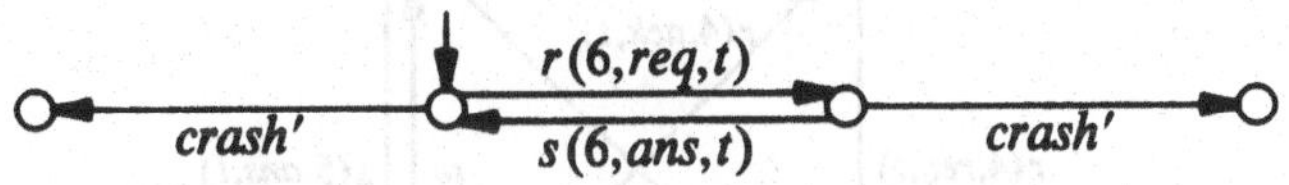

$$SV \;= \sum_{t \in T} r(6,req,t) \cdot SV_{2,t} + crash'$$

$$SV_{2,t} = s(6,ans,t) \cdot SV \; + crash'$$

3.2.3.2. The server's interface is roughly analogous to its counterpart on the client's side. Initially, the interface awaits a request and relays it to the server. If the answer doesn't seem to come immediately, the interface acknowledges receipt of the request and awaits further events. If an enquiry message from an impatient client arrives, the *TLSN* waits some more and sends another acknowledgement. This gives rise to the following system of equations:

$$TLSN = TS_1$$

$$TS_1 \;= \sum_{t \in T} r(4,req,t) \cdot TS_{2,t} + \sum_{t \in T} r(4,enq,t) \cdot TS_1 + crash'$$

$$TS_{2,t} = s(6,req,t) \cdot TS_{3,t} + \sum_{m \in M} r(4,m) \cdot TS_{2,t} + crash'$$

$$TS_{3,t} = to \cdot TS_{4,t} + r(6,ans,t) \cdot TS_{6,t} + \sum_{m \in M} r(4,m) \cdot TS_{3,t} + crash'$$

$$TS_{4,t} = s(5,ack,t) \cdot TS_{5,t} + r(6,ans,t) \cdot TS_{6,t} + \sum_{m \in M} r(4,m) \cdot TS_{4,t} + crash'$$

$$TS_{5,t} = r(4,enq,t) \cdot TS_{3,t} + r(6,ans,t) \cdot TS_{6,t} + \sum_{\substack{m \in M \\ m \neq (enq,t)}} r(4,m) \cdot TS_{5,t} + crash' \quad (*)$$

$$TS_{6,t} = s(5,ans,t) \cdot TS_{7,t} + \sum_{m \in M} r(4,m) \cdot TS_{6,t} + crash'$$

$$TS_{7,t} = r(4,req,t^+)\cdot TS_{2,t^+} + r(4,ack,t)\cdot TS_1 + to\cdot TS_{8,t} + \\ + \sum_{\substack{m\in M\\ m\neq(req,t^+)\\ m\neq(ack,t)}} r(4,m)\cdot TS_{7,t} + crash'$$

$$TS_{8,t} = r(4,req,t^+)\cdot TS_{2,t^+} + r(4,ack,t)\cdot TS_1 + s(5,ans,t)\cdot TS_1 + \\ + s(5,ans,t)\cdot TS_{7,t} + \sum_{\substack{m\in M\\ m\neq(req,t^+)\\ m\neq(ack,t)}} r(4,m)\cdot TS_{8,t} + crash'$$

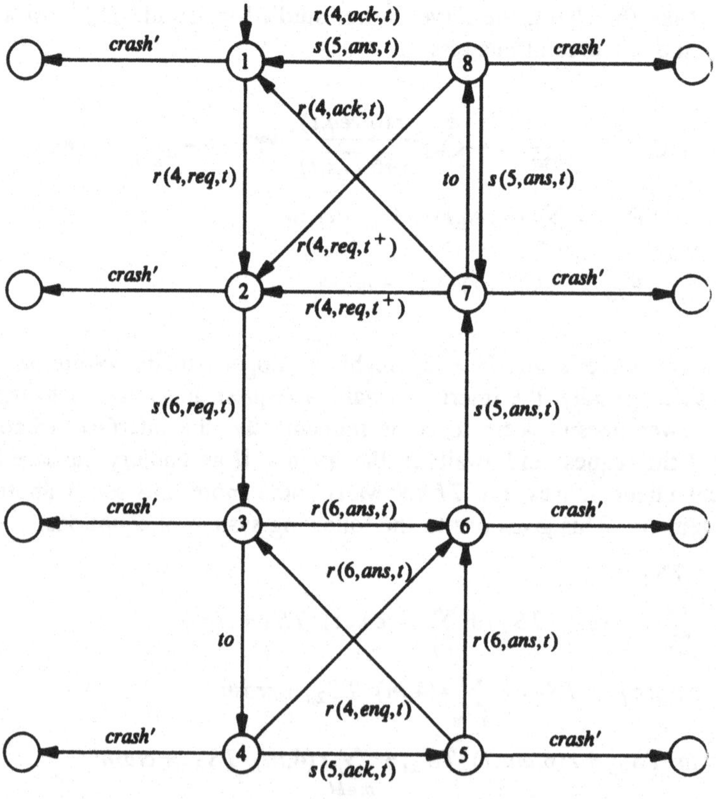

FIGURE 3. Process graph of the *TLSN*. Note that the loops $n \xrightarrow{r(4,m)} n$ are not shown.

Contrary to its counterpart on the client's node, the *TLSN* is always willing to accept and ignore the wrong input. The asymmetry arises because it is the client's role to get impatient if the computation takes a lot of time, and then to generate a message that might be inappropriate by the time it arrives. These loops are not shown in Figure 3. Also not shown is the incrementing of the sequence numbers.

Another minor difference is that the *TLSN* does not remember the request sequence number while the server is idle. The prime reason for doing so is to cope with the situation that a server has crashed and a new one is started. The new one should not insist on starting with request number 1, for that has already been served by its predecessor.

3.2.4. In the next subsection, we will study the subsystem consisting of the *Server* and the *Channel*, properly linked. For want of a better name, we will call this combination *System*:

$$System = \partial_{H_{(4,5)}}(Channel \| Server).$$

3.3. The requirements

This section summarises the requirements from Sections 2.3 through 2.8, with all i's dotted and some t's crossed. In particular, we will try to be clear on the position of the communication channel and the precise subsets of A occurring in various equations.

3.3.1. Client crashes apart, the client and server are exchanging requests and answers (from 2.8):

$$\tau_I \partial_{H_{(2,3)}}(\partial_{\{crash\}}(Client) \| System) = \tau \cdot \prod_{n \in \mathbb{N}} c(3, ans, 1, n)$$

where $I = A - \{c(3, ans, 1, n) \mid n \in \mathbb{N}\}$ as before.

3.3.2. While it is computing an answer, the *System* generates acknowledgement messages (from 2.4):

$$\tau_{I_n} \partial_{\{c(6, ans, 1, n)\}}(\partial_{\{crash\}}(Client) \| System) = \tau \cdot c(3, ack, 1, n)^{\omega}$$

where $I_n = A - \{c(3, ack, 1, n)\}$. Here we use the notation X^{ω} for $\prod_{n \in \mathbb{N}} X$. Recall that $c(6, ans, 1, n)$ is the event that the server establishes the n-th answer.

3.3.3. In a two-client system, even if one client crashes, the other will be served (from 2.7):

$$\tau_I \partial_H(Client \| \rho_g(Client) \| System) = \tau_I(Amoeba)$$

where $I = A - \{c(p, d, 1, n) \mid p \in \{2, 3\}, d \in \{req, ans\}, n \in \mathbb{N}\}$, and ρ_g is the renaming operator induced by $g: A \to A$ defined by:

$$g(a) = \begin{cases} r(3, d, 2, n) & \text{if } a = r(3, d, 1, n), d \in D,\ n \in \mathbb{N} \\ s(2, d, 2, n) & \text{if } a = s(2, d, 1, n), d \in D,\ n \in \mathbb{N} \\ a & \text{otherwise} \end{cases}$$

Note that τ_I abstracts from (among others) all events pertaining to the second client.

3.3.4. Finally, the system does not abuse crashes to escape from illegal states. In other words, the equations above are also satisfied if the system is not allowed to crash:

$$\tau_I \partial_{\{crash\}}(Amoeba) = \tau \cdot \prod_{n \in \mathbb{N}} c(3,ans,1,n)$$

$$\tau_{I_n} \partial_{\{crash, c(6,ans,1,n)\}}(Amoeba) = \tau \cdot c(3,ack,1,n)^{\omega}$$

$$\tau_I \partial_{\{crash\}} \partial_H(Client \| \rho_g(Client) \| System) = \tau_I \partial_{\{crash\}}(Amoeba)$$

3.4. A problematic situation

When we tried to establish algebraically that the Amoeba system satisfies the requirements in 3.3, we discovered that it does not.

To be specific, the system described in 3.2 does not satisfy the second requirement in 3.3.4. I.e., it may happen that the client and server's interfaces do not enter the phase where they exchange enquiries and acknowledgements while the server proper is establishing a reply. This situation ends when the reply comes, or if one of the parties crashes. If we block both these escapes we will observe livelock: the *TLCN* keeps repeating its request and the *TLSN* does not respond.

3.4.1. Trouble starts if the server's interface acknowledges receipt of a request, and this acknowledgement fails to arrive. When the *TLCN* times out, it assumes that the request was not delivered properly and repeats the request. The server's interface, however, is in a state where it does not accept requests on the ground that the server proper is busy. This interface is expecting an enquiry message. Thus, the parties are out of sync and will remain so until the server comes up with a reply, for that is the only event that both parties are willing to accept at their respective stages.

3.4.2. The shortest trace that leads to the problematic situation is:

$$c(1,req) \cdot c(2,req,1,1) \cdot i \cdot c(4,req,1,1) \cdot c(6,req,t) \cdot to \cdot s(5,ack,1,1) \cdot i,$$

where the *to* is the one that takes the *TLSN* from state 3 to state 4 and the last i is the one in the $i \cdot \rho_f(OWC)$ summand of $\rho_f(OWC_{2,(ack,1,1)})$. This leads to a state $S =$

$$\partial_{\{crash, c(6,ans,1,1)\}} \partial_H(\partial_{H_{(1)}}(CL_2 \| TC_{3,1,1}) \| OWC \| \rho_f(OWC) \| \partial_{H_{(6)}}(SV_{2,1} \| TS_{5,1,1})).$$

Inspecting the specifications, we see that the only possible transition in this state is a *to* that brings *TLCN* in state 2,1,1. Next, a $c(2,req,1,1)$ action brings *TLCN* back to state 3,1,1 and *OWC* to 2,(2,*req*, 1, 1), from where it can choose between an i action or an i action followed by a $c(4,req,1,1)$ action. In both cases the global state reverts to S. Consequently we are in a livelock situation.

3.4.3. The problem is easily mended. The point is that the *TLSN* ignores all requests while the server is busy. This policy is wrong: it should check whether the request is in fact a retransmission of the request the server is currently serving. If so, this indicates that the original acknowledgement message was lost in the return channel. Hence it should be retransmitted. In other words, a term $+r(4,req,t)\cdot TS_{3,t}$ should be added to the equation (*) for state $TS_{5,t}$ in Section 3.2.3.2.

4. THE VERIFICATION

4.0. In this section we will formally verify that the corrected *Amoeba* protocol satisfies all requirements mentioned in 3.3. If the reader has read verifications in process algebra before, he will probably not find anything new in this section.

4.1. For reference, we include the revised version of the *TLSN* specification:

$$TLSN = TS_1$$

$$TS_1 = \sum_{t\in T} r(4,req,t)\cdot TS_{2,t} + \sum_{t\in T} r(4,enq,t)\cdot TS_1 + crash'$$

$$TS_{2,t} = s(6,req,t)\cdot TS_{3,t} + \sum_{m\in M} r(4,m)\cdot TS_{2,t} + crash'$$

$$TS_{3,t} = to\cdot TS_{4,t} + r(6,ans,t)\cdot TS_{6,t} + \sum_{m\in M} r(4,m)\cdot TS_{3,t} + crash'$$

$$TS_{4,t} = s(5,ack,t)\cdot TS_{5,t} + r(6,ans,t)\cdot TS_{6,t} + \sum_{m\in M} r(4,m)\cdot TS_{4,t} + crash'$$

$$TS_{5,t} = (r(4,enq,t) + r(4,req,t))\cdot TS_{3,t} + r(6,ans,t)\cdot TS_{6,t} + \\ + \sum_{\substack{m\in M\\ m\neq (enq,t),(req,t)}} r(4,m)\cdot TS_{5,t} + crash'$$

$$TS_{6,t} = s(5,ans,t)\cdot TS_{7,t} + \sum_{m\in M} r(4,m)\cdot TS_{6,t} + crash'$$

$$TS_{7,t} = r(4,req,t^+)\cdot TS_{2,t^+} + r(4,ack,t)\cdot TS_1 + to\cdot TS_{8,t} + \\ + \sum_{\substack{m\in M\\ m\neq (req,t^+)\\ m\neq (ack,t)}} r(4,m)\cdot TS_{7,t} + crash'$$

$$TS_{8,t} = r(4,req,t^+)\cdot TS_{2,t^+} + r(4,ack,t)\cdot TS_1 + s(5,ans,t)\cdot TS_1 + s(5,ans,t)\cdot TS_{7,t} + \\ + \sum_{\substack{m\in M\\ m\neq (req,t^+)\\ m\neq (ack,t)}} r(4,m)\cdot TS_{8,t} + crash'$$

4.2. We start by showing that the presence of the CL process is redundant:

LEMMA. *Client* $= \rho_h(TLCN)$ *where* ρ_h *is the renaming induced by* $h: A \to A$ *defined by:*

$$h(a) = \begin{cases} c(1,req) & \text{if } a = r(1,req) \\ c(1,ans) & \text{if } a = s(1,ans) \\ crash & \text{if } a = crash' \\ a & \text{otherwise} \end{cases}$$

PROOF. By direct calculation, one shows that the vector:

$$\left[\partial_{H_{(1)}}(CL \| TC_{1,t}),\ \partial_{H_{(1)}}(CL_2 \| TC_{2,t}),\ \ldots,\ \partial_{H_{(1)}}(CL_2 \| TC_{7,t}),\ \partial_{H_{(1)}}(CL \| TC_{8,t}),\ \partial_{H_{(1)}}(CL \| TC_{9,t})\right]$$

satisfies the (renamed) equations 3.2.1.2. The result then follows by RSP. □

4.3. LEMMA. *Server* $= \rho_{h'}(TLSN)$ *where* $\rho_{h'}$ *is the renaming induced by* $h': A \to A$ *defined by:*

$$h'(a) = \begin{cases} c(6,req,t) & \text{if } a = s(6,req,t),\ t \in T \\ c(6,ans,t) & \text{if } a = r(6,req,t),\ t \in T \\ crash & \text{if } a = crash' \\ a & \text{otherwise} \end{cases}$$

PROOF. Analogous to 4.2. □

4.4. For the sake of clarity, we will first consider the requirements from 3.3.4, the ones without server crashes. In this subsection, we will tackle:

$$\tau_I \partial_{\{crash\}}(Amoeba) = \tau \cdot \prod_{n \in \mathbb{N}} c(1,ans,1,n). \qquad (\star)$$

4.4.1. NOTATION. Let us denote, for $n > 1$:

$$Amoeba_n = \tau_I \partial_{\{crash\} \cup H_{(2,3)}}(\rho_h(TC_{2,1,n}) \| \partial_{H_{(4,5)}}(Channel_{n-1} \| \sum_{k \in \{1,7,8\}} \rho_{h'}(TS_{k,1,n-1})))$$

where $Channel_n = OWC_n \| \rho_f(OWC_n)$ and $OWC_n = \sum_{\substack{k \in \{1,2,3\} \\ d \in D}} OWC_{k,(d,1,n)}$, where we take $OWC_{1,m}$ to mean OWC as specified in 3.2.2.1. We will write $OWC_{1,\varnothing}$ if we want to emphasise that the channel is actually empty. For $n = 1$ reference would be made to messages pertaining to request number 0. Because this does not exists, we have to define $Amoeba_1$ separately:

$$Amoeba_1 = \tau_I \partial_{\{crash\}}(Amoeba).$$

4.4.2. LEMMA. $Amoeba_n = \tau \cdot c(3, ans, 1, n) \cdot Amoeba_{n+1}$.

The proof naturally breaks in two halves. Denote:

$Halfway_n =$

$$= \tau_I \partial_{\{crash\} \cup H_{(2,3)}} \Big(\sum_{2 \leq k \leq 6} \rho_h(TC_{k,n}) \| \partial_{H_{(4,5)}}(OWC_n \| \rho_f(OWC_{n-1})) \| \rho_{h'}(TS_{6,n}) \Big)$$

4.4.3. LEMMA. *For* $n > 1$: $Amoeba_n = \tau \cdot Halfway_n$.

PROOF. Notice that the set of states

$$\{\partial_{\{crash\} \cup H_{(2,3)}}(\rho_h(TC_{i,n}) \| \partial_{H_{(4,5)}}(OWC_{j,m} \| \rho_f(OWC_{k,m'})) \| \rho_{h'}(TS_{l,n'}))) \mid$$

$$\mid 2 \leq i \leq 6,\ j \leq 3,\ k \leq 3,\ m = (d, 1, n),$$

$$l = 1 \vee (2 \leq l \leq 5 \wedge n' = n) \vee (7 \leq l \leq 8 \wedge n' = n-1),$$

$$d = req \vee d = enq,\ (m' = (ans, 1, n-1) \vee m' = (ack, 1, n))\}$$

forms a (huge) cluster. The exits of this cluster are the summands of $Halfway_n$. The result now follows by CFAR [3]. □

4.4.4. LEMMA. $Amoeba_1 = \tau \cdot Halfway_1$.

PROOF. This is just a watered-down version of the previous lemma, the difference being that in this case the reverse channel cannot contain a message pertaining to the previous cycle. So the possible states are the elements of

$$\{\partial_{\{crash\} \cup H_{(2,3)}}(\rho_h(TC_{i,(1,1)})) \| \partial_{H_{(4,5)}}(OWC_{j,m} \| \rho_f(OWC_{1,\varnothing})) \| \rho_{h'}(TS_{l,(1,1)}))) \mid$$

$$\mid i \leq 6,\ j \leq 3,\ l \leq 5,\ m = (d, 1, 1),\ d \in \{req, enq\}\}$$

As before, this forms a cluster, and the result follows by CFAR. □

4.4.5. LEMMA. $Halfway_n = \tau \cdot c(1, ans, 1, n) \cdot Amoeba_{n+1}$.

PROOF. To begin with, the set of states

$$\{\partial_{\{crash\} \cup H_{(2,3)}}(\rho_h(TC_{i,n}) \| \partial_{H_{(4,5)}}(OWC_{j,m} \| \rho_f(OWC_{k,m'})) \| \rho_{h'}(TS_{l,n'}))) \mid$$

$$\mid 2 \leq i \leq 6,\ j \leq 3,\ k \leq 3,\ l \in \{7, 8, 1\},\ m = (d, 1, n),\ d = req \vee d = enq,$$

$$m' = (d', 1, n'),\ d' = ack \vee d' = ans,\ n' \in \{n-1, n\}\}$$

forms a huge cluster, all of whose exits are of the form $c(3, ans, 1, n) \cdot X$, with X an element of the set S below. Hence by CFAR:

$$Halfway_n = \tau \cdot \sum_{X \in S} c(1, ans, 1, n) \cdot X$$

where

$$S = \{\partial_{\{crash\}\cup H_{(2,3)}}(\rho_h(TC_{i,(1,n)}) \| \partial_{H_{(4,5)}}(OWC_{j,m} \| \rho_f(OWC_{k,m'}) \| \rho_{h'}(TS_{l,(1,n)}))) \mid$$
$$\mid i\in\{7,8,9,1\},\ j\leqslant 3,\ k\leqslant 3,\ l\leqslant 8,$$
$$m=(d,1,n),\ d\in\{req,enq,ack\},\ m'=(ans,1,n)\}.$$

Again S is a cluster, so by CFAR: $\forall X\in S: X = \tau\cdot Amoeba_{n+1}$.

Summing up, we have:

$$Halfway_n = \tau\cdot \sum_{X\in S} c(1,ans,1,n)\cdot X$$
$$= \tau\cdot c(1,ans,1,n)\cdot\tau\cdot Amoeba_{n+1}$$
$$= \tau\cdot c(1,ans,1,n)\cdot Amoeba_{n+1}$$ □

Equation (*) in 4.4 follows from the three lemmas above by observing that $\tau_I(Amoeba) = Amoeba_1$ (by definition) and cancelling all τ's except the initial one.

4.5. In this section we will establish the second equation from 3.3.4:

Lemma. $\tau_{I_n}\partial_{\{crash,c(6,ans,1,n)\}}(Amoeba) = \tau\cdot c(3,ack,1,n)^{\omega}$.

Proof. As always, this boils down to applying CFAR to a suitable set of states, in this case:

$$\{\partial_{\{crash,c(6,ans,1,n)\}\cup H}(\rho_h(TC_{i,(1,n)}) \| \partial_{H_{(4,5)}}(OWC_{j,m} \| \rho_f(OWC_{k,m'}) \| \rho_{h'}(TS_{l,n_2}))) \mid$$
$$i\leqslant 9,\ j,k\leqslant 3,\ l\leqslant 8,\ m=(d,1,n_3),\ m'=(d',1,n_4),\ d,d'\in D,$$
$$n_1,n_2,n_3,n_4\leqslant n,\ n_2=n_1 \vee n_2=n_1-1,\ n_2\leqslant n_3\leqslant n_1,\ n_3=n\rightarrow d\neq ack,$$
$$n_4=n\vee n_4=n-1,\ n_1=n\rightarrow i\leqslant 6,\ n_2=n\rightarrow l\leqslant 5,\ n_4=n\rightarrow d'\neq ans\}$$

As before, we have to convince ourselves that from each state in this set there is a path to a $c(3,ack,1,n)$ exit. After all, the trouble in the original specification was that from some states this was no longer possible. Consider any state σ in the repaired version. If either channel contains a message, then the receiving process is willing to accept that message. So it is possible that these messages are delivered. Now, if the n-th request hasn't yet been sent, it is possible that all requests up to the $(n-1)$st are sent and replied to promptly. Next, it is possible that the client (re)sends a $(req,1,n)$ or an $(enq,1,n)$ message. This may arrive and the *TLSN* may timeout and reply with an $(ack,1,n)$ message, which may also arrive. So we see that from each state within the cluster there is a possible sequence of events leading to a $c(3,ack,1,n)$ exchange.

4.6. The third equation from 3.3.4:

$$\tau_I \partial_{\{crash\}} \partial_H(Client \| \rho_g(Client) \| System) = \tau_I \partial_{\{crash\}}(Amoeba)$$

At first one is tempted to use the CA rules to show that the τ_I-operator abstracts from all actions pertaining to the second client. However, this does not, and should not, work, as the second client interferes with the system. In fact, the point of the whole exercise is to show that the second client cannot clog up the system forever. Once we have established that the first client has a chance to proceed after finitely many steps of his colleague, and consequently infinitely many such chances, CFAR guarantees us that it will eventually proceed.

So we are to convince ourselves that:

$$\{\tau_I \partial_{\{crash\}} \partial_H(TC_{i,n_1} \| \rho_g(TC_{i',n_2}) \| \partial_{H_{(4,5)}}(OWC_{j,m} \| \rho_f(OWC_{k,m'}) \| \rho_{h'}(TS_{l,n_3}))) \mid$$
$$i \leqslant 9,\ n_1 \leqslant n,\ n_1 = n \rightarrow i \leqslant 6,\ i' \leqslant 9,\ n_2 \in \mathbb{N},\ j,k \leqslant 3,\ l \leqslant 8,$$
$$m = (d,c,p),\ d = req \vee d = enq,\ m' = (d',c',p'),\ d' = ans \vee d' = ack,$$
$$(c' = 1 \wedge (p' = n_1 \vee p' = n_1 - 1)) \vee (c' = 2 \wedge (p' = n_2 \vee p' = n_2 - 1)),$$
$$(c = 1 \wedge p = n_1) \vee (c = 2 \wedge p = n_2),\ n_3 \in \{n_1, n_1 - 1, n_2, n_2 - 1\}\}$$

indeed forms a cluster with exits of the form $c(3, ans, 1, n) \cdot X$.

The hard part here is to convince oneself that from each point within this cluster there is a path to an exit. If we compare the specifications of the channels and the *TLxN*'s we can see that in each of the states mentioned above it is possible that the channels deliver any messages they may contain; next, if the $\rho_{h'}(TLSN)$ is not in its initial state, it is possible that it completes the transaction it is dealing with, and if that was not the n-th transaction for *Client* 1, then it is possible that the system goes on to carry out transactions with *Client* 1, until it has completed the n-th. So we see that indeed from each point in the cluster there is a path to an exit.

4.7. Having satisfied ourselves that the system behaves as promised if it doesn't crash, we turn to cases where the server does crash and is restarted from scratch. If this happens while the old server was busy and the client knew this, i.e. it had received an acknowledgement but not yet an answer, the client will send a number of *enq* messages, to which the server doesn't respond[1]. After a while the client guesses what has happened, resends its request and reverts to state 2,(1,n).

What we set out to verify in this section, is that if the client makes this cycle through states 2-6 and the client possibly crashes, then the parallel composition of these four processes just runs around some gigantic cluster and never

1. In the data set as described in [9] there is a *nak* message which seems applicable here, but there is no mention of it ever being used. In the actual *Amoeba* system it is, of course, used in this situation.

gets stuck in a dark corner of it.

4.7.1. In order to establish equation 3.3.1:

$$\tau_I \partial_{H_{(2,3)}}(\partial_{crash}(Client) \| System) = \tau \cdot \prod_{n \in \mathbb{N}} c(1, ans, 1, n)$$

we denote:

$$Amoeba_n = \tau_I \partial_{H_{(2,3)}}(\partial_{\{crash\}}(\rho_h(TC_{2,n})) \| \partial_{H_{(4,5)}}(Channel_{n-1} \| \sum_{l \in \{1,7,8\}} \rho_{h'}(TS_{k,(1,n-1)})))$$

where $Channel_n$ is the same as in 4.4.1. Note that $Amoeba_n$ is not the same: here the server may crash, whereas in 4.4.1 it may not.

4.7.2. LEMMA. $Amoeba_n = \tau \cdot c(1, ans, 1, n) \cdot Amoeba_{n+1}$.

PROOF. The set of states

$$\{\partial_{H_{(2,3)}}(\partial_{\{crash\}}(\rho_h(TC_{i,n})) \| \partial_{H_{(4,5)}}(OWC_{j,m} \| \rho_f(OWC_{k,m'}) \| \rho_{h'}(TS_{l,n'}))) \mid$$
$$\mid 2 \leq i \leq 6,\ j \leq 3,\ k \leq 3,\ l \leq 8,$$
$$n' = n \vee (7 \leq l \leq 8 \wedge n' = n-1),\ m = (d, 1, n),\ d = req \vee d = enq,$$
$$m' = (ans, 1, n-1) \vee m' = (ack, 1, n) \vee m' = (ans, 1, n)\}$$

forms a cluster whose exits are of the form $c(1, ans, 1, n) \cdot X$, with X in the set S below. In particular, if the server crashes and is restarted, it goes to state $1,(1,n)$, which is still in this cluster. Applying CFAR yields:

$$Amoeba_n = \tau \cdot \sum_{X \in S} c(1, ans, 1, n) \cdot X$$

where

$$S = \{\partial_{H_{(2,3)}}(\partial_{\{crash\}}(\rho_h(TC_{i,n})) \| \partial_{H_{(4,5)}}(OWC_{j,m} \| \rho_f(OWC_{k,m'}) \| \rho_{h'}(TS_{l,n'}))) \mid$$
$$\mid i \in \{7,8,9,1\},\ j \leq 3,\ k \leq 3,$$
$$l \in \{7,8,1\},\ m = (d, 1, n),\ d \in \{req, enq, ack\},\ m' = (ans, 1, n)\}.$$

S is a cluster, too, and by CFAR $\forall X \in S : X = \tau \cdot Amoeba_{n+1}$. So we conclude:

$$Amoeba_n = \tau \cdot c(3, ans, 1, n) \cdot Amoeba_{n+1}. \qquad \square$$

4.7.3. To complete the proof of 3.3.1, we have to show that $\tau_I(Amoeba) = \tau \cdot c(3, ans, 1, 1) \cdot Amoeba_2$. In this case the reverse channel cannot contain a message $(ans, 1, 0)$, so the cluster simplifies to:

$$\{\partial_{H_{(2,3)}}(\partial_{\{crash\}}(\rho_h(TC_{i,1})) \| \partial_{H_{(4,5)}}(OWC_{j,m} \| \rho_f(OWC_{k,m'}) \| \rho_{h'}(TS_{l,1}))) \mid$$
$$\mid 2 \leq i \leq 6,\ j \leq 3,\ k \leq 3,\ l \leq 8,\ m = (d, 1, 1),$$
$$d = req \vee d = enq,\ m' = (ack, 1, 1) \vee m' = (ans, 1, 1)\}.$$

The rest of the proof is entirely analogous to 4.7.2. $\square$

4.7.4. The proofs of 3.3.2 and 3.3.3 are entirely analogous to those in 4.5 and 4.6 and will therefore be omitted. The point is that even if the server crashes and begins afresh, the system does not leave the relevant cluster. The *crash* transition provides an extra path from certain states to the exit, but we have already established in 4.5 and 4.6 that such paths exist in the revised version of the protocol.

5. CONCLUSIONS

We have demonstrated that it is possible to describe in process algebra equations what liveness and safety properties a communication protocol is meant to have. Theoretically it is also possible to derive that a specific implementation indeed possesses these properties but this usually boils down to apply the CFAR rule to large and intricate clusters and process algebra offers little means to handle these gracefully. One seems to need a criterion that guarantees that all states satisfying some assertion form a cluster and that CFAR may be applied to it. The state operator [1] might provide such a means, but as of now we do not see how to use it for this purpose.

ACKNOWLEDGEMENT

The author wishes to thank Frits Vaandrager for his careful proofreading and several improvements he suggested.

REFERENCES

1. J.C.M. BAETEN, J.A. BERGSTRA (1988). Global renaming operators in concrete process algebra. *Information and Computation 78(3)*, 205-245.
2. J.A. BERGSTRA (1988). *A Mode Transfer Operator in Process Algebra*, Report P8808, Programming Research Group, University of Amsterdam.
3. J.A. BERGSTRA, J.W. KLOP (1989). *An Introduction to Process Algebra.* This volume.
4. J.A. BERGSTRA, J.W. KLOP (1984). Process algebra for synchronous communication. *Information and Control 60 (1/3)*, 109-137.
5. J.A. BERGSTRA, J.W. KLOP (1986). Process algebra: specification and verification in bisimulation semantics. M. HAZEWINKEL, J.K. LENSTRA, L.G.L.T. MEERTENS (eds.). *Mathematics and Computer Science II*, CWI Monograph 4, North-Holland, Amsterdam, 61-94.
6. J.A. BERGSTRA, J.W. KLOP (1986). Algebra of communicating processes. J.W. DE BAKKER, M. HAZEWINKEL, J.K. LENSTRA (eds.). *Mathematics and Computer Science*, CWI Monograph 1, North-Holland, Amsterdam, 89-138.
7. E. BRINKSMA (ed.) (1987). ISO *Information processing systems – Open systems interconnection – LOTOS – A Formal Description Technique Based on the Temporal Ordering of Observational Behaviour*, ISO/TC97/SC21N DIS8807.
8. C.P.J. KOYMANS, J.C. MULDER (1989). *A Modular Approach to Protocol Verification using Process Algebra.* This volume.
9. S.J. MULLENDER (1985). *Principles of Distributed Operating System*

Design, Ph.D. Thesis, Free University, Amsterdam.

Process Algebra Semantics of POOL

Frits W. Vaandrager
Centre for Mathematics and Computer Science
P.O. Box 4079, 1009 AB Amsterdam, The Netherlands

In this article we describe a translation of the Parallel Object-Oriented Language POOL to the language of ACP, the Algebra of Communicating Processes. This translation provides us with a large number of semantics for POOL. It is argued that an optimal semantics for POOL does not exist: what is optimal depends on the application domain one has in mind. We show that the select statement in POOL makes a semantical description of POOL with handshaking communication between objects incompatible with a description level where message queues are used. Attention is paid to the question how fairness and successful termination can be included in the semantics. Finally it is shown that integers and booleans in POOL can be implemented in various ways.

1. Introduction

At this moment there are a lot of programming languages which offer facilities for concurrent programming. The basic notions of some of these languages, for example CSP [18], occam [19] and LOTOS [20], are rather close to the basic notions in ACP, and it is not very difficult to give semantics of these languages in the framework of ACP. Milner [23] showed how a simple high level concurrent language can be translated into CCS. However, it is not obvious at first sight how to give process algebra semantics of more complex concurrent programming languages like Ada [6], Pascal-Plus [13] or POOL [1-3]. This is an important problem because of the simple fact that a lot of concurrent systems are specified in terms of these languages. In this article we will tackle the problem, and give process algebra semantics of the language POOL.

In order to modularize the problems we first give, in Section 2, a translation to process algebra of a simple sequential programming language: with each element of the language a process is associated, specified in terms of the operators $\cdot$, $+$, $\gg$ (sequential and alternative composition, and chaining).

In Section 3, we give process algebra semantics of a representative subset of the programming language POOL-T (see [1]). POOL is an acronym for 'Parallel Object-Oriented Language'. It stands for a family of languages designed at Philips Research Laboratories in Eindhoven. The 'T' in POOL-T stands for 'Target'. POOL is a language that permits the programming of systems with a

Partial support received from the European Community under ESPRIT project no. 432, An Integrated Formal Approach to Industrial Software Development (METEOR).

large amount of parallelism, using object-oriented programming. In [4] an operational semantics is given of a language from the POOL-family. Our semantics of POOL is to a large extent inspired by this paper. A denotational semantics of POOL is presented in [5].

In order to deal with the complexity of POOL (compared to the toy language of Section 2) we make use of attribute grammars. We associate with each (abstract) POOL program a process specified in the signature of ACP together with some additional operators. As soon as the translation of a programming language into the signature of ACP (+additional operators) is accomplished, the whole range of process algebras becomes available as possible semantics of the language. We think this is a major advantage of our approach. Especially when dealing with concurrent programming languages, the answer to the question what is to be considered as the optimal semantics, is heavily influenced by the application one has in mind: if the system that executes the program is placed in a glass box and does not communicate with the external world, one can work with a more identifying semantics (allowing for simpler proofs) than in the case in which the system is part of a network and does communicate with the external world. Issues like fairness and the presence of interrupt mechanism are also relevant in the choice of the optimal semantics. The axioms we will give correspond to bisimulation semantics. In this semantics relatively few processes are identified, and therefore all the results we will prove are also valid in a large number of other semantics.

The process algebra semantics are very operational: we can define a term rewriting machine that executes the process algebra specification we relate to a program. Interestingly, the semantics are also (to a large extent) compositional: the value denoted by a construct is specified in terms of the values denoted by its syntactic subcomponents.

A good theory of semantics of programming languages is a method which makes it possible to predict the behaviour of a computer that executes a program. Furthermore a good theory assists people in building new predictable computers. This implies that a theory of semantics of programming languages should provide tools which make it possible to substantiate the claim that the mathematical models in which the language constructs are interpreted indeed model reality. In our framework such a tool is the abstraction operator τ_I. This operator makes it possible to prove that the semantics of POOL as presented in Section 3 has a common abstraction with a number of other semantics of the language, which are closer to implementation.

In an implementation of the language POOL there will be message queues in which the incoming messages for an object are stored. On the conceptual level, there are no queues and we have handshaking communication between the objects. In Section 4 an example is presented which shows that these two views are in contradiction with each other. The problem is due to the so-called 'select statement', which is part of the language POOL-T. A minor change in the definition of the select statement is proposed in order to remove this difficulty[1]. However, it is shown that even with the new language definition the two descriptions are different in bisimulation semantics. Although we think that the two views of a POOL system are equivalent in failure semantics, we have not proved this.

A similar question is dealt with in Section 6: on the conceptual level each integer and boolean in POOL is an object which has a data part and a process part. In an implementation this is of course not the case. Instead, an implementation will contain some special circuits for arithmetical and logical operations. We prove that these views of the system have a common abstraction.

In Section 5 we discuss a trace semantics of the language POOL. A lot of things can be proved with more ease in this semantics, but we show that this semantics does not describe deadlock behaviour in a situation in which the POOL system interacts with the environment. We also pay some attention to the question how issues like fairness and successful termination can be included in a semantical description of POOL.

Section 7 contains a number of conclusions.

At the end of this introduction we give the definition of the *renaming operators* and *chaining operators*. These operators will pay an important role in the rest of the paper, but are not described in the introduction of this volume.

1.1. Renaming operators (RN)

For every function $f: A_{\tau\delta} \to A_{\tau\delta}$ with the property that $f(\delta)=\delta$ and $f(\tau)=\tau$, we define an operator $\rho_f: P \to P$. Axioms for ρ_f are given in Table 1.1. (Here $a \in A_{\tau\delta}$.)

$\rho_f(a) = f(a)$	RN1
$\rho_f(x+y) = \rho_f(x)+\rho_f(y)$	RN2
$\rho_f(xy) = \rho_f(x)\cdot\rho_f(y)$	RN3

TABLE 1.1

For $t \in A_{\tau\delta}$, and $H \subseteq A$ we define the function $r_{t,H}: A_{\tau\delta} \to A_{\tau\delta}$ by:

$$r_{t,H}(a) = \begin{cases} t & \text{if } a \in H \\ a & \text{otherwise} \end{cases}$$

We use t_H as a notation for the operator $\rho_{r_{t,H}}$. The operators ∂_H and δ_H are considered to be equal.

1. In a more recent offspring of the POOL-family of languages, called POOL2 (see [3]), the select statement has been removed altogether. Instead this language contains a 'conditional answer statement'. It seems that this construct does not lead to semantical problems like the select statement.

1.2. Chaining operators (CH)
A basic situation we will encounter is one in which there are processes which input and output values in a domain D. Often we want to 'chain' two processes in such a way that the output of the first one becomes the input of the second. In order to describe this, we define *chaining* operators $\ggg$ and $\gg$. In the process $x \ggg y$ the output of process x serves as input of process y. Operator $\gg$ is identical to operator $\ggg$, but hides in addition the communications that take place at the internal communication port. The reason for introducing two operators is a technical one: the operator $\gg$ (in which we are interested most) often leads to *unguarded recursion.* We will define the chaining operators in terms of the operators of ACP$_\tau$+RN. In this way we obtain a finite axiomatisation of the operator (if the alphabet of atomic actions is finite).

First we make a number of assumptions about the alphabet A and the communication function γ. Let for $d \in D$, $\downarrow d$ be the action of reading d, and $\uparrow d$ be the action of sending d. Let A' be the following set

$$A' = \{\uparrow d, \downarrow d, s(d), r(d), c(d) \mid d \in D\}.$$

We assume $A' \subseteq A$ and furthermore that for $a,b \in A - A'$: $\gamma(a,b) \notin A'$. On A' communication is defined by

$$\gamma(s(d), r(d)) = c(d)$$

and all other communications give δ. Define $H_{CH} = \{s(d), r(d) \mid d \in D\}$. The renaming functions f and g are defined by

$$f(\uparrow d) = s(d) \quad \text{and} \quad g(\downarrow d) = r(d) \quad (d \in D)$$

and $f(a) = g(a) = a$ for every other $a \in A_{\tau\delta}$. Now the 'concrete' chaining of processes x and y, notation $x \ggg y$, is defined by means of the axiom

$$x \ggg y = \partial_{H_{CH}}(\rho_f(x) \| \rho_g(y)) \qquad \text{CHC}$$

Figure 1.1 contains a graphical display of the construction.

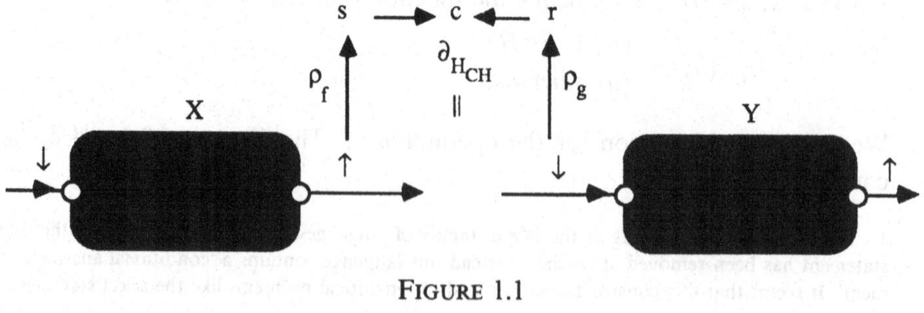

FIGURE 1.1

Define the set $I_{CH} = \{c(d) \mid d \in D\}$. The 'abstract' chaining of processes x and y, notation $x \gg y$, is defined by means of the axiom

$$x \gg y = \tau_{I_{CH}}(x \ggg y) \qquad \text{CHA}$$

One of the properties of the chaining operators we use most is that they are associative (under some very weak assumptions). The conditional axioms below state that the chaining operators are associative if the actions of H_{CH} do not occur in the alphabets of the components. In [26] it is shown that, if we add some natural axioms about alphabets to the axiom system, these two axioms become derivable.

$$\frac{\alpha(x) \cap H_{CH} = \alpha(y) \cap H_{CH} = \alpha(z) \cap H_{CH} = \varnothing}{(x \ggg y) \ggg z = x \ggg (y \ggg z)} \qquad \text{CC1}$$

$$\frac{\alpha(x) \cap H_{CH} = \alpha(y) \cap H_{CH} = \alpha(z) \cap H_{CH} = \varnothing}{(x \gg y) \gg z = x \gg (y \gg z)} \qquad \text{CC2}$$

The module consisting of axioms CHC, CHA, CC1 and CC2 is denoted CH.

1.2.1. Notation. For the term

$$x \ggg (\sum_{d_1 \in D_1} \downarrow d_1 \cdots \sum_{d_n \in D_n} \downarrow d_n \cdot y_{d_1, \ldots, d_n})$$

(where $D_1, \ldots, D_n \subseteq D$) we write

$$x \ggg_{d_1, \ldots, d_n} y_{d_1, \ldots, d_n}$$

In all applications it will be clear from the context what $D_1, \ldots, D_n$ are. A similar notation is used for the $\gg$-operator.

2. A SIMPLE SEQUENTIAL PROGRAMMING LANGUAGE

The following definition of a simple programming language is adopted from [9]. In the definition a choice between different versions of a rule is indicated by a vertical bar ('|').

2.1. DEFINITION (syntax of *Iexp*, *Bexp* and *Stat*). Let *Ivar*, with typical elements $v, w, u, \ldots$, and *Icon*, with typical elements $\alpha, \ldots$, be given finite sets of symbols.

a. The class *Iexp*, with typical elements $s, t, \ldots$, is defined by

$$s ::= v \mid \alpha \mid s_1 + s_2 \mid \cdots \mid \textbf{if } b \textbf{ then } s_1 \textbf{ else } s_2 \textbf{ fi}$$

(Expressions such as $s_1 - s_2$, $s_1 \times s_2$, ... may be added at the position of the ..., if desired.)

b. The class *Bexp*, with typical elements b, ..., is defined by

$$b ::= \mathbf{true} \mid \mathbf{false} \mid s_1 = s_2 \mid \cdots \mid \neg\, b \mid b_1 \supset b_2$$

(Expressions such as $s_1 < s_2$, ... may be added at the position of the ..., if desired.)

c. The class *Stat*, with typical elements S, ..., is defined by

$$S ::= v := s \mid S_1 ; S_2 \mid \mathbf{if}\, b\, \mathbf{then}\ S_1\ \mathbf{else}\ S_2\ \mathbf{fi} \mid \mathbf{while}\, b\, \mathbf{do}\, S\, \mathbf{od}$$

2.2. *Note.* In contrast to [9], we require the sets *Ivar* and *Icon* to be finite. If we would allow them to be infinite this would lead to infinite sums in our process algebra specifications. It is trivial to add an infinite sum operator to, for example, the term model defined in [16]. However, the combination of such an operator and the abstraction operators τ_I leads to a number of non-trivial questions that are worth separate investigation. For this reason we will confine ourselves to the finite case in this article.

2.3. *Semantics of the toy language.* We will now relate to each element of the language defined in Section 2.1, a recursive specification in the signature of the operators $\cdot$, $+$ and $\ggg$. The first thing we have to do is to give the parameters of ACP: the alphabet A and the communication function. The value domain D of the chaining operator is

$$D = (Ivar \rightarrow Icon) \cup Icon \cup \{\mathbf{true}, \mathbf{false}\}.$$

Here $Ivar \rightarrow Icon$ is the set of all functions from variables to their values. The set A of atomic actions is the set A' as described in Section 1.2. Communication on A' is also as described in Section 1.2.

2.4. *Notation.* Let $\sigma \in Ivar \rightarrow Icon$, $v \in Ivar$ and $\alpha \in Icon$. We use the well-known notation $\sigma\{\alpha / v\}$ to denote the element of $Ivar \rightarrow Icon$ that satisfies for each $v' \in Ivar$

$$\sigma\{\alpha / v\}(v') = \begin{cases} \alpha & \text{if } v' = v \\ \sigma(v') & \text{otherwise} \end{cases}$$

2.5. Below we give a number of process algebra equations. The variables in these equations are elements of the toy language with semantical brackets ('$[\![$' and '$]\!]$') placed around them, often sub- and super-scripted with elements of D. The process corresponding to execution of language element $w \in Iexp \cup Bexp \cup Stat$, with an initial memory configuration $\sigma \in Ivar \rightarrow Icon$, is the solution of this system, with

$$[\![w]\!]^{\sigma}$$

taken as root variable. Throughout the rest of this section $\alpha,\alpha' \in Icon$, $\beta,\beta' \in \{\mathbf{true},\mathbf{false}\}$ and $\sigma,\sigma' \in Ivar \to Icon$.

2.6. The class *Iexp*

$$[\![v]\!]^\sigma = \uparrow\sigma(v)$$

$$[\![\alpha]\!]^\sigma = \uparrow\alpha$$

$$[\![s_1+s_2]\!]^\sigma = [\![s_1]\!]^\sigma \cdot [\![s_2]\!]^\sigma \gg\!\!\!>_{\alpha,\alpha'} \uparrow sum(\alpha,\alpha')$$

$$[\![\mathbf{if}\, b\, \mathbf{then}\, s_1\, \mathbf{else}\, s_2\, \mathbf{fi}]\!]^\sigma = [\![b]\!]^\sigma \gg\!\!\!> (\downarrow\mathbf{true}\cdot[\![s_1]\!]^\sigma + \downarrow\mathbf{false}\cdot[\![s_2]\!]^\sigma)$$

2.7. The class *Bexp*

$$[\![\mathbf{true}]\!]^\sigma = \uparrow\mathbf{true}$$

$$[\![\mathbf{false}]\!]^\sigma = \uparrow\mathbf{false}$$

$$[\![s_1=s_2]\!]^\sigma = [\![s_1]\!]^\sigma \cdot [\![s_2]\!]^\sigma \gg\!\!\!>_{\alpha,\alpha'} [\![=]\!]_{\alpha,\alpha'}$$

$$[\![=]\!]_{\alpha,\alpha'} = \begin{cases} \uparrow\mathbf{true} & \text{if } \alpha=\alpha' \\ \uparrow\mathbf{false} & \text{otherwise} \end{cases}$$

$$[\![\neg b]\!]^\sigma = [\![b]\!]^\sigma \gg\!\!\!> (\downarrow\mathbf{true}\cdot\uparrow\mathbf{false} + \downarrow\mathbf{false}\cdot\uparrow\mathbf{true})$$

$$[\![b_1 \supset b_2]\!]^\sigma = [\![b_1]\!]^\sigma \gg\!\!\!> (\downarrow\mathbf{true}\cdot[\![b_2]\!]^\sigma + \downarrow\mathbf{false}\cdot\uparrow\mathbf{true})$$

2.8. The class *Stat*

$$[\![v := s]\!]^\sigma = [\![s]\!]^\sigma \gg\!\!\!>_\alpha \uparrow\sigma\{\alpha/v\}$$

$$[\![S_1\,;S_2]\!]^\sigma = [\![S_1]\!]^\sigma \gg\!\!\!>_{\sigma'} [\![S_2]\!]^{\sigma'}$$

$$[\![\mathbf{if}\, b\, \mathbf{then}\, S_1\, \mathbf{else}\, S_2\, \mathbf{fi}]\!]^\sigma = [\![b]\!]^\sigma \gg\!\!\!> (\downarrow\mathbf{true}\cdot[\![S_1]\!]^\sigma + \downarrow\mathbf{false}\cdot[\![S_2]\!]^\sigma)$$

$$[\![\mathbf{while}\, b\, \mathbf{do}\, S\, \mathbf{od}]\!]^\sigma = [\![b]\!]^\sigma \gg\!\!\!>$$
$$(\downarrow\mathbf{true}\cdot([\![S]\!]^\sigma \gg\!\!\!>_{\sigma'} [\![\mathbf{while}\, b\, \mathbf{do}\, S\, \mathbf{od}]\!]^{\sigma'}) + \downarrow\mathbf{false}\cdot\uparrow\sigma)$$

The following theorem shows that the specification presented above singles out a unique process.

2.9. THEOREM. *The specification defined in 2.6-2.8 is guarded.*

PROOF. Define a relation $\xrightarrow{u}$ between elements of Ξ by

$$X \xrightarrow{u} Y \Leftrightarrow Y \text{ occurs unguarded in } t_X.$$

It is enough to show that the relation $\xrightarrow{u}$ is well founded (i.e. there is no infinite sequence $X_1 \xrightarrow{u} X_2 \xrightarrow{u} X_3 \cdots$). This can be done by defining a function $m : \Xi \to \mathbb{N}$ such that for $X, Y \in \Xi$

$$X \xrightarrow{u} Y \quad \Rightarrow \quad m(Y) < m(X).$$

The definition goes by induction on the complexity of the language elements in the variables. We give only a very small part of it. This should convince the reader that it is possible to give a complete definition, which has the desired property.

$$m([\![v]\!]^\sigma) = 1$$

$$m([\![\alpha]\!]^\sigma) = 1$$

$$m([\![s_1 + s_2]\!]^\sigma) = m([\![s_1]\!]^\sigma) + m([\![s_2]\!]^\sigma)$$

etc. □

2.10. Note. As a direct consequence of axiom CC1 we have that ';' is associative:

$$[\![(S_1;S_2);S_3]\!]^\sigma = [\![S_1;(S_2;S_3)]\!]^\sigma.$$

2.11. Remark. In the equation for $[\![s_1 + s_2]\!]^\sigma$ we say that, in order to evaluate $s_1 + s_2$, we first have to evaluate s_1 and thereafter s_2. Other possibilities would have been

$$[\![s_1 + s_2]\!]^\sigma = [\![s_2]\!]^\sigma \cdot [\![s_1]\!]^\sigma \gg_{\alpha,\alpha'} \uparrow sum(\alpha,\alpha')$$

(evaluation in the reverse order), or

$$[\![s_1 + s_2]\!]^\sigma = ([\![s_1]\!]^\sigma \| [\![s_2]\!]^\sigma) \gg_{\alpha,\alpha'} \uparrow sum(\alpha,\alpha')$$

(evaluation in parallel). The three resulting semantics are all different. One can prove however that they are identical after appropriate abstraction.

2.12. Remark. It is easy to define a term rewriting system which, for given guarded specification $E = \{X = t_X \mid X \in \Xi\}$, rewrites a given term t in the signature of $ACP_\tau + RN + CH$ with variables in Ξ, into a term of the form $\Sigma a_i \cdot t_i + \Sigma b_j$. Now the simple data flow network of Figure 2.1 represents a machine that 'executes' specification E. Here *TRS* is a component that implements the term rewriting system described above, and N is a nondeterministic device that for each input $\Sigma a_i \cdot t_i + \Sigma b_j$ chooses either one summand $a_i \cdot t_i$, and thereafter sends term t_i to the input port and atomic action a_i to the output port, or chooses one summand b_j and sends this to the output port.

The following theorem says that the operators + and $\gg$ can be eliminated in favour of the sequential composition operator $\cdot$. This means that in the case of the toy language the nondeterministic device N of Section 2.12 never has a real choice.

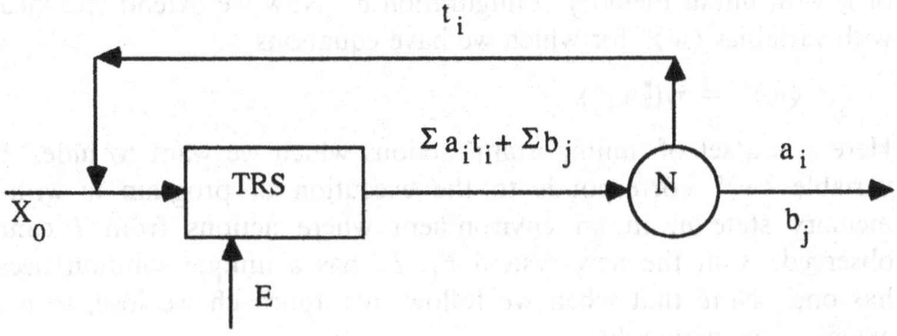

FIGURE 2.1

2.13. THEOREM. *Using the axioms of ACP+RN+CH+RDP+PR+AIP⁻ we can prove:*

(1) $\forall s \in Iexp\ \forall \sigma \in (Ivar \to Icon)\ \exists d_1, ..., d_n \in D\ \exists \alpha \in Icon$:

$$[\![s]\!]^\sigma = c(d_1) \cdots c(d_n) \cdot \uparrow \alpha$$

(2) $\forall b \in Bexp\ \forall \sigma \in (Ivar \to Icon)\ \exists d_1, ..., d_n \in D\ \exists \beta \in \{\textbf{true}, \textbf{false}\}$:

$$[\![b]\!]^\sigma = c(d_1) \cdots c(d_n) \cdot \uparrow \beta$$

(3) $\forall S \in Stat\ \forall \sigma \in (Ivar \to Icon)$:
$(\exists d_1, ..., d_n \in D\ \exists \sigma' \in (Ivar \to Icon): [\![S]\!]^\sigma = c(d_1) \cdots c(d_n) \cdot \uparrow \sigma')$
$\vee (\exists d_1, d_2, ... : [\![S]\!]^\sigma = c(d_1) \cdot c(d_2) \cdots)$

PROOF. By induction on the complexity of the language elements. □

2.14. REMARK. The reason why we used the operator $\ggg$ instead of operator $\gg$ in the definitions above is that the use of $\gg$ would lead to unguarded systems of equations. There exist models of ACP_τ (for example the term model discussed in [16]) in which we can relate to each specification (so also the unguarded ones) a special solution. If we would work in these models it would be possible to use the operator $\gg$ instead of the operator $\ggg$. But as stated before, we do not want to restrict ourselves to one single model. In the axiomatic framework the following approaches are available if one wants to obtain 'abstract' semantics:

1. *Partial abstraction.* In the system of equations defining the semantics of the toy language (Sections 2.6-2.8) we can replace all occurrences of operator $\ggg$ in the equations for the classes *Iexp* and *Bexp* by an operator $\gg$. Using induction on the structure of the elements of *Iexp* and *Bexp* one can prove that the resulting system is still guarded. It is not possible to replace occurrences of $\ggg$ in the equations for elements of the class *Stat* by $\gg$. Consequently this approach will not lead to 'full abstractness'.
2. *Delayed abstraction.* Let E be a guarded specification that contains no τ-steps or abstraction operator. For a language element w and a memory configuration σ, $[\![w]\!]^\sigma$ is the formal variable that corresponds to execution

of w with initial memory configuration σ. Now we extend specification E with variables $\langle w \rangle^{\sigma}$ for which we have equations

$$\langle w \rangle^{\sigma} = \tau_I([\![w]\!]^{\sigma}).$$

Here I is a set of 'unimportant' actions which we want to hide. Formal variable $\langle w \rangle^{\sigma}$ corresponds to the execution of program w with initial memory state σ, in an environment where actions from I cannot be observed. Call the new system E_I. E_I has a unique solution because E has one. Note that when we follow this approach we lose, to a certain extent, compositionality.

3. Combination of 1 and 2.

3. Translation of POOL to process algebra

3.1. In this section we give a translation to process algebra of a (representative) subset of the programming language POOL-T. POOL is an acronym for 'Parallel Object-Oriented Language'. It stands for a family of languages designed at Philips Research Laboratories in Eindhoven. The 'T' in POOL-T stands for 'Target'. Below we give, by means of a context-free grammar, the definition of a language POOL-⊥-CF. This language is a subset of the context free syntax of POOL-T, as presented in [1][1]. In this section we will give process algebra semantics of a language POOL-⊥, defined by:

$$\text{POOL-}\bot = \text{POOL-T} \cap \text{POOL-}\bot\text{-CF}.$$

By giving a definition in this way we do not have to give an exhaustive enumeration of all the context conditions. Because most of the context conditions in POOL are rather obvious ('all instance variables are declared in the current class definition', etc.), this is not a serious omission. Moreover, we will mention context conditions whenever we need them.

First we will define a mapping $SPEC_C$ that relates a process algebra specification to each element of the language POOL-⊥. The subscript C indicates that the resulting specification is in the signature of concrete process algebra, as opposed to the specification we will present in Section 3.11, which contains an abstraction operator.

3.2. Context-free languages. Although the notions of a context-free grammar and the language generated by it will be commonly known, we give a formal definition, because we will need this later on.

1. Except for the fact that the expression denoting the destination object in a send-expression can be **nil** in POOL-⊥-CF, which is not the case in the context-free syntax of POOL-T.

3.2.1. DEFINITION. A *context-free grammar* is a 4-tuple $G = (T,N,S,P)$, where T and N are finite sets of *terminal* resp. *nonterminal symbols*; $V = T \cup N$ is called the *vocabulary* of symbols; $S \in N$ is the *start symbol*, and P is a finite set of *production rules* of the form $X_0 \rightarrow X_1 \cdots X_n$ with $X_0 \in N$, $n > 0$, and $X_1, ..., X_n \in V - \{S\}$.

3.2.2. DEFINITION. Let $G = (T,N,S,P)$ be a context-free grammar, and let $V = T \cup N$. Let $\mathfrak{N} = (\mathbb{N} - \{0\})^*$ be the set of sequences of positive natural numbers. We write ϵ for the empty string, and use $\sigma.0$ as a notation for sequence σ. A *derivation tree* of G is a 2-tuple $t = (nodes(t), label(t))$, where $nodes(t)$ is a nonempty finite subset of $\mathfrak{N}$ such that for all $\sigma \in \mathfrak{N}$ and $m,n \in \mathbb{N} - \{0\}$:
1. $\sigma.n \in nodes(t) \Rightarrow \sigma \in nodes(t)$
2. $\sigma.n \in nodes(t) \wedge m < n \Rightarrow \sigma.m \in nodes(t)$

and $label(t)$ is a function from $nodes(t)$ into V such that if $\sigma.n \in nodes(t)$ and $\sigma.(n+1) \notin nodes(t)$, and $label(t)(\sigma.j) = X_j$ for $0 \leqslant j \leqslant n$, then production $(X_0 \rightarrow X_1 \cdots X_n)$ is in P. $(X_0 \rightarrow X_1 \cdots X_n)$ is called the production *applied at* σ. An element $\sigma \in nodes(t)$ is called a *leaf* if $\sigma.1 \notin nodes(t)$. A derivation tree is called *complete* if the labels of all the leaves are in T. Let $\sigma_1 \cdots \sigma_n$ be the sequence consisting of all the leaves of t, ordered lexicographically. Now $yield(t)$ is the sequence $label(\sigma_1) \cdots label(\sigma_n)$.

3.2.3. DEFINITION. Let $G = (T,N,S,P)$ be a context-free grammar. The *language* $L(G)$ generated by G is the set

$$L(G) = \{yield(t) \mid t \text{ is a complete derivation tree of } G \text{ and } label(t)(\epsilon) = S\}.$$

3.3. Objects in POOL. A system that executes a POOL-program can be decomposed into *objects*. An object possesses some internal *data*, and also a *process*, that has the ability to act on these data. Each object has a clear separation between its inside and its outside: the data of an object cannot be accessed directly by (the process part of) other objects.

Interaction between objects takes place in the form of so-called *method calls*. One object can send a message to another object, requesting it to perform a certain *method* (a kind of procedure). The result of the method execution is sent back to the sender. In this way one object can access the data of another object. However, because the object that receives a method call decides whether and when to execute this method, every object has its own responsibility of keeping its internal data in a consistent state.

The programs of POOL are called *units*. A unit consists of a number of *class definitions*. A *class* is a description of the behaviour of a set of objects. All objects in one class (the *instances* of that class) have the same data domain, the same methods for answering messages, and the same local process (called the object's *body*).

If a unit is to be executed, a new instance of the last class defined in the unit is created and its body is started. The body of an object can contain instructions for the creation of new objects. This makes it possible for the first object to start the whole system up.

When several objects have been created, their bodies may execute in parallel, thus introducing parallelism into the language. However, the sender of a message always waits until the destination object has returned its answer (this mechanism is known as *rendez-vous* message passing).

A number of standard classes are already predefined in the language (e.g. *Integer* and *Boolean*). They can be used in any program without defining them, but they also cannot be redefined.

The symbol **nil** denotes for each class a special object present in the system. Sending a message to such an object will always result in an error. The initial value of variables that are not parameters of a procedure is **nil**.

Because numbers are also objects, the addition of 3 and 4 is indicated in POOL by sending a message with method name *add* and parameter 4 to the object 3.

We first give, in Section 3.4, the formal definition of POOL-⊥-CF. Section 3.5 contains some remarks concerning this definition, and the relation with POOL-T and POOL-⊥.

3.4. DEFINITION (POOL-⊥-CF). We assume that two finite sets, *LId* and *UId*, of syntactic elements are given. These sets correspond to the lower-identifiers resp. upper-identifiers in POOL-T. Elements of *LId* are strings starting with a lower case letter, elements of *UId* start with an upper case letter. We define: $Id = LId \cup UId$. Let $N_0 \in \mathbb{N}$ be given. The set *Int* of integers in POOL-⊥ is

$$Int = \{-N_0, ..., -1, 0, 1, ..., N_0\}.$$

N_0 can not be ω because that would lead to infinite sums and infinite merges. The set *Bool* of booleans is

$$Bool = \{\mathbf{true}, \mathbf{false}\}.$$

Now the context-free grammar *G*, which defines POOL-⊥-CF, is

$$G = (T, N, U, P)$$

where

$$T = Id \cup Int \cup Bool \cup \{\mathbf{root}, \mathbf{unit}, \mathbf{class}, \mathbf{var}, \mathbf{body}, \mathbf{end}, \mathbf{method}, \mathbf{routine}, \mathbf{local}, \mathbf{in}, \mathbf{nil}$$

$$\mathbf{return}, \mathbf{post}, \mathbf{if}, \mathbf{then}, \mathbf{else}, \mathbf{fi}, \mathbf{do}, \mathbf{od}, \mathbf{sel}, \mathbf{les}, \mathbf{or}, \mathbf{answer}, \mathbf{self}, \mathbf{new}, \;;\;, \cdot\,, \leftarrow, \;!\;, \;,\;, \;:\;\}$$

$$N = \{U, RU, CDL, CD, MDL, MD, RDL, RD, PD, VDL, VD, SS, S, SE,$$

$$GCL, GC, AN, MIL, E, CO, SN, RC, MC, EL, CI, MI, RI, VI\}$$

P : see Table 3.1

In Table 3.1, optional syntactical elements are enclosed in square brackets ('[' and ']').

Syntax of POOL-⊥

<table>
<tr><th>No</th><th>Description</th><th>Syntactic Rule</th></tr>
<tr><td>1</td><td>unit</td><td>U→RU</td></tr>
<tr><td>2</td><td>root unit</td><td>RU→root unit CDL</td></tr>
<tr><td>3</td><td>class definition list</td><td>CDL→CD [,CDL]</td></tr>
<tr><td>4</td><td>class definition</td><td>CD→class CI [varVDL][RDL][MDL]
body SS end CI</td></tr>
<tr><td>5</td><td>method definition list</td><td>MDL→MD [MDL]</td></tr>
<tr><td>6</td><td>method definition</td><td>MD→method MI PD end MI</td></tr>
<tr><td>7</td><td>routine definition list</td><td>RDL→RD [RDL]</td></tr>
<tr><td>8</td><td>routine definition</td><td>RD→routine RI PD end RI</td></tr>
<tr><td>9</td><td>procedure denotation</td><td>PD→([VDL]) CI : [local VDL in] [SS]
return E [post SS]</td></tr>
<tr><td>10</td><td>variable declaration list</td><td>VDL→VD [,VDL]</td></tr>
<tr><td>11</td><td>variable declaration</td><td>VD→VI : CI</td></tr>
<tr><td>12</td><td>statement sequence</td><td>SS→S [; SS]</td></tr>
<tr><td>13</td><td>statement</td><td>S→ VI←E
| AN
| if E then SS [else SS] fi
| do E then SS od
| SE
| SN
| MC
| RC</td></tr>
<tr><td>14</td><td>select statement</td><td>SE→sel GCL les</td></tr>
<tr><td>15</td><td>guarded command list</td><td>GCL→GC [or GCL]</td></tr>
<tr><td>16</td><td>guarded command</td><td>GC→ E [AN] then SS</td></tr>
</table>

17	answer statement	$AN \rightarrow$ **answer** (MIL)
18	method identifier list	$MIL \rightarrow MI\,[,MIL]$
19	expression	$E \rightarrow VI$ | **self** | CO | **new** | SN | MC | RC | **nil**
20	constant	$CO \rightarrow c$ (for $c \in Bool \cup Int$)
21	send expression	$SN \rightarrow E\,!\,MI\,([EL])$
22	method call	$MC \rightarrow MI\,([EL])$
23	routine call	$RC \rightarrow CI \cdot RI\,([EL])$
24	expression list	$EL \rightarrow E\,[,EL]$
25	class identifier	$CI \rightarrow C$ (for $C \in UId$)
26	method identifier	$MI \rightarrow m$ (for $m \in LId$)
27	routine identifier	$RI \rightarrow r$ (for $r \in LId$)
28	variable identifier	$VI \rightarrow v$ (for $v \in LId$)

TABLE 3.1

3.5. Remarks (numbers refer to productions).

(1) In POOL-T a unit can also be a specification unit or an implementation unit. This makes it possible to group a set of class definitions together into a logically coherent collection and to specify a clear interface with other units.

(2) The names of the classes defined in a unit must be different (similar context conditions in (5), (7), (9) and (10)). There are 4 standard classes: *Integer*, *Boolean*, *Read_File* and *Write_File*. The definitions of these classes can be found in Section 3.9.3. The standard classes can be used in any program without defining them, but they also cannot be redefined. Elements of *Int* are instances of class *Integer* and elements of

Bool are instances of class *Boolean*.

(4) The class identifier following the **end** must be identical to the initial class identifier (similar context conditions in (6) and (8)).

(8) Routines are procedural abstractions related to a **class**, rather than to an individual object. They can be called also by objects from another class. Two objects can call and execute a routine concurrently as though each has its own version of the routine.

(9) The first variable declaration list is the formal parameter list, the second one contains the local variables of the method or routine. Only in the case of a method, a post-processing section may be present. The type of the return expression must be the same as the class identifier in the procedure denotation.

(11) A strong typing mechanism is included in the language: each variable is associated to a class (its *type*) and may contain the names of objects of that class only.

(13) The statement $VI \leftarrow E$ is called an assignment and executed as follows: First the expression on the right hand side is evaluated and its result (a reference to an object) is determined. Then the variable is made to contain this reference.

The statement **do** *E* **then** *SS* **od** is the classical while statement.

A send expression, a method call and a routine call can occur as statement as well as expression. If they occur as statement, the corresponding expression is evaluated, and its result is discarded. So only the side-effects of the evaluation are important.

(14) The select statement is the most complicated construct in the language. It specifies the conditional answering of messages. A select statement is executed as follows:

- All the expressions (called: guards) of the guarded commands are evaluated in the order in which they occur in the text. If any of them results in **nil**, an error occurs.
- The guarded commands whose expressions result in **false** are discarded, they do not play a role in the rest of the execution of the select statement. Only the ones with **true** (the open guarded commands) remain. If there are no open guarded commands, an error occurs.
- Now the object may choose to execute the (textually) first open guarded command without an answer statement, or it may choose to answer a message with a method identifier which occurs in one of the answer statements of an open guarded command that has no open guarded command without an answer statement before it. In the last case it must select the first open guarded command in which the method identifier of the chosen message occurs.
- If the object has chosen to answer a message, this is done.
- After that in either case the statement after **then** is executed, and the select statement terminates.

(17) An object executing an answer statement waits for a message with a method name that is present in the list. Then it executes the method (after initializing parameters). The result is sent back to the sender of the message, and the answer statement terminates.

(19) The symbol **self** always denotes the object that is executing the expression itself.
The expression **new** may only occur in a routine. When a **new** expression is evaluated, a new object of the class where the routine is defined, is created, and execution of its body is started. The result of the **new** expression is a reference to that new object.

(21) When a send expression is evaluated, first the expression before the '!' is evaluated. The result will be the destination for the message. Then the expressions in the expression list are evaluated from left to right. The resulting objects will be the parameters of the message. Thereafter the message, consisting of the indicated method identifier and the parameters, is sent to the destination object. The answer of the destination object is the result of the send expression.

(22) An object may not send a message to itself. If an object wants to invoke one of its own methods, this can be done by means of a method call. A method call may not occur in a routine.

3.6. Attribute grammars. The complexity of the language POOL does not allow for a translation into process algebra which is as straightforward as in the case of the toy language of Section 2. Several problems arise, e.g. how to establish the relation between a method call and the corresponding method declaration, the semantics of a **new** expression, etc.

The main tool we will use in order to manage this complexity is the formalism of *attribute grammars*. This is not the place to give an extensive introduction into the theory of attribute grammars. For this we refer to e.g. [12, 14, 21].

Informally an attribute grammar is a context-free grammar in which we add to each nonterminal a finite number of *attributes*. For each occurrence of a nonterminal in a derivation tree these attributes have a *value*. With each production rule of the context-free grammar we associate a number of *semantic rules*. These rules define the values of the attributes. Some of the attributes are based on the attributes of the descendants of the nonterminal symbol. These are called *synthesized* attributes. Other attributes, called *inherited* attributes, are based on the attributes of the ancestors.

In the theory of abstract data types one presents specifications of the stack, Petri net people model the producer/consumer problem, and in the field of communication protocols one verifies the Alternating Bit Protocol. The example one always encounters in an introduction into the theory of attribute grammars is the one, first presented in [21], in which the binary notation for numbers is defined. We do not want to break with this tradition, and will also give the famous example.

3.6.1. EXAMPLE. We start with a context-free grammar that generates binary notations for numbers: the terminal symbols are ·, 0, 1; the nonterminal symbols are B, L and N, standing respectively for bit, list of bits, and number; the starting symbol is N; and the productions are

$$B \to 0 \mid 1$$

$$L \to B \mid LB$$

$$N \to L \mid L \cdot L$$

Strings in the corresponding language are for instance '0', '010', '0.010' and '1010.101'. Now we introduce the following attributes

1. Each B has a 'value' $v(B)$ which is a rational number.
2. Each B has a 'scale' $s(B)$ which is an integer.
3. Each L has a 'value' $v(L)$ which is a rational number.
4. Each L has a 'length' $l(L)$ which is an integer.
5. Each L has a 'scale' $s(L)$ which is an integer.
6. Each N has a 'value' $v(N)$ which is a rational number.

These attributes can be defined as follows:

Syntactic Rules	Semantic Rules
$B \to 0$	$v(B) = 0$
$B \to 1$	$v(B) = 2^{s(B)}$
$L \to B$	$v(L) = v(B); s(B) = s(L); l(L) = 1$
$L_1 \to L_2 B$	$v(L_1) = v(L_2) + v(B); s(B) = s(L_1);$
	$s(L_2) = s(L_1) + 1; l(L_1) = l(L_2) + 1$
$N \to L$	$v(N) = v(L); s(L) = 0$
$N \to L_1 \cdot L_2$	$v(N) = v(L_1) + v(L_2); s(L_1) = 0;$
	$s(L_2) = -l(L_2)$

TABLE 3.2

(In the fourth and sixth rules subscripts have been used to distinguish between occurrences of like nonterminals.) If one looks for some time at this equations, one sees (hopefully) that for each complete derivation tree t with $label(t)(\epsilon) = N$ there is a unique valuation of the attributes such that the semantic rules hold.

Furthermore the v attribute of the root nonterminal gives the value of the string generated by the tree.

Below we give a formal definition of an attribute grammar. There are many (often essentially different) definitions possible. The following one is a simplified version of the definition presented in [14].

3.6.2. DEFINITION. The elements of an *attribute grammar G* are:

1. A context-free grammar $G_0 = (T,N,S_0,P)$.
2. A *semantic domain* (or set of data types) $D = \langle\Omega,\Phi\rangle$, where Ω is a finite set of sets and Φ is a set of functions of type $V_1 \times \cdots \times V_m \rightarrow V_{m+1}$ for $m \geqslant 0$ and $V_i \in \Omega$. In the case $m=0$, Φ can contain elements of V (for $V \in \Omega$). We demand that for each $V \in \Omega$ there is a $v \in V$ with $v \in \Phi$.
3. An *attribute description* consisting of
   a. Two finite disjoint sets *S-Att* and *I-Att* of *synthesized* or *s-attributes* resp. *inherited* or *i-attributes*; $Att = S\text{-}Att \cup I\text{-}Att$ is the set of *attributes*.
   b. For $X \in N$, $S(X)$ and $I(X)$ are subsets of *S-Att* resp. *I-Att*; $A(X) = S(X) \cup I(X)$ is the set of *attributes* of X. We demand $I(S_0) = \varnothing$.
   c. For each $\alpha \in Att$, $V(\alpha) \in \Omega$ is the (possibly infinite) set of *attribute values* of α.
4. First some intermediate terminology:
   For each production rule $p: X_0 \rightarrow X_1 \cdots X_n$, we define the set $A(p)$ of *attributes* of p, by

$$A(p) = \{\langle\alpha,j\rangle \mid 0 \leqslant j \leqslant n,\ \alpha \in A(X_j)\}.$$

   Intuitively $\langle\alpha,j\rangle$ is an attribute of the occurrence of X_j on the j-th position in p. Furthermore the sets $INT(p)$ and $EXT(p)$ of *internal* resp. *external* attributes of p are defined by

$$INT(p) = \{\langle\alpha,j\rangle \mid (j=0 \wedge \alpha \in S(X_0)) \vee (1 \leqslant j \leqslant n \wedge \alpha \in I(X_j))\}$$

$$EXT(p) = \{\langle\alpha,j\rangle \mid (j=0 \wedge \alpha \in I(X_0)) \vee (1 \leqslant j \leqslant n \wedge \alpha \in S(X_j))\}$$

   A *semantic rule* for p is a string of the form

$$\langle\alpha,j\rangle = f(\langle\alpha_1,k_1\rangle, \ldots, \langle\alpha_m,k_m\rangle) \qquad (*)$$

   with $\langle\alpha,j\rangle \in INT(p)$, $m \geqslant 0$, $\langle\alpha_i,k_i\rangle \in EXT(p)$ for $1 \leqslant i \leqslant m$, and $f \in \Phi$ is a function from $V(\alpha_1) \times \cdots \times V(\alpha_m)$ into $V(\alpha)$.
   Now we continue the definition:
   For each $p \in P$, $R(p)$ is a finite set of semantic rules for p. We demand that for each $p \in P$ and $\langle\alpha,j\rangle \in INT(p)$, $R(p)$ contains exactly one semantic rule.

The definition above gives the 'syntax' of attribute grammars. To define the 'semantics' of an attribute grammar, we need again some terminology:

3.6.3. DEFINITION. Let G be an attribute grammar. Let t be a derivation tree of the corresponding context-free grammar. The *attributes* of t are defined by

$$A(t) = \{\langle\alpha,\sigma\rangle \mid \sigma\in nodes(t),\ \alpha\in A(label(t)(\sigma))\}$$

(the notation $A(.)$ is clearly overloaded, but always means 'attributes of ... ').
A *decoration* of t is a function

$$val : A(t)\rightarrow\{v \mid \exists\alpha\in A(t) : v\in V(\alpha)\}$$

such that for each $\langle\alpha,\sigma\rangle\in A(t)$, $val(\alpha,\sigma)\in V(\alpha)$.
Suppose $\sigma\in nodes(t)$ and $p : X_0\rightarrow X_1 \cdots X_n$ is a production applied at σ. If $R(p)$ contains a semantic rule (*) (see Definition 3.6.2), then the string

$$\langle\alpha,\sigma.j\rangle = f(\langle\alpha_1,\sigma.k_1\rangle, ..., \langle\alpha_m,\sigma.k_m\rangle) \qquad (**)$$

is called a *semantic instruction* of t.

3.6.4. DEFINITION. A decoration val of t is called a *correct decoration* if for each semantic instruction (**) of t

$$val(\alpha,\sigma.j) = f(val(\alpha_1,\sigma.k_1), ..., val(\alpha_m,\sigma.k_m))$$

(this is a serious equality, not a string!)

3.6.5. It follows from the Definitions 3.6.2 and 3.6.3, that for each attribute $\langle\alpha,\sigma\rangle$ there is exactly one semantic instruction in $R(t)$ of the form $\langle\alpha,\sigma\rangle = ...$ This means that each attribute of t is defined by exactly one equation in the system of equations $R(t)$. A sufficient condition to solve this system is that the system of equations contains no circularities. In [21], an algorithm is given which detects for an arbitrary attribute grammar whether or not the semantic rules can possibly lead to circular definition of some attributes. All the attribute grammars we will employ, contain no circularities, and therefore there is for each complete derivation tree precisely one correct decoration. This decoration can be computed if the functions which occur in the semantic rules are computable.

3.7. State Operator (SO). In [8], state operators λ_σ^m are introduced. Here m is member of a set M, the set of objects. These objects are very much like the objects in POOL: they posses some internal data, and there is a local process which can act upon these data. The object can block actions of the process, or rename then, depending on the data. $\lambda_\sigma^m(x)$ is a process corresponding to object m in state σ, executing process x. We can visualize as in Figure 3.1.

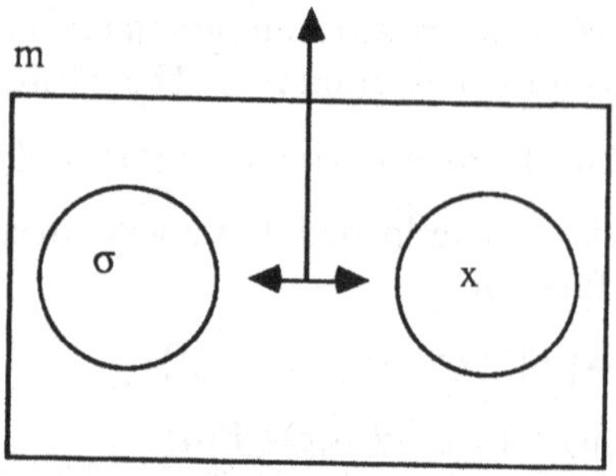

FIGURE 3.1

Below we give the formal definition of the state operators.

3.7.1. DEFINITION. Let M and Σ be two given sets. Elements of M are called *objects*, elements of Σ are called *states*. Suppose two functions *act* and *eff* are given

$$act:\ A \times M \times \Sigma \rightarrow A_{\tau\delta} \quad \text{(action function)}$$

$$eff:\ A \times M \times \Sigma \rightarrow \Sigma \quad \text{(effect function)}$$

Now we extend the signature with operators

$$\lambda_\sigma^m : P \rightarrow P \quad (\text{for } m \in M,\ \sigma \in \Sigma)$$

and extend the set of axioms by ($a \in A$; $x,y \in P$; $m \in M$; $\sigma \in \Sigma$)

$\lambda_\sigma^m(\delta) = \delta$	SO1
$\lambda_\sigma^m(\tau) = \tau$	SO2
$\lambda_\sigma^m(ax) = act(a,m,\sigma) \cdot \lambda_{eff(a,m,\sigma)}^m(x)$	SO3
$\lambda_\sigma^m(\tau x) = \tau \cdot \lambda_\sigma^m(x)$	SO4
$\lambda_\sigma^m(x+y) = \lambda_\sigma^m(x) + \lambda_\sigma^m(y)$	SO5

TABLE 3.3

The state operators can be defined in terms of the operators and constants of ACP_τ + RN (see [26]).

3.8. Parameters of the axiom system. We will relate to POOL-⊥ programs specifications in the signature of ACP+RN+CH+SO. The first thing we have to do is to specify the parameters of the axiom system. We will not give a complete list of all the atomic actions. The alphabet A of atomic actions simply consists of all the atomic actions we mention.

3.8.1. Objects. Let N_1 be a fixed natural number. N_1 gives an upperbound on the number of active (or non-standard) POOL objects which can be created during the execution of a POOL-⊥ program. The set $AObj$ contains references to these potential objects.

$$AObj = \{\hat{0}, \hat{1}, ..., \hat{N}_1\}$$

The hats are needed to distinguish between the names of the non-standard objects and the names of the standard objects which are always present in the system:

$$SObj = Int \cup Bool \cup \{\textbf{nil}\} \cup \{\textbf{input}, \textbf{output}\}.$$

The set $Obj = SObj \cup AObj$ gives the domain of values of variables in POOL-⊥ programs. It is also the value domain of the chaining operator we will employ; this means that the alphabet contains actions $\uparrow\alpha, \downarrow\alpha$, etc. for $\alpha \in Obj$).

3.8.2. Communication. Objects in POOL communicate by sending *frames* to each other. These frames are built up as follows

destination	type of message	message	sender

The field 'sender' contains a reference to the object which sends the message; the field 'destination' contains a reference to the object which reads the message. There are two types of messages:

mc: The sender asks the destination to perform a method-call. The field 'message' contains the name of the method together with the actual parameters. So a *mc*-frame looks as follows

$$(\alpha, mc, m(\alpha_1, ..., \alpha_n), \beta) \tag{3.8.2.1}$$

an: After an object has executed a method call, an *an*-frame is sent back to the object which originated the method call. The field 'message' contains the answer (a reference to an object):

$$(\beta, an, \gamma, \alpha) \tag{3.8.2.2}$$

Let N_2 be a fixed natural number. N_2 gives an upperbound on the length of a variable declaration list of a procedure denotation. The set $\mathfrak{M}$ of messages that occurs in a method call frame is:

$$\mathfrak{M} = \{m(\alpha_1, ..., \alpha_n) \mid m \in LId, 0 \leq n \leq N_2, \alpha_1, ..., \alpha_n \in Obj\} \quad (3.8.2.3)$$

and the set $\mathfrak{F}$ of frames is:

$$\mathfrak{F} = \{(\alpha, mc, d, \beta) \mid \alpha, \beta \in Obj, d \in \mathfrak{M}\} \cup \{(\beta, an, \gamma, \alpha) \mid \alpha, \beta, \gamma \in Obj\}. \quad (3.8.2.4)$$

For each frame $f \in \mathfrak{F}$, we have atomic actions $read(f)$, $send(f)$ and $comm(f)$. The communication function on these actions is given by

$$read(f) | send(f) = comm(f) \quad \text{for } f \in \mathfrak{F}. \quad (3.8.2.5)$$

The set J of forbidden actions that will be encapsulated is

$$J = \{read(f), send(f) \mid f \in \mathfrak{F}\}. \quad (3.8.2.6)$$

3.8.3. Renamings. A POOL object is fully determined by its class and by its name. For each class we will specify a process that gives the *general* behaviour of the instances (the objects) of that class. Now the only thing we have to do in order to define the process corresponding to a *specific* object, is to give a renaming function which renames the actions of the process which is related to the class of that object. This renaming function gives the object its identity, a name. The frames which are sent and received by an object, contain the name of that object. But since on the level of a class this name is not known, the process related to a class contains 'unfinished' *read* and *send* actions: actions $rd(uf)$ and $sn(uf)$, where uf is an unfinished frame in which the field that gives the identity of the object is absent. Actions of the form $rd(uf)$ and $sn(uf)$ do not communicate.

For each $\alpha \in Obj$ we define a renaming function f_α by:

$$f_\alpha(sn(\beta, mc, m(\alpha_1, ..., \alpha_n))) = send(\beta, mc, m(\alpha_1, ..., \alpha_n), \alpha) \quad (3.8.3.1)$$

$$f_\alpha(rd(mc, m(\alpha_1, ..., \alpha_n), \beta)) = read(\alpha, mc, m(\alpha_1, ..., \alpha_n), \beta) \quad (3.8.3.2)$$

$$f_\alpha(sn(\beta, an, \gamma)) = send(\beta, an, \gamma, \alpha) \quad (3.8.3.3)$$

$$f_\alpha(rd(an, \beta, \gamma)) = read(\alpha, an, \beta, \gamma) \quad (3.8.3.4)$$

If an object executes a **self** expression, the corresponding process on class level contains a non-deterministic choice between actions $eqs(\beta)$ for $\beta \in Obj$. The following equations for the renaming functions make that, for a specific instance of the class, the action which will be actually performed is the right one.

$$f_\alpha(eqs(\beta)) = \begin{cases} skip & \text{if } \beta = \alpha \\ \delta & \text{otherwise} \end{cases} \quad (3.8.3.5)$$

If an object answers a method call, the result of the return expression in the procedure denotation has to be sent back to the sender of the method call. To model this we introduce renaming functions g_α. The function g_α interprets a $\uparrow\beta$ action as a $sn(\alpha, an, \beta)$ action:

$$g_\alpha(\uparrow\beta) = sn(\alpha, an, \beta). \quad (3.8.3.6)$$

3.8.4. Process creation. For $d \in \mathcal{N} \times AObj$ we introduce atomic actions $create(d)$, $create^*(d)$ and $\underline{create}(d)$. $create(d)$ stands for: ask for the creation of a process on basis of initial information d. $create^*(d)$ means: receive a request for creation. $\underline{create}(d)$ indicates that process creation has taken place.

Elements of $\mathcal{N}$ (see Definition 3.2.2) play the role of formal variables in the process algebra specification that we will construct in order to give the semantics of POOL-$\perp$. In general the process denoted by the first parameter of a create action will give the behaviours of a certain class, and the second parameter gives the name of the instance of that class to be created.

We extend the communication function by

$$create(d) \mid create^*(d) = \underline{create}(d). \tag{3.8.4.1}$$

Create actions are not involved in any other proper communication. Let

$$K = \{create(d), create^*(d) \mid d \in \mathcal{N} \times AObj\}. \tag{3.8.4.2}$$

Actions from K will be encapsulated.

Our way of dealing with process creation in POOL is inspired by the mechanism described in [10]. We have chosen however not to use the process creation operator E_φ presented there, because of the lack of proof rules for this operator.

3.8.5. State operator. In the semantical description of the toy language of Section 2 the state of the memory was a parameter of the formal variables in the specification. In principle this approach can also be followed in the case of the language POOL-$\perp$. But since in POOL objects of a different class have, in general, different variables and the language contains recursion, which leads to the creation of new instances of variables, the memory state of a POOL object can become rather complicated. For this reason we prefer to keep track of the memory state in a different way: namely by means of a state operator. For each variable $v \in LId$ and value $\alpha \in Obj$, λ_α^v represents a memory cell with name v in state α. A value β can be assigned to variable v by means of an atomic action $ass(v,\beta)$:

$$\lambda_\alpha^v(ass(v,\beta) \cdot x) = skip \cdot \lambda_\beta^v(x). \tag{3.8.5.1}$$

If in the evaluation of an expression the value of a variable v is needed, this can be expressed at the level of process algebra by means of an alternative composition of actions $eqv(v,\beta)$. The following equation makes that in an environment with variable cell v, the correct action will be actually performed:

$$\lambda_\alpha^v(eqv(v,\beta) \cdot x) = \begin{cases} skip \cdot \lambda_\alpha^v(x) & \text{if } \alpha = \beta \\ \delta & \text{otherwise} \end{cases} \tag{3.8.5.2}$$

Notice that in the case of nested λ_α^v operators, actions $ass(v,\beta)$ and $eqv(v,\beta)$ interact with the innermost λ_α^v operator. This is relevant for nested method calls, etc.

The initial object, which starts the system up, has name $\hat{0}$. An object *counter* counts the number of objects which have been created. It also provides an environment in which new objects obtain new names. An error occurs when more than N_1 objects have been created. For $n \in \mathbb{N}$ we have

$$\lambda_n^{counter}(\overline{create}(X,\alpha)\cdot x) = \begin{cases} skip \cdot \lambda_{n+1}^{counter}(x) & \text{if } \alpha = \hat{n} \wedge n < N_1 \\ error \cdot \lambda_{n+1}^{counter}(x) & \text{if } n = N_1 \\ \delta & \text{otherwise} \end{cases} \qquad (3.8.5.3)$$

3.8.6. Formal variables. The set Ξ of formal variables of the process algebra specification related to POOL-$\perp$ consists of the elements of $\mathfrak{N}$, possibly sub- and superscripted with elements of *LId* and *Obj**. Formally we have:

$$\Xi = \mathfrak{N} \cup \mathfrak{N} \times LId \cup \mathfrak{N} \times (Obj^*) \cup \mathfrak{N} \times LId \times (Obj^*). \qquad (3.8.6.1)$$

We define $node : \Xi \rightarrow \mathfrak{N}$ to be the projection function which relates to each variable the corresponding element of $\mathfrak{N}$.

3.8.7. Note. From now on, when we speak about a POOL-$\perp$ program, what we mean is an extended program, in which the class definition list begins with the class definitions of the standard classes (see Section 3.9.3).

3.9. Attribute description. Table 3.4 contains a list of all the attributes we will employ for the semantical description of POOL-$\perp$. In Section 3.9.1 we give a detailed description of these attributes. Section 3.9.2 contains all the semantical rules which were not already given in Section 3.9.1, and in Section 3.9.3 the standard classes are defined.

3.9.1. Remarks.

1. We make the names of the nodes in a derivation tree explicit by means of an inherited attribute $[\![.]\!]$. With each node in a derivation tree we will relate a number of process algebra equations with variables in Ξ. The values of the attribute $[\![.]\!]$ (which are elements of Ξ) will be the 'most important' or 'key' variables in this specification. The semantic rules for this attribute are as follows
   - For production $U \rightarrow RU$ the rule is $[\![RU]\!] = 1$
   - If $X_0 \rightarrow X_1 \cdots X_n$ is a production with $X_0 \neq U$, and if $X_i \in N$ for certain $1 \leqslant i \leqslant n$ then we have the rule $[\![X_i]\!] = [\![X_0]\!].i$.
2. The value of synthesized attribute *id* is (one of) the identifier(s) generated by the corresponding nonterminal.
3. Attribute *vd* collects variables declared in a variable declaration list.
4. Attribute *pd* gives the information concerning a procedure declaration that we need: a formal variable denoting the process related to the procedure, and the number of parameters of the procedure.
5. The attribute *rd* gives for each routine in a routine definition list the essential information: a process variable and the number of parameters. The value of *rd* is arbitrary for elements of *LId* which are not the name of a routine.

Name attr.	*i/s*	*Description*	*Attribute value*	*Nonterminals*
$[\![\cdot]\!]$	i	Key variable	$\mathfrak{N}$	N-{U}
id	s	Identifier	*LId*	{VI,RI,MI,CI, VD,RD,MD,CD}
vd	s	Variable declarations	LId^*	{VDL}
pd	s	Procedure declaration	$\mathfrak{N}\times\mathbb{N}$	{PD,RD,MD}
rd	s	Routine declarations	$LId\rightarrow\mathfrak{N}\times\mathbb{N}$	{RDL,CD}
md	s	Method declarations	$LId\rightarrow\mathfrak{N}\times\mathbb{N}$	{MDL,CD}
cd	s	Class declarations	$UId\rightarrow\mathfrak{N}$	{CDL}
rdc	s	Routine decl. of a CDL	$UId\times LId\rightarrow\mathfrak{N}\times\mathbb{N}$	{CDL}
mdc	s	Method decl. of a CDL	$UId\times LId\rightarrow\mathfrak{N}\times\mathbb{N}$	{CDL}
cdf	i	Class definitions	$UId\rightarrow\mathfrak{N}$	N-{U,RU}
rdf	i	Routine definitions	$UId\times LId\rightarrow\mathfrak{N}\times\mathbb{N}$	N-{U,RU}
mdf	i	Method definitions	$UId\times LId\rightarrow\mathfrak{N}\times\mathbb{N}$	N-{U,RU}
class	i	Class	*UId*	N-{U,RU,CDL,CD}
l	s	Length	$\mathbb{N}$	{EL}
mis	s	Method ident. set	*Pow*(*LId*)	{MIL,AN,GC}
misl	s	Method ident. set list	$(Pow(LId))^*$	{GCL}
peq	s	Process equations	Sets of eq. over ACP+RN+CH+SO with variables in Ξ	N-{U,VI,RI,MI,CI, VD,VDL,RD,RDL, MD,MDL}
spec	s	Specification	Sets of eq. over ACP+RN+CH+SO with variables in Ξ	N-{VI,RI,MI,CI, VD,VDL,RD,RDL, MD,MDL}

TABLE 3.4

6. The meaning of attribute *md* is similar to the meaning of *rd*.
7. The attribute *cd* gives the essential information for each class definition in a class definition list: the process corresponding to the general behaviour of that class. The value of *cd* is arbitrary for elements of *UId* which are not present in the class definition list.
8. Attribute *rdc* is like *rd* but now for a list of class definitions.
9. Attribute *mdc* is like *md* but now for a list of class definitions.
10. All the information that is gathered in the s-attribute *cd* is distributed over the parse tree by means of the i-attribute *cdf*:
    - For production $RU\rightarrow$**root unit** CDL we have the rule $cdf(CDL) = cd(CDL)$.
    - If $X_0\rightarrow X_1 \cdots X_n$ is a production ($X_0\neq U,RU$), and if $X_i\in N$ for certain $1\leqslant i\leqslant n$, then $cdf(X_i) = cdf(X_0)$.

11. Attribute *rdf* is like attribute *cdf*.
12. Attribute *mdf* is like attribute *cdf*.
13. In order to define the semantics of, for example, a new expression, we need to know in which class definition this expression occurs. Therefore we define an i-attribute *class* with domain *UId*:
    - For production

      $$CD \to \mathbf{class}\ CI_1\ [\mathbf{var}\ VDL\ ][\ RDL\ ][\ MDL\ ]\ \mathbf{body}\ SS\ \mathbf{end}\ CI_2$$

      we have rules

      $$[\,class(VDL)=\,]\ [\,class(RDL)=\,]\ [\,class(MDL)=\,]\,class(SS)=id(CI_1)$$

    - If $X_0 \to X_1 \cdots X_n$ is a production ($X_0 \neq U, RU, CDL, CD$), and if $X_i \in N$ for certain $1 \leq i \leq n$, then $class(X_i) = class(X_0)$.
14. In the semantic rules for the send expression we need information about the length of the expression list. This information is contained in attribute *l*.
15. The attribute *mis* gives the method identifiers which occur in the method identifier list of an answer statement. The attribute is used to define the semantics of the select statement.
16. The attribute *misl* gives a list of the method identifier sets which occur in the answer statements in a guarded command list.
17. The value of the attribute *peq* is a set of equations in the signature of ACP+RN+CH+SO with variables in Ξ. We will define the attribute in such a way that for each nonterminal X:

    $$(Y = t_Y) \in peq(X) \ \Rightarrow\ node(Y) = [\![X]\!].$$

    Furthermore we take care that for each nonterminal X, $peq(X)$ never contains two equations for the same variable. These conditions make that the union for all the nodes in a derivation tree of the values of attribute *peq* never contains two equations for the same variable.
18. The s-attribute *spec* collects the values of attribute *peq*. The value of the attribute *spec* belonging to the root of the derivation tree (which has label U) is the specification we relate to the parse tree. We have the following semantic rules:
    - Let $X_0 \to X_1 \cdots X_n$ be a production such that $X_0 \neq U$ has attribute *spec*. Let $S \subseteq \{1, ..., n\}$ be the set of indices i for which X_i has an attribute *spec*. Then:

      $$spec(X_0) = peq(X_0) \cup \bigcup_{i \in S} spec(X_i)$$

    - For production $U \to RU$ we have:

      $$spec(U) = spec(RU) \cup$$

      $$\cup\ \{(X = \delta) \mid X \in \Xi \text{ and there is no equation for } X \text{ in } spec(RU)\}.$$

3.9.2. Semantic rules. In case a production contains an optional syntactical element, we will often use a fraction notation in the semantic rules: the numerator corresponds to the semantic rule for the production *with* the optional element, the denominator corresponds to the production *without* the optional element. **In case of a semantic rule** $peq(X) = \{E_1, E_2, ...\}$**, we only write down the equations** $E_1, E_2, ...$**!!!** Numbers refer to the numbering of productions in Table 3.1.

$VI \rightarrow v \quad (v \in LId)$ (28)

$$id(VI) = v$$

$RI \rightarrow r \quad (r \in LId)$ (27)

$$id(RI) = r$$

$MI \rightarrow m \quad (m \in LId)$ (26)

$$id(MI) = m$$

$CI \rightarrow C \quad (C \in UId)$ (25)

$$id(CI) = C$$

$EL_0 \rightarrow E\,[\,,EL_1\,]$ (24)

$$l(EL_0) = 1[\,+\,l(EL_1)]$$

$$[\![EL_0]\!] = [\![E]\!][\,\cdot\,[\![EL_1]\!]]$$

○ We state again that the equation for $[\![EL_0]\!]$ is not to be considered as a semantic rule defining attribute $[\![.]\!]$, but as an element of the set defining attribute *peq*. The equation says that execution of an expression list consists of sequential execution of all the expressions from left to right.

$RC \rightarrow CI \cdot RI(\,)$ (23.1)

Let

$$rdf(RC)(id(CI), id(RI)) = (X\ n)$$

then

$$[\![RC]\!] = skip \cdot X_\epsilon$$

○ In a correct POOL-⊥ program *n* will be 0. The *skip* action is needed in order to keep the specification guarded.

$RC \rightarrow CI \cdot RI\,(EL)$ (23.2)

Let

$$rdf(RC)(id(CI), id(RI)) = (X\ n)$$

then

$$[\![RC]\!] = [\![EL]\!] \gg_{\alpha_1, \ldots, \alpha_n} X_{\alpha_1, \ldots, \alpha_n}$$

○ First the expressions of the parameter list are evaluated. Thereafter the routine call is executed, with the actual parameters instantiated. In a correct program the number of actual parameters equals the number of formal parameters: $l(EL) = n$.

$MC \rightarrow MI(\,)$ (22.1)

Let

$$mdf(MC)(class(MC), id(MI)) = (X\ n)$$

then

$$[\![MC]\!] = skip \cdot X_\epsilon$$

$MC \rightarrow MI(EL)$ (22.2)

Let

$$mdf(MC)(class(MC), id(MI)) = (X\ n)$$

then

$$[\![MC]\!] = [\![EL]\!] \gg_{\alpha_1, \ldots, \alpha_n} X_{\alpha_1, \ldots, \alpha_n}$$

$SN \rightarrow E\,!\,MI(\,)$ (21.1)

Let

$$id(MI) = m$$

then

$$[\![SN]\!] = [\![E]\!] \gg_\alpha [\![SN]\!]_\alpha$$

$$[\![SN]\!]_\alpha = \begin{cases} error & \text{if } \alpha = \textbf{nil} \\ sn(\alpha, mc, m(\,)) \cdot \sum_{\beta \in Obj} rd(an, \beta, \alpha) \cdot \uparrow \beta & \text{otherwise} \end{cases}$$

○ First the expression on the left is evaluated. If the result is **nil** an error occurs. Otherwise the result of the expression is the destination of the message. Now the message is sent and the answer awaited. This answer (if it comes) is the result of the send expression. In a correct POOL program the type of expression E will be a class that contains a method m without parameters.

$SN \rightarrow E\,!\,MI(EL)$ (21.2)

Let

$$id(MI) = m$$

$$l(EL) = n$$

then

$$[\![SN]\!] = [\![E]\!] \gg_\alpha [\![SN]\!]_\alpha$$

$$[\![SN]\!]_{\mathbf{nil}} = error$$

and for $\alpha \neq \mathbf{nil}$:

$$[\![SN]\!]_\alpha = [\![EL]\!] \gg_{\alpha_1, \ldots, \alpha_n} sn(\alpha, mc, m(\alpha_1, \ldots, \alpha_n)) \cdot \sum_{\beta \in Obj} rd(an, \beta, \alpha) \cdot \uparrow\beta$$

○ Like 21.1 but now with parameters.

$CO \rightarrow c \quad (c \in Bool \cup Int)$ (20)

$$[\![CO]\!] = \uparrow c$$

$E \rightarrow VI$ (19.1)

$$[\![E]\!] = \sum_{\alpha \in Obj} eqv(id(VI), \alpha) \cdot \uparrow\alpha$$

○ Cf. equation 3.8.5.2.

$E \rightarrow \mathbf{self}$ (19.2)

$$[\![E]\!] = \sum_{\alpha \in Obj} eqs(\alpha) \cdot \uparrow\alpha$$

○ Cf. equation 3.8.3.5.

$E \rightarrow CO$ (19.3)

$$[\![E]\!] = [\![CO]\!]$$

$E \rightarrow \mathbf{new}$ (19.4)

Let

$$cdf(E)(class(E)) = X$$

then

$$[\![E]\!] = \sum_{\alpha \in AObj} create(X, \alpha) \cdot \uparrow\alpha$$

○ Process creation takes place in an environment (cf. equation 3.8.5.3) that takes care of the naming of new objects, and always allows only one of the actions $create(X, \alpha)$ to occur.

$E \rightarrow SN$ (19.5)

$$[\![E]\!] = [\![SN]\!]$$

$E \rightarrow MC$ (19.6)

$$[\![E]\!] = [\![MC]\!]$$

$E \rightarrow RC$ (19.7)

$$[\![E]\!] = [\![RC]\!]$$

$E \rightarrow \mathbf{nil}$ (19.8)

$$[\![E]\!] = \uparrow\mathbf{nil}$$

$MIL_0 \rightarrow MI\,[\,,MIL_1\,]$ (18)

Let

$$id(MI) = m$$

$$mdf\,(MIL_0)(class\,(MIL_0),m) = (X\ n)$$

then

$$mis\,(MIL_0) = \{m\}\,[\,\cup mis\,(MIL_1)\,]$$

$$[\![MIL_0]\!]_m = \sum_{\alpha_1,\ \ldots,\alpha_n,\alpha \in Obj} rd(mc,m(\alpha_1,\ \ldots,\alpha_n),\alpha)\cdot \rho_{g_\alpha}(X_{\alpha_1,\ \ldots,\alpha_n})$$

$$[\![MIL_0]\!]_{\overline{m}} = \frac{[\![MIL_1]\!]_{\overline{m}}}{\delta} \quad \text{if } \overline{m} \neq m$$

○ For the m which occur in the method identifier list, $[\![MIL_0]\!]_m$ gives the process that describes the answering of a message m: first a method call with identifier m is read, then the method is executed, and the result is returned to the sender (cf. equation 3.8.3.6). For m not in MIL_0, $[\![MIL_0]\!]_m = \delta$.

$AN \rightarrow \mathbf{answer}\,(\,MIL\,)$ (17)

$$mis\,(AN) = mis\,(MIL)$$

$$[\![AN]\!]_m = [\![MIL]\!]_m$$

$$[\![AN]\!] = \sum_{m \in LId} [\![MIL]\!]_m$$

○ The variables $[\![AN]\!]_m$ will be needed for the description of the select statement.

The semantic rules for the nonterminals MIL, AN, GC, GCL and SE are rather complicated. This is because the semantics of the select statement is to a large extent not compositional: it is not defined in terms of the semantics of the answer statements which occur in the guarded commands, but in terms of the individual method identifiers of these answer statements. The formalism of attribute grammars has difficulties in dealing with such a case.

$GC \rightarrow E$ **then** SS (16.1)

$$mis\,(GC) = \varnothing$$

$$[\![GC]\!] = [\![E]\!]$$

$$[\![GC]\!]_\epsilon = skip \cdot [\![SS]\!]$$

○ The prefix *skip* in the equation for variable $[\![GC]\!]_\epsilon$ is needed because we want to give a different semantics to the following two select statements:

sel

  true answer(m_1) **then** $x \leftarrow 1$ **or**

  true answer(m_2) **then** $x \leftarrow 2$

les

and

sel

  true answer(m_1) **then** $x \leftarrow 1$ **or**

  true then answer(m_2) ; $x \leftarrow 2$

les

If the environment offers a method call with method identifier m_1, but no method call with method identifier m_2, then the first select statement will answer m_1. The second select statement however may choose to execute the second guarded command, which will result in a deadlock.

$GC \rightarrow E\ AN$ **then** SS (16.2)

$$mis(GC) = mis(AN)$$

$$[\![GC]\!] = [\![E]\!]$$

$$[\![GC]\!]_m = [\![AN]\!]_m \cdot [\![SS]\!]$$

$GCL \rightarrow GC$ (15.1)

Let

$$mis(GC) = M$$

then

$$misl(GCL) = (M)$$

$$[\![GCL]\!] = [\![GC]\!]$$

$$[\![GCL]\!]_\epsilon^\alpha = \begin{cases} [\![GC]\!]_\epsilon & \text{if } \alpha = \mathbf{true} \wedge M = \varnothing \\ \delta & \text{otherwise} \end{cases}$$

$$[\![GCL]\!]_m^\alpha = \begin{cases} [\![GC]\!]_\epsilon & \text{if } \alpha = \mathbf{true} \wedge M = \varnothing \\ [\![GC]\!]_m & \text{if } \alpha = \mathbf{true} \wedge m \in M \\ \delta & \text{otherwise} \end{cases}$$

○ See remark about production 14.

$GCL_0 \rightarrow GC$ **or** GCL_1 (15.2)

Let

$$mis(GC) = M_0$$

$$misl(GCL_1) = (M_1, ..., M_n)$$

then

$$misl(GCL_0) = (M_0, M_1, ..., M_n)$$

$$[\![GCL_0]\!] = [\![GC]\!] \cdot [\![GCL_1]\!]$$

$$[\![GCL_0]\!]_\epsilon^{\alpha_0, ..., \alpha_n} = \begin{cases} [\![GC]\!]_\epsilon & \text{if } \alpha_0 = \mathbf{true} \wedge M_0 = \varnothing \\ [\![GCL_1]\!]_\epsilon^{\alpha_1, ..., \alpha_n} & \text{otherwise} \end{cases}$$

$$[\![GCL_0]\!]_m^{\alpha_0, ..., \alpha_n} = \begin{cases} [\![GC]\!]_\epsilon & \text{if } \alpha_0 = \mathbf{true} \wedge M_0 = \varnothing \\ [\![GC]\!]_m & \text{if } \alpha_0 = \mathbf{true} \wedge m \in M_0 \\ [\![GCL_1]\!]_m^{\alpha_1, ..., \alpha_n} & \text{otherwise} \end{cases}$$

O See remark about production 14.

$SE \rightarrow$ **sel** GCL **les** (14)

Let

$$misl(GCL) = (M_1, ..., M_n)$$

then

$$[\![SE]\!] = [\![GCL]\!] \ggg_{\alpha_1, ..., \alpha_n} [\![SE]\!]_{\alpha_1, ..., \alpha_n}$$

$$[\![SE]\!]_{\alpha_1, ..., \alpha_n} = error \text{ if } (\exists i : \alpha_i = \mathbf{nil}) \vee (\forall i : \alpha_i = \mathbf{false})$$

$$[\![SE]\!]_{\alpha_1, ..., \alpha_n} = \sum_{m \in LId \cup \{\epsilon\}} [\![GCL]\!]_m^{\alpha_1, ..., \alpha_n} \text{ otherwise}$$

O Execution of a select statement starts with evaluation of the expressions in the guarded commands. If one expression yields **nil** or all expressions yields **false** an error occurs. The intuitive meaning of variable

$$[\![GCL]\!]_\epsilon^{\alpha_1, ..., \alpha_n}$$

is: Execute the first open guarded command without an answer statement, assuming that evaluation of the expressions yields values $\alpha_1, ..., \alpha_n$. If there is no open guarded command without an answer statement the result is δ. Analogously, for $m \in LId$, the intuitive meaning of variable

$$[\![GCL]\!]_m^{\alpha_1, ..., \alpha_n}$$

is: Execute the first open guarded command without an answer statement or with m in the method identifier list of the answer statement.

$S \rightarrow VI \leftarrow E$ (13.1)

$$[\![S]\!] = [\![E]\!] \ggg_\alpha ass(id(VI), \alpha)$$

O Cf. equation 3.8.5.1.

$S \rightarrow AN$ (13.2)

$$[\![S]\!] = [\![AN]\!]$$

$S \rightarrow$ **if** E **then** SS_1 [**else** SS_2] **fi** (13.3)

$$[\![S]\!] = [\![E]\!] \ggg_\alpha [\![S]\!]_\alpha$$

$$[\![S]\!]_\alpha = \begin{cases} [\![SS_1]\!] & \text{if } \alpha = \mathbf{true} \\ \dfrac{[\![SS_2]\!]}{skip} & \text{if } \alpha = \mathbf{false} \\ error & \text{otherwise} \end{cases}$$

$S \rightarrow$ **do** E **then** SS **od** (13.4)

$$[\![S]\!] = [\![E]\!] \ggg_\alpha [\![S]\!]_\alpha$$

$$[\![S]\!]_\alpha = \begin{cases} [\![SS]\!] \cdot [\![S]\!] & \text{if } \alpha = \mathbf{true} \\ skip & \text{if } \alpha = \mathbf{false} \\ error & \text{otherwise} \end{cases}$$

$S \rightarrow SE$ (13.5)

$$[\![S]\!] = [\![SE]\!]$$

$S \rightarrow SN$ (13.6)

$$[\![S]\!] = [\![SN]\!] \ggg (\sum_{\alpha \in Obj} \downarrow\alpha)$$

○ The send expression is evaluated and afterwards the result is discarded.

$S \rightarrow MC$ (13.7)

$$[\![S]\!] = [\![MC]\!] \ggg (\sum_{\alpha \in Obj} \downarrow\alpha)$$

$S \rightarrow RC$ (13.8)

$$[\![S]\!] = [\![RC]\!] \ggg (\sum_{\alpha \in Obj} \downarrow\alpha)$$

$SS_0 \rightarrow S\,[\,;SS_1\,]$ (12)

$$[\![SS_0]\!] = [\![S]\!][\cdot[\![SS_1]\!]]$$

$VD \rightarrow VI : CI$ (11)

$$id(VD) = id(VI)$$

$VDL_0 \rightarrow VD\ [\ ,\ VDL_1\ ]$ (10)

$$vd(VDL_0) = (id(VD))[\star vd(VDL_1)]$$

○ The function $\star$ denotes concatenation of lists.

$PD \rightarrow ([\ VDL_1\ ])\ CI : [\ \textbf{local}\ VDL_2\ \textbf{in}\ ]\ [\ SS_1\ ]\ \textbf{return}\ E\ [\ \textbf{post}\ SS_2\ ]$ (9)

Let

$$vd(VDL_1) = (v_1, ..., v_n)$$

$$vd(VDL_2) = (w_1, ..., w_k)$$

($n = 0$ or $k = 0$ if there is no VDL_1 resp. VDL_2)
then

$$pd(PD) = ([\![PD]\!]\ n)$$

$$[\![PD]\!]_{\alpha_1, ..., \alpha_n} = \lambda_{\alpha_1}^{v_1} \circ \cdots \circ \lambda_{\alpha_n}^{v_n} \circ \lambda_{\mathbf{nil}}^{w_1} \circ \cdots \circ \lambda_{\mathbf{nil}}^{w_k}([\,[\![SS_1]\!]\cdot\,][\![E]\!][\,\cdot[\![SS_2]\!]\,])$$

○ Process $[\![PD]\!]_{\alpha_1, ..., \alpha_n}$ corresponds to execution of the procedure with parameters $\alpha_1, ..., \alpha_n$.

$RD \rightarrow \textbf{routine}\ RI_1\ PD\ \textbf{end}\ RI_2$ (8)

$$id(RD) = id(RI_1)$$

$$pd(RD) = pd(PD)$$

$RDL_0 \rightarrow RD\ [\ RDL_1\ ]$ (7)

$$rd(RDL_0) = \frac{rd(RDL_1)}{rd_0}\{pd(RD)/\,id(RD)\}$$

○ We use the notation for function modification of Section 2.4. rd_0 is an arbitrarily chosen element out of the domain of attribute rd. We use similar conventions in the semantic rules for productions 5, 4 and 3.

$MD \rightarrow \textbf{method}\ MI_1\ PD\ \textbf{end}\ MI_2$ (6)

$$id(MD) = id(MI_1)$$

$$pd(MD) = pd(PD)$$

$MDL_0 \rightarrow MD\ [\ MDL_1\ ]$ (5)

$$md(MDL_0) = \frac{md(MDL_1)}{md_0}\{pd(MD)/\,id(MD)\}$$

$CD \rightarrow \textbf{class}\ CI_1\ [\ \textbf{var}\ VDL\ ]\ [\ RDL\ ]\ [\ MDL\ ]\ \textbf{body}\ SS\ \textbf{end}\ CI_2$ (4)

Let

$$vd(VDL) = (v_1, ..., v_n)$$

then

$$id(CD) = id(CI_1)$$

$$md(CD) = \frac{md(MDL)}{md_0}$$

$$rd(CD) = \frac{rd(RDL)}{rd_0}$$

$$[\![CD]\!] = \lambda_{\mathbf{nil}}^{v_1} \circ \cdots \circ \lambda_{\mathbf{nil}}^{v_n}([\![SS]\!])$$

$CDL_0 \rightarrow CD\,[\,,CDL_1\,]$ (3)

$$cd(CDL_0) = \frac{cd(CDL_1)}{cd_0}\{[\![CD]\!]/id(CD)\}$$

$$mdc(CDL_0) = \frac{mdc(CDL_1)}{mdc_0}\{md(CD)/id(CD)\}$$

$$rdc(CDL_0) = \frac{rdc(CDL_1)}{rdc_0}\{rd(CD)/id(CD)\}$$

$$[\![CDL_0]\!] = \frac{[\![CDL_1]\!]}{[\![CD]\!]}$$

○ Process $[\![CDL_0]\!]$ gives the behaviour of the last class defined in CDL_0.

$RU \rightarrow$ **root unit** CDL (2)

Let

$$cd(CDL)(Integer) = I$$

$$cd(CDL)(Boolean) = B$$

$$cd(CDL)(Read\_File) = R$$

$$cd(CDL)(Write\_File) = W$$

$$\mathcal{C} = \{cd(CDL)(C) \mid C \in UId\}$$

$$ACTIVE = \mathop{\|}_{\alpha \in AObj} \Big(\sum_{X \in \mathcal{C}} create^*(X, \alpha) \cdot \rho_{f_\alpha}(X)\Big)$$

$$STANDARD = \Big(\mathop{\|}_{\alpha \in Int} \rho_{f_\alpha}(I)\Big) \| \rho_{f_{\mathbf{true}}}(B) \| \rho_{f_{\mathbf{false}}}(B) \| \rho_{f_{\mathbf{input}}}(R) \| \rho_{f_{\mathbf{output}}}(W)$$

then

$$[\![RU]\!] = \lambda_0^{counter} \circ \partial_J \circ \partial_K(create([\![CDL]\!], \hat{0}) \| ACTIVE \| STANDARD)$$

○ The environment in which a POOL-⊥ unit is to be executed consists of encapsulation operators ∂_J and ∂_K (cf. equations 3.8.2.6 and 3.8.4.2), and the object *counter* (cf. equation 3.8.5.3). In the scope of these operators we have the 'sleeping' active objects and the standard objects (except for **nil**, which is in our semantics a kind of virtual object). Now execution of a POOL-⊥ unit starts with an action that orders for the creation of an instance of the last class defined in the unit.

3.9.3. Standard classes. In POOL-T there are a number of classes that are predefined. Four of them, the classes *Integer*, *Boolean*, *Read_File* and *Write_File*, are, although in simplified form, also present in POOL-⊥. The standard classes can, to a large extent, be defined in terms of POOL-⊥. To make a complete definition possible, we extend the language POOL-⊥ with a new construct:

$$E \rightarrow \textbf{acp}\ t\ \textbf{pca}$$

for each closed term t in the signature of ACP. The corresponding semantic rule is

$$peq(E) = \{[\![E]\!] = t\}.$$

The standard classes are described by the following class definitions:

3.9.3.1. The Booleans. This is a class with as only objects **true**, **false** and the virtual **nil**. The methods of the class generate an error if a parameter is **nil**. Surprisingly, we can describe this class completely in terms of POOL itself.

class *Boolean*

var *result* : *Boolean*

method *or* (*b* : *Boolean*) *Boolean* :

if self then

if *b* **then** *result*←**true else** *result*←**true fi else**

if *b* **then** *result*←**true else** *result*←**false fi**

fi

return *result*

end *or*

method *and* (*b* : *Boolean*) *Boolean* :

if self then

if *b* **then** *result*←**true else** *result*←**false fi else**

if *b* **then** *result*←**false else** *result*←**false fi**

fi

return *result*

end and

method *not* ( ) *Boolean* :

if self then *result*←**false else** *result*←**true fi**

return *result*

end *not*

method *equal* (*b* : *Boolean*) *Boolean* :

if self then

if *b* **then** *result*←**true else** *result*←**false fi else**

if *b* **then** *result*←**false else** *result*←**true fi**

fi

return *result*

end *equal*

body do true then answer (*or,and,not,equal*) **od**

end *Boolean*

3.9.3.2. The Integers. This class contains all the integers from *Int* (plus **nil**). The methods of the class generate an error if the parameter is **nil.** In case of overflow the result of a method call is **nil** (so, for example $sum(N_0,N_0)$ = **nil**). Another option would have been to generate an error. We only give the definition of the method *add.* The other method definitions are similar.

class *Integer*

method *add* (*i* : *Integer*) *Integer* :

$$\textbf{return acp} \sum_{\alpha\in Int} eqs(\alpha)\Big(\sum_{\beta\in Int} eqv(i,\beta)\cdot\uparrow sum(\alpha,\beta) + eqv(i,\textbf{nil})\cdot error\Big) \textbf{ pca}$$

end *add*

etc., etc.

body do true then answer(*add, sub, mul, div, mod, power, minus,*

less, less_or_equal, equal, greater, greater_or_equal) **od**

end *Integer*

3.9.3.3. The classes Read_File and Write_File. In POOL-T it is possible to open new input and output files. These options are not present in POOL-⊥: there is only one object of class *Read_File* (the object **input**), and one object of class *Write_File* (the object **output**). These objects communicate with the external world by means of actions *input* (*d*) and *output* (*d*), for $d \in Int \cup Bool$.

class *Read_File*

routine *standard_in* ( ) *Read_File* :

return acp ↑**input pca**

end *standard_in*

method *read_int* ( ) *Integer* :

$$\textbf{return acp} \sum_{\alpha\in Int} input(\alpha)\cdot\uparrow\alpha \textbf{ pca}$$

end *read_int*

method *read_bool* ( ) *Boolean* :

$$\textbf{return acp} \sum_{\beta \in Bool} input(\beta) \cdot \uparrow\beta \ \textbf{pca}$$

end *read_bool*

body do true then answer(*read_int*, *read_bool*) **od**

end *Read_File*

class *Write_File*

routine *standard_out* ( ) *Write_File* :

$$\textbf{return acp} \uparrow \textbf{output pca}$$

end *standard_out*

method *write_int* (*i* : *Integer*) *Write_File* :

$$\textbf{return acp} \sum_{\alpha \in Int} eqv(i, \alpha) \cdot output(\alpha) \cdot \uparrow\textbf{output} + eqv(i, \textbf{nil}) \cdot error \ \textbf{pca}$$

end *write_int*

method *write_bool* (*b* : *Boolean*) *Write_File* :

$$\textbf{return acp} \sum_{\beta \in Bool} eqv(b, \beta) \cdot output(\beta) \cdot \uparrow\textbf{output} + eqv(b, \textbf{nil}) \cdot error \ \textbf{pca}$$

end *write_bool*

body do true then answer(*write_int*, *write_bool*) **od**

end *Write_File*

3.10. THEOREM. *For each program* $w \in$ POOL-$\perp$ *the specification* $SPEC_C(w)$ *is guarded.*

PROOF. Introduce a new *s*-attribute *height* for those nonterminals which have attribute *peq*. Let the value domain of this new attribute be the set $\mathbb{N}$ of natural numbers. Let $X_0 \rightarrow X_1 \cdots X_n$ be a production where X_0 has attribute *height*. Then the semantic rule for the attribute *height* is:

$$height(X_0) = \max(\{0\} \cup \{height(X_i) \mid 1 \leq i \leq n \text{ and } X_i \text{ has attribute } height\}) + 1$$

Using the same technique as in the proof of Theorem 2.9, the proof that for each POOL-$\perp$ program the corresponding specification is guarded can now be given by means of straightforward induction on the value of attribute *height*. □

3.11. Abstraction. Most of the atomic actions which were used in the description of the semantics for POOL will be invisible in an actual implementation of the language. If one looks at a computer executing a POOL program, one most likely cannot observe that one object sends a message to another object. In general the only visible actions will be the actions by means of which the POOL system communicates with the external world: the *error* action and the actions $input(d)$ and $output(d)$ $(d \in Int \cup Bool)$ as defined in Section 3.9.3.3. Therefore we define:

$$I = \{c(d) \mid d \in D\} \cup \{comm(f) \mid f \in \mathcal{F}\} \cup \{skip\} \tag{3.11.1}$$

and introduce a new formal variable *ROOT*, which will be the root variable of the specification corresponding to a given POOL-$\perp$ unit. The equation for *ROOT* is:

$$ROOT = \tau_I([\![RU]\!]). \tag{3.11.2}$$

ROOT gives the abstract behaviour of a POOL system executing a given unit. We call the corresponding function from POOL units to process algebra expressions $SPEC_A$.

3.12. Models. A lot of semantics (models, Σ-algebras) have been given of the signature that is used in this section. In this article we are only interested in models where the principles RDP and RSP are valid. For each of these models M, there exists a mapping INT_M that relates to every guarded specification E the unique solution of this system in the model. As examples of models we mention the semantics $\mathcal{Q}(BS)$ of terms modulo bisimulation equivalence presented in [16], the semantics $\mathcal{Q}(FS)$ of process graphs modulo failure equivalence described in [11], and the trace model that is presented in [28].

4. Message queues

In the description of POOL as presented in the previous section, communication between objects takes place by means of handshaking. However, in the official language definition (see [1]) communication is described differently: All messages sent to a certain object will be stored there in a queue in the order in which they arrive. When that object executes an answer statement, the first message in the queue whose name occurs in the method identifier list of the answer statement will be answered. Below we present a modified process algebra description of POOL, in which each object has its own message queue. This description, which, due to the select statement, turns out to be rather complicated, corresponds to the language definition in [1]. We call the new translation function $SPEC_{AQ}$. Thereafter, in Section 4.5, we discuss the important question for which models M the mappings $INT_M \circ SPEC_A$ and $INT_M \circ SPEC_{AQ}$ are identical.

4.1. New channels. If we view the field 'type of message' of a frame (cf. Section 3.8.2) as the name of a channel, then we can depict the situation in which there are two objects α and β, connected by channel *mc*, 'classically' as follows:

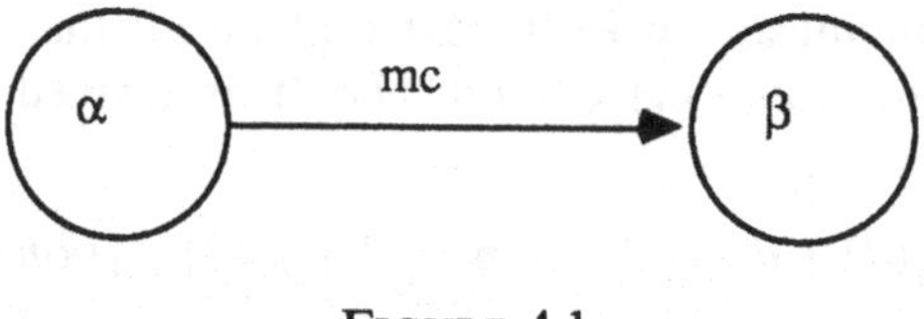

FIGURE 4.1

In this section we introduce for each object β a message queue $\rho_{f_\beta}(Q)$. Furthermore we have new channels (message types) *iq*, *om* and *fm*. The new version of Figure 4.1 becomes:

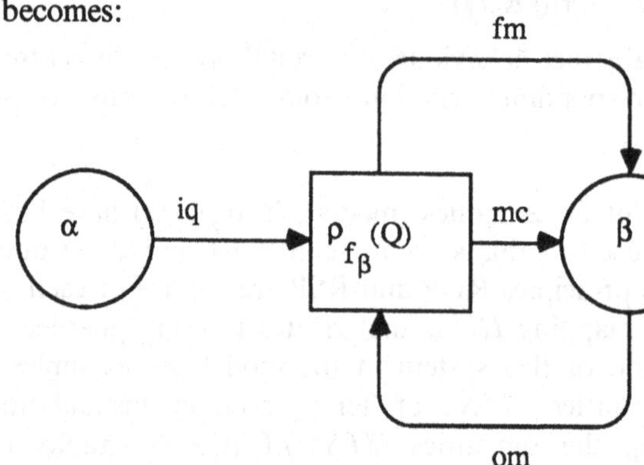

FIGURE 4.2

First we discuss the new message types.

iq: (in queue). If object α wants to send a message to object β, it must send this message by channel *iq* to the queue of object β. We have the following new semantic rules for the send expression:

$SN \rightarrow E\,!\,MI(\,)$ (21.1)

Let

$$id(MI) = m$$

then

$$[\![SN]\!] = [\![E]\!] \ggg_\alpha [\![SN]\!]_\alpha$$

$$[\![SN]\!]_\alpha = \begin{cases} error & \text{if } \alpha = \mathbf{nil} \\ sn(\alpha, iq, m(\,)) \cdot \sum_{\beta \in Obj} rd(an, \beta, \alpha) \cdot \uparrow\beta & \text{otherwise} \end{cases}$$

(production 21.2 is changed analogously).

om: (order message). Let $L \subseteq LId$. By sending message L along channel *om* to its queue, object β orders the queue to deliver the first message with a message identifier in L. The message type *om* occurs in the new semantic rules for the answer statement:

$AN \rightarrow$ **answer** (MIL) (17)

Let

$$M = mis(MIL)$$

then

$$mis(AN) = M$$

$$[\![AN]\!]_m = sn(om, \{m\}) \cdot [\![MIL]\!]_m$$

$$[\![AN]\!] = sn(om, M) \cdot \sum_{m \in M} [\![MIL]\!]_m$$

fm: (first method). During the execution of a select statement object β sometimes needs to know, for given $L \subseteq LId$, if there is a message in its queue with a method identifier in L, and if so, what is the method identifier of the first one. This information is passed along channel *fm* (the negative answer is coded as ϵ). The new semantic rules for the select statement are:

$SE \rightarrow$ **sel** GCL **les** (14)

Let

$$misl(GCL) = (M_1, ..., M_n)$$

$$M_{\alpha_1, ..., \alpha_n} = \bigcup_{\{i \mid \alpha_i = \textbf{true}\}} M_i$$

then

$$[\![SE]\!] = [\![GCL]\!] \gg_{\alpha_1, ..., \alpha_n} [\![SE]\!]_{\alpha_1, ..., \alpha_n}$$

$$[\![SE]\!]_{\alpha_1, ..., \alpha_n} = error$$

if $(\exists i : \alpha_i = \textbf{nil}) \vee (\forall i : \alpha_i = \textbf{false})$,

$$[\![SE]\!]_{\alpha_1, ..., \alpha_n} = \sum_{m \in LId} rd(fm, (M_{\alpha_1, ..., \alpha_n}, m)) \cdot [\![GCL]\!]_m^{\alpha_1, ..., \alpha_n}$$

if $\forall i : \alpha_i = \textbf{true} \Rightarrow M_i \neq \varnothing$, and

$$[\![SE]\!]_{\alpha_1, ..., \alpha_n} = \sum_{m \in LId \cup \{\epsilon\}} rd(fm, (M_{\alpha_1, ..., \alpha_n}, m)) \cdot [\![GCL]\!]_m^{\alpha_1, ..., \alpha_n}$$

otherwise.

O $M_{\alpha_1, ..., \alpha_n}$ is the set of all method identifiers occurring in the answer statement of an open guarded command. If there is no message in the queue whose method identifier is in $M_{\alpha_1, \ldots, \alpha_n}$, and there are open guarded commands without an answer statement ($M_i = \emptyset$ for some i), then the (textually) first of them is selected. If there is no message in the queue whose method identifier is in $M_{\alpha_1, \ldots, \alpha_n}$, and there is no open guarded command without an answer statement, the object waits until a message that belongs to $M_{\alpha_1, \ldots, \alpha_n}$ arrives, and then proceeds with this message. This waiting may last forever. If there is a message in the queue with method identifier in $M_{\alpha_1, \ldots, \alpha_n}$ this message is selected. The first guarded command is chosen that has either no answer statement or whose answer statement contains the method named in the message.

4.2. The process Q. We introduce a new object q as parameter of the state operator. The state of this object (the content of the queue) will be an element of $(\mathfrak{M} \times Obj)^*$ (for definition $\mathfrak{M}$, see equation 3.8.2.3): a list of pairs of method calls and references to the senders of these calls. We need four fresh formal variables Q, R, S and A. The process Q gives the behaviour of an 'unfinished' queue, a queue that is not yet associated with one specific object. We have the following equation:

$$Q = \lambda_\epsilon^q(R \| S \| A). \tag{4.2.1}$$

Q consists of the merge of three processes, R, S and A, which operate in an environment in which the content of the queue is known. The job of process R is to read messages in the queue:

$$R = \sum_{d \in \mathfrak{M}} \sum_{\alpha \in Obj} rd(iq, d, \alpha) \cdot R. \tag{4.2.2}$$

The relevant equation for the state operator is:

$$\lambda_\sigma^q(rd(iq, d, \alpha) \cdot x) = rd(iq, d, \alpha) \cdot \lambda^q_{(d,\alpha)*\sigma}(x). \tag{4.2.3}$$

The process S first waits for an order to deliver a message with method identifier in a certain set L, and thereafter delivers the first message in the queue with this property. When such a message is not in the queue, process S waits until it arrives.

$$S = \sum_{L \subseteq LId} rd(om, L) \cdot sn(mc, L) \cdot S. \tag{4.2.4}$$

In order to define the interaction between actions $sn(mc, L)$ and operator λ_σ^q we need three auxiliary functions. The function $mf(L, \sigma)$ picks the first message in σ with a method identifier in L, and returns ϵ if there is no such message. The function is recursively defined by:

$$mf(L, \epsilon) = \epsilon \tag{4.2.5}$$

$$mf(L, \sigma * (m(\alpha_1, \ldots, \alpha_n), \alpha)) = \begin{cases} m(\alpha_1, \ldots, \alpha_n) & \text{if } m \in L \\ mf(L, \sigma) & \text{otherwise} \end{cases} \tag{4.2.6}$$

The function $sf(L, \sigma)$ returns the sender of the first message in σ with method identifier in L, or returns ϵ.

$$sf(L,\epsilon) = \epsilon \tag{4.2.6}$$

$$sf(L,\sigma\star(m(\alpha_1, ..., \alpha_n),\alpha)) = \begin{cases} \alpha & \text{if } m \in L \\ sf(L,\sigma) & \text{otherwise} \end{cases} \tag{4.2.7}$$

The function $of(L,\sigma)$ omits the first element of σ with method identifier in L.

$$of(L,\epsilon) = \epsilon \tag{4.2.8}$$

$$of(L,\sigma\star(m(\alpha_1, ..., \alpha_n),\alpha)) = \begin{cases} \sigma & \text{if } m \in L \\ of(L,\sigma)\star(m(\alpha_1, ..., \alpha_n),\alpha) & \text{otherwise} \end{cases} \tag{4.2.9}$$

Now we can define:

$$\lambda_\sigma(sn(mc,L)\cdot x) = \begin{cases} sn(mc,mf(L,\sigma),sf(L,\sigma))\cdot\lambda^q_{of(L,\sigma)}(x) & \text{if } mf(L,\sigma)\neq\epsilon \\ \delta & \text{otherwise} \end{cases} \tag{4.2.10}$$

The process A gives an answer to questions of the form: 'Is there a message in the queue with method identifier in a set L, and if so, what is the method identifier of the first one?'.

$$A = \sum_{L\subseteq LId} \sum_{m\in LId\cup\{\epsilon\}} sn(fm,(L,m))\cdot A. \tag{4.2.11}$$

Again we need an auxiliary function: $if(L,\sigma)$ gives the identifier of the first message in σ with identifier in L.

$$if(L,\epsilon) = \epsilon \tag{4.2.12}$$

$$if(L,\sigma\star(m(\alpha_1, ..., \alpha_n),\alpha)) = \begin{cases} m & \text{if } m \in L \\ if(L,\sigma) & \text{otherwise} \end{cases} \tag{4.2.13}$$

The relevant equation for the state operator is:

$$\lambda^q_\delta(sn(fm,(L,m))\cdot x) = \begin{cases} sn(fm,(L,m))\cdot\lambda^q_\delta(x) & \text{if } if(L,\sigma) = m \\ \delta & \text{otherwise} \end{cases} \tag{4.2.14}$$

4.3. Extensions. We add the new frames which were introduced in the previous section to the set $\mathcal{F}$ of frames (see equation 3.8.2.4), we introduce actions $rd(f)$, $sn(f)$, $read(f)$, $send(f)$ and $comm(f)$ for the new frames, and extend the communication function in the obvious way. Furthermore the set J of encapsulated actions (see equation 3.8.2.4) is extended. For the new atoms the renaming functions f_α are defined by:

$$f_\alpha(sn(\beta,iq,d)) = send(\beta,iq,d,\alpha) \tag{4.3.1}$$

$$f_\alpha(rd(iq,d,\beta)) = read(\alpha,iq,d,\beta) \tag{4.3.2}$$

$$f_\alpha(sn(om,M)) = send(\alpha,om,M,\alpha) \tag{4.3.3}$$

$$f_\alpha(rd(om,M)) = read(\alpha,om,M,\alpha) \tag{4.3.4}$$

$$f_\alpha(sn(fm, (M,m))) = send(\alpha, fm, (M,m), \alpha) \tag{4.3.5}$$

$$f_\alpha(rd(fm, (M,m))) = read(\alpha, fm, (M,m), \alpha) \tag{4.3.6}$$

4.4. Root unit. Now we change the semantic rule for the root unit as follows:

RU→**root unit** *CDL* (2)

Let

$$cd(CDL)(Integer) = I$$

$$cd(CDL)(Boolean) = B$$

$$cd(CDL)(Read\_File) = R$$

$$cd(CDL)(Write\_File) = W$$

$$\mathcal{C} = \{cd(CDL)(C) \mid C \in UId\}$$

$$ACTIVE = \mathop{\|}_{\alpha \in AObj} \Big(\sum_{X \in \mathcal{C}} create^*(X, \alpha) \cdot \rho_{f_\alpha}(X) \Big)$$

$$STANDARD = \Big(\mathop{\|}_{\alpha \in Int} \rho_{f_\alpha}(I) \Big) \| \rho_{f_{true}}(B) \| \rho_{f_{false}}(B) \| \rho_{f_{input}}(R) \| \rho_{f_{output}}(W)$$

$$QUEUE = \mathop{\|}_{\alpha \in Obj} (\rho_{f_\alpha}(Q))$$

then

$$[\![RU]\!] = \lambda_0^{counter} \circ \partial_J \circ \partial_K (create([\![CDL]\!], \hat{0}) \| ACTIVE \| STANDARD \| QUEUE)$$

4.5. The incompatibility of $SPEC_A$ and $SPEC_{AQ}$. Clearly the mapping $SPEC_{AQ}$ is much more complicated than the mapping $SPEC_A$. Therefore we would like to work with $SPEC_A$ instead of $SPEC_{AQ}$. But since $SPEC_{AQ}$ corresponds to the official language definition in [1] and $SPEC_A$ does not, we first have to show that the two mappings lead to the same semantics of POOL. Unfortunately this is not possible: for any model M of ACP_τ which preserves fairness and liveness properties we have

$$INT_M \circ SPEC_A \neq INT_M \circ SPEC_{AQ}.$$

Stated informally, the fairness we require of the models is that (1) all processes that become permanently enabled, must execute infinitely often, and (2) two processes that can communicate infinitely often will do so infinitely often. These fairness requirements correspond to the fairness requirements formulated in [1]. The issue of fairness is discussed in more detail in Section 5.4.

The notions of safety and liveness are frequently used in the literature. Roughly, safety means that something bad cannot happen, while liveness means that something good will eventually happen. In the context of POOL, liveness implies that a program that will certainly perform a certain action is different from a program which may not do this.

Now consider the situation in which an object executes the following piece of POOL text:

$b \leftarrow$**true** ;

do b **then sel**

true answer(m_1) **then** $b \leftarrow$**false or**

true then $b \leftarrow b$ **or**

true answer(m_2) **then** $b \leftarrow$**false or**

les od ;

Write_File . standard_out( ) ! *write_bool*(b)

Suppose the object operates in a system with message queues, and that at the moment at which the object starts execution of the POOL text, the message queue of the object contains two messages: first a message with method identifier m_2, and after that a message with method identifier m_1. Now execution of the POOL text takes place as follows: first b is set to **true**, then the object enters the do-loop and the select statement is executed. The set of method identifiers occurring in an open guarded command is $\{m_1, m_2\}$. The first message in the queue with a method identifier in this set is m_2. Now the first guarded command is chosen that has either no answer statement or whose answer statement contains m_2. In our case this is the second guarded command. The trivial statement part of this guarded command is executed, and the select statement terminates. But since variable b is still equal to **true**, the select statement is immediately executed for the second time. Again b remains **true**. It will be clear that the select statement never terminates.

However, if the object operates in a system without message queues, the select statement *will* terminate! In the situation with handshaking communication there is one object that wants to send a message with identifier m_1, and one object that wants to send a message with identifier m_2. Due to the fairness requirement communication of the message with identifier m_1 will eventually take place, b is set to **false**, the do-loop terminates, and **false** is printed. This means that there is a difference with respect to liveness between the situation with, and the situation without message queues.

A good semantics of POOL should preserve fairness and liveness properties. The example presented above shows that in a semantical description employing handshaking communication between the objects instead of communication by means of message queues, liveness properties get lost almost inevitably.

4.6. In this section we propose a minor change in the language definition of POOL, which removes the difficulty of Section 4.5. In the example of Section 4.5 it is clear from the beginning that the third guarded command will never be chosen. But instead of leaving the turmoil of battle, the third guarded command starts helping his neighbour, the second guarded command. Because of this the competition between the first and the second guarded command is not fair and the second guarded command always wins. The modification of the language definition we propose consists of the removal of all open guarded commands in a select statement which have an open guarded command without an answer statement before them. Formally this means that we replace the definition of sets $M_{\alpha_1,\ldots,\alpha_n}$ in the semantic rules for the select statement in Section 4.1 by:

$$M_{\alpha_1,\ldots,\alpha_n} = \{m \mid \exists i : m \in M_i \wedge \alpha_i = \mathbf{true} \wedge (\forall j < i : \alpha_j = \mathbf{true} \Rightarrow M_j \neq \emptyset)\}.$$

The modified version of $SPEC_{AQ}$ is called $SPEC_{AQ'}$.

4.7. Even after modification of the language definition, the semantical description with handshaking communication is not equivalent to the description using message queues. The following theorem shows that it is impossible to prove equivalence if one only uses the axioms presented thus far. However, whereas the difficulty of Section 4.5 was a *general* difficulty, present in all semantical descriptions employing handshaking communication between the objects, the difficulty pointed out in the following theorem is *specific*, and only present in bisimulation semantics and other semantics which distinguish processes that cannot be distinguished by observation.

4.7.1. THEOREM. $INT_{@(BS)} \circ SPEC_A \neq INT_{@(BS)} \circ SPEC_{AQ'}$.

PROOF. Below we present a POOL-⊥ unit u with the property that in the term model modulo bisimulation the unique solutions of specifications $SPEC_A(u)$ and $SPEC_{AQ'}(u)$ are different. The program is a very simple one: the initial object of class *Root* creates 3 objects of class *Number* and these three objects ask the standard output object to print resp. numbers 1, 2 and 3.

root unit

class *Number*

var *m* : *Integer*

routine *new* ( ) *Number* :

  return new

end *new*

method *init* (*n* : *Integer*) *Number* :

  m←*n* **return self**

end *init*

body *answer*(*init*); *Write_File* . *standard_out* ( ) ! *write_int*(*m*)

end *Number*,

class *Root*

body *Number . new*( ) ! *init*(1) ; *Number . new*( ) ! *init*(2) ; *Number . new*( ) ! *init*(3)

end *Root*

Writing down $SPEC_A(u)$ and $SPEC_{AQ'}(u)$ is a long and tedious job which we happily leave to the reader. However, it is easy to see that the process graphs that correspond to these specifications can not be bisimilar. If there is a message queue before the standard output object, it is possible that at a certain moment during execution of the program the three method calls of the three objects of class *Number* are waiting in the queue. Because, for given method, an object answers the methods calls in the queue in the order in which they have arrived, the order in which the actions *output*(1), *output*(2) and *output*(3) will be performed, is completely determined in such a state. However, in the case where there are no message queues there is no state in which no output action has taken place but still the order in which the output actions will occur is known. Therefore the process graphs corresponding to $SPEC_A$ and $SPEC_{AQ'}$ are not bisimilar. □

What we learn from Theorem 4.7.1 is that we can either do bisimulation semantics based on a translation of units in which we use queues (this leads to very long and complicated proofs), or add some axioms to our theory in such a way that we can prove equivalence of $SPEC_A$ and $SPEC_{AQ'}$. We conjecture that

$$INT_{\mathcal{A}(FS)} \circ SPEC_A = INT_{\mathcal{A}(FS)} \circ SPEC_{AQ'}$$

and that equivalence can be proved if we add to our theory the axioms of failure semantics as presented in [11]. The proof however will be long and complicated, and we do not give it in this article.

5. Trace semantics, fairness and successful termination

5.1. The trace model as presented in [28], is not a good semantic domain for POOL in the sense that it identifies too much and does not describe deadlock behaviour. In $\mathcal{A}(TR_{den})$ we have for example:

$$output(0) = output(0) + \tau \cdot \delta.$$

We do not want to identify these processes because the first one will definitely output a 0, whereas the second one may not.

5.2. It is well-known that it is not possible to give a trace model of ACP in which one looks at the terminating (and infinite) traces, and the trace sets do not have to be prefix closed. In such a model $a(b+c)$ and $ab+ac$ would be identical. This is problematic since $\partial_{\{c\}}(a(b+c)) = ab$ and $\partial_{\{c\}}(ab+ac) = ab + a\delta$ are different.

5.3. However, there exist some interesting semantics of POOL based on trace sets. The basic idea of the approach which is, although in a different setting, followed in [4], is that one first interprets a specification in a domain in which not very many processes are identified (the domain of transition systems, the model $\mathcal{G}(BS)$) and then takes the set of terminating (and infinite) traces of this process. In this approach one typically looks at

$$YIELD \circ INT_{\mathcal{G}(BS)} \circ SPEC_A(u)$$

where *YIELD* is a function that gives the set of terminating (and infinite) traces of elements of $\mathcal{G}(BS)$. The resulting semantic domain is not a model of ACP but for most applications that does not matter. An advantage of the approach is that it allows for simple solutions to a number of problems.

5.4. Fairness. The fairness problem for example can be solved easily. In [1] a fairness condition concerning POOL is formulated by stating that the execution 'speed' of any object is arbitrary but positive. Whenever an object can proceed with its execution without having to wait for a message or a message result, it will eventually do so. A second fairness requirement on the execution of a POOL program is the condition that all messages sent to a certain object will be stored there in one queue in the order in which they arrive. In process algebra we have deliberately chosen to ignore the exact timing of occurrences of events. Fortunately the fairness requirements concerning POOL can be defined without referring to timing aspects. The first fairness requirement is called *weak process fairness* or *justice* in the literature:

All processes that become permanently enabled, must execute infinitely often

The second requirement is called *strong channel fairness:*

Two processes that can communicate infinitely often will do so infinitely often

For reviews of the literature on fairness we refer to [15, 24]. We think that the Petri net model for ACP based on occurrence nets, which is presented in [17], preserves enough information for a description of the fairness requirements of POOL. More research is needed to make this explicit. In the trace set approach the solution is very simple: one omits all the unfair traces and looks at:

$$YIELD_F \circ INT_{\mathcal{G}(BS)} \circ SPEC_C(u)$$

where $YIELD_F$ gives the set of fair terminating and infinite traces of elements of $\mathcal{G}(BS)$.

5.4.1. Fair abstraction. If we work with 'abstract' translation functions like $SPEC_A$ and $SPEC_{AQ}$, then it is possible to give a 'more or less' fair semantics of POOL without using a $YIELD_F$ function. This employs the fact that Koomen's Fair Abstraction Rule (KFAR) is valid in (for example) the model $\mathcal{G}(BS)$. Consider the following unit *f*:

root unit

class *Out*

routine *new*( ) *Out* :

return new

end *new*

body *Write_File* . *standard_out* ! *write_int* (0)

end *Out*,

class *Chatter*

var *x* : *Integer*

body *Out* . *new*( ) ; **do true then** $x \leftarrow 1$ **od**

end *Chatter*

It can be proved that in any model *M* in which KFAR holds:

$$INT_M \circ SPEC_A(f) = \tau \cdot output(0) \cdot \delta.$$

This means that the object of class *Out* will make progress despite the infinite chatter of the object of class *Chatter*. Note that KFAR equates infinite chatter and deadlock.

5.4.2. KFAR is too fair. We give an example which shows that sometimes KFAR is too fair. Consider the architecture of Figure 5.1.

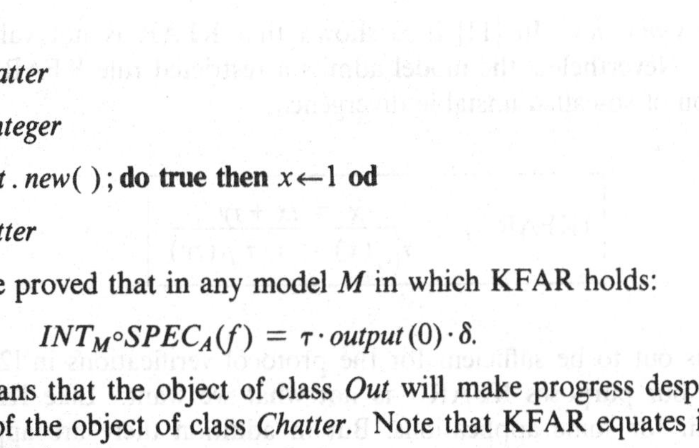

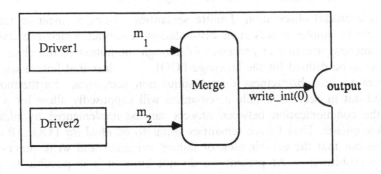

FIGURE 5.1

There are two objects *Driver1* and *Driver2*. The only thing these objects do is sending method calls to an object *Merge*. *Driver1* all the time asks *Merge* to perform method m_1 and analogously *Driver2* asks *Merge* to perform method m_2. The object *Merge* has the task to perform statement **answer**(m_1,m_2) until doomsday. Every time when it has answered method m_1 two times consecutively, the object *Merge* asks the object **output** to print a 0. We leave it to the reader to write down the corresponding POOL program.

The point we want to make is this. According to the language definition in [1], the execution where object *Merge* answers messages of *Driver1* and *Driver2* in turn (m_1, m_2, m_1, m_2,...) will be fair. Hence it is possible that *Merge* never orders to print a 0. However, in a semantics where KFAR holds, a 0 will be printed: the only way for the system to get out of the 'cluster' of internal actions is to perform an action *output*(0). This action is always possible during execution of the program. KFAR says that therefore it will occur. Again we leave it to the reader to fill in the formal details.

5.4.3. Failure semantics. In [11] it is shown that KFAR is not valid in the model $\mathcal{Q}(FS)$. Nevertheless the model admits a restricted rule KFAR$^-$ for the fair abstraction of so-called unstable divergence:

$$(\text{KFAR}^-) \qquad \frac{x = ix + \tau y}{\tau_{\{i\}}(x) = \tau \cdot \tau_{\{i\}}(\tau y)}$$

KFAR$^-$ turns out to be sufficient for the protocol verifications in [22, 25, 27]. However, for our purposes KFAR$^-$ is not what we want. Like KFAR, the rule is too fair for some applications. But in addition there are applications where KFAR$^-$ is not fair enough. KFAR$^-$ does not allow for a proof that the object of class *Out* in the example of Section 5.4.1 will make progress. We even have:

$$\pi_1(INT_{\mathcal{Q}(FS)} \circ SPEC_A(f)) \neq \tau \cdot output(0) \cdot \delta.$$

This is a crucial observation. Failure semantics - being a linear semantics - often yields simpler proofs than bisimulation semantics which preserves the full branching structure of processes. Although the notion of full abstractness still has to be defined for the language POOL, it is clear that failure semantics is closer to full abstractness than bisimulation semantics. Furthermore, as pointed out in Section 4, failure semantics will supposedly allow for a proof that the communication between objects can be implemented by means of message queues. Thus failure semantics seems to be ideal for POOL. But now it turns out that the combination of failure semantics and weak process fairness is problematic. At present we do not know if it is possible to give a semantics of POOL which is 'fully abstract' and also 'fair'.

5.5. Deadlock behaviour. A limit on the applicability of the trace approach sketched in Section 5.3 is that it only describes the behaviour of a POOL system in situations in which this system is placed in a 'glass' box, and does not communicate with the environment. Below we present two POOL-$\perp$ units $u1$ and $u2$ with the property that

$$YIELD \circ INT_{@(BS)} \circ SPEC_A(u1) = YIELD \circ INT_{@(BS)} \circ SPEC_A(u2)$$

although

$$INT_{@(BS)} \circ SPEC_A(u1) \neq INT_{@(BS)} \circ SPEC_A(u2)$$

(we even have

$$INT_{@(FS)} \circ SPEC_A(u1) \neq INT_{@(FS)} \circ SPEC_A(u2) \;).$$

The root object of unit $u1$ creates an object that performs the job of outputting a 0. After ordering for the creation, the root object inputs a value.

root unit

class *Out*

routine *new*( ) *Out* :

return new

end *new*

body *Write_File . standard_out* ! *write_int* (0)

end *Out*,

class *In*

body *Out . new*( ) ; *Read_File . standard_in*( ) ! *read_int*( )

end *In*

In unit $u2$ the root object of class *Semaphore* creates two objects: one object has to output a 0, and the other object inputs a value. But before the I/O actions can take place the objects have to decrease a semaphore. After an object has decreased a semaphore, it can perform the I/O action. After that, it increases the semaphore again. If during execution of $u2$ the input actions are blocked (the enemy has bombed the input device), it can happen (if the object that has to input a value is the first one to decrease the semaphore) that the output action will not take place. In this respect $u2$ differs from $u1$: if during execution of $u1$ the input actions are blocked, the output action will still happen.

root unit

class *Out*

var *sem* : *Semaphore*

routine *new*( ) *Out* :

return new

end *new*

```
method init (s : Semaphore) Out :
        sem←s  return self
end init
body
        answer(init) ;
        sem ! down( ) ;
        Write_File . standard_out( ) ! write_int(0) ;
        sem ! up( )
end Out ,

class In
var sem : Semaphore
routine new( ) In :
        return new
end new
method init (s : Semaphore) In :
        sem←s  return self
end init
body
        answer ;
        sem ! down( ) ;
        Read_File . standard_in( ) ! read_int( ) ;
        sem ! up( )
end In ,

class Semaphore
method down ( ) Semaphore :
        return self
end down
method up ( ) Semaphore :
        return self
```

end *up*

body

Out . *new* ( ) ! *init* (**self**) ;

In . *new* ( ) ! *init* (**self**) ;

do true then answer(*down*) ; **answer** (*up*) **od**

end *Semaphore*

We can prove in the theory that:

(1) The following x_1 is a solution of $SPEC_A(u1)$:

$$x_1 = \tau \cdot (output(0) \| \sum_{\alpha \in Int} input(\alpha)) \cdot \delta$$

(2) The following x_2 is a solution of $SPEC_A(u2)$:

$$x_2 = \tau \cdot (\tau \cdot output(0) \cdot (\sum_{\alpha \in Int} input(\alpha)) + \tau \cdot (\sum_{\alpha \in Int} input(\alpha)) \cdot output(0)) \cdot \delta$$

Let $B = \{input(\alpha) \mid \alpha \in Int\}$ be the set of blocked actions. Then

$$\partial_B(x_1) = \tau \cdot output(0) \cdot \delta$$

$$\partial_B(x_2) = \tau \cdot (\tau \cdot output(0) \cdot \delta + \tau \cdot \delta)$$

Thus units $u1$ and $u2$ behave differently in an environment which does not offer certain actions: in environment ∂_B $u1$ will certainly output a 0, whereas $u2$ may not do this.

5.6. Successful termination. For arbitrary POOL units u_1 and u_2, and for an arbitrary model M we have that:

$$INT_M \circ SPEC_A(u_1) \cdot INT_M \circ SPEC_A(u_2) = INT_M \circ SPEC_A(u_1).$$

This is because the process corresponding to a unit is infinite or ends in a deadlock. If one wants to describe a situation where after execution of a POOL unit, something else can be done, one has to change the semantics. In the trace set approach of the previous section this is simple: one simply defines the operation sequential composition in the obvious way. In the axiomatic approach things are not that easy. We propose (but do not work out) a solution in the spirit of [7]: one defines a program transformation that transforms the original program (in the case of POOL also the definitions of the standard classes have to be transformed). The transformation introduces a number of new program variables and statements in such a way that the resulting program can terminate successfully. In this approach it is possible to differentiate between various ways in which a unit can terminate: one option is that a unit terminates successfully if all active objects have finished execution of their body; another option says that a unit terminates successfully if there is no object (or pair of objects) that can do a step.

6. Integers and booleans

On the conceptual level, each integer and each boolean is represented by a different object. In an implementation of the language it will of course not be possible to point at different processors saying: 'This is object **true**' or 'That processor over there implements object 4370578', etc. On the level of implementation integers and booleans certainly will not be objects. Instead an implementation will contain some special circuits for arithmetical and logical operations. The aim of this section is to make it plausible that, when speaking about integers and booleans, the conceptual and implementation view of the system are not in contradiction with each other (although there is a problem).

6.1. Simple expressions for integer and Boolean objects. The first two equations in a $SPEC_A$ specification have the form (cf. equation 3.11.2 and the semantic rule for production (2) in Section 3.9.2):

$$ROOT = \tau_I([\![RU]\!])$$

$$[\![RU]\!] = \lambda_0^{counter} \circ \partial_J \circ \partial_K(create([\![CDL]\!],\hat{0}) \| ACTIVE \| STANDARD)$$

Here $I = \{c(d) \mid d \in D\} \cup \{comm(f) \mid f \in \mathcal{F}\} \cup \{skip\}$. If we define

$$I' = \{c(d) \mid d \in D\} \cup \{skip\}$$

then we can prove, using the conditional axioms, that this is equivalent to:

$$ROOT = \tau_I([\![RU]\!])$$

$$[\![RU]\!] = \lambda_0^{counter} \circ \partial_J \circ \partial_K(create([\![CDL]\!],\hat{0}) \| ACTIVE \| \tau_{I'}(STANDARD))$$

Applying the conditional axioms again gives that $\tau_{I'}(STANDARD)$ equals

$$(\mathop{\|}_{\alpha \in Int} \tau_{I'} \circ \rho_{f_\alpha}(I)) \| \tau_{I'} \circ \rho_{f_{\mathbf{true}}}(B) \| \tau_{I'} \circ \rho_{f_{\mathbf{false}}}(B) \| \tau_{I'} \circ \rho_{f_{\mathbf{input}}}(R) \| \tau_{I'} \circ \rho_{f_{\mathbf{output}}}(W).$$

The processes corresponding to the objects of class *Integer* and *Boolean* are very simple. For the object **true** we can derive:

$$\tau_{I'} \circ \rho_{f_{\mathbf{true}}}(B) =$$

$$= \tau \cdot (\sum_{\beta \in Bool} \sum_{\alpha \in Obj} read(\mathbf{true}, mc, or(\beta), \alpha) \cdot send(\alpha, an, \mathbf{true}, \mathbf{true}) \cdot \tau_{I'} \circ \rho_{f_{\mathbf{true}}}(B)$$

$$+ \sum_{\alpha \in Obj} read(\mathbf{true}, mc, or(\mathbf{nil}), \alpha) \cdot error \cdot \tau_{I'} \circ \rho_{f_{\mathbf{true}}}(B)$$

$$+ \sum_{\beta \in Obj - Bool - \{\mathbf{nil}\}} \sum_{\alpha \in Obj} read(\mathbf{true}, mc, or(\beta), \alpha) \cdot \delta + \cdots).$$

The dots at the end of the equation stand for similar summands corresponding to the other methods of class *Boolean*. In a correct POOL-⊥ program the parameter of a message with method identifier *or* will always be an element of $Bool \cup \{\mathbf{nil}\}$. Therefore the summand $\Sigma_{\beta \in Obj - Bool - \{\mathbf{nil}\}}(\cdot)$ is redundant in the context in which it is placed, and we can omit it (the corresponding summands of the other methods can of course also be omitted). A formal proof of this obvious fact can be given using the theorems about the notion of 'redundancy in a context' of [28].

After this simplification the process that gives the behaviour of object **true** can be written into the following form:

$$X_{\mathbf{true}} = \tau\cdot(\sum read(\mathbf{true},mc, ...,\beta)\cdot send(\beta,an, ...,\mathbf{true}) + \sum read(\mathbf{true},mc, ...,\beta)\cdot error)\cdot X_{\mathbf{true}}.$$

Using the identity $\tau x\|y=\tau(x\|y)$, we can replace the equation for variable *ROOT* by:

$$ROOT = \tau\cdot\tau_I([\![RU]\!])$$

and omit the initial τ in the equation for $X_{\mathbf{true}}$:

$$X_{\mathbf{true}} = (\sum read(\mathbf{true},mc, ...,\beta)\cdot send(\beta,an, ...,\mathbf{true}) + \sum read(\mathbf{true},mc, ...,\beta)\cdot error)\cdot X_{\mathbf{true}}.$$

We claim that all the processes corresponding to objects of class *Integer* and *Boolean* can be specified analogously. Let for $\alpha\in Int\cup Bool$, $\mathbb{S}_\alpha\subseteq\mathfrak{F}$ be the set of frames that can be sent to object α:

$$\mathbb{S}_\alpha = \{(\alpha,mc,d,\beta) \mid d\in\mathfrak{M},\ \beta\in Obj \text{ and } d \text{ correct for } \alpha\}.$$

Message d is correct for object α if the method identifier of d occurs in the class description of α, the number of parameters is correct, and the parameters are of the right type. For each $\alpha\in Int\cup Bool$ process X_α is defined by:

$$X_\alpha = \sum_{f\in\mathbb{S}_\alpha} read(f)\cdot an_f\cdot X_\alpha.$$

Here an_f is an atomic action, the answer to the method call f. This can be a *send* action or the *error* action. For example:

$$an_{(1,mc,add(1),\hat{1})} = send(\hat{1},an,2,1)$$

$$an_{(1,mc,minus(\mathbf{nil}),\hat{0})} = error$$

Now we define:

$$INT = \mathop{\|}_{\alpha\in Int} X_\alpha$$

$$BOOL = X_{\mathbf{true}}\|X_{\mathbf{false}}$$

$$I/O = \tau_{I'}\circ\rho_{f_{input}}(R)\|\tau_{I'}\circ\rho_{f_{output}}(W)$$

Let $SPEC_{AA}$ be the same function as $SPEC_A$ except for the fact that the term for variable *ROOT* is prefixed with a τ and that in the equation for $[\![RU]\!]$ *STANDARD* is replaced by $INT\|BOOL\|I/O$. We have for all models M:

$$INT_M\circ SPEC_A = INT_M\circ SPEC_{AA}.$$

6.2. Monadic objects. The processes $STANDARD$ and $INT \| BOOL \| I/O$ both consist of the merge of a number of objects. Each object answers all the messages for one integer or boolean, and different objects answer messages for different integers or booleans.

We now introduce processes INT_M and $BOOL_M$. These processes are composed of a huge amount of 'monadic' objects. For each frame there is a monadic object which has nothing else to do but answering that frame. There is for example a monadic object answering the message from object $\hat{0}$ to object 1 in which it asks to perform method *add* with parameter 3:

$$M_{(1,mc,add(3),\hat{0})} = read(1,mc,add(3),\hat{0}) \cdot send(\hat{0},an,4,1) \cdot M_{(1,mc,add(3),\hat{0})}.$$

Let $\mathbb{S}_{INT} = \bigcup_{\alpha \in Int} \mathbb{S}_\alpha$ and $\mathbb{S}_{BOOL} = \mathbb{S}_{\mathbf{true}} \cup \mathbb{S}_{\mathbf{false}}$. We define for $f \in \mathbb{S}_{INT} \cup \mathbb{S}_{BOOL}$ the process M_f by:

$$M_f = read(f) \cdot an_f \cdot M_f.$$

Processes INT_M and $BOOL_M$ are defined by:

$$INT_M = \mathop{\|}_{f \in \mathbb{S}_{INT}} M_f \quad \text{and} \quad BOOL_M = \mathop{\|}_{f \in \mathbb{S}_{BOOL}} M_f.$$

Let $SPEC_{AM}$ be the same as $SPEC_{AA}$ except for the fact that in the equation for $[\![RU]\!]$, $INT \| BOOL$ is replaced by $INT_M \| BOOL_M$.

6.3. The error action. We would like to prove for all models M:

$$INT_M \circ SPEC_{AA} = INT_M \circ SPEC_{AM}.$$

This would be a nice theorem because the same argument used to 'ungroup' the standard objects into monadic objects, can, when reversed, also be used to 'group' the monadic objects into a new configuration (a single object **integer** and a single object **boolean**, or separate objects for the various methods, etc.).

Unfortunately the two semantics are different. The problem, which has to do with the *error* action, is illustrated by the following POOL unit *m*:

root unit

class *One_plus_one*

var *n* : *Integer*

routine *new*( ) *One_plus_one* :

  return new

end *new*

body $n \leftarrow 1 \,!\, add(1)$; *Write_File* · *standard_out*( ) ! *write_int*(*n*)

end *One_plus_one*,

class *One_minus_nil*

body *One_plus_one* · *new*( ) ; 1 ! *minus* (**nil**)

end *One_minus_nil*

In the $SPEC_{AA}$ case where integers are objects, it can happen that object 1 first answers the method call *minus* (**nil**). This leads to a state in which no external action has been performed but the order in which the actions will be executed is fully determined, namely first the *error* action and then the action *output* (2). In the $SPEC_{AM}$ case such a state cannot be reached since there are different monadic objects for frames $(1, mc, minus(\mathbf{nil}), \hat{0})$ and $(1, mc, add(1), \hat{1})$, and these monadic objects work independently. If the *error* action is blocked it can happen in the $SPEC_{AA}$ case that the action *output* (2) will not be performed. In the $SPEC_{AM}$ case the *output* (2) action will always be performed in such a situation. As a result of this:

$$INT_{@(FS)} \circ SPEC_{AA}(m) \neq INT_{@(FS)} \circ SPEC_{AM}(m).$$

6.4. Ostrich policy. The problem is not typical for the 'monadic' implementation of the integers and booleans but arises in every implementation different from the one suggested by $SPEC_{AA}$. However, it has to be noticed that in the trace set approach of Section 5.3, $SPEC_{AA}$ and $SPEC_{AM}$ (and thereby all other implementations) lead to the same semantics. In case we do not want to describe the system in terms of trace semantics, the best solution seems to be to abstract from the *error* action. We replace the equation for variable *ROOT* in $SPEC_{AA}$ and $SPEC_{AM}$ by

$$ROOT = \tau \cdot \tau_{I \cup \{error\}}([\![RU]\!]).$$

Call the new functions $SPEC_{AAO}$ and $SPEC_{AMO}$ (the 'O' from ostrich policy).

CLAIM. For all models M:

$$INT_M \circ SPEC_{AAO} = INT_M \circ SPEC_{AMO}.$$

We will not give a rigorous proof of this claim but confine ourselves to a sketch of it.

6.5. DEFINITION. A specification $E = \{X = t_X \mid X \in \Xi\}$ is called *strictly linear* if for every $X \in \Xi$:

$t_X = \tau$ or

$t_X = \delta$ or

$\exists m \geqslant 1$

$\exists a_1, ..., a_m \in A_\tau$

$\exists X_1, ..., X_m \in \Xi$ such that

$$t_X = \sum_{k=1}^{m} a_k \cdot X_k$$

6.6. THEOREM. *For every guarded specification E there exists a strictly linear guarded specification F with the same solution.*

6.7. *Structure of active objects.* Although a POOL system contains a large amount of parallelism, the individual objects work in a totally sequential way. The process algebra equations which define the behaviour of these objects contain chaining operators but, beside value passing, the process on the right hand side always starts after termination of the left hand side process. This observation (which of course can be expressed formally) motivates the following claim.

CLAIM. For every $\alpha \in AObj$ there exists a strictly linear guarded system of equations with root variable X_α such that

$$X_\alpha = \sum_{V \in \mathcal{C}} create^*(V,\alpha) \cdot \rho_{f_\alpha}(V)$$

and with the property (cf. semantic rules for production 21) that atomic actions $send(\alpha, mc, m(\alpha_1, ..., \alpha_n), \beta)$ only occur in equations of the form:

$$X = send(\alpha, mc, m(\alpha_1, ..., \alpha_n), \beta) \cdot Y$$

where Y is a variable for which we have an equation of the form:

$$Y = \sum_{\gamma \in Obj} read(\beta, an, \gamma, \alpha) \cdot Z_\gamma.$$

This means that every time when an active object performs an action $send(\alpha, mc, m(\alpha_1, ..., \alpha_n), \beta)$, the next action will be of the form $read(\beta, an, \gamma, \alpha)$.

6.8. We rewrite the equations for INT, $BOOL$, INT_M and $BOOL_M$ into the following form:

$$INT = \sum_{f \in \mathbb{S}_{INT}} read(f) \cdot INT^f$$

$$INT^f = (\mathop{\|}_{\beta \in Int - \{\alpha\}} X_\beta) \| an_f \cdot X_\alpha \quad \text{for } f \in \mathbb{S}_\alpha$$

$$BOOL = \sum_{f \in \mathbb{S}_{BOOL}} read(f) \cdot BOOL^f$$

$$BOOL^f = (\mathop{\|}_{\beta \in Bool - \{\alpha\}} X_\beta) \| an_f \cdot X_\alpha \quad \text{for } f \in \mathbb{S}_\alpha$$

$$INT_M = \sum_{f \in \mathbb{S}_{INT}} read(f) \cdot INT_M^f$$

$$INT_M^f = (\mathop{\|}_{g \in \mathbb{S}_{INT} - \{f\}} M_g) \| an_f \cdot M_f$$

$$BOOL_M = \sum_{f \in \mathbb{S}_{BOOL}} read(f) \cdot BOOL_M^f$$

$$BOOL^f_M = (\underset{g \in S_{BOOL} - \{f\}}{\|} M_g) \| an_f \cdot M_f$$

Define:

$$I'' = \{comm(\alpha, an, \beta, \gamma) \mid \alpha, \beta \in Obj;\ \gamma \in Int \cup Bool\} \cup \{error\}.$$

Application of the conditional axioms gives that, in order to prove the claim of Section 6.4, it is enough to show:

$$LHS = RHS$$

where

$$LHS = \tau_{I''} \circ \partial_J \circ \partial_K (create([\![CDL]\!], \hat{0}) \| (\underset{\alpha \in AObj}{\|} X_\alpha) \| INT \| BOOL \| I/O)$$

$$RHS = \tau_{I''} \circ \partial_J \circ \partial_K (create([\![CDL]\!], \hat{0}) \| (\underset{\alpha \in AObj}{\|} X_\alpha) \| INT_M \| BOOL_M \| I/O)$$

A quick inspection of the semantic rules defining $SPEC_{AAO}$ learns us that *LHS* is specifiable by means of guarded equations for all $n \in \mathbb{N}$. Therefore it is enough to show that for every $n \in \mathbb{N}$:

$$\pi_n(LHS) = \pi_n(RHS).$$

6.9. Definition. For X a variable and t a term, the relation *X occurs open in t* is defined inductively by:

1. X occurs open in X
2. if X occurs open in t then X occurs open in $t \cdot s$, $t \mathbin{\|\!\_} s$, $t+s$, $s+t$, $t \| s$, $s \| t$, $t \mid s$, $s \mid t$, $\partial_H(t)$, $\tau_I(t)$, $\rho_f(t)$ and $\pi_n(t)$.

An occurrence of a variable X in a term t is *needed* if t contains a subterm of the form $\pi_n(s)$ and X occurs open in s.

6.10. Definition. For given specification E, $\vec{E}$ is the term rewriting system consisting of the axioms from ACP_τ + RN + CH + SO + PR + RC-AT together with the equations of E (read from left to right). Here RC is the rewrite rule:

$$a \mid b = \gamma(a,b)$$

that rewrites a term $a \mid b$ into the corresponding communication, and AT is the set of axioms consisting of A1, A2, C1-3 and T1-3.

6.11. Theorem. *Let E be a guarded specification with root variable* X_0. *Let* $n \in \mathbb{N}$. *Then the term* $\pi_n(X_0)$ *will be rewritten into a closed term if we apply the rewrite rules of* $\vec{E}$, *following the strategy that only needed occurrences of variables are replaced.*

6.12. Choose a $n \in \mathbb{N}$. We have to prove:

$$\pi_n(LHS) = \pi_n(RHS).$$

The specifications that specify *LHS* and *RHS* are almost the same. We relate variables LHS and RHS, INT and INT_M, INT^f and INT_M^f, $BOOL$ and $BOOL_M$, $BOOL^f$ and $BOOL_M^f$, and furthermore all variables with the same name. Now we start to rewrite the term $\pi_n(LHS)$ into a closed term. Simultaneously we start rewriting $\pi_n(RHS)$ *in exactly the same way.* If on the left hand side a variable is rewritten, then we also rewrite the corresponding variable on the right hand side, etc. The problem with this imitation game is of course that the equations for INT^f and INT_M^f, $BOOL^f$ and $BOOL_M^f$ are different. What we do in order to solve this problem is that, when during the rewrite process a variable INT^f or $BOOL^f$ becomes needed, we rewrite the left and right hand side in such a way that:

1. The new left and right hand side are equivalent modulo names of variables.
2. No variable INT^f or $BOOL^f$ occurs needed in the left hand side.
3. It is clear that this intermediate 'surgery' will not slow down the process of rewriting $\pi_n(LHS)$ into a closed term.

Using the imitation + surgery strategy we rewrite $\pi_n(LHS)$ and $\pi_n(RHS)$ into the same closed term. Because n was chosen arbitrarily that finishes the proof of the claim of Section 6.4.

6.13. Surgery. Let $\alpha \in Int$ and $f = (\alpha, mc, d, \beta) \in \mathbb{S}_\alpha$ (the boolean case can be dealt with analogously). Suppose that after some rewrite step variable INT^f becomes needed in the left hand side term. We claim that INT^f occurs in a subterm which can be brought into the form:

$$comm(f) \cdot \pi_m \circ \tau_{I''} \circ \partial_H \circ \partial_K(\cdots \| INT^f \| \sum_{\gamma \in Obj} read(\beta, an, \gamma, \alpha) \cdot Z_\gamma).$$

If we rewrite variable INT^f this becomes:

$$comm(f) \cdot \pi_m \circ \tau_{I''} \circ \partial_H \circ \partial_K(\cdots \| (\mathop{\|}_{\kappa \in Int - \{\alpha\}} X_\kappa) \| an_f \cdot X_\alpha \| \sum_{\gamma \in Obj} read(\beta, an, \gamma, \alpha) \cdot Z_\gamma).$$

The corresponding right hand side subterm can be brought into the form:

$$comm(f) \cdot \pi_m \circ \tau_{I''} \circ \partial_H \circ \partial_K(\cdots \| (\mathop{\|}_{g \in \mathbb{S}_{INT} - \{f\}} M_g) \| an_f \cdot M_f \| \sum_{\gamma \in Obj} read(\beta, an, \gamma, \alpha) \cdot Z_\gamma).$$

If $an_f = error$ we bring the ostrich policy into practice: because $error \in I''$ we can replace the *error* action by τ in both terms. The next step is to eliminate these τ's using the identity $\tau x \| y = \tau(x \| y)$. But then the subterm on the left contains the merge for all $\alpha \in Int$ of X_α. This is equal to INT. The subterm on the right contains the merge for all $f \in \mathbb{S}_{INT}$ of processes M_f, which is equal to INT_M. This finishes the surgery activities for the case $an_f = error$.

In the other case we have $an_f = send(\beta, an, \overline{\gamma}, \alpha)$ for some $\overline{\gamma} \in Obj$. Using the conditional axioms we can replace the left hand side subsubterm (excusez le mot):

$$an_f \cdot X_\alpha \| \sum_{\gamma \in Obj} read(\beta, an, \gamma, \alpha) \cdot Z_\gamma$$

by

$$\tau_{\{comm(\beta,an,\overline{\gamma},\alpha)\}} \circ \partial_{\{send(\beta,an,\overline{\gamma},\alpha)\}}(send(\beta,an,\overline{\gamma},\alpha)\cdot X_\alpha \| \sum_{\gamma\in Obj} read(\beta,an,\gamma,\alpha)\cdot Z_\gamma)$$

which is equal to

$$\tau\cdot\tau_{\{comm(\beta,an,\overline{\gamma},\alpha)\}} \circ \partial_{\{send(\beta,an,\overline{\gamma},\alpha)\}}(X_\alpha \| Z_{\overline{\gamma}}) +$$
$$+ \sum_{\gamma\in Obj} read(\beta,an,\gamma,\alpha)\cdot\tau_{\{comm(\beta,an,\overline{\gamma},\alpha)\}} \circ \partial_{\{send(\beta,an,\overline{\gamma},\alpha)\}}(send(\beta,an,\overline{\gamma},\alpha)\cdot X_\alpha \| Z_\gamma).$$

The second summand is redundant in the context in which it occurs and can be omitted. Using the conditional axioms again, together with identity $\tau x \| y = \tau(x \| y)$, yields that the term can be replaced by:

$$X_\alpha \| Z_{\overline{\gamma}}.$$

Now we have brought the left hand side subterm in a form which contains the merge for all $\alpha\in Int$ of X_α. This merge we can replace by INT. The same strategy that was used to rewrite the left hand side can be used to rewrite the right hand side. The result is the same term as obtained on the left hand side, except that we have variable INT_M instead of INT.

7. Conclusions

1. In this paper we showed that it is possible to give semantics of a realistic concurrent programming language by means of process algebra. The translation of POOL programs into process algebra is complicated, but this is mainly caused by the complexity of POOL, in particular by the complexity of the select statement. The attribute grammar which we used for the translation made it possible to give the semantics in a modular way.
2. This paper contains an application of ACP where the sequential composition operator is used in full generality. It would have been more involved to give semantics of POOL in a signature containing prefixing (an operator $A\times P\rightarrow P$) instead of sequential composition. Three auxiliary operators, the renaming operator, the chaining operator and the state operator, turned out to be useful.
3. Because we have no infinite sum and infinite merge operators in the signature, we had to choose the value domain of POOL variables finite. Furthermore the number of objects which can be created during execution of a POOL unit is finite. Although it would be useful to have these infinitary operators available, we do not think that their absence in the present paper is a real deficiency: the memory of each computer is finite, and no computer will function eternally.
4. The approach followed in this paper can also be used to give semantics of other concurrent programming languages. From the point of view of process algebra we see no fundamental difference between the object-oriented approach from POOL, and the imperative, logic or functional approaches followed in other languages. However, at present it is difficult to give process algebra semantics of a language in which real-time aspects play a role.

5. KFAR does not completely capture the notion of fairness in POOL. In Section 5.4.3 we pointed out that combination of failure semantics and weak process fairness is especially problematic. An open question is whether or not the two concepts can be combined in a consistent manner.
6. There is not one single 'optimal' semantics of POOL. Depending on the application domain one has in mind one can try to find an optimum. There are a lot of features which can be included in the semantical description of the language: infinite domains of variables, fairness, error behaviour, termination behaviour, etc. An important parameter in the choice of a semantics is the type of interaction between the environment and the POOL system. In case one wants to use the semantics to build an executable prototype, the semantics has to be operational. In case the semantics is used for the construction of proof systems or for the correctness proof of implementations, one requires abstractness and compositionality. It might be the case that the combination of all these requirements leads to inconsistencies.
7. The translation of POOL into process algebra can be used for prototyping of the language. The shortest route seems to be a translation into an algebraic specification formalism. The attribute grammar which we used can be specified algebraically in a straightforward way. The process algebra part is already specified algebraically but some work has to be done in order to deal with a number of notational conventions, for example the sum operator and the numerous '...' occurring in the equations. There are several alternatives for transforming algebraic specifications into executable prototypes, for example by means of a transformation into a complete (conditional) term rewriting system and execution by means of an existing rewrite rule interpreter, or by means of a transformation into a set of Horn clauses and using an existing Prolog system for their execution.
8. It would be interesting to construct a proof system, based on our process algebra semantics, which can be used to prove correctness of POOL programs.
9. A semantical description of POOL with handshaking communication between the objects is incompatible with the description in [1], where message queues are used. A minor change in the language definition is proposed in order to remove this difficulty. In our opinion this result shows that, when dealing with concurrent programming languages, questions like: 'Is this semantical description in accordance with the language definition?' and 'Is this a correct implementation of the language?' are highly relevant.
10. An important problem to be solved is in our view the development of techniques which make it possible to prove that two semantics of POOL have a common abstraction. In Section 6 we gave a sketch of such a proof, showing that the Integers and Booleans can be implemented in a lot of ways. In Section 4 we discussed the question whether or not the

communication between objects can be implemented by message queues. We showed that, even after modification of the language definition, this is not possible in bisimulation semantics. An open question is the equivalence in failure semantics.

ACKNOWLEDGEMENTS
I would like to thank Pierre America, Joost Kok, Jan Rutten and all the participants of the PAM seminar for their valuable criticism and many inspiring discussions.

REFERENCES

1. P. AMERICA (1985). *Definition of the Programming Language POOL-T,* ESPRIT project 415, Doc. Nr. 91, Philips Research Laboratories, Eindhoven.
2. P. AMERICA (1986). *Rationale for the Design of POOL,* ESPRIT project 415, Doc. Nr. 53, Philips Research Laboratories, Eindhoven.
3. P. AMERICA (1987). *A Sketch for POOL2,* ESPRIT project 415, Doc. Nr. 240, Philips Research Laboratories, Eindhoven.
4. P. AMERICA, J.W. DE BAKKER, J.N. KOK, J.J.M.M. RUTTEN (1986). Operational semantics of a parallel object-oriented language. *Conference Record of the 13th ACM Symposium on Principles of Programming Languages,* St. Petersburg, Florida, 194-208.
5. P. AMERICA, J.W. DE BAKKER, J.N. KOK, J.J.M.M. RUTTEN (1986). *A Denotational Semantics of a Parallel Object-oriented Language,* CWI Report CS-R8626, Centre for Mathematics and Computer Science, Amsterdam. To appear in *Information and Computation.*
6. ANSI (1983). *Reference Manual for the Ada Programming Language,* ANSI/MIL-STD 1815 A, United States Department of Defense Washington D.C.
7. K.R. APT, N. FRANCEZ (1984). Modelling the distributed termination convention of CSP. *TOPLAS 6(3),* 370-379.
8. J.C.M. BAETEN, J.A. BERGSTRA (1988). Global renaming operators in concrete process algebra. *Information and Computation 78(3),* 205-245.
9. J.W. DE BAKKER (1980). *Mathematical Theory of Program Correctness,* Prentice-Hall.
10. J.A. BERGSTRA (1989). *A Process Creation Mechanism in Process Algebra.* This volume.
11. J.A. BERGSTRA, J.W. KLOP, E.-R. OLDEROG (1987). Failures without chaos: a new process semantics for fair abstraction. M. WIRSING (ed.). *Proc. IFIP Conf. on Formal Description of Programming Concepts - III,* Ebberup 1986, North-Holland, Amsterdam, 77-103.
12. G.V. BOCHMAN (1976). Semantic evaluation from left to right. *Communications of the ACM 19(2),* 55-62.
13. D.W. BUSTARD (1980). An introduction to Pascal-Plus. R.M. MCKEAG, A.M. MACNAGHTEN (eds.). *On the construction of programs - an advanced course,* Cambridge University Press, 1-57.

14. J. ENGELFRIET (1984). *Formele Talen en Automaten 2,* Department of Computer Science, State University of Leiden, lecture notes (in Dutch).
15. N. FRANCEZ (1986). *Fairness*, Springer-Verlag, Berlin.
16. R.J. VAN GLABBEEK (1987). Bounded nondeterminism and the approximation induction principle in process algebra. F.J. BRANDENBURG, G. VIDAL-NAQUET, M. WIRSING (eds.). *Proc. STACS 87,* LNCS 247, Springer-Verlag, 336-347.
17. R.J. VAN GLABBEEK, F.W. VAANDRAGER (1987). Petri net models for algebraic theories of concurrency (extended abstract). J.W. DE BAKKER, A.J. NIJMAN, P.C. TRELEAVEN (eds.). *Proceedings PARLE conference, Eindhoven, Vol. II (Parallel Languages),* LNCS 259, Springer-Verlag, 224-242.
18. C.A.R. HOARE (1985). *Communicating Sequential Processes,* Prentice-Hall.
19. INMOS, LTD. (1984). *The Occam Programming Manual,* Prentice-Hall.
20. ISO (1987). *A Formal Description Technique.* ISO/TC97/SC21/WG16-1 DP8807.
21. D.E. KNUTH (1968). Semantics of context-free languages. *Mathematical Systems Theory, 2,* 127-145. Correction: *Mathematical Systems Theory 5,* 1971, 95-96.
22. C.P.J. KOYMANS, J.C. MULDER (1989). *A Modular Approach to Protocol Verification using Process Algebra,* This volume.
23. R. MILNER (1980). *A Calculus of Communicating Systems,* LNCS 92, Springer-Verlag.
24. J. PARROW (1985). *Fairness Properties in Process Algebra - with Applications in Communication Protocol Verification,* DoCS 85/03, Ph.D. Thesis, Department of Computer Systems, Uppsala University.
25. F.W. VAANDRAGER (1986). *Verification of Two Communication Protocols by means of Process Algebra,* CWI Report CS-R8608, Centre for Mathematics and Computer Science, Amsterdam.
26. F.W. VAANDRAGER (1986). *Process Algebra Semantics of POOL,* CWI Report CS-R8629, Centre for Mathematics and Computer Science, Amsterdam.
27. F.W. VAANDRAGER (1989). *Some Observations on Redundancy in a Context.* This volume.
28. F.W. VAANDRAGER (1989). *Two Simple Protocols,* This volume.

Some Observations on Redundancy in a Context

Frits W. Vaandrager

Centre for Mathematics and Computer Science
P.O. Box 4079, 1009 AB Amsterdam, The Netherlands

Let x be a process which can perform an action a when it is in state s. In this article we consider the situation where x is placed in a context which blocks a whenever x is in s. The option of doing a in state s is *redundant* in such a context and x can be replaced by a process x' which is identical to x, except for the fact that x' cannot do a when it is in s (irrespective of the context). A simple, compositional proof technique is presented, which uses information about the traces of processes to detect redundancies in a process specification. As an illustration of the technique, a modular verification of a workcell architecture is presented.

1. Introduction

We are interested in the verification of distributed systems by means of algebraic manipulations. In process algebra, verifications often consist of a proof that the behaviour of an implementation *IMPL* equals the behaviour of a specification *SPEC*, after abstraction from internal activity: $\tau_I(IMPL) = SPEC$.

The simplest strategy to prove such a statement is to derive first the transition system (process graph) for the process *IMPL* with the expansion theorem, apply an abstraction operator to this transition system, and then simplify the resulting system to the system for *SPEC* using the laws of (for instance) bisimulation semantics. This 'global' strategy however, is often not very practical due to combinatorial state explosion: the number of states of *IMPL* can be of the same order as the product of the number of states of its components. Another serious problem with this strategy is that it provides almost no 'insight' in the structure of the system being verified. It is impossible to use the approach for the design of distributed systems, i.e. the stepwise construction of an implementation starting from a specification. This makes that there is a strong need for proof methods with a more *modular/compositional* character.

Partial support received from the European Community under ESPRIT project no. 432, An Integrated Formal Approach to Industrial Software Development (METEOR).

1.1. Modularity and compositionality. For the purpose of verification, we are interested in proof principles which transform a system locally, so that for a correctness proof of a local transformation one does not have to deal with the complexity of the system as a whole. A *modular* verification transforms an expression $\tau_I(IMPL)$ gradually into $SPEC$ by a sequence of local transformation steps. Consider, as an example, the case where $IMPL$ represents the parallel composition of components X_1, X_2 and X_3, where the actions in a set H have to synchronise: $IMPL = \partial_H(X_1 \| X_2 \| X_3)$. A possible step in a modular verification could be that X_1 and X_2 are replaced by Y_1 and Y_2. In that case one has to prove that:

$$\tau_I \circ \partial_H(X_1 \| X_2 \| X_3) = \tau_I \circ \partial_H(Y_1 \| Y_2 \| X_3).$$

It is sufficient to prove that $X_1 \| X_2 = Y_1 \| Y_2$. However, this will not be possible in general. It can be the case that processes $X_1 \| X_2$ and $Y_1 \| Y_2$ are only equal in the context $\tau_I \circ \partial_H(\cdots \| X_3)$. And even if the processes are equal, then still it is often not a good strategy to prove this. If one shows that two processes are equal, then one shows that they are interchangeable in any context, not only in the context in which they actually occur. In order to bring about successful substitutions, it is therefore desirable (or even necessary) to incorporate information about the context in which components are placed in correctness proofs of substitutions. A proof technique which allows one to do this to a sufficiently large degree is called modular. It is also possible to use a modular proof system the other way around. In that case one starts with a specification, which is refined to an implementation by a sequence of transformation steps.

A proof rule is called *compositional* if it helps to prove properties of the system as a whole from properties of the individual components. Compositional proof rules are essential for modular verifications.

In this article we present a proof principle which can be used to enhance the modularity of verifications. We claim that the principle captures a simple intuition about the behaviour of concurrent systems, and moreover makes it possible to give short, modular proofs in quite a large number of situations.

1.2. Example. We give a specification of a Dutch coffee machine similar to the one described in [14]:

$$KM = \overline{30c} \cdot (\overline{kof} + \overline{choc}) \cdot zoem \cdot KM.$$

After inserting 30 cents, the user may select 'koffie' or 'chocolade'. Dutch coffee machines make a humming sound ('zoemen') when they produce a drink. The behaviour of a typical Dutch user of such a machine can be described by the recursive equation below:

$$DU = (kof + 30c \cdot kof) \cdot talk \cdot DU.$$

Dutch people are widely known for their thrift, and they will never spend 30 cents for a cup of coffee if they can get it for free*. Synchronisation of actions

* Dutch users do not occur in [14]. In the modelling as presented here, the thrift of the Dutch user is not really taken into account: we can think of an environment where process DU performs

is given by: $\gamma(kof,\overline{kof})=kof^*$, $\gamma(30c,\overline{30c})=30c^*$ and $\gamma(choc,\overline{choc})=choc^*$. Let $H=\{kof, \overline{kof}, choc, \overline{choc}, 30c, \overline{30c}\}$. Consider the system $\partial_H(DU \| KM)$. It will be clear that in this environment the thrift of the Dutch user makes no sense. This behaviour is *redundant in the given context*. More 'realistic' is the behaviour $\overline{DU} = 30c \cdot kof \cdot talk \cdot \overline{DU}$, because $\partial_H(DU \| KM) = \partial_H(\overline{DU} \| KM)$.

1.3. Redundancy in a context. The example above is an instance of a situation which occurs very often: a process x has, in principle, the possibility to perform an action a when it is in state s, but is placed in an environment $\partial_H(\cdots \| y)$ which blocks a whenever the process is in s. In situations like this, the a-step from s is *redundant in the context* $\partial_H(\cdots \| y)$. We want to have the possibility to replace x by a component $\overline{x}$, that is identical to x except for the fact that $\overline{x}$ cannot do action a when it is in state s (irrespective of the context). For a compositional proof of the correctness of this type of substitutions new proof rules are needed. In this article we will show that in most situations partial information about the *(finite, sequential) traces* of processes is sufficient to prove that a summand in a specification is redundant and can be omitted. The notion 'redundancy in a context' was introduced in [16]. The present article can be viewed as a thorough revision of Section 6 from that paper.

1.4. Trace-specifications. It is argued by many authors (see for instance [5]), that if one is interested in program development by stepwise refinement, one needs to have the possibility of mixing programming notation with specification parts. A natural way to specify aspects of concurrent processes, advocated by [9, 14, 15, 17], is to give information about the traces, ready pairs and failure pairs of these processes. This leads to the notation

$$x \textbf{ sat } S$$

which expresses that process x satisfies property S. When we use the notation in this article, S will always be a property of the traces of x. Without any problem we can also include other information in S but we don't need that here.

In recent years it has become abundantly clear that there are many notions of 'process'. For instance, the idea that a process, in general, *is* the set of its traces, ready pairs or failure pairs is just false, because these notions of process do not capture features like real-time and fairness. Therefore we are interested in proof rules which express 'universal' truths about processes, and which are not tied to some particular model.

The point which is new in this article is that we use statements of the form x **sat** S, i.e. information about the traces of processes, in proofs that processes are equal in a sense different from (and finer than) trace equivalence. Thus we combine the advantages of a linear trace semantics with the distinctive power of finer equivalences.

an action $30c$ even though it has the possibility to perform an action *kof* instead. Preference of a process for certain actions can be modelled by means of the 'priority operator' of [2].

1.5. Workcell architecture. As an illustration of our technique, we present in Section 5 of this article a specification and verification of a workcell architecture, i.e. a system consisting of a number of workcells which cooperate in order to manufacture a certain product. The verification is not only modular, but also short when compared with the non-modular verifications of the same system by Biemans and Blonk [4], and Mauw [13]. In the first steps of the verification we remove the redundant summands in the process specification of the workcell architecture. Often the information that some summand is redundant has some importance of its own. It allows one to replace one component by another which is simpler cq. cheaper. In our modular proof this information becomes available as a by-product.

1.6. Related work. This is not the first article which is concerned with modular verification in the setting of process algebra. Work in this area has also been done by Larsen and Milner [11, 12], and Koymans and Mulder [10]. We think that our approach has basically two advantages when compared with this work. The first advantage is that our approach is technically speaking much simpler. People have strong intuitions concerning the trace behaviour of concurrent systems. Our proof rule makes it possible to use these intuitions quite directly in verifications. The intuitions behind the techniques of [10-12] are more involved and a lot of technical machinery is needed to formalize them. Our approach is probably less general than the approaches of [10-12], but we think that for almost all practical applications it can be used just as well.

The second advantage of our technique is that it is independent of the particular process semantics which is used. This in contrast to the work of [10-12], which is tied heavily to bisimulation semantics. In the discussion below we employ the laws of interleaved bisimulation semantics. However, we could just as well work with the laws of failure equivalence, ready equivalence or trace equivalence. Working with bisimulation semantics only makes our results stronger. We conjecture that the proof rule based on trace-specifications, as presented in this article, also holds in partial order semantics (see [7]). Probably the correctness proof of the workcell architecture which is presented in Section 5, when reorganized a little bit, is also valid in partial order semantics. It is a topic for future research to substantiate these claims.

2. Traces and trace-specifications

A *trace* of a process is a finite sequence that gives a possible order in which atomic actions can be performed by that process. A trace can end with the symbol $\surd$ (pronounce 'tick'), to indicate that, after execution of the last atomic action, successful termination can occur. After some preliminary definitions we give, in Section 2.3, axioms that relate processes to trace sets.

2.1. Definition.

1. For any alphabet Σ, we use Σ^* to denote the set of finite sequences over alphabet Σ. We write λ for the empty sequence and a for the sequence consisting of the single symbol $a \in \Sigma$. By $\sigma \star \sigma'$, often abbreviated $\sigma\sigma'$, we

denote the concatenation of sequences σ and σ'.

2. Let σ be a sequence and V be a set of sequences. We use notation $\sigma\star V$ (or σV) for the set $\{\sigma\star\rho \mid \rho\in V\}$, and notation $V\star\sigma$ (or $V\sigma$) for the set $\{\rho\sigma \mid \rho\in V\}$.
3. By $\sharp\sigma$ we denote the length of a sequence σ.
4. On sequences we define a partial ordering $\leqslant$ (the *prefix ordering*) by: $\sigma\leqslant\rho$ if and only if, for some sequence σ', $\sigma\sigma'=\rho$. A set of sequences V is *closed under prefixing* if, for all $\sigma\leqslant\rho$, $\rho\in V$ implies that $\sigma\in V$.
5. $A_{\surd}=A\cup\{\surd\}$ is the set of atomic actions together with the termination symbol. Elements from $(A_{\surd})^*$ are called *traces* or *histories*. τ acts as the identity over $(A_{\surd})^*$ and is therefore replaced by λ when occurring in traces.
6. $\mathbb{T}$ is the set of nonempty, countable subsets of $T = A^* \cup A^*\star\surd$ which are closed under prefixing.

2.2. DEFINITION. Let $a,b\in A$, $V,W\in\mathbb{T}$, $\sigma,\sigma_1,\sigma_2\in T$. We define the following ACP-operators on trace sets*:

1. Sequential composition.
   $V\cdot W ::= (V\cap A^*) \cup \{\sigma_1\star\sigma_2 \mid \sigma_1\surd\in V \text{ and } \sigma_2\in W\}$.
2. Parallel composition. $V\|W ::= \{\sigma \mid \exists\sigma_1\in V,\ \sigma_2\in W : \sigma\in\sigma_1\|\sigma_2\}$. The set $\sigma_1\|\sigma_2$ of traces is defined inductively by:

$$a\sigma_1\|b\sigma_2 = \begin{cases} a(\sigma_1\|b\sigma_2)\cup b(a\sigma_1\|\sigma_2)\cup\gamma(a,b)(\sigma_1\|\sigma_2) & \text{if } \gamma(a,b)\in A \\ a(\sigma_1\|b\sigma_2)\cup b(a\sigma_1\|\sigma_2) & \text{otherwise} \end{cases}$$

$$\lambda\|a\sigma = a\sigma\|\lambda = a(\lambda\|\sigma), \quad \lambda\|\lambda = \{\lambda\}, \quad \surd\|\sigma = \sigma\|\surd = \{\sigma\}.$$

   Here $\gamma: A_\delta\times A_\delta\rightarrow A_\delta$ is a given function which describes the synchronisation between atomic actions. γ is commutative, associative and has δ as zero-element.
3. Encapsulation. Let $H\subseteq A$. $\partial_H(V) ::= V\cap(A_{\surd}-H)^*$.
4. Abstraction. Let $I\subseteq A$. $\tau_I(V) ::= \{\tau_I(\sigma) \mid \sigma\in V\}$. The function τ_I on traces is given by:

$$\tau_I(a\star\sigma) = \begin{cases} \tau_I(\sigma) & \text{if } a\in I \\ a\star\tau_I(\sigma) & \text{otherwise} \end{cases}$$

$$\tau_I(\lambda) = \lambda, \quad \tau_I(\surd) = \surd.$$

5. Renaming. Let $f: A_{\tau\delta}\rightarrow A_{\tau\delta}$ with $f(\tau)=\tau$ and $f(\delta)=\delta$. $\rho_f(V) ::= \{\rho_f(\sigma) \mid \sigma\in V\}$. The function ρ_f on traces is given by:

$$\rho_f(a\star\sigma) = \begin{cases} f(a)\star\rho_f(\sigma) & \text{if } f(a)\neq\delta \\ \lambda & \text{otherwise} \end{cases}$$

*The auxiliary operator $\lfloor\!\lfloor$ cannot be defined on trace sets. For a discussion of this issue we refer to [8].

$$\rho_f(\lambda) = \lambda, \quad \rho_f(\surd) = \surd.$$

6. Projection. Let $n \in \mathbb{N}$.
$\pi_n(V) ::= \{\sigma \in V \cap A^* \mid \sharp\sigma \leqslant n\} \cup \{\sigma\surd \in V \mid \sharp\sigma \leqslant n\}^{\dagger}$.
7. Alphabets. $\alpha(V) ::= \{\alpha(\sigma) \mid \sigma \in V\}$. The function $\alpha: T \rightarrow Pow(A)$ is given by:

$$\alpha(a \star \sigma) = \{a\} \cup \alpha(\sigma), \quad \alpha(\lambda) = \alpha(\surd) = \varnothing.$$

2.3. The Trace Operator (TO). Let P be the sort of processes. The *trace operator* $tr: P \rightarrow \mathbb{T}$ relates to every process the set of traces that can be executed by that process. The operator satisfies the axioms of Table 1. ($a \in A$, $x,y \in P$, $H,I \subseteq A$, $f: A_{\tau\delta} \rightarrow A_{\tau\delta}$ with $f(\tau)=\tau$ and $f(\delta)=\delta$, and $n \in \mathbb{N}$)

$tr(\delta) = \{\lambda\}$	TO1	$tr(\partial_H(x)) = \partial_H(tr(x))$	TO7
$tr(\tau) = \{\lambda, \surd\}$	TO2	$tr(\tau_I(x)) = \tau_I(tr(x))$	TO8
$tr(a) = \{\lambda, a, a\surd\}$	TO3	$tr(\rho_f(x)) = \rho_f(tr(x))$	TO9
$tr(x+y) = tr(x) \cup tr(y)$	TO4	$tr(\pi_n(x)) = \pi_n(tr(x))$	TO10
$tr(x \cdot y) = tr(x) \cdot tr(y)$	TO5	$\alpha(x) = \alpha(tr(x))$	TO11
$tr(x \| y) = tr(x) \| tr(y)$	TO6		

TABLE 1. Axioms for the trace operator

When calculating with trace sets we implicitly use ZF. This means that the considerations of this paper are not of a completely algebraic nature. We restrict our attention to the models of the theory ACP_τ with recursion and auxiliary operators that can be mapped homomorphically to the trace algebra. This is no serious restriction because all 'interesting' process algebras are in this class. A similar approach is followed in [1].

2.3.1. Examples.

$$tr(x) = tr(\delta + x) = tr(\delta) \cup tr(x) = \{\lambda\} \cup tr(x). \tag{1}$$

So λ is member of the trace set of every process.

$$tr(ax) = tr(a) \cdot tr(x) = \{\lambda, a, a\surd\} \cdot tr(x) = \{\lambda, a\} \cup a \star tr(x) \overset{(1)}{=} \tag{2}$$
$$= \{\lambda\} \cup \{a\} \cup a \star (tr(x) \cup \{\lambda\}) = \{\lambda\} \cup a \star tr(x).$$

Let X be given by the recursive equation $X = aX$.

$$tr(X) = \bigcup_{n \geqslant 0} \pi_n(tr(X)) = \bigcup_{n \geqslant 0} tr(\pi_n(X)) = \bigcup_{n \geqslant 0} tr(a^n \cdot \delta) \tag{3}$$

† The π_n-operators we define here, satisfy the same axioms as the ones defined in [6]: $\pi_n(\tau) = \tau$, $\pi_0(ax) = \delta$, $\pi_{n+1}(ax) = a \cdot \pi_n(x)$, etc.

$$= \{\lambda\} \cup \{\lambda, a\} \cup \{\lambda, a, aa\} \cup \cdots = \{\lambda, a, aa, \ldots\}.$$

The first identity in derivation (3) follows from the structure of $\mathbb{T}$ and the definition of the π_n-operators on $\mathbb{T}$.

2.4. Trace-specifications. A *trace-specification* is a predicate. A trace-specification S describes the set of traces which, when assigned to free occurrences of a chosen variable σ of type trace in S, make the predicate true: $\{\sigma | S\}$. The syntax for trace-specifications we have in mind is a first-order language with integers, actions, traces, some simple functions like addition and multiplication, taking the i-th element of a trace, $\sharp\sigma$, $\rho_i(\sigma)$, equality predicates for the integers, actions and traces, and quantification over integers and traces. This syntax is almost equivalent to the syntax proposed in [14], except for the fact that we moreover have multiplication. This increases the expressiveness of our logic, and makes it for instance possible to define for each regular trace-language L a predicate S_L such that $L = \{\sigma | S_L\}$. In Section 4.5 it will be argued that such predicates are useful. All predicates that we will use in this article are definable in terms of the syntax which is described informally above.

A process x *satisfies* a trace-specification S for trace variable σ, notation

$$x \ \mathbf{sat}_\sigma \ S,$$

if

$$\forall \sigma \in tr(x): S.$$

Because in nearly all cases we will use a fixed trace-variable σ, we often omit the subscript σ and write x **sat** S. In this article we regard x **sat** S merely as a notation. The proofs take place on the more elementary level of the tr-operator and trace sets. In [9] an elegant proof system is given which takes x **sat** S as a primitive notion. This system contains for instance rules like

$$\frac{x \ \mathbf{sat} \ S, \ x \ \mathbf{sat} \ S'}{x \ \mathbf{sat} \ S \wedge S'} \qquad \frac{x \ \mathbf{sat} \ S, \ S \Rightarrow S'}{x \ \mathbf{sat} \ S'}.$$

2.4.1. Notation. Let $\sigma \in T$, $B \subseteq A$ and $a \in A$.

1. $\sigma \upharpoonright B$ gives the *projection* of trace σ onto the actions of B: $\sigma \upharpoonright B = \tau_{A-B}(\sigma)$.
2. $\sigma \downarrow a$ denotes the number of occurrences of a in σ:

$$\sigma \downarrow a = \begin{cases} \sharp(\sigma \upharpoonright \{a\}) - 1 & \text{if } \sigma = \sigma' \surd \\ \sharp(\sigma \upharpoonright \{a\}) & \text{otherwise} \end{cases}$$

3. Even though our trace-specification language contains no alphabet operator, we can talk about alphabets in predicates: $\alpha(\sigma) \subseteq B \Leftrightarrow \sigma \upharpoonright B = \sigma$.

2.4.2. Example. The coffee machine from Example 1.2 satisfies

$$KM \textbf{ sat } \alpha(\sigma) \subseteq \{\overline{kof}, \overline{choc}, \overline{30c}, zoem\} \wedge (\sigma \downarrow \overline{kof} \leqslant \sigma \downarrow \overline{30c}).$$

The number of cups of 'koffie' produced by the machine is always less or equal to the number of times 30 cents have been paid. The Dutch user however, takes care that never more than 30 cents are paid in advance:

$$DU \textbf{ sat } \alpha(\sigma) \subseteq \{kof, 30c, talk\} \wedge (\sigma \downarrow kof \geqslant (\sigma \downarrow 30c - 1)).$$

2.4.3. Remark. Sometimes we write a specification as $S(\sigma)$, to indicate that the specification will normally contain σ as a free variable. In that case we use the notation $S(te)$ to denote the predicate obtained from $S(\sigma)$ by substituting all free occurrences of σ by an expression te of sort trace, avoiding name clashes.

3. Observability and localisation

The parallel combinator $\|$ is in some sense related to the cartesian product construction. In the graph model of [3], the set of nodes of a graph $g\|h$ is defined as the set of ordered pairs of the nodes of g and h. Still the $\|$-operator lacks an important property of cartesian products, namely the existence of projection operators. It is not possible in general to define operators l and r such that $l(x\|y)=x$ and $r(x\|y)=y$. In this section we show that, if we impose a number of constraints on the communication function, and on x and y, it becomes possible to define an operator which, given the alphabet of x, can recover x almost completely from $x\|y$:

$$\tau \cdot \rho_{\nu(\alpha(x))}(x\|y) \cdot \delta = \tau \cdot x \cdot \delta.$$

The conditions on x and y make that x is *observable*, the operator $\rho_{\nu(\alpha(x))}$ *localises* x in $x\|y$.

3.1. Communication. For the specification of distributed systems, we mostly use the read/send communication scheme, or communications of type $\gamma(kof, \overline{kof}) = kof^*$. Following [10], such communication functions will be characterized as *trijective*. The assumption that communication is trijective will simplify the discussion of this article.

3.1.1. DEFINITION. A communication function γ is *trijective* if three pairwise disjoint subsets $R, S, C \subseteq A$ can be given, and bijections $\overline{\ }: R \rightarrow S$ and $^\circ: R \rightarrow C$ such that for every $a, b, c \in A$:

$$\gamma(a,b)=c \Rightarrow (a \in R \wedge b = \overline{a} \wedge c = a^\circ) \vee (b \in R \wedge a = \overline{b} \wedge c = b^\circ).$$

In the rest of this article we assume that communication is trijective.

3.1.2. Remark. Observe that a trijective communication function γ satisfies the following three properties, and that each γ satisfying these properties is trijective ($a,b,c,d \in A$):

1. $\gamma(a,a) = \delta$,
2. if $\gamma(a,b) \neq \delta$ and $\gamma(a,c) \neq \delta$ then $b = c$ (γ is 'monogamous'),
3. if $\gamma(a,b) = \gamma(c,d) \neq \delta$ then $a = c$ or $a = d$ (γ is 'injective').

Observe further that a trijective γ satisfies $\gamma(\gamma(a,b),c) = \delta$ ('handshaking').

3.2. Observability. We are interested in the behaviour of a process x when it is placed in a context $\cdots \| y$. In order to keep things simple, we will always choose x and y in such a way that x is observable in context with y: every action of $x \| y$ is either an action from x, or an action from y, or a synchronisation between x and y. In the last case we moreover know which action from x participates in the synchronisation. Below we give a formal definition of this notion of observability.

3.2.1. DEFINITION. Let $B \subseteq A$ be a set of atomic actions. B is called *observable* if for each triple $a,b,c \in A$ with $\gamma(a,b) = c$ at most one element of $\{a,b,c\}$ is a member of B.

Let for $A_1, A_2 \subseteq A$: $A_1 | A_2 = \{\gamma(a_1,a_2) \in A \mid a_1 \in A_1, a_2 \in A_2\}$. From the fact that a set B of actions is observable, we can conclude that $B \cap B|A = \emptyset$. Because γ is injective, we know in addition that γ has an 'inverse' on $B|A$: for each $c \in B|A$, there is exactly one $b \in B$ such that an $a \in A$ exists with $\gamma(a,b) = c$. In this case we write $b = \gamma_B^{-1}(c)$.

3.2.2. DEFINITION. Let x,y be processes. Process x is called *observable in context* $\cdots \| y$, if $\alpha(x)$ is observable, and $\alpha(y)$ is disjoint from $\alpha(x)$ and $\alpha(x)|A$.

If a process x is observable in a context $\cdots \| y$, then one can tell for each action from $x \| y$ whether it is from x, from y, or from x and y together. In the last case one can also tell which action from x participates in the communication. Observe that the fact that x is observable in context $\cdots \| y$ does not imply that y is observable in context $\cdots \| x$.

3.3. Localisation. The 'localisation' of actions from x in a context $\cdots \| y$ as described informally above, can be expressed formally by means of renaming operators. In the literature other definitions of the notions observability and localisation can be found (see [1] and [16]). In the choice of the definitions, there is a trade-off between the degree of generality (the capability of operators to localise actions) and the length of the definitions.

3.3.1. DEFINITION. Let $B \subseteq A$ be observable. The *localisation function* $\nu(B)$: $A_{\tau\delta} \rightarrow A_{\tau\delta}$ is the renaming function defined by:

$$\nu(B)(a) = \begin{cases} a & \text{if } a \in B \cup \{\tau,\delta\} \\ \gamma_B^{-1}(a) & \text{if } a \in B|A \\ \tau & \text{otherwise} \end{cases}$$

3.3.2. Example. The communication function in Example 1.2 is trijective. Furthermore $\alpha(DU) = \{kof, 30c, talk\}$ is observable. Process DU is observable in the context $\cdots \| KM$. DU is however not observable in the context $\cdots \|(DU\|KM)$. The expression

$$\rho_{\nu(\alpha(DU))} \circ \partial_H(DU\|KM)$$

denotes the process corresponding to the behaviour of the Dutch user in a context $\partial_H(\cdots \|KM)$. We derive:

$$\begin{aligned}
&\rho_{\nu(\alpha(DU))} \circ \partial_H(DU\|KM) = \\
&\quad = \rho_{\nu(\alpha(DU))}(30c^* \cdot kof^* \cdot (talk \cdot zoem + zoem \cdot talk) \cdot \partial_H(DU\|KM)) \\
&\quad = 30c \cdot kof \cdot (talk \cdot \tau + \tau \cdot talk) \cdot \rho_{\nu(\alpha(DU))} \circ \partial_H(DU\|KM) \\
&\quad = 30c \cdot kof \cdot talk \cdot \rho_{\nu(\alpha(DU))} \circ \partial_H(DU\|KM)
\end{aligned}$$

Hence $\rho_{\nu(\alpha(DU))} \circ \partial_H(DU\|KM)$ and $\overline{DU}$ satisfy the same guarded recursion equation. Application of the *Recursive Specification Principle (RSP)* now gives that both processes are equal.

3.3.3. Remark. It may seem that one needs the τ-law T2 ($\tau x = \tau x + x$) in the verification above. Surprisingly we can perform the verification using only the τ-law T1 ($x\tau = x$):

$$kof \cdot (talk \cdot \tau + \tau \cdot talk) = kof \cdot (\tau \| talk) = kof \cdot \tau \lfloor\!\lfloor talk = kof \lfloor\!\lfloor talk = kof \cdot talk.$$

In fact we claim that all the verifications in this article can be done using the τ-law T1 only. So we also do not need the law T3 ($a(\tau x + y) = a(\tau x + y) + ax$).

3.3.4. **Theorem.** *Let p,q be closed terms with p observable in context* $..\|q$. *Then* $\mathrm{ACP}_\tau + \mathrm{RN} + \mathrm{AB} \vdash \tau \cdot \rho_{\nu(\alpha(p))}(p\|q) \cdot \delta = \tau \cdot p \cdot \delta$.

Proof. Easy. □

3.3.5. **Theorem.** *Let x,y be processes, with x observable in context* $..\|y$. *Then we can prove using the axioms TO that:* $tr(\rho_{\nu(\alpha(x))}(x\|y)) \subseteq tr(x)$.

Proof. Using the axioms from Table 1, we rewrite the statement we have to prove into:

$$\rho_{\nu(\alpha(tr(x)))}(tr(x)\|tr(y)) \subseteq tr(x).$$

Because $tr(x), tr(y) \in \mathbb{T}$, it is sufficient to prove that for every $V, W \in \mathbb{T}$ with $\alpha(V)$ observable and $\alpha(W)$ disjoint from $\alpha(V)$ and $\alpha(V)|A$:

$$\rho_{\nu(\alpha(V))}(V\|W) \subseteq V.$$

First we apply the definition of the merge-operator on trace sets:

$$\rho_{\nu(\alpha(V))}(V\|W) = \rho_{\nu(\alpha(V))}(\{\sigma \mid \exists v \in V,\ w \in W : \sigma \in v\|w\}).$$

The theorem is proved if we show for all $v \in V$ and $w \in W$ that:

$$\rho_{\nu(\alpha(V))}(v \| w) \subseteq V.$$

We prove a slightly stronger fact: Let $v = v_1 \star v_2 \in V$ and let $w \in W$. Then:

$$v_1 \star \rho_{\nu(\alpha(V))}(v_2 \| w) \subseteq V.$$

The proof goes by means of simultaneous induction on the structure of v_2 and w.

Case 1: $v_2 = \surd$

$$v_1 \star \rho_{\nu(\alpha(V))}(\surd \| w) = v_1 \star \rho_{\nu(\alpha(V))}(\{w\}) = v_1 \star \{\rho_{\nu(\alpha(V))}(w)\} \subseteq v_1 \star \{\lambda, \surd\} \subseteq V$$

Here we use that V is closed under prefixing.

Case 2: $w = \surd$

$$v_1 \star \rho_{\nu(\alpha(V))}(v_2 \| \surd) = v_1 \star \rho_{\nu(\alpha(V))}(\{v_2\}) = v_1 \star \{\rho_{\nu(\alpha(V))}(v_2)\} = v_1 \star \{v_2\} = \{v\} \subseteq V$$

Case 3.1: $v_2 = \lambda$ en $w \in A^\star$

$$v_1 \star \rho_{\nu(\alpha(V))}(\lambda \| w) = v_1 \star \rho_{\nu(\alpha(V))}(\{w\}) = v_1 \star \{\rho_{\nu(\alpha(V))}(w)\} = v_1 \star \{\lambda\} = \{v\} \subseteq V$$

Case 3.2: $v_2 = \lambda$ en $w = w_1 \surd$

$$v_1 \star \rho_{\nu(\alpha(V))}(\lambda \| w_1 \surd) = v_1 \star \rho_{\nu(\alpha(V))}(\{w_1\}) = v_1 \star \{\rho_{\nu(\alpha(V))}(w_1)\} = v_1 \star \{\lambda\} = \{v\} \subseteq V$$

Case 4.1: $v_2 \in A^\star$ en $w = \lambda$

$$v_1 \star \rho_{\nu(\alpha(V))}(v_2 \| \lambda) = v_1 \star \rho_{\nu(\alpha(V))}(\{v_2\}) = v_1 \star \{\rho_{\nu(\alpha(V))}(v_2)\} = v_1 \star \{v_2\} = \{v\} \subseteq V$$

Case 4.2: $v_2 = v_3 \surd$ en $w = \lambda$

$$v_1 \star \rho_{\nu(\alpha(V))}(v_3 \surd \| \lambda) = v_1 \star \rho_{\nu(\alpha(V))}(\{v_3\}) = v_1 \star \{\rho_{\nu(\alpha(V))}(v_3)\} = v_1 \star \{v_3\} = \{v_1 \star v_3\} \subseteq V$$

(V is closed under prefixing.)

Case 5.1: $v_2 = av_3$, $w = bw_1$ en $\gamma(a,b) = \delta$

$$\begin{aligned} v_1 \star \rho_{\nu(\alpha(V))}(av_3 \| bw_1) &= v_1 \star \rho_{\nu(\alpha(V))}(a(v_3 \| bw_1) \cup b(av_3 \| w_1)) \\ &= v_1 \star a \star \rho_{\nu(\alpha(V))}(v_3 \| bw_1) \cup v_1 \star \rho_{\nu(\alpha(V))}(av_3 \| w_1) \subseteq V \end{aligned}$$

(Apply induction hypothesis.)

Case 5.2: $v_2 = av_3$, $w = bw_1$ en $\gamma(a,b) \in A$

$$v_1 \star \rho_{\nu(\alpha(V))}(av_3 \| bw_1) = v_1 \star \rho_{\nu(\alpha(V))}(a(v_3 \| bw_1) \cup b(av_3 \| w_1) \cup \gamma(a,b)(v_3 \| w_1))$$

$$= v_1 \star a \star \rho_{\nu(\alpha(V))}(v_3 \| b w_1) \cup v_1 \star \rho_{\nu(\alpha(V))}(a v_3 \| w_1) \cup$$
$$\cup v_1 \star a \star \rho_{\nu(\alpha(V))}(v_3 \| w_1) \subseteq V$$

(Apply induction hypothesis.) $\square$

Notice that the $\subseteq$-sign in Theorem 3.3.5 cannot be changed into an $=$-sign. If $tr(y)$ contains no traces ending on $\surd$, then $tr(\rho_{\nu(\alpha(x))}(x \| y)$ will also contain no such traces, even if they are in $tr(x)$.

3.3.6. THEOREM. *Let x,y be processes, with x observable in context ..$\|y$, and let $H \subseteq A$. Then we can prove using the axioms TO that: $tr(\rho_{\nu(\alpha(x))} \circ \partial_H(x \| y)) \subseteq tr(x)$.*

PROOF. Just like we did in the proof of Theorem 3.3.5, we reformulate the statement. Let $V, W \in \mathbb{T}$ with $\alpha(V)$ observable, and $\alpha(W)$ disjoint from $\alpha(V)$ and $\alpha(V)|A$. We have to prove:

$$\rho_{\nu(\alpha(V))} \circ \partial_H(V \| W) \subseteq V.$$

For $X, Y \in \mathbb{T}$ we have that $\partial_H(X) \subseteq X$ and $X \subseteq Y \Rightarrow \rho_f(X) \subseteq \rho_f(Y)$. Hence

$$\rho_{\nu(\alpha(V))} \circ \partial_H(V \| W) \subseteq \rho_{\nu(\alpha(V))}(V \| W).$$

From the proof of Theorem 3.3.5 we conclude:

$$\rho_{\nu(\alpha(V))}(V \| W) \subseteq V. \quad \square$$

The following corollary of Theorem 3.3.6 plays an important role in this article because it allows us to derive a property of a system as a whole from a property of a component (this is the essence of compositionality).

3.3.7. COROLLARY. *Let x,y be processes, with x observable in context ..$\|y$, let $H \subseteq A$ and suppose $f = \nu(\alpha(x))$. If x* **sat** *$S(\sigma)$, then:*

$$\rho_f \circ \partial_H(x \| y) \ \mathbf{sat}\ S(\sigma)$$

and consequently

$$\partial_H(x \| y) \ \mathbf{sat}\ S(\rho_f(\sigma)).$$

3.4. REMARK. The formal definitions of the notions 'observable' and 'localisation' in this section are quite complex. The definitions are much simpler if one works with the synchronisation-merge $\|_A$ of Olderog and Hoare [15] instead of the parallel combinator $\|$ of ACP. In fact the whole discussion of this article can be simplified considerably if one uses the $\|_A$-combinator. The main reason for this is that the combinator corresponds quite directly with logical conjunction of trace-specifications (see [14]).

Still, one cannot say that $\|_A$ is a better operator than $\|$ in general. The synchronisation format of the $\|$-operator is very flexible and often allows for elegant specifications. An unpleasant property of the $\|_A$-operator is that it is not associative (in general $(x\|_B y)\|_C z \neq x\|_B(y\|_C z)$). We think that the operators $\|$ and $\|_A$ are both very useful and that therefore notions like 'observable', 'localisation' and 'redundancy in context' should be worked out for both.

4. Redundancy in a context

We want to prove, in a compositional way, that in a given context a summand in a specification can be omitted. We will restrict ourselves in this article to the case where the summand occurs in a 'linear' equation.

4.1. Definition. Let $E = \{X=t_X \mid X\in V_E\}$ be a recursive specification. A set $C\subseteq V_E$ of variables is called a *cluster* if for each $X\in C$, t_X is of the form:

$$\sum_{k=1}^{m} a_k\cdot X_k + \sum_{l=1}^{n} Y_l$$

for actions $a_k\in A_\tau$, variables $X_k\in C$ and $Y_l\in V_E-C$. Cluster C is called *isolated* if variables from C do not occur in the terms for the variables from V_E-C.

4.2. Definition. Let $E = \{X=t_X \mid X\in V_E\}$ be a recursive specification and let C be an isolated cluster in E. Let $X_0,X_1,X_2\in C$, $a\in A_\tau$ and let aX_2 be a summand of t_{X_1}. Let E' be obtained from E by replacing summand aX_2 in t_{X_1} by a 'fresh' atom t. Write $p\equiv\langle X_0|E\rangle$ and $p'\equiv\langle X_0|E'\rangle$. Let y be a process with p observable in context $..\|y$. Let $H\subseteq A$. The summand aX_2 of p *is redundant in the context* $\partial_H(..\|y)$ if:

$$tr(\rho_{\nu(\alpha(p))}\circ\partial_H(p\|y))\cap\{\sigma a\mid\sigma t\in tr(p')\}=\varnothing.$$

4.2.1. Comment. One can say that the set $\{\sigma a\mid\sigma t\in tr(p')\}$ is the contribution of summand aX_2 to $tr(p)$. Theorem 3.3.6 gives that $tr(\rho_{\nu(\alpha(p))}\circ\partial_H(p\|y))$ is also a subset of $tr(p)$. If summand aX_2 is redundant, this means that all behaviours of p of the form 'go from state X_1 with an a-step to state X_2' are not possible if p is placed in the context $\partial_H(..\|y)$.

We give an example which shows why we require in Definition 4.2 that cluster C is isolated. Assume a trijective communication function γ with $\gamma(a,\bar{a})=a^*$ and $\gamma(b,\bar{b})=b^*$. Assume further that $H=\{a,\bar{a},b,\bar{b}\}$ en $I=\{a^*,b^*\}$. Consider the following recursive specification E:

$$X_0 = aX_0 + X_1$$

$$X_1 = b\cdot\tau_I\circ\partial_H(X_0\|\bar{a}\cdot c)$$

In this system X_0 forms a cluster which is not isolated. We derive:

$$X_0 = aX_0 + b\cdot c\cdot\delta.$$

From this equation it is easy to see that X_0 is observable in context $..\|\bar{b}$. We have:

$$\rho_{\nu(\alpha(X_0))} \circ \partial_H(X_0 \| \overline{b}) = b \cdot c \cdot \delta.$$

If the condition in Definition 4.2 that C is isolated would be absent, then the summand aX_0 would (by definition) be redundant in context $\partial_H(.. \| \overline{b})$. However, the summand cannot be omitted: outside the cluster it plays an essential role!

We can now formulate the central proof principle of this article:

A redundant summand can be omitted.

Below we formally present this principle as a theorem.

4.3. THEOREM. *Let $p \equiv \langle X_0 | E \rangle$ and $q \equiv \langle Y_0 | F \rangle$, with E and F guarded recursive specifications, and p observable in context $.. \| q$. Let $H \subseteq A$. Let C be an isolated cluster in E with $X_0, X_1, X_2 \in C$, $a \in A_\tau$ and aX_2 a summand of t_{X_1}. Let E' and $\overline{E}$ be obtained from E by resp. replacing aX_2 by a fresh atom t, and omitting it. Let $p' \equiv \langle X_0 | E' \rangle$ and $\overline{p} \equiv \langle X_0 | \overline{E} \rangle$. Suppose that* ACP$_\tau$ + RDP + RN + PR + TO *proves that summand aX_2 is redundant. Then:* ACP$_\tau$ + RDP + RN + PR + AIP$^-$ $\vdash \partial_H(p \| q) = \partial_H(\overline{p} \| q)$.

PROOF. Omitted. The proof uses a bisimulation model generated by Plotkin like action rules. It is proved that the (infinitary) axiom system ACP$_\tau$ + RDP + RN + PR + AIP$^-$ is sound and complete for processes represented by a guarded specification. Consequently it is enough to prove that $\partial_H(p \| q)$ and $\partial_H(\overline{p} \| q)$ are bisimilar. The proof that the obvious candidate for a bisimulation between these processes indeed *is* a bisimulation uses the fact that every trace of actions in the transition system of an expression p is also a (provable) element of $tr(p)$. □

4.4. *Remark.* A summand which can be omitted is in general not redundant. In every context the second summand of the equation

$$X = aX + aX$$

can be omitted, even if it is not redundant. At present we have no idea how a 'reversed version' of Theorem 4.3 would look like.

4.5. *Proving redundancies.* Now we know that a redundant summand can be omitted, it becomes of course interesting to look for techniques which allow us to prove that summands are redundant. The following strategy works in most cases.

Let E, C, X_0, etc., be as given in Definition 4.2. In order to prove that the summand is redundant, it is enough to show that for some predicate $S(\sigma)$:

$$p' \textbf{ sat } \forall \sigma' : \sigma = \sigma' t \Rightarrow S(\sigma' a) \quad \text{and}$$

$$\rho_{\nu(\alpha(p))} \circ \partial_H(p \| y) \textbf{ sat } \neg S(\sigma).$$

If the cluster C is finite, then $\{\sigma a \mid \sigma t \in tr(p')\}$ is a regular language and can be denoted by a predicate in the trace-specification language of Section 2.4. Consequently we can in such cases always express that a summand is redundant.

4.6. Example. We return to Example 1.2 and show how the statement

$$\partial_H(DU \| KM) = \partial_H(\overline{DU} \| KM)$$

can be proved with the notions presented in this section. KM is observable in context $DU\|..$, and DU is observable in context $..\|KM$. The specification of DU contains no isolated clusters, but using RSP we can give an equivalent specification where the set of variables as a whole forms an isolated cluster ($DU = UD$).

UD	$=$	$30c \cdot UD_1 + kof \cdot UD_2$
UD_1	$=$	$kof \cdot UD_2$
UD_2	$=$	$talk \cdot UD$

TABLE 2. Specification of DU

In Example 2.4.2 we already observed that:

$$KM \text{ sat } \sigma\!\downarrow\!\overline{kof} \leqslant \sigma\!\downarrow\!\overline{30c}.$$

Because of Corollary 3.3.7 we also have:

$$\rho_{\nu(\alpha(KM))} \circ \partial_H(UD \| KM) \text{ sat } \sigma\!\downarrow\!\overline{kof} \leqslant \sigma\!\downarrow\!\overline{30c}.$$

The alphabet of process $\partial_H(UD \| KM)$ contains no actions $\overline{kof}$ or $\overline{30c}$, because these actions are in H. This implies that occurrences of these actions in traces from $tr(\rho_{\nu(\alpha(KM))} \circ \partial_H(UD \| KM))$ 'originated' (by renaming) from actions kof^* and $30c^*$. Hence:

$$\partial_H(UD \| KM) \text{ sat } \sigma\!\downarrow\!kof^* \leqslant \sigma\!\downarrow\!30c^*.$$

But since the alphabet of $\partial_H(UD \| KM)$ contains no actions kof and $30c$, this implies:

$$\rho_{\nu(\alpha(UD))} \circ \partial_H(UD \| KM) \text{ sat } \sigma\!\downarrow\!kof \leqslant \sigma\!\downarrow\!30c.$$

Define UD' by:

UD'	$=$	$30c \cdot UD'_1 + t$
UD'_1	$=$	$kof \cdot UD'_2$
UD'_2	$=$	$talk \cdot UD'$

Of course we have

$$UD' \textbf{ sat } \forall\sigma' : \sigma=\sigma' t \Rightarrow (\sigma' kof)\downarrow kof > (\sigma' kof)\downarrow 30c.$$

This shows that the second summand in the equation from UD is redundant. □

In the example above, we gave a long proof of a trivial fact. The nice thing about the proof is however that it is compositional and only uses general properties of the separate components. This makes that the technique can be used also in less trivial situations where the number of states of the components is large.

In the sequel we will speak about redundant summands of equations which are not part of a cluster. What we mean in such a case is that the corresponding system of equations can be transformed into another system, that a certain summand in the new system is redundant, and that the system which results from omitting this summand is equivalent to the system obtained by omitting the summand in the original system that was called 'redundant'.

5. A WORKCELL ARCHITECTURE

In this section we present a modular verification of a small system which is described in [4, 13].

One can speak about *Computer Integrated Manufacturing (CIM)* if computers play a role in all phases of an industrial production process. In the CIM-philosophy one views a plant as a (possibly hierarchically organized) set of concurrently operating *workcells*. Each workcell is responsible for a well-defined part of the production process, for instance the filling and closing of bottles of milk.

In principle it is possible to specify the behaviour of individual workcells in process algebra. A composite workcell, or even a plant, can then be described as the parallel composition of a number of more elementary workcells. Proof techniques from process algebra can be applied to show that a composite workcell has the desired external behaviour.

In general, not all capabilities of a workcell which is part of a CIM-architecture will be used. A robot which can perform a multitude of tasks, can be part of an architecture where its only task is to fasten a bolt. Other possibilities of the robot will be used only when the architecture is changed. A large part of the behaviours of workcells will be redundant in the context of the CIM-architecture of which they are part. Therefore it can be expected that the notions which are presented in the previous sections of this article, will be useful in the verification of such systems.

5.1. *Specification*

5.1.1. The external behaviour. We want to construct a composite workcell which satisfies the following specification.

$$SPEC = \sum_{n=0}^{N} r\,1(n) \cdot SPEC^n \cdot SPEC$$

$$SPEC^0 = s\,0(r) \qquad SPEC^{n+1} = s\,10(proc(p\,1)) \cdot SPEC^n$$

TABLE 3. Specification of a composite workcell

Via port 1, the workcell accepts an order to produce n products of type $proc(p\,1)$ and to deliver these products at port 10. Here $0 \leqslant n \leqslant N$ for a given upperbound $N > 0$. After execution of the order, the workcell gives a signal r at port 0, and returns to its initial state (r = ready).

5.1.2. Architecture. The architecture of the system that has to implement this specification is depicted in Figure 1.

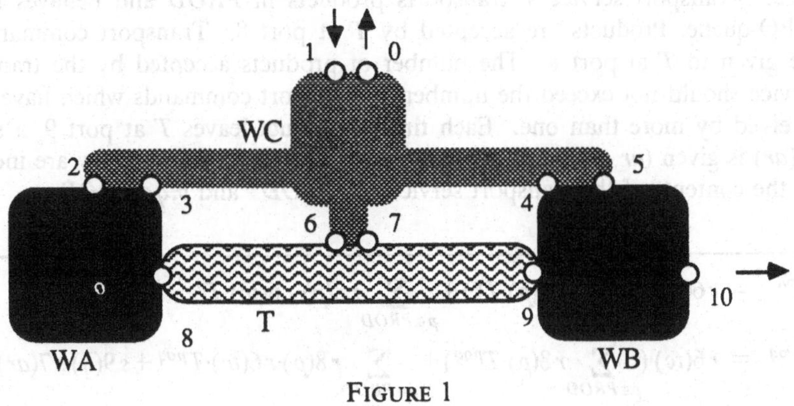

FIGURE 1

There are four components: Workcell A (WA), Workcell B (WB), the Transport service T, and the Workcell Controller WC.

5.1.3. Workcell A. By means of a signal n at port 2, Workcell A receives the order to produce n products of type $p\,1$. The cell performs the job and delivers the products to the Transport service T at port 8. Thereafter a message r is sent at port 3, to indicate that a next order can be given.

$$WA = \sum_{n=0}^{N} r\,2(n) \cdot XA^n$$

$$XA^0 = s\,3(r) \cdot WA \qquad XA^{n+1} = s\,8(p\,1) \cdot XA^n$$

TABLE 4. Specification of Workcell A

5.1.4. Workcell B. By means of a signal n at port 4, Workcell B receives the order to process n products. B receives products from a set $PROD$ at port 9. An incoming product p is processed and the result $proc(p) \in PROD$ is delivered at port 10 ($proc$ = processed). Thereafter a message r is sent at port 5 and the workcell returns to its initial state. We assume that $p1 \in PROD$.

$$WB = \sum_{n=0}^{N} r4(n) \cdot XB^n$$

$$XB^0 = s5(r) \cdot WB \qquad XB^{n+1} = \sum_{p \in PROD} r9(p) \cdot s10(proc(p)) \cdot XB^n$$

TABLE 5. Specification of Workcell B

5.1.5. Transport service T transports products in $PROD$ and behaves like a FIFO-queue. Products are accepted by T at port 8. Transport commands tc are given to T at port 6. The number of products accepted by the transport service should not exceed the number of transport commands which have been received by more than one. Each time a product leaves T at port 9, a signal $s7(ar)$ is given (ar = arrival). Variables in the specification below are indexed by the contents of the transport service: $\sigma \in PROD^*$ and $p,q \in PROD$.

$$T^{\lambda} = r6(tc) \cdot (\sum_{p \in PROD} r8(p) \cdot T^p) + \sum_{p \in PROD} r8(p) \cdot r6(tc) \cdot T^p$$

$$T^{\sigma q} = r6(tc) \cdot (\sum_{p \in PROD} r8(p) \cdot T^{p\sigma q}) + \sum_{p \in PROD} r8(p) \cdot r6(tc) \cdot T^{p\sigma q} + s9(q) \cdot s7(ar) \cdot T^{\sigma}$$

TABLE 6. Specification of Transport service

5.1.6. Workcell Controller WC is the boss of components WA, T and WB. From his superiors (via port 1), WC can get the order to take care of the manufacturing of n products $proc(p1)$. In order to execute this order, WC sends a stream of commands to his subordinates, receiving progress reports from these subordinates in between. When the controller thinks that the task has been completed, he generates a signal $s0(r)$.

$$WC = \sum_{n=0}^{N} r1(n) \cdot s4(n) \cdot XC^n$$

$$XC^0 = r5(r) \cdot s0(r) \cdot WC \qquad XC^{n+1} = s2(1) \cdot r3(r) \cdot s6(tc) \cdot r7(ar) \cdot XC^n$$

TABLE 7. Specification of Workcell Controller

5.1.7. $\mathbb{D} = \{n \mid 0 \leqslant n \leqslant N\} \cup \{r, tc, ar\} \cup PROD$ is the set of objects which can be communicated in the system, and $\mathbb{P} = \{0,1,...,10\}$ is the set of port-names used. Communication takes place following the read/send-scheme:

$$\gamma(rp(d), sp(d)) = cp(d) \quad \text{for } p \in \mathbb{P},\ d \in \mathbb{D}$$

and γ yields δ in all other cases. Important sets of actions are:

$$H = \{rp(d), sp(d) \mid 2 \leqslant p \leqslant 9 \text{ and } d \in \mathbb{D}\} \quad \text{and}$$

$$I = \{cp(d) \mid 2 \leqslant p \leqslant 9 \text{ and } d \in \mathbb{D}\}.$$

The implementation as a whole can now be described by:

$$\boxed{IMPL = \partial_H(WC \| WA \| T^\lambda \| WB)}$$

5.2. THEOREM (CORRECTNESS IMPLEMENTATION).

$$\text{ACP}_\tau + \text{SC} + \text{RDP} + \text{PR} + \text{AIP}^- + \text{AB} + \text{CA} \vdash \tau_I(IMPL) = SPEC.$$

PROOF. In seven steps we transform $\tau_I(IMPL)$ to $SPEC$. Before we start with the 'real' calculations, we show in the first three steps that in the specifications of components WA, T and WB, a large number of summands can be omitted. Notice that communication is trijective and that each component of $IMPL$ is observable in context with the other components.

First we use that the only command which is given by the controller to Workcell A is a request to produce a single product $p\,1$. This means that:

$$IMPL \ \textbf{sat} \ \sigma{\downarrow}c\,2(n) = 0 \quad \text{for } n \neq 1.$$

Consequently

$$\rho_{\nu(\alpha(WA))}(IMPL) \ \textbf{sat} \ \sigma{\downarrow}r\,2(n) = 0 \quad \text{for } n \neq 1.$$

Using the approach of Section 4.5, together with Theorem 4.3, we obtain that all the summands in the specification of WA which correspond to the acceptance of a command different from $r\,2(1)$ are redundant. We have

$$IMPL = \partial_H(WC \| \overline{WA} \| T^\lambda \| WB),$$

where $\overline{WA}$ is given by:

$$\boxed{\overline{WA} = r\,2(1) \cdot s\,8(p\,1) \cdot s\,3(r) \cdot \overline{WA}}$$

Hence:

$$\tau_I(IMPL) = \tau_I \circ \partial_H(WC \| \overline{WA} \| T^\lambda \| WB). \qquad \text{(step 1)}$$

Also component T^λ is clearly a candidate for simplification. With some simple trace-theoretic arguments we show that nearly all summands in the specification of T^λ are redundant.

The only product which is delivered by $\overline{WA}$ at port 8 is $p\,1$. This means that:

$$IMPL \textbf{ sat } \sigma{\downarrow}c\,8(p) = 0 \quad \text{for } p \neq p\,1. \tag{1}$$

From the behaviour of component WC we conclude:

$$IMPL \textbf{ sat } \sigma{\downarrow}c\,6(tc) \leqslant \sigma{\downarrow}c\,3(r). \tag{2}$$

Further we deduce from the behaviour of $\overline{WA}$:

$$IMPL \textbf{ sat } \sigma{\downarrow}c\,3(r) \leqslant \sigma{\downarrow}c\,8(p\,1). \tag{3}$$

From (2) and (3) together we conclude that the number of transport commands at port 6 is less or equal to the number of products $p\,1$ that are handed to the transport service at port 8:

$$IMPL \textbf{ sat } \sigma{\downarrow}c\,6(tc) \leqslant \sigma{\downarrow}c\,8(p\,1). \tag{4}$$

From the specification of $\overline{WA}$ we learn that A does not deliver products without being asked for:

$$IMPL \textbf{ sat } \sigma{\downarrow}c\,8(p\,1) \leqslant \sigma{\downarrow}c\,2(1). \tag{5}$$

Further it follows from the specification of WC that the number of commands given to A by the controller, never exceeds the number of ar-signals with more than one:

$$IMPL \textbf{ sat } \sigma{\downarrow}c\,2(1) \leqslant \sigma{\downarrow}c\,7(ar) + 1. \tag{6}$$

From (5) and (6) together we conclude:

$$IMPL \textbf{ sat } \sigma{\downarrow}c\,8(p\,1) \leqslant \sigma{\downarrow}c\,7(ar) + 1. \tag{7}$$

From formulas (1), (4) and (7) it follows that nearly all summands in the specification of T^λ are redundant.

$$\tau_I \circ \partial_H(WC \| \overline{WA} \| T^\lambda \| WB) = \tau_I \circ \partial_H(WC \| \overline{WA} \| T \| WB) \qquad \text{(step 2)}$$

where T is given by:

$$\boxed{T = r\,8(p\,1) \cdot r\,6(tc) \cdot s\,9(p\,1) \cdot s\,7(ar) \cdot T}$$

The transport service delivers at port 9 only products of type $p\,1$. Therefore all summands in the specification of WB which correspond to the acceptance of another product, are redundant.

$$\tau_I \circ \partial_H(WC \| \overline{WA} \| T \| WB) = \tau_I \circ \partial_H(WC \| \overline{WA} \| T \| \overline{WB}) \qquad \text{(step 3)}$$

where $\overline{WB}$ is given by:

$$\overline{WB} = \sum_{n=0}^{N} r\,4(n)\cdot\overline{XB}^n$$

$$\overline{XB}^0 = s\,5(r)\cdot\overline{WB} \qquad \overline{XB}^{n+1} = r\,9(p\,1)\cdot s\,10(proc(p\,1))\cdot\overline{XB}^n$$

We will now 'zoom in' on components WC, $\overline{WA}$ and T. Define:

$$H' = \{rp(d), sp(d) \mid p \in \{2,3,6,7,8\} \text{ and } d \in \mathbb{D}\} \quad \text{and}$$
$$I' = \{cp(d) \mid p \in \{2,3,6,7,8\} \text{ and } d \in \mathbb{D}\}.$$

Application of the conditional axioms CA gives:

$$\tau_I \circ \partial_H(WC \| \overline{WA} \| T \| \overline{WB}) = \tau_I \circ \partial_H(\tau_{I'} \circ \partial_{H'}(WC \| \overline{WA} \| T) \| \overline{WB}). \quad \text{(step 4)}$$

Let W be given by:

$$W = \sum_{n=0}^{N} r\,1(n)\cdot s\,4(n)\cdot W^n$$

$$W^0 = r\,5(r)\cdot s\,0(r)\cdot W \qquad W^{n+1} = \tau\cdot s\,9(p\,1)\cdot W^n$$

We prove that $W = \tau_{I'} \circ \partial_{H'}(WC \| \overline{WA} \| T)$, by showing that process $\tau_{I'} \circ \partial_{H'}(WC \| \overline{WA} \| T)$ satisfies the defining equations of W.

$$\tau_{I'} \circ \partial_{H'}(WC \| \overline{WA} \| T) = \sum_{n=0}^{N} r\,1(n)\cdot s\,4(n)\cdot \tau_{I'} \circ \partial_{H'}(XC^n \| \overline{WA} \| T)$$

$$\tau_{I'} \circ \partial_{H'}(XC^0 \| \overline{WA} \| T) = r\,5(r)\cdot s\,0(r)\cdot \tau_{I'} \circ \partial_{H'}(WC \| \overline{WA} \| T)$$

$$\tau_{I'} \circ \partial_{H'}(XC^{n+1} \| \overline{WA} \| T) =$$
$$= \tau_{I'}(c\,2(1)\cdot\partial_{H'}(s\,3(r)\cdot s\,6(tc)\cdot r\,7(ar)\cdot XC^n \| s\,8(p\,1)\cdot s\,3(r)\cdot \overline{WA} \| T))$$
$$= \tau\cdot\tau_{I'}(c\,8(p\,1)\cdot\partial_{H'}(s\,3(r)\cdot s\,6(tc)\cdot r\,7(ar)\cdot XC^n \| s\,3(r)\cdot \overline{WA} \| r\,6(tc)\cdot s\,9(p\,1)\cdot s\,7(ar)\cdot T))$$
$$= \tau\cdot\tau\cdot\tau_{I'}(c\,3(r)\cdot\partial_{H'}(s\,6(tc)\cdot r\,7(ar)\cdot XC^n \| \overline{WA} \| r\,6(tc)\cdot s\,9(p\,1)\cdot s\,7(ar)\cdot T))$$
$$= \tau\cdot\tau_{I'}(c\,6(tc)\cdot\partial_{H'}(r\,7(ar)\cdot XC^n \| \overline{WA} \| s\,9(p\,1)\cdot s\,7(ar)\cdot T))$$
$$= \tau\cdot\tau_{I'}(s\,9(p\,1)\cdot\partial_{H'}(r\,7(ar)\cdot XC^n \| \overline{WA} \| s\,7(ar)\cdot T))$$
$$= \tau\cdot s\,9(p\,1)\cdot\tau_{I'}(c\,7(ar)\cdot\partial_{H'}(XC^n \| \overline{WA} \| T))$$
$$= \tau\cdot s\,9(p\,1)\cdot\tau_{I'} \circ \partial_{H'}(XC^n \| \overline{WA} \| T)$$

We have now derived:

$$\tau_I \circ \partial_H(\tau_{I'} \circ \partial_{H'}(WC \| \overline{WA} \| T) \| \overline{WB}) = \tau_I \circ \partial_H(W \| \overline{WB}). \quad \text{(step 5)}$$

Let V be given by:

$$V = \sum_{n=0}^{N} r1(n)\cdot V^n$$

$$V^0 = \tau\cdot s0(r)\cdot V \qquad V^{n+1} = \tau\cdot s10(proc(p1))\cdot V^n$$

We show that $\tau_I\circ\partial_H(W\|\overline{WB})$ satisfies the defining equations of V.

$$\begin{aligned}\tau_I\circ\partial_H(W\|\overline{WB}) &= \sum_{n=0}^{N} r1(n)\cdot\tau_I\circ\partial_H(s4(n)\cdot W^n\|(\sum_{m=0}^{N} r4(m)\cdot\overline{XB}^m))\\ &= \sum_{n=0}^{N} r1(n)\cdot\tau_I(c4(n)\cdot\partial_H(W^n\|\overline{XB}^n))\\ &= \sum_{n=0}^{N} r1(n)\cdot\tau\cdot\tau_I\circ\partial_H(W^n\|\overline{XB}^n)\end{aligned}$$

$$\tau\cdot\tau_I\circ\partial_H(W^0\|\overline{XB}^0) = \tau\cdot\tau_I(c5(r)\cdot\partial_H(s0(r)\cdot W\|\overline{WB}))\ \tau\cdot s0(r)\cdot\tau_I\circ\partial_H(W\|\overline{WB})$$

$$\begin{aligned}\tau\cdot\tau_I\circ\partial_H(W^{n+1}\|\overline{XB}^{n+1}) &= \tau\cdot\tau_I(c9(p1)\cdot\partial_H(W^n\|s10(proc(p1))\cdot\overline{XB}^n))\\ &= \tau\cdot s10(proc(p1))\cdot\tau_I\circ\partial_H(W^n\|\overline{XB}^n)\end{aligned}$$

(here we use that $\tau(\tau x\|y)=\tau\tau x\lfloor\!\lfloor y=\tau x\lfloor\!\lfloor y=\tau(x\|y)$). From the above derivation it follows that:

$$\tau_I\circ\partial_H(W\|\overline{WB}) = V. \qquad \text{(step 6)}$$

We show that $SPEC$ satisfies the defining equations of V.

$$SPEC = \sum_{n=0}^{N} r1(n)\cdot(\tau\cdot SPEC^n\cdot SPEC)$$

$$\tau\cdot SPEC^0\cdot SPEC = \tau\cdot s0(r)\cdot SPEC$$

$$\tau\cdot SPEC^{n+1}\cdot SPEC = \tau\cdot s10(proc(p1))\cdot(\tau\cdot SPEC^n\cdot SPEC)$$

Hence:

$$V = SPEC. \quad \square \qquad \text{(step 7)}$$

This example shows that a combination of trace-theoretic arguments and the use of alphabet calculus makes it possible to verify simple systems in a compositional and modular way.

ACKNOWLEDGEMENTS
I would like to thank the participants of the PAM seminar, especially Jos Baeten, Jan Bergstra and Hans Mulder, for their comments on earlier versions of this article.

REFERENCES

1. J.C.M. BAETEN, J.A. BERGSTRA (1988). Global renaming operators in concrete process algebra. *Information and Computation 78(3)*, 205-245.
2. J.C.M. BAETEN, J.A. BERGSTRA, J.W. KLOP (1986). Syntax and defining equations for an interrupt mechanism in process algebra. *Fundamenta Informaticae IX(2)*, 127-168.
3. J.C.M. BAETEN, J.A. BERGSTRA, J.W. KLOP (1987). On the consistency of Koomen's Fair Abstraction Rule. *Theoretical Computer Science, 51(1/2)*, 129-176.
4. F. BIEMANS, P. BLONK (1986). On the formal specification and verification of CIM architectures using LOTOS. *Computers in Industry 7(6)*, 491-504.
5. E.W. DIJKSTRA (1976). *A Discipline of Programming*, Prentice-Hall, Englewood Cliff.
6. R.J. VAN GLABBEEK (1987). Bounded nondeterminism and the approximation induction principle in process algebra. F.J. BRANDENBURG, G. VIDAL-NAQUET, M. WIRSING (eds.). *Proceedings STACS 87*, LNCS 247, Springer-Verlag, 336-347.
7. R.J. VAN GLABBEEK, F.W. VAANDRAGER (1987). Petri net models for algebraic theories of concurrency. J.W. DE BAKKER, A.J. NIJMAN, P.C. TRELEAVEN (eds.). *Proceedings PARLE Conference, Eindhoven, Vol. II (Parallel Languages)*, LNCS 259, Springer-Verlag, 224-242.
8. R.J. VAN GLABBEEK, F.W. VAANDRAGER (1988). *Modular Specifications in Process Algebra - With Curious Queues*, CWI Report CS-R8821, Centre for Mathematics and Computer Science, Amsterdam. Extended abstract to appear in *Proceedings of the METEOR Workshop on Algebraic Methods: Theory, Tools and Applications*, LNCS, Springer-Verlag.
9. C.A.R. HOARE (1985). *Communicating Sequential Processes*, Prentice-Hall.
10. C.P.J. KOYMANS, J.C. MULDER (1989). *A Modular Approach to Protocol Verification using Process Algebra.* This volume.
11. K.G. LARSEN (1986). *Context-dependent Bisimulation between Processes*, Ph. D. Thesis, Department of Computer Science, University of Edinburgh.
12. K.G. LARSEN, R. MILNER (1987). A complete protocol verification using relativized bisimulation. TH. OTTMANN (ed.). *Proceedings 14th ICALP, Karlsruhe*, LNCS 267, Springer-Verlag, 126-135.
13. S. MAUW (1989). *Process Algebra as a Tool for the Specification and Verification of CIM-architectures.* This volume.
14. E.-R. OLDEROG (1986). Process theory: semantics, specification and verification. J.W. DE BAKKER, W.-P. DE ROEVER, G. ROZENBERG (eds.). *Current Trends in Concurrency*, LNCS 224, Springer-Verlag, 442-509.
15. E.-R. OLDEROG, C.A.R. HOARE (1986). Specification-oriented semantics

for communicating processes. *Acta Informatica 23*, 9-66.

16. F.W. VAANDRAGER (1986). *Verification of Two Communication Protocols by Means of Process Algebra*, CWI Report CS-R8608, Centre for Mathematics and Computer Science, Amsterdam.
17. J. ZWIERS (1988). *Compositionality, Concurrency and Partial Correctness: Proof Theories for Networks of Processes, and their Connection*, Ph.D. Thesis, Technical University Eindhoven.

A Modular Approach to Protocol Verification using Process Algebra

C.P.J. Koymans
Department of Philosophy, State University of Utrecht
Heidelberglaan 2, 3584 CS Utrecht, The Netherlands

J.C. Mulder
Programming Research Group, University of Amsterdam
P.O. Box 41882, 1009 DB Amsterdam, The Netherlands

A version of the Alternating Bit Protocol is verified by means of process algebra. To avoid a combinatorial explosion, a notion of 'modules' is introduced and the protocol is divided in two such modules. A method is developed for verifying conglomerates of modules and applied to the motivating example.

One of the basic problems in protocol verification is the following: data are to be transmitted from A to B via some unreliable medium M. A protocol has been proposed for doing so correctly and perhaps efficiently. A rigorous mathematical proof of the correctness claim is desired.

Now protocol verification aims at providing the techniques for giving such a proof. Several formalisms have been advocated, but as yet none has been widely accepted.

The framework we adhere to is process algebra. The first protocol correctness proof by means of process algebra is in Bergstra and Klop [2], where a simple version of the Alternating Bit Protocol is verified.

We have tried our hands at a more complicated version, called the Concurrent Alternating Bit Protocol (CABP) and found that the number of possible state transitions was prohibitively large. In this article we propose a divide-and-conquer strategy. We group processes into modules, describe and verify their behaviour and finally combine them. For different approaches, see [4,5,6,7].

In Section 1 we deal with the Concurrent Alternating Bit Protocol (CABP). In Section 2 we present the modular approach. Modules are introduced in Section 3, whereas the verification of the CABP is given in Section 4.

Partial support received from the European Community under ESPRIT project no. 432, An Integrated Formal Approach to Industrial Software Development (METEOR).

1. THE CONCURRENT ALTERNATING BIT PROTOCOL

1.1. Architecture

The architecture of the protocol can be depicted as in Figure 1.1:

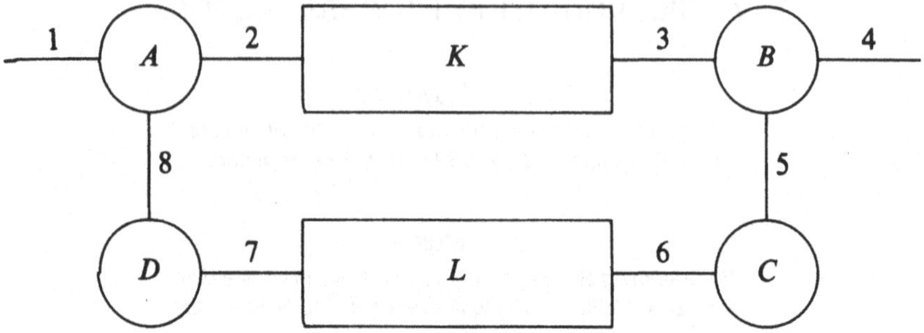

FIGURE 1.1

There are six components:

A: *Data transmitter.* A reads data from port 1 and transmits them repeatedly via channel K until an acknowledgement has been received from D.

K: *Data transmission channel.* K transfers data from A to B and may make two sorts of mistakes: a datum may be corrupted, i.e. changed into some error value e recognizable as such, or it may be lost altogether. However K is supposed to be fair in the sense that it will not make infinitely many mistakes consecutively.

B: *Data receiver.* B receives data from K, outputs them at port 4, and sends an acknowledgement to C via port 5.

C: *Acknowledgement transmitter.* C receives an acknowledgement from B and repeatedly transmits it via L to D.

L: *Acknowledgement transmission channel.* L transfers acknowledgements from C to D. It makes similar mistakes as K.

D: *Acknowledgement receiver.* D receives acknowledgements from L and passes them on to A.

1.2. Remarks

1.2.1. One might propose to collapse A and D into a sender process, and B plus C into a receiver process. The resulting processes would be more complicated and in the correctness proof we would have to decompose them again. Consequently, we present them as separate processes in the first place. Of course, if the reader feels more comfortable when he thinks of A and D as running interleaved on the same physical processor, he is free to do so.

1.2.2. This version of the Alternating Bit Protocol is called 'concurrent' to emphasize the fact that A and C do not wait for a negative response before retransmitting. The idea is that one can freely retransmit in what otherwise would have been idle time, whereas performance gain will occur if the channel malfunctions, because in this version retransmissions start earlier and occur more often.

1.2.3. In [2] it was assumed that neither K nor L ever 'forget' a datum, whereas in [7] a timeout mechanism was added to overcome such a mishap. In Petri-net terms, those protocols pass around a single token. If it ever gets lost, things stop moving, unless a time-out mechanism introduces a fresh token.

In the CABP however, processes A and C keep on firing, so that the rest will have to throw away many tokens to prevent the system from being flooded. In any case, activity never stops, for C never waits for input.

1.3. Data and actions

1.3.1. Data

D is the finite set of data to be transferred from port 1 to port 4.
$B=\{0,1\}$ is the set of acknowledgement bits sent at port 6.
$D \times B$, the Cartesian product set, will be transferred at port 2.
$B \cup \{e\}$, where e is the error value, is used at port 7.
$D \times B \cup \{e\}$ may be sent at port 3.
$\{ac\}$, where ac is an acknowledgement, occurs at ports 5 and 8.
$\mathbb{D} = D \cup D \times B \cup \{0,1,e,ac\}$ is the set of
all transferable data.

1.3.2. Actions

For $d \in \mathbb{D}$ and $p \in \{1, \ldots, 8\}$ there are read, send and transfer actions:

$r(d,p)$: read datum d at port p.
$s(d,p)$: send datum d at port p.
$t(d,p)$: transfer datum d at port p.

In fact $t(d,p)$ is a communication action: $t(d,p) = r(d,p) | s(d,p)$. There are six more atomic actions. They are called *ik*, *jk*, *kk*, *il*, *jl* and *kl* and they are internal actions of K and L corresponding to internal choices. And, of course, there are the inevitable constants δ and τ.

The entire alphabet is then:

$$A = \{r(d,p), s(d,p), t(d,p) \mid d \in \mathbb{D}, 1 \leqslant p \leqslant 8\} \cup \{ik, jk, kk, il, jl, kl\}.$$

The communication function $\cdot|\cdot : A \times A \rightarrow A$ is:

$$a|b = \begin{cases} c \text{ if } \exists d \in \mathbf{D}\ \exists p \in \{1,\dots,8\}\ [\{a,b\} = \{r(d,p), s(d,p)\} \wedge c = t(d,p)] \\ \delta \text{ otherwise.} \end{cases}$$

Two relevant subsets of A are:

$$H = \{r(d,p), s(d,p) \mid d \in \mathbf{D},\ p \in \{2,3,5,6,7,8\}\}$$
$$I = \{t(d,p) \mid d \in \mathbf{D}, 1 \leqslant p \leqslant 8\} \cup \{ik, jk, kk, il, jl, kl\}$$

The process we are investigating is $\tau_I \partial_H(A \| K \| B \| C \| L \| D)$, where $A, \dots, D$ are specified in Section 1.4.

1.4. The individual components
We will describe each component twice, viz. by a state transition diagram and by a recursive set of equations. These states are parameterised by parameters $b \in \{0,1\}$ and $d, d' \in \mathbf{D}$.

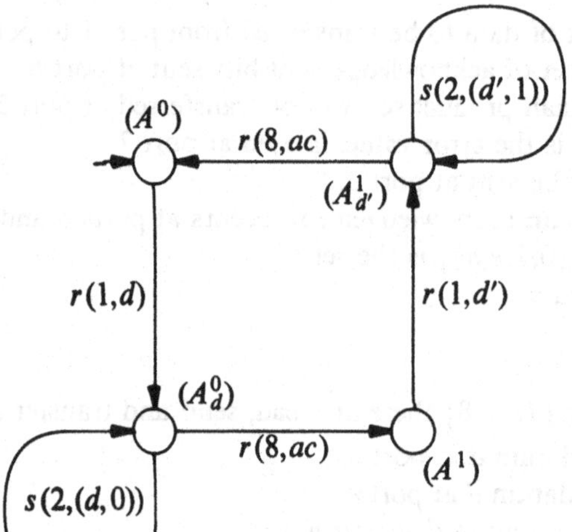

FIGURE 1.2

$$A: \quad A = A^0$$
$$A^b = \sum_{d \in D} r(1,d) \cdot A^b_d$$
$$A^b_d = s(2,(d,b)) \cdot A^b_d + r(8,ac) \cdot A^{1-b}$$

$$K: \quad K = \sum_{x \in D \times B} r(2,x) \cdot (ik \cdot s(3,x) + jk \cdot s(3,e) + kk) \cdot K$$

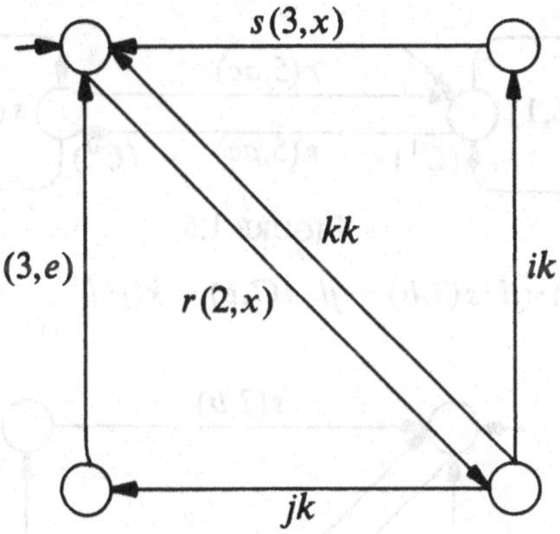

FIGURE 1.3

$$B: \quad B = B^0$$

$$B^b = (r(3,e) + \sum_{d \in D} r(3,(d,1-b))) \cdot B^b + \sum_{d \in D} r(3,(d,b)) \cdot s(4,d) \cdot s(5,ac) \cdot B^{1-b}$$

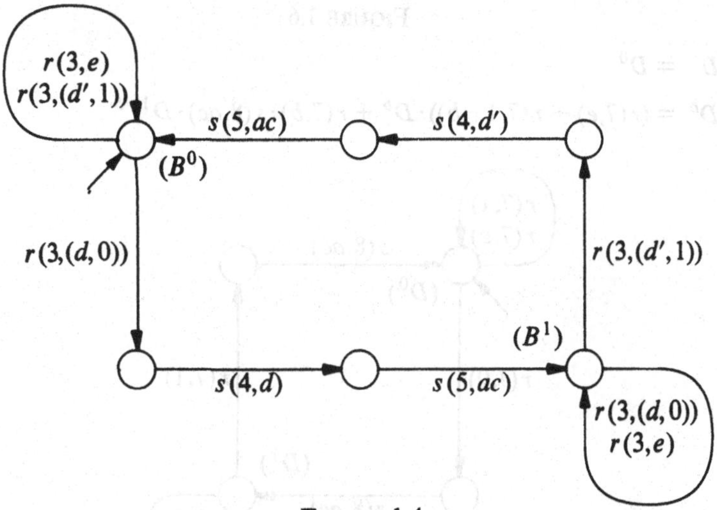

FIGURE 1.4

NOTE. A doubly labelled arrow 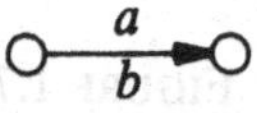 stands for two arrows 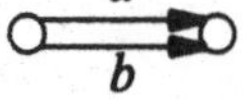

C: $C = C^1$ (N.B. *not* C^0)

$C^b = r(5,ac) \cdot C^{1-b} + s(6,b) \cdot C^b$

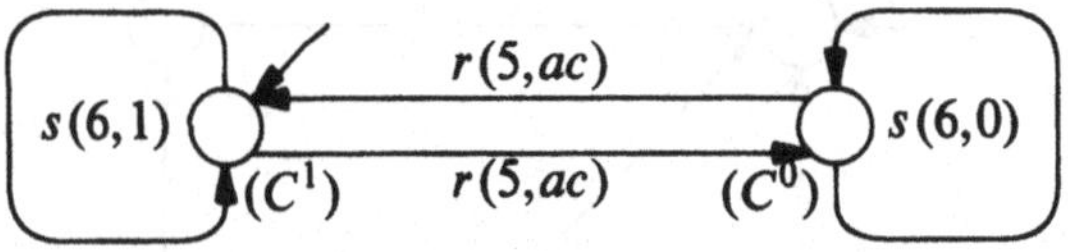

FIGURE 1.5

L: $L = \sum_{b \in B} r(6,b) \cdot (il \cdot s(7,b) + jl \cdot s(7,e) + kl) \cdot L$

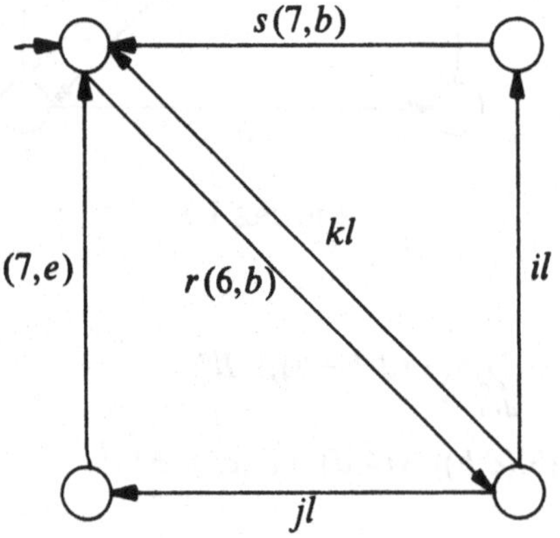

FIGURE 1.6

D: $D = D^0$

$D^b = (r(7,e) + r(7,1-b)) \cdot D^b + r(7,b) \cdot s(8,ac) \cdot D^{1-b}$

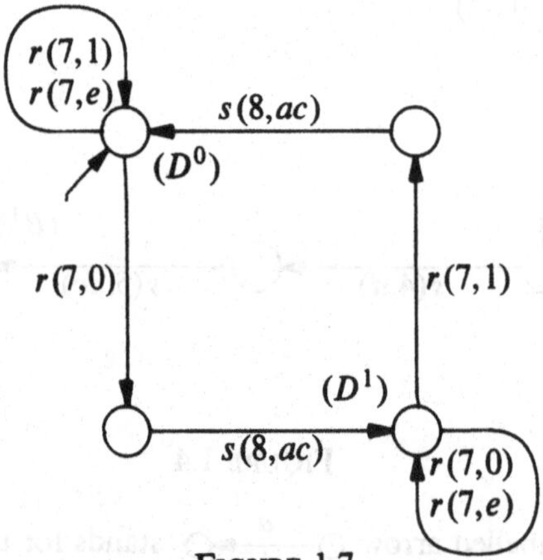

FIGURE 1.7

2. The modular approach

2.1. Running example

When irrelevant details are stripped off, CABP consists of six processes looking like this:

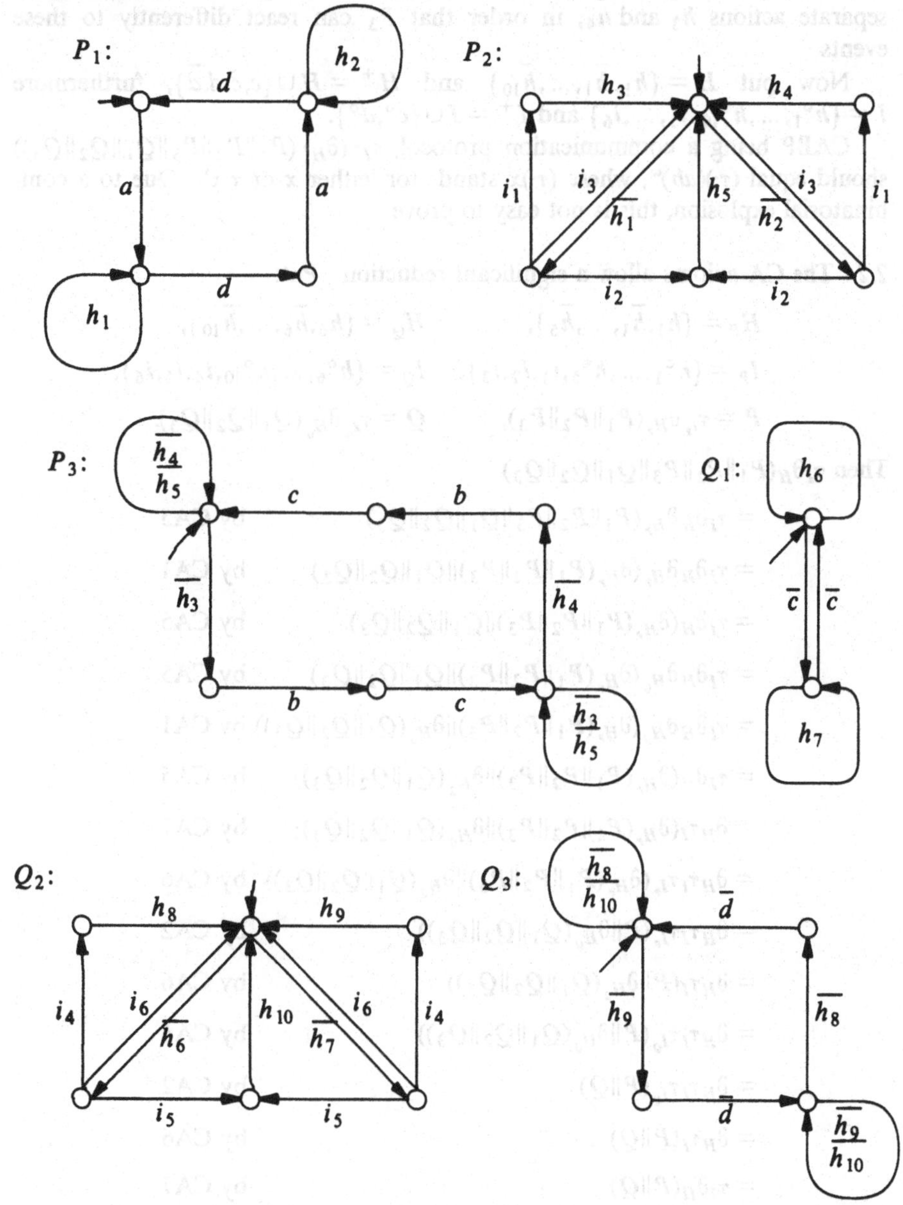

FIGURE 2.1

Here $l|\bar{l} = l^\circ$ for those l that occur overlined.

We put P_1,P_2,P_3,Q_1,Q_2,Q_3 for A,K,B,C,L,D, respectively. The atomic actions have been given more systematic names, too. This renaming forces us to 'unfold' the state transition diagrams of the channels. E.g. where Figure 1.3 contains a single edge labelled $s(3,b)$, P_2 in Figure 2.1 must contain separate actions h_3 and h_4, in order that P_3 can react differently to these events.

Now put $H = \{h_1, \bar{h}_1, \ldots, \bar{h}_{10}\}$ and $H^+ = H \cup \{c, \bar{c}, d, \bar{d}\}$, furthermore $I = \{h^\circ{}_1, \ldots, h^\circ{}_{10}, i_1, \ldots, i_6\}$ and $I^+ = I \cup \{c^\circ, d^\circ\}$.

CABP being a communication protocol, $\tau_{I^+}(\partial_{H^+}(P_1 \| P_2 \| P_3 \| Q_1 \| Q_2 \| Q_3))$ should equal $(\tau\cdot)(ab)^\omega$, where $(\tau\cdot)x$ stands for 'either x or $\tau\cdot x$'. Due to a combinatorial explosion, this is not easy to prove.

2.2. The CA axioms allow a significant reduction. Put:

$$H_P = \{h_1, \bar{h}_1, \ldots, \bar{h}_5\}, \qquad H_Q = \{h_6, \bar{h}_6, \ldots, \bar{h}_{10}\},$$

$$I_P = \{h^\circ{}_1, \ldots, h^\circ{}_5, i_1, i_2, i_3\}, \quad I_Q = \{h^\circ{}_6, \ldots, h^\circ{}_{10}, i_4, i_5, i_6\},$$

$$P = \tau_{I_P}\partial_{H_P}(P_1 \| P_2 \| P_3), \qquad Q = \tau_{I_Q}\partial_{H_Q}(Q_1 \| Q_2 \| Q_3).$$

Then $\tau_I\partial_H(P_1 \| P_2 \| P_3 \| Q_1 \| Q_2 \| Q_3)$

$$\begin{aligned}
&= \tau_I\partial_H\partial_{H_P}(P_1 \| P_2 \| P_3 \| Q_1 \| Q_2 \| Q_3) && \text{by CA5}\\
&= \tau_I\partial_H\partial_{H_P}(\partial_{H_P}(P_1 \| P_2 \| P_3) \| Q_1 \| Q_2 \| Q_3) && \text{by CA1}\\
&= \tau_I\partial_H(\partial_{H_P}(P_1 \| P_2 \| P_3) \| Q_1 \| Q_2 \| Q_3) && \text{by CA5}\\
&= \tau_I\partial_H\partial_{H_Q}(\partial_{H_P}(P_1 \| P_2 \| P_3) \| Q_1 \| Q_2 \| Q_3) && \text{by CA5}\\
&= \tau_I\partial_H\partial_{H_Q}(\partial_{H_P}(P_1 \| P_2 \| P_3) \| \partial_{H_Q}(Q_1 \| Q_2 \| Q_3)) && \text{by CA1}\\
&= \tau_I\partial_H(\partial_{H_P}(P_1 \| P_2 \| P_3) \| \partial_{H_Q}(Q_1 \| Q_2 \| Q_3)) && \text{by CA5}\\
&= \partial_H\tau_I(\partial_{H_P}(P_1 \| P_2 \| P_3) \| \partial_{H_Q}(Q_1 \| Q_2 \| Q_3)) && \text{by CA7}\\
&= \partial_H\tau_I\tau_{I_P}(\partial_{H_P}(P_1 \| P_2 \| P_3) \| \partial_{H_Q}(Q_1 \| Q_2 \| Q_3)) && \text{by CA6}\\
&= \partial_H\tau_I\tau_{I_P}(P \| \partial_{H_Q}(Q_1 \| Q_2 \| Q_3)) && \text{by CA2}\\
&= \partial_H\tau_I(P \| \partial_{H_Q}(Q_1 \| Q_2 \| Q_3)) && \text{by CA6}\\
&= \partial_H\tau_I\tau_{I_Q}(P \| \partial_{H_Q}(Q_1 \| Q_2 \| Q_3)) && \text{by CA6}\\
&= \partial_H\tau_I\tau_{I_Q}(P \| Q) && \text{by CA2}\\
&= \partial_H\tau_I(P \| Q) && \text{by CA6}\\
&= \tau_I\partial_H(P \| Q) && \text{by CA7}
\end{aligned}$$

So we may first calculate P and Q separately, and then combine them.

This yields:[1]

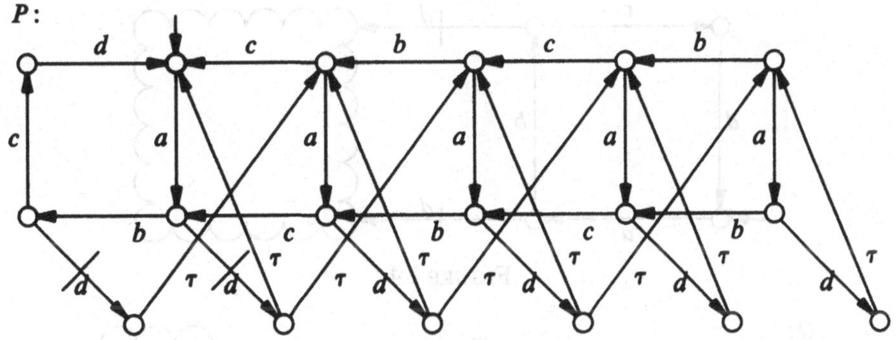

FIGURE 2.2

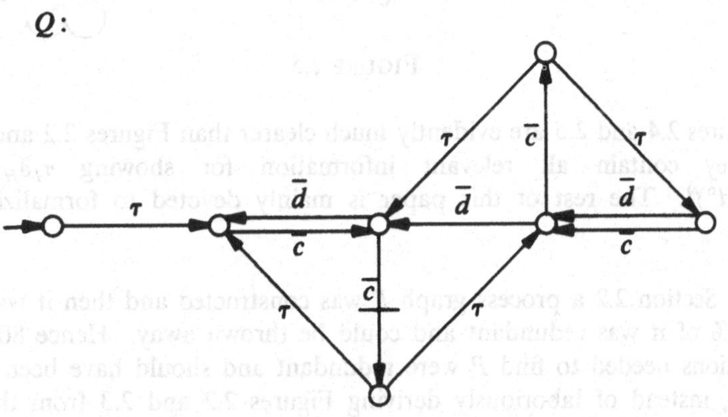

FIGURE 2.3

When merging these processes, one finds that the edges marked with a crossbar (⟶ with crossbar) are redundant in the sense of Vaandrager [7], i.e. they do not communicate and are encapsulated out when P and Q are combined.

It is evident that any edge that can be reached from the root only via one of these redundant edges is itself redundant, too. Inspection of Figures 2.2 and 2.3 shows that this is the case in about 80% of both P and Q. So 80% of these graphs is irrelevant information. We only need to know that they look somewhat like this:

1. This diagram is meant as an illustration only. In the sequel we will argue that this calculation would be a rather cumbersome way of verifying CABP, which is why we left it out.

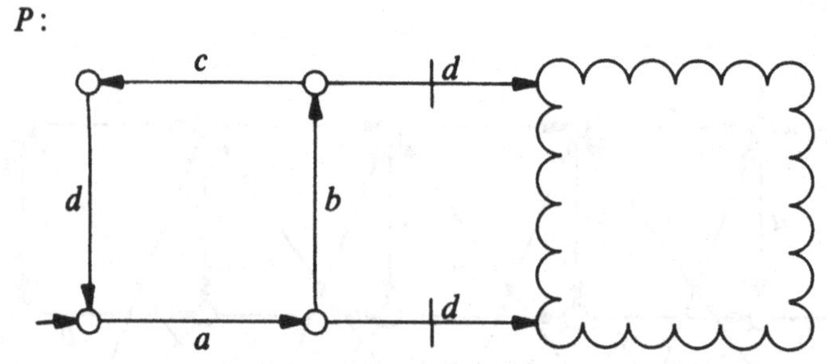

FIGURE 2.4

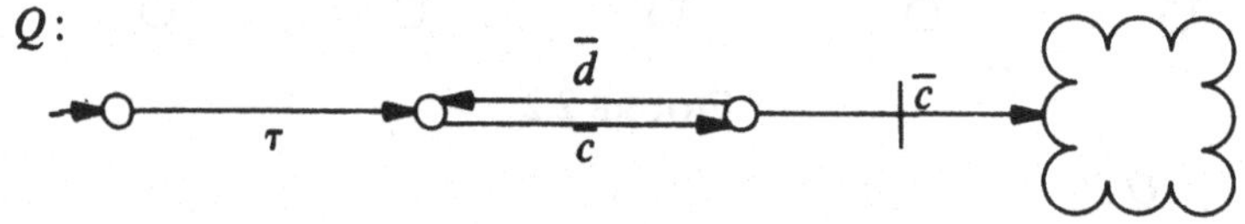

FIGURE 2.5

Figures 2.4 and 2.5 are evidently much clearer than Figures 2.2 and 2.3 and yet they contain all relevant information for showing $\tau_I \partial_H(P \| Q) = \tau(abc^\circ d^\circ)^\omega$. The rest of this paper is mainly devoted to formalizing these ideas.

2.3. In Section 2.2 a process graph P was constructed and then it was argued that 80% of it was redundant and could be thrown away. Hence 80% of the calculations needed to find P were redundant and should have been avoided. That is, instead of laboriously deriving Figures 2.2 and 2.3 from the CABP specification and then simplifying to Figure 2.4 we should have conjectured Figure 2.4 from the information in Section 1, and we should have proved this conjecture by methods to be developed in Section 3. In fact this programme will be carried out in Section 4.

2.4. Figure 2.6 is a simplified version of Figure 1.1:

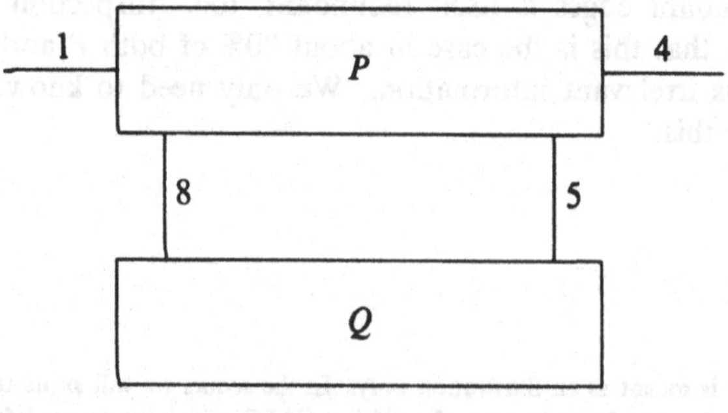

FIGURE 2.6

Recall that P is supposed to communicate at ports 1, 4, 5 and 8, in that order, repeatedly. In this section we denote these communications as a,b,c and d, so a first approximation to P should be $P^* = abcd \cdot P^*$.

2.5. In Section 2.4 it was argued that P 'should be' $(abcd)^\omega$. Of course, it isn't. For, if it were, process Q would not be needed. Q has to pass signals from port 5 to port 8. As these signals do not contain any information, all Q actually does, is ensuring that communication at port 8 occurs later than communication at port 5.

P is ready to communicate at port 8 at any time after communicating at 1. In contrast, the other ports of P only communicate when it is their turn. We will call a port ***robust*** if it always awaits its turn before communicating. Here 'its turn' is defined by a specification, so in case of doubt we may have to talk about robustness relative to a certain specification. For example, in process P, port 8 is not robust relative to P^*, port 5 is not robust relative to $ab\delta$ and all ports are robust relative to P itself.

As a general design principle, whenever we connect two modules via a channel, we will see to it that at least one end is a robust port and hence blocks the channel when it should be inactive. Usually the robust end will be thought of as sending the signal.

2.6. DEFINITION. A ***module specification*** S is a pair $(F(S), R(S))$, where $F(S)$ is a process called the ***functional part,*** and $R(S)$ is a subset of $\alpha(R(S))$ called the ***robustness set.***

Think of a module specification as describing an imperfect black box: $F(S)$ describes the intended behaviour, and the complement of $R(S)$ describes possible deviations from $F(S)$.

EXAMPLES. $S_P = ((abcd)^\omega, \{a,b,c\})$, $S_Q = ((\bar{c}\bar{d})^\omega, \{\bar{d}\})$.
Processes P and Q are to 'implement' S_P and S_Q respectively.

2.7. In Section 3.8 we will define a notion of 'P implements M', define an algebraic criterion for this relation, describe how modules are assembled into larger modules, and prove that a robust module meets its specification.

2.8. REMARK. The terms 'specification' and 'implementation' are meant to suggest that module implementations are interchangeable: if some assembly of modules performs a certain function, then any implementations of these modules will do the job.

For example, channels K and L in Section 1.4 can buffer at most one item at a time. If they are replaced by channels with a larger capacity, P and Q still implement S_P and S_Q, so the combination still works.

3. Modules

3.1. Definition. A *module* is a finitely branching, rooted, directed, connected multigraph with two sorts of edges: *normal* ($\longrightarrow$), and *barred* ($\not\longrightarrow$). Moreover, both sorts of edges are labeled with labels from a finite set $A \cup \{\delta,\tau\}$.

3.2. Notation. $\mathbf{M}$ is the set of modules. If $M \in \mathbf{M}$, then

$r(M)$ is the root of M,
$N(M)$ is the set of nodes of M,
$E(M)$ is its set of edges,
$\alpha(M)$ is its alphabet, i.e. its set of node labels,
$e: n \xrightarrow{a} m$ means that e is an edge from n to m labeled a,
$\pi: n \xrightarrow{\sigma} m$ means that π is a path from n to m, and the labels along π other than τ spell the word $\sigma \in A^*$. If $n = m$, π may be empty. Notice that σ never contains δ.
$\mathbf{G} = \{M \in \mathbf{M} \mid M$ contains no barred edges$\}$. An element of $\mathbf{G}$ will be called a *robust module*.
$\leftrightarrows_{r\tau}$ denotes rooted τ-bisimulation on $\mathbf{G}$, denoted by $\leftrightarrows$ in [1].
$\leftrightarrows_{\tau}$ denotes τ-bisimulation on $\mathbf{G}$, definable by: $g \leftrightarrows_{\tau} h$ iff $\tau \cdot g \leftrightarrows_{r\tau} \tau \cdot h$.

3.3. Definition. With each module specification S we associate a module $M(S)$ in the following way:
Take a process graph G of the functional part $F(S)$ of S, with normal edges, and add barred edges $n \overset{a}{\not\longrightarrow} \cdot$ for each non-robust action a (i.e. $a \in A - R(S)$) and for each node n from which no edge $n \xrightarrow{a} \cdot$ emerges. The destination of the barred edges is immaterial. For definiteness we will make them end in new terminal nodes.

Example. $M(S_P) = M(((abcd)^\omega, \{a,b,c\}))$ becomes:

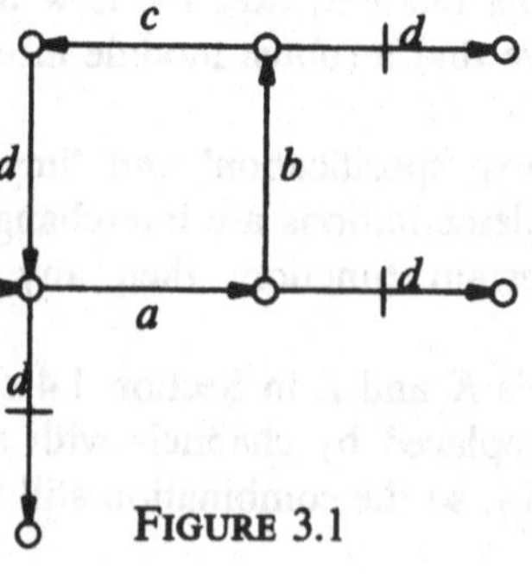

Figure 3.1

3.4. The reader might notice that Figure 3.1 contains one more $\overset{d}{+\!\!\longrightarrow}\cdot$ edge than does Figure 2.4. This is because Figure 3.1 expresses '*P* might always do *d*', whereas Figure 2.4 is based on a careful analysis of exactly when '*P* really can do *d*'. When a port *p* is 'partially' robust, i.e. it is sometimes but not always willing to communicate when it shouldn't, then a module can describe exactly when it is robust and when it isn't, whereas robustness sets can only express that *p* is not completely robust. This is why we study graphs rather than algebraic specifications.

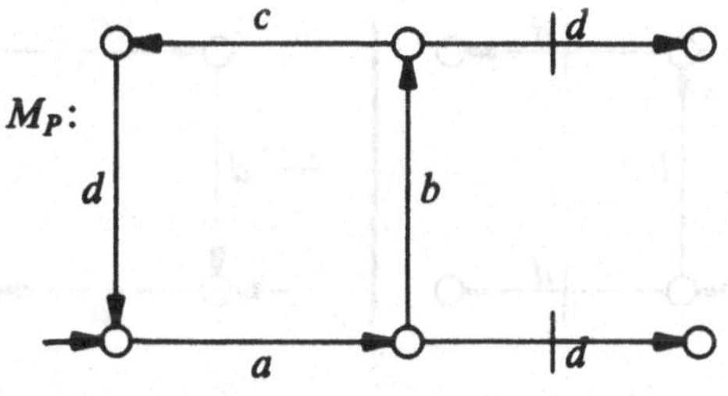

FIGURE 3.2

In the sequel, our running example will be M_P, depicted in Figure 3.2. This is the exact counterpart of Figure 2.4.

3.5. DEFINITION. A node *l* is called *loopy* if its outgoing edges are (precisely) $l \overset{a}{\longrightarrow} l$ for all $a \in A$, i.e. loops labeled with all letters of the alphabet *A*.

EXAMPLE. If $A = \{a,b,c,d\}$, then 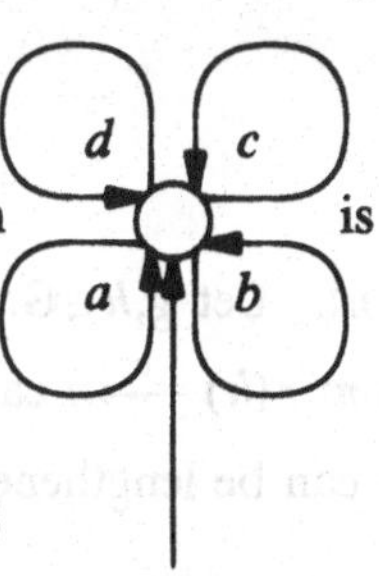 is loopy.

FIGURE 3.3

In the sequel we will abbreviate multiple edges connecting the same nodes, and in particular loops, by multi-labeled edges (as in 1.4), like this:

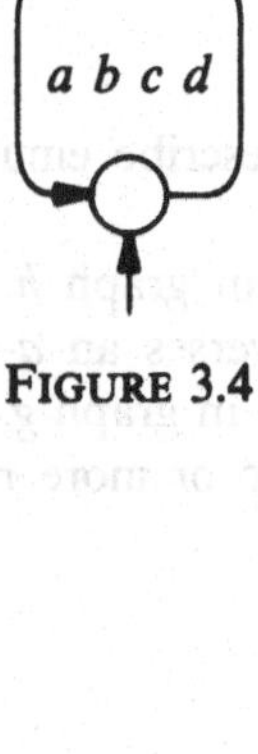

FIGURE 3.4

3.6. DEFINITION. We will need two operations from **M** to **G**:

$|\cdot|$: leave out all barred edges, and

$!\cdot!$: add a loopy node l, and replace each $n \overset{a}{\not\longrightarrow} \cdot$ by $n \overset{a}{\longrightarrow} l$.

In these and all subsequent operations on graphs it is tacitly implied that whenever a graph becomes disconnected, only those parts that can be reached from the root are retained.

EXAMPLES.

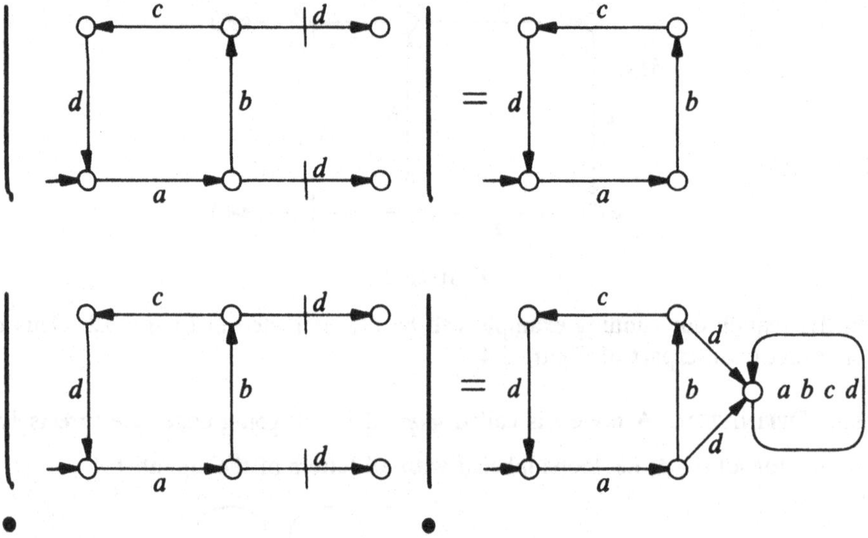

FIGURE 3.5

3.7.1. DEFINITION. Let $g,h \in \mathbf{G}$. Then $g \underline{\leftarrow} h$ (pronounced 'g emulates h') iff whenever a path π: $r(h) \overset{\sigma}{\longrightarrow} n$ can be lengthened to $r(h) \overset{\sigma}{\longrightarrow} n \overset{\sigma'}{\longrightarrow} m$ then all paths $r(g) \overset{\sigma}{\longrightarrow} k$ can be lengthened to $r(g) \overset{\sigma}{\longrightarrow} k \overset{\sigma'}{\longrightarrow} \cdot$.

3.7.2. REMARK. Note that if $g \underline{\leftarrow} h$ and there exists a path $r(h) \overset{\sigma}{\longrightarrow} n$, then there is at least one path $r(g) \overset{\sigma}{\longrightarrow} k$, because the empty path $r(g) \overset{\epsilon}{\longrightarrow} r(g)$ can be lengthened to $r(g) \overset{\epsilon}{\longrightarrow} r(g) \overset{\sigma}{\longrightarrow} k$, so the condition 'for all paths ...' never holds vacuously.

3.7.3. A more playful way to describe emulation is the following two-player game:

Player H runs down a path in graph h. When he traverses a τ-edge, he remains silent, but when he traverses an a-edge, he says 'a', and his turn is over. Player G runs down a path in graph g. When H announces he traversed an a-edge, G tries to traverse zero or more τ-edges, and then an a-edge. If he fails, he loses; if he succeeds, it is *H*'s turn again.

Some obvious rules: both players start at the roots of their own graphs; they do not traverse δ-edges; they do not reveal which path they are following, but only the labels they encounter; *G* wins if he does not lose, etc.

Now *g* emulates h iff *G* can not lose, no matter how stupid he may play.

3.7.4. EXAMPLES.

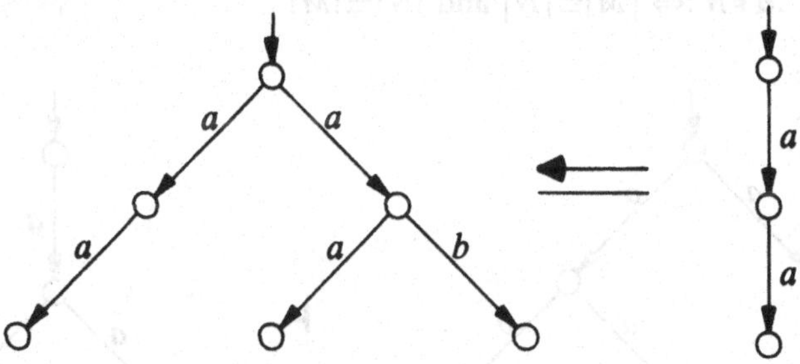

FIGURE 3.6

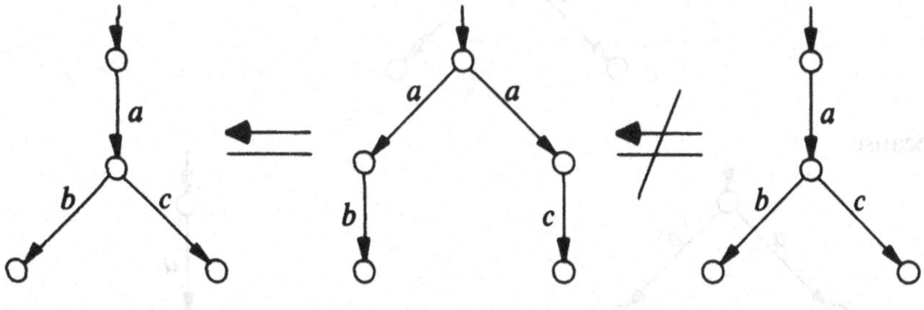

FIGURE 3.7

Emulation is not reflexive, in other words a graph does not necessarily emulate itself:

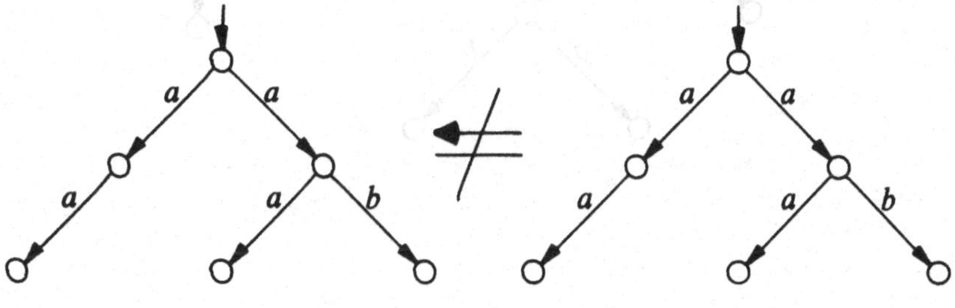

FIGURE 3.8

The rightmost $\xrightarrow{\langle a\rangle}$ can be lengthened to $\xrightarrow{\langle a,b\rangle}$ whereas the leftmost $\xrightarrow{\langle a\rangle}$ can be lengthened to $\xrightarrow{\langle a,a\rangle}$ only.

3.7.5. Remark. There are several notions of *emulation, simulation* and *implementation* in the literature. We invented this one while trying to verify CABP and it turns out that our notion is usable in this case. Experience will show which notion is 'best', most universal, easiest to comprehend, etc.

3.8. Definition. The main relation on $\mathbf{M}\times\mathbf{M}$ is called *implementation:*

$$M \models N :\Leftrightarrow |M| \sqsubseteq |N| \text{ and } !N! \sqsubseteq !M!$$

Examples.

i)

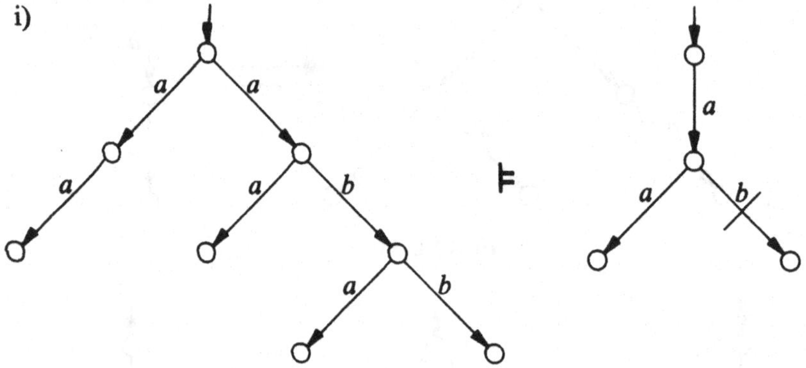

because

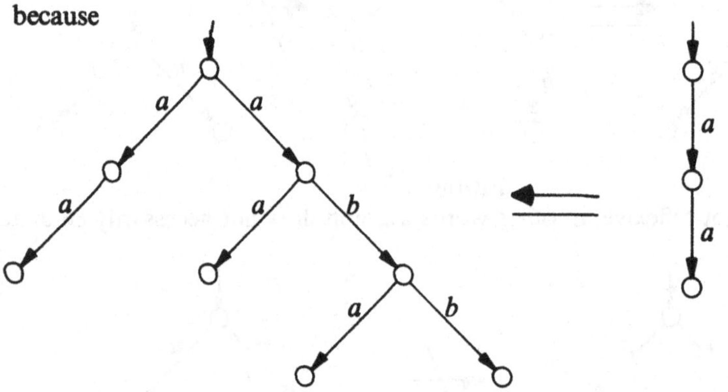

and

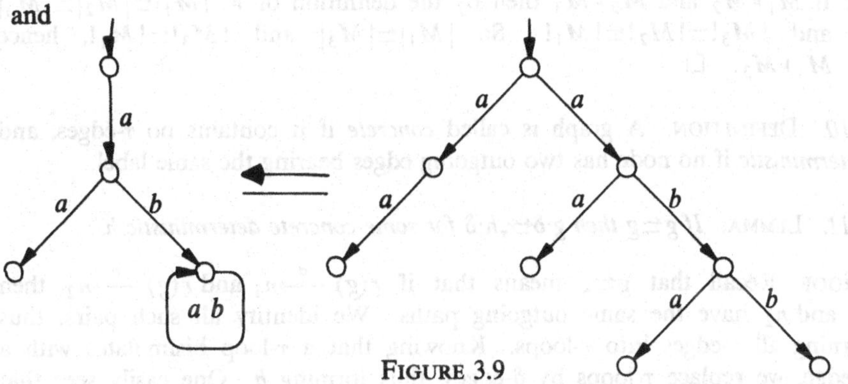

FIGURE 3.9

ii)
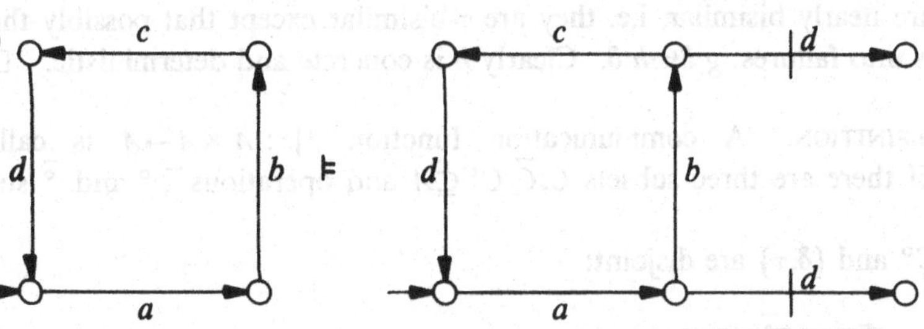

FIGURE 3.10

iii)
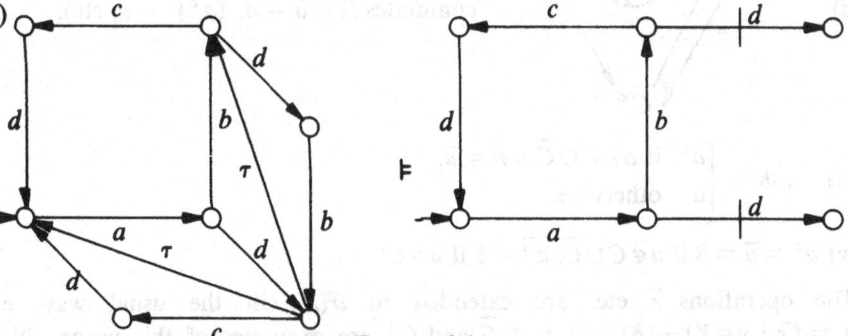

FIGURE 3.11

3.9. LEMMA. $\Leftarrow$ and $\models$ *are transitive.*

PROOF.

$\Leftarrow$:Suppose $g_1 \Leftarrow g_2$ and $g_2 \Leftarrow g_3$ and π: $r(g_3) \xrightarrow{\sigma} n_3 \xrightarrow{\sigma'} k_3$ and $r(g_1) \xrightarrow{\sigma} n_1$. Then Remark 3.7.2 grants the existence of a path $r(g_2) \xrightarrow{\sigma} n_2$. Then there is a path $r(g_2) \xrightarrow{\sigma} n_2 \xrightarrow{\sigma'} k_2$ by the definition of $\Leftarrow$, and for the same reason there is a path $r(g_1) \xrightarrow{\sigma} n_1 \xrightarrow{\sigma'} k_1$.

$\models$: If $M_1 \models M_2$ and $M_2 \models M_3$ then by the definition of $\models$, $|M_1| \underline{\leftarrow} |M_2| \underline{\leftarrow} |M_3|$ and $!M_3! \underline{\leftarrow} !M_2! \underline{\leftarrow} !M_1!$. So $|M_1| \underline{\leftarrow} |M_3|$ and $!M_3! \underline{\leftarrow} !M_1!$, hence $M_1 \models M_3$. □

3.10. Definition. A graph is called *concrete* if it contains no τ-edges, and *deterministic* if no node has two outgoing edges bearing the same label.

3.11. Lemma. *If $g \underline{\leftarrow} g$ then $g \cdot \delta \underline{\leftrightarrow}_\tau h \cdot \delta$ for some concrete deterministic h.*

Proof. Recall that $g \underline{\leftarrow} g$ means that if $r(g) \xrightarrow{\sigma} n_1$ and $r(g) \xrightarrow{\sigma} n_2$ then n_1 and n_2 have the same outgoing paths. We identify all such pairs, thus turning all τ-edges into τ-loops. Knowing that a τ-loop bisimulates with a δ-edge, we replace τ-loops by δ-edges, thus forming h. One easily sees that g and h are nearly bisimilar, i.e. they are τ-bisimilar except that possibly their end nodes into failures: $g \cdot \delta \underline{\leftrightarrow} h \cdot \delta$. Clearly h is concrete and deterministic. □

3.12. Definition. A communication function $\cdot|\cdot : A \times A \rightarrow A$ is called *trijective* if there are three subsets $C, \bar{C}, C^{\circ} \subseteq A$ and operations $\bar{\cdot}, \cdot^{\circ}$ and $\cdot^{\bar{\circ}}$ such that:

i) $C, \bar{C}, C^{\circ}$ and $\{\delta, \tau\}$ are disjoint;

ii) 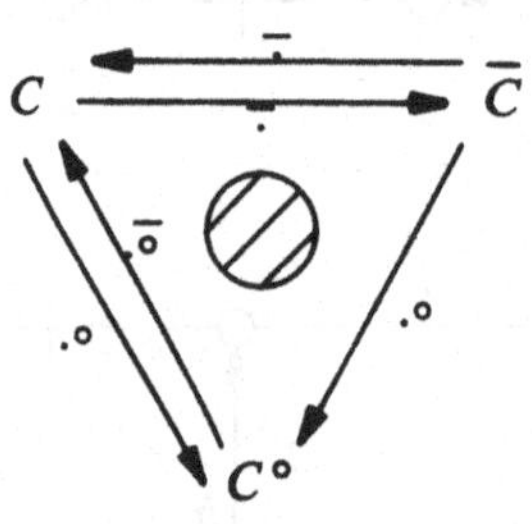

commutes (i.e. $\bar{\bar{a}} = a$, $(a^{\circ})^{\bar{\circ}} = a$, etc);

iii) $a|b = \begin{cases} a^{\circ} & \text{if } a \in C \cup \bar{C} \wedge b = \bar{a}, \\ \delta & \text{otherwise.} \end{cases}$

iv) $a^{\circ} = \bar{a} = \delta$ if $a \notin C \cup \bar{C}$, $a^{\bar{\circ}} = \delta$ if $a \notin C^{\circ}$.

The operations $\bar{\cdot}$ etc. are extended to $\mathcal{P}(A)$ in the usual way, e.g. $\bar{X} = \{\bar{x} \mid x \in X\} - \{\delta\}$. In fact $\bar{C}$ and C° are examples of this usage. Note that in fact $\bar{A} = \bar{C}$, $\bar{\bar{A}} = C$ and $A^{\circ} = C^{\circ}$.

Also note that trijectivity implies HA: $a|b|c = \delta$, unless $a|b = \bar{c}$. However $a|b \in C^{\circ} \cup \{\delta\}$, while $\bar{c} \in C \cup \bar{C} \cup \{\delta\}$. Furthermore C° and $C \cup \bar{C}$ are disjoint, so $a|b = \bar{c}$ implies $a|b = \bar{c} = \delta$, but then $a|b|c = \delta$, too.

3.13. Fair FIFO queues satisfy an algebraic criterion [3], viz. X is a queue if and only if $\tau \cdot \partial_H(X \| T) \cdot \delta = \tau \cdot \partial_H(Q \| T) \cdot \delta$ where Q is a standard example of a queue, and H and T are suitably chosen. In other words, X is a queue if and only if it behaves like one in a suitably chosen test environment. In the sequel we will generalize this idea to a large class of modules. In Section 3.14 we will define a *tester* $T(M)$ for this larger class of modules and in Section 3.20 we will prove $\tau \cdot \partial_H(X \| T(M)) \cdot \delta = \tau \cdot \partial_H(M \| T(M)) \cdot \delta \Rightarrow X \models M$ modulo some reasonable restrictions.

3.14. DEFINITION. Suppose the communication function is trijective. Let M be a concrete module. Now apply the following transformations to M (strictly in this order):

1. For each $n \in N(M)$, and for each $a \in \alpha(M)$, if there is neither an edge $n \xrightarrow{a} \cdot$ nor an edge $n \overset{a}{\nrightarrow} \cdot$, then add an edge $n \xrightarrow{a} n_0$ to some new terminal node n_0. These extra edges are called traps or trap edges.
2. Apply $\bar{\cdot}$ to all edge labels.
3. Apply $|\cdot|$ to the graph. The resulting graph $T(M)$ is called the tester for M. If S is a specification, $T(M(S))$ may be abbreviated $T(S)$.

3.15. EXAMPLES.

i) $S(Q) = ((\bar{c}\bar{d})^\omega, \{\bar{d}\})$.

$M(Q) = M(S(Q)) =$

$T(Q) = T(S(Q)) =$

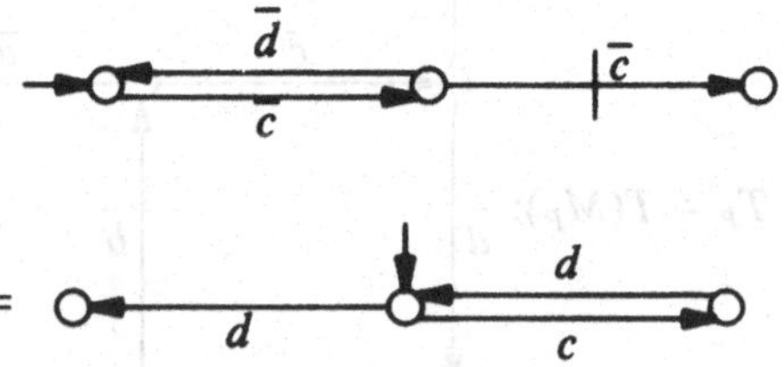

FIGURE 3.12

ii) A one-bit buffer $B = (r(0,1) \cdot s(0,2) + r(1,1) \cdot s(1,2)) \cdot B$, where port 2 is robust:

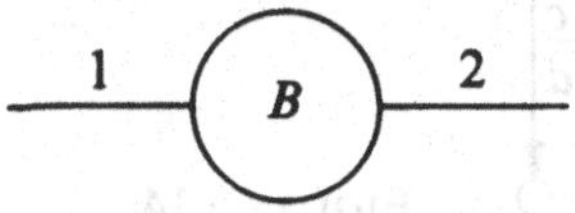

Here $C = \{r(d,p) \mid p \in \{1,2\}, d \in \{0,1\}\}$, $\bar{C} = \{s(d,p) \mid p \in \{1,2\}, d \in \{0,1\}\}$, $C^\circ = \{t(d,p) \mid p \in \{1,2\}, d \in \{0,1\}\}$, $\overline{r(d,p)} = s(d,p)$, $\overline{s(d,p)} = r(d,p)$, $r(d,p) = t(d^\circ,p)$, and $t(\bar{d^\circ},p) = r(d,p)$. This is sometimes called *read-send communication*.

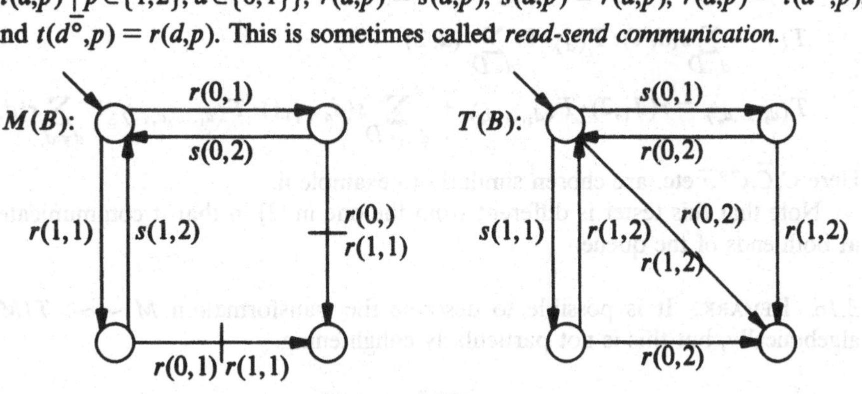

FIGURE 3.13

iii) Our running example:

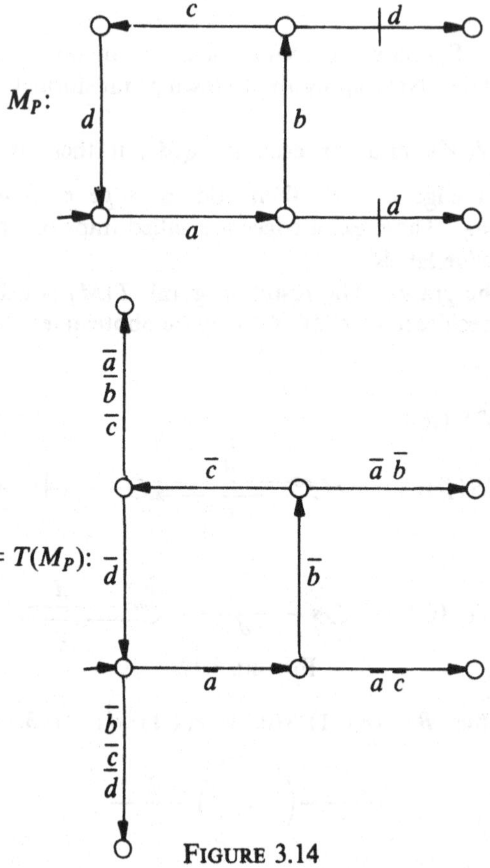

FIGURE 3.14

iv) Our tester for a robust queue over some finite alphabet D would have infinitely many states, indexed by finite sequences over D:

$$T\langle\rangle = \sum_{d \in D} s(d, 1) \cdot T\langle d \rangle + \sum_{d \in D} r(d, 2)$$

$$T\langle d_1, \ldots, d_n \rangle = r(d_1, 2) \cdot T\langle d_2, \ldots, d_n \rangle + \sum_{d_{n+1} \in D} s(d_{n+1}, 1) \cdot T\langle d_1, \ldots, d_{n+1} \rangle + \sum_{d \neq d_1} r(d, 2)$$

Here $C, \overline{C}, C^{\circ}, \bar{\cdot}$ etc. are chosen similarly to example ii.

Note that this tester is different from the one in [3] in that it communicates at both ends of the queue.

3.16. REMARK. It is possible to describe the transformation $M \rightsquigarrow T(M)$ algebraically, but this is not particularly enlightening.

3.17. In order to do anything nontrivial with modules, we need the whole bunch of operations and relations traditionally defined for graphs.

3.17.1. The constructions for $+, \cdot, \partial_H$, and τ_I can be copied verbatim from [1].

3.17.2. The constructions for $\|, \lfloor\!\lfloor$, and $|$ are the usual Cartesian product constructions, augmented with a clause that diagonal edges representing successful communication are barred if and only if at least one of the composing edges is barred.

3.17.3. The definition of $\leftrightarrows_\tau$ is augmented with a clause that barred edges should correspond to barred edges (bearing the same label, of course). This implies that $\overset{\tau}{+\!\!\!\longrightarrow}$ edges can only correspond to $\overset{\tau}{+\!\!\!\longrightarrow}$ edges.

3.18. EXAMPLES.

i)

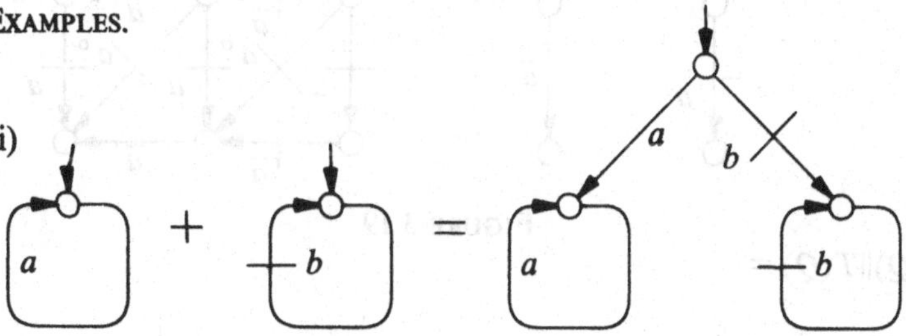

FIGURE 3.15

ii)

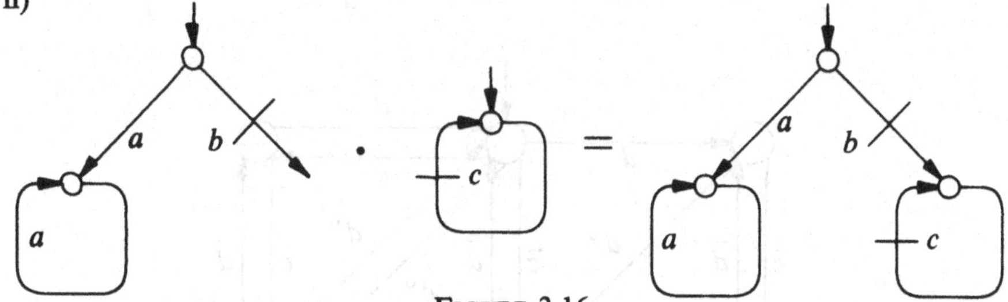

FIGURE 3.16

iii)

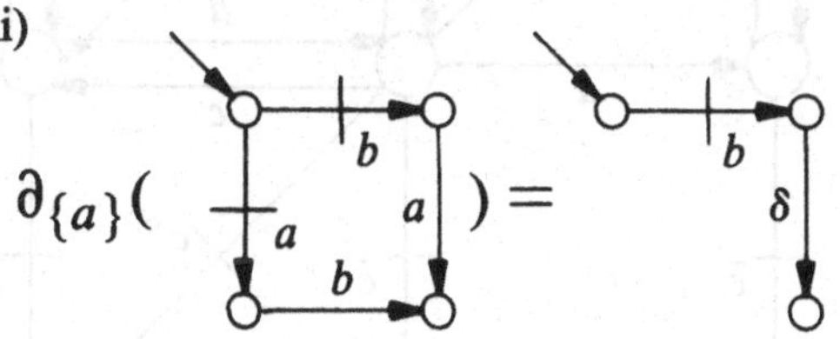

FIGURE 3.17

iv)

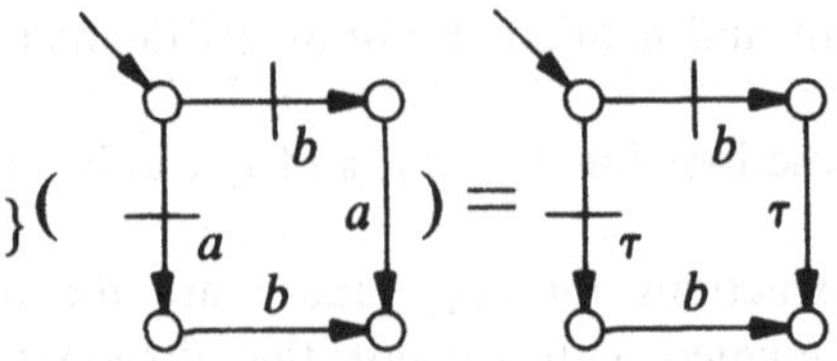

FIGURE 3.18

v)

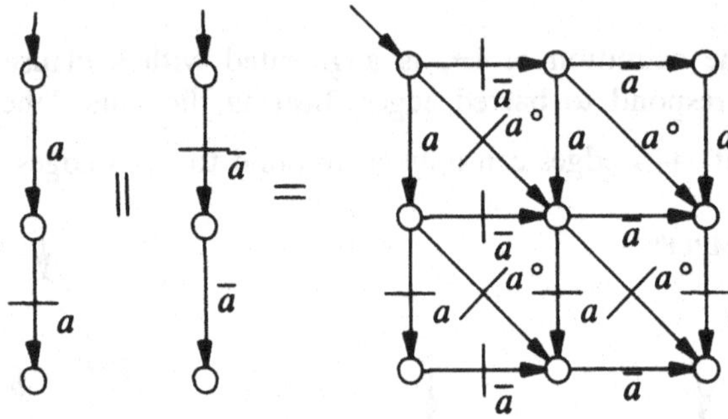

FIGURE 3.19

vi) $M(Q) \| T(Q) =$

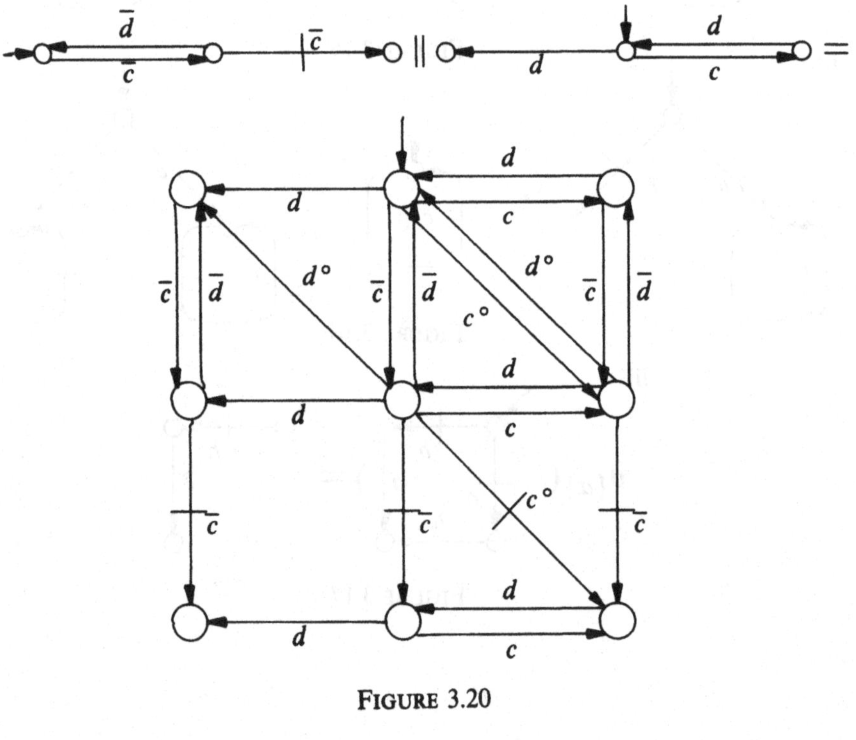

FIGURE 3.20

vii)

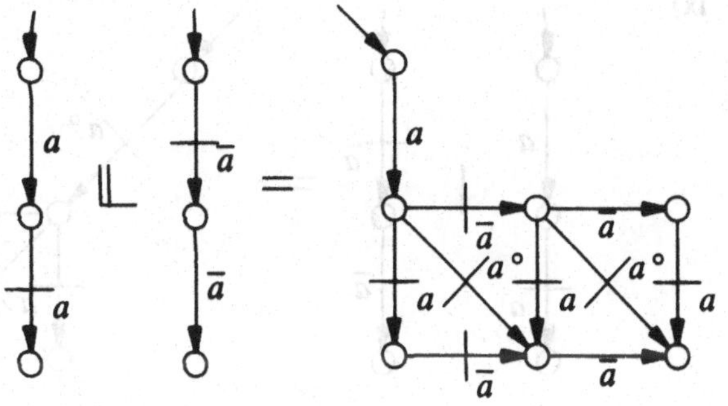

FIGURE 3.21

viii) $M(Q) \| \!\!\lfloor T(Q) =$

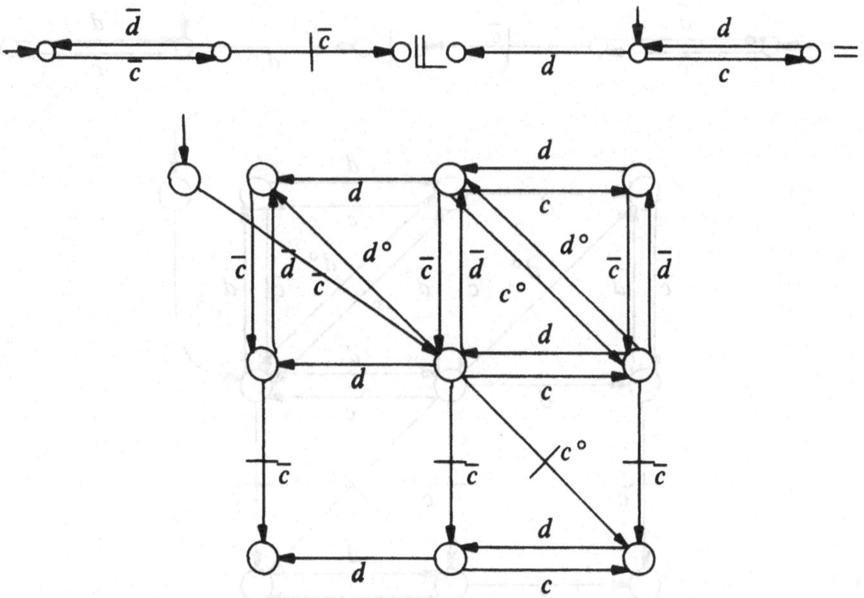

FIGURE 3.22

ix)

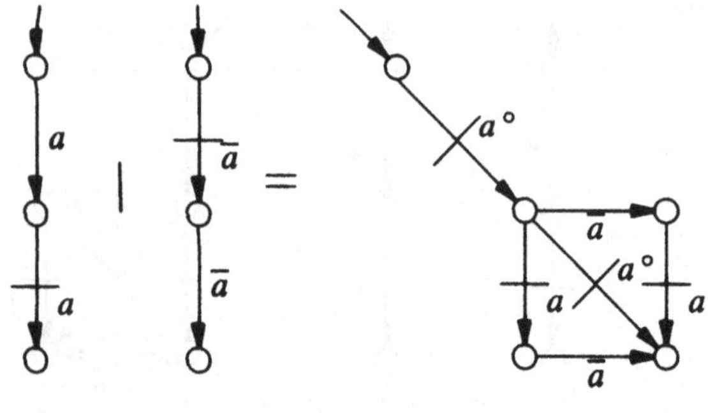

FIGURE 3.23

x) $M(Q)|T(Q) =$

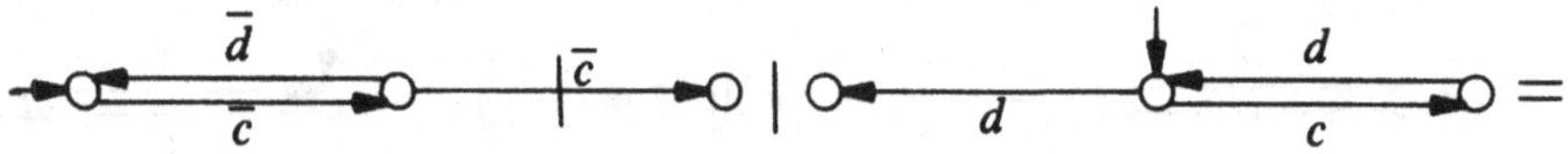

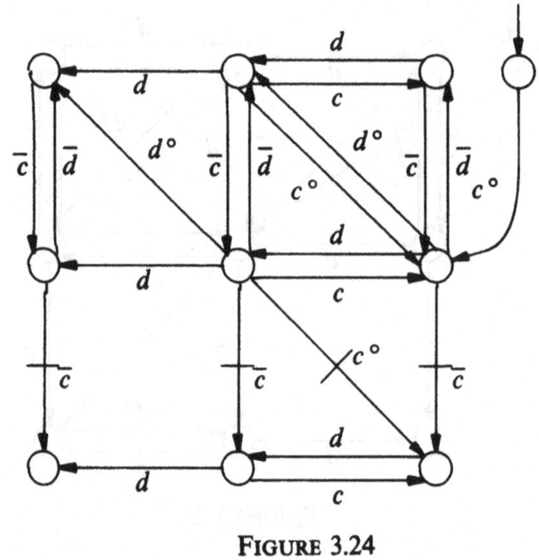

FIGURE 3.24

xi)

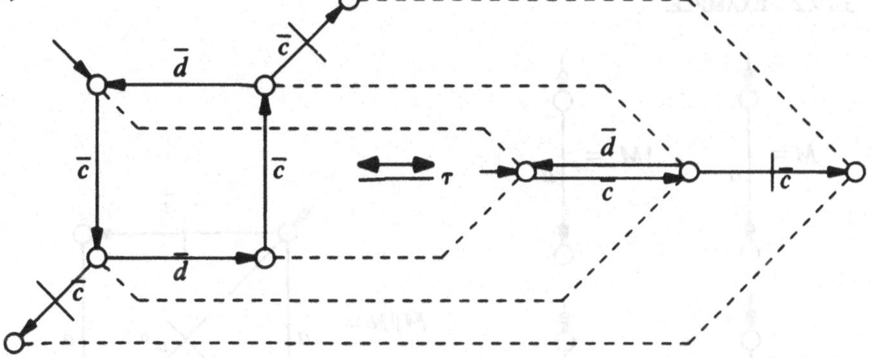

FIGURE 3.25

3.19.1. LEMMA.

i) $|M|\,\|\,|N| = |M\|N|$

ii) $!M!\,\|\,!N! \leftrightarrows_\tau !M\|N!$

PROOF.

i) Follows trivially from the definitions.

ii) Call a point in the Cartesian product graph *semi-loopy* if at least one of its coordinates is loopy. If l is the loopy node in $!M!$ then any edge $n \xrightarrow{a} m$ in $!N!$ will give rise to an edge $(l,n) \xrightarrow{a} (l,m)$, and similarly with N and M reversed. Those and the loops $(l,n) \xrightarrow{a} (l,n)$ are precisely the outgoing edges of the semi-loopy nodes in $!M!\|\|!N!$. Consequently, any outgoing path from a semi-loopy node ends in a semi-loopy node (possibly the same), and any sequence of labels can be obtained. Hence we can bisimulate $!M!\|\|!N!$ and $!M\|N!$ by relating the semi-loopy points in $!M!\|\|!N!$ to the loopy point in $!M\|N!$ and the rest to 'themselves'. □

3.19.2. EXAMPLE.

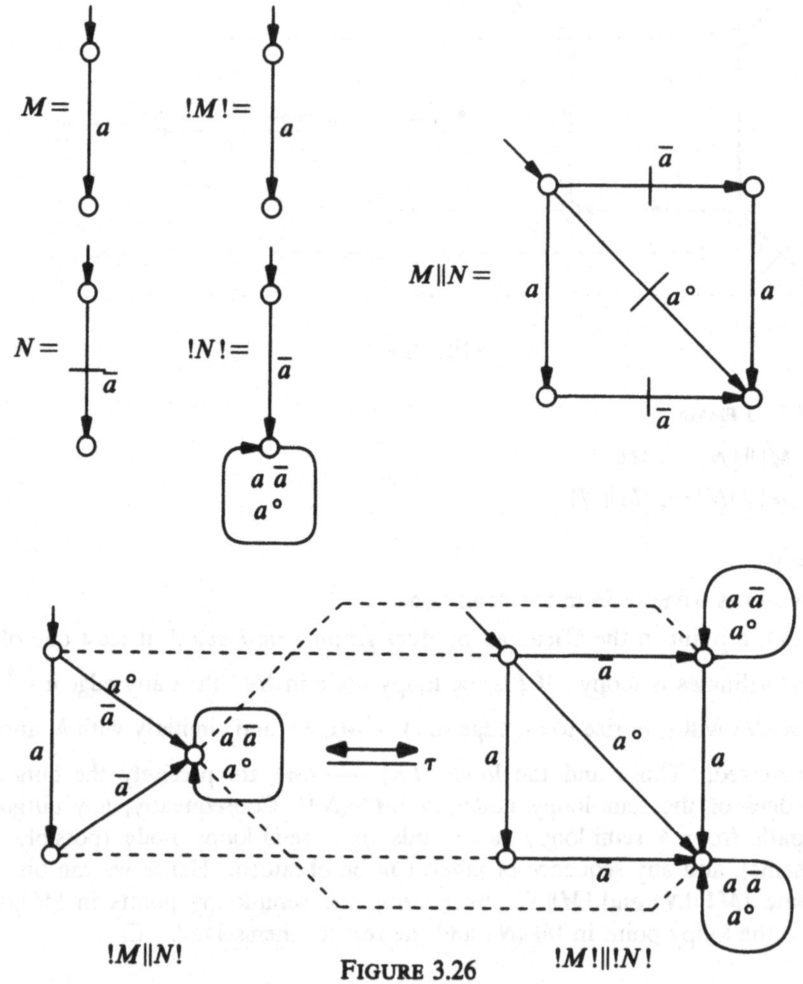

FIGURE 3.26

3.20. THEOREM. (TEster Principle, or TEP). *Let M be a module, $T=T(M)$ its tester, X any process. Suppose*:

1. *Communication is trijective.*
2. *$!M!$ is concrete and deterministic.*
3. *$\alpha(X)=\alpha(M)\subseteq C=\overline{A}$, i.e. X and M consist of communication actions only.*
4. *$\partial_H(X\|T)\cdot\delta \leftrightarrows_\tau \partial_H(M\|T)\cdot\delta$, where $H=\alpha(M)\cup\overline{\alpha(M)}$.*

Then $X \models M$.

PROOF. Abbreviate: $L:=\partial_H(X\|T)\cdot\delta$, $R:=\partial_H(M\|T)\cdot\delta$.

$|X|\leftleftharpoons|M|$: Suppose that a path π_M: $r(|M|) \xrightarrow{\sigma} m_1$ can be lengthened to

π'_M: $r(|M|) \xrightarrow{\sigma} m_1 \xrightarrow{\sigma'} m_2$ and $|X|$ also contains a path π_X: $r(|X|) \xrightarrow{\sigma} x_1$. $|M|$ being concrete, we may assume without loss of generality that σ' is in fact a singleton $\langle a \rangle$. By construction, T contains a path π'_T: $r(T) \xrightarrow{\bar{\sigma}} t_1 \xrightarrow{\bar{a}} t_2$. Note that $\bar{a} \neq \delta$ in view of condition 3. Consequently, there is a path π'_R: $r(R) \xrightarrow{\sigma^\circ} r_1 \xrightarrow{a^\circ} r_2$. Moreover this r_1 is unique, for trijectivity implies that the decomposition $\sigma^\circ = \sigma | \bar{\sigma}$ is unique, condition 3 implies that σ can only come from $|M|$ and also that $\alpha(T) \subseteq \overline{\alpha(M)} \subseteq \bar{C}$, so $\bar{\sigma}$ can only come from T; finally, $|M|$ being deterministic implies that π_M is the unique path labeled σ, and that its tester T is also deterministic, hence π_T: $r(T) \xrightarrow{\bar{\sigma}} t_1$ is the unique path labeled $\bar{\sigma}$. The presence of paths π_X: $r(|X|) \xrightarrow{\sigma} x_1$ in $|X|$ and π_T: $r(T) \xrightarrow{\bar{\sigma}} t_1$ in T gives rise to the existence of a path π_L: $r(|L|) \xrightarrow{\sigma^\circ} l_1$ in L. In the bisimulation relation asserted by $|L| \leftrightarrows_\tau |R|$, l_1 must be related to r_1 above, because the path $r(|R|) \xrightarrow{\sigma^\circ} r_1$ in $|R|$ is unique. As $r_1 \xrightarrow{a^\circ} r_2$ there must be a path $l_1 \xrightarrow{\langle a^\circ \rangle} l_2$. By trijectivity and condition 3 this can only come from a path $x_1 \xrightarrow{\langle a \rangle} x_2$ (and the matching path in T, of course).

So we see that we can lengthen any path $r(|X|) \xrightarrow{\sigma} x_1$ to $r(|X|) \xrightarrow{\sigma} x_1 \xrightarrow{\langle a \rangle} x_2$.

$!M! \leftarrow !X!$: Note that $!X! = X$ and $!M! = M$. Suppose a path π_x: $r(!X!) \xrightarrow{\sigma} x_1$ can be lengthened to $r(!X!) \xrightarrow{\sigma} x_1 \xrightarrow{\sigma'} x_2$. We are to show that any path $r(!M!) \xrightarrow{\sigma} m_1$ can be lengthened to $r(!M!) \xrightarrow{\sigma} m_1 \xrightarrow{\sigma'} m_2$. $!M!$ being deterministic, this is equivalent to showing that $!M!$ contains a path labeled $\sigma_0 = \sigma * \sigma'$. We distinguish two cases:

Case 1: $!L!$ contains a path labeled σ_0. Then $!R!$ does so, too. Trijectivity and condition 3 now imply that we can 'project' this path down to M, and from there to $!M!$.

Case 2: We can find some, possibly empty, initial segment σ°_1 of σ°_0 in $!L!$ (i.e. a path bearing that label), σ°_1 maximal, but shorter than σ°_0. Consider the 'projection' onto T: $r(T) \xrightarrow{\bar{\sigma}_1} t_1$. Since trap edges of T do not communicate with actions of X by conditions 2 and 4, a corresponding path $r(!M!) \xrightarrow{\bar{\sigma}_1} m_1$ exists.

Now, since σ°_1 is not all of σ°_0, the rest of σ°_0 must begin with some atom a°. So now $!X!$ contains a path $r(!X!) \xrightarrow{\sigma_1} x_1 \xrightarrow{\langle a \rangle} x_3$ and $!L!$ does not contain a similar path $r(!L!) \xrightarrow{\sigma^\circ_1} l_1 \xrightarrow{\langle a^\circ \rangle} \cdot$. Apparently, T

does not contain an edge $t_1 \xrightarrow{\bar{a}} \cdot$. Now t_1 can not be the end node of one of the trap edges added in step 3.14.1 for those edges do not communicate with edges of M by construction (of T). So we can deduce that this can only happen if M contains an edge $m_1 \overset{a}{+\!\!\!\longrightarrow} m_3$. But then $!M!$ contains an edge $m_1 \xrightarrow{a} m_l$, with m_l loopy. Hence we can complete our path $r(!M!) \xrightarrow{\sigma_1} m_1 \xrightarrow{a} m_l \xrightarrow{\sigma_2} m_l$. □

3.21. **Remark.** The role of the δ's in condition 4 of Section 3.20 is not evident from the proof, to say the least. Inspection of the proof shows that the theorem also holds without them. In fact one can derive that result more easily by noting that it is just a weakening of Section 3.20. Stated differently, condition 4 as given is a weakening of the version without delta's and consequently the theorem as a whole is stronger than the variation. For example, consider

$$M = \to\bigcirc \xrightarrow{a} \bigcirc \overset{a}{+\!\!\!\longrightarrow} \bigcirc,$$

$$N = \to\bigcirc \xrightarrow{\tau} \bigcirc \xrightarrow{a} \bigcirc.$$

One easily sees that $N \models M$.

We calculate:

$$T(M) = \to\bigcirc \xrightarrow{\bar{a}} \bigcirc;$$

$$L = \partial_{\{a,\bar{a}\}}(M \| T(M)) = \to\bigcirc \xrightarrow{a^{\circ}} \bigcirc \xrightarrow{\delta} \bigcirc;$$

$$R = \partial_{\{a,\bar{a}\}}(N \| T(M)) = \to\bigcirc \xrightarrow{\tau} \bigcirc \xrightarrow{a^{\circ}} \bigcirc.$$

We see that L and R are 'equal up to leading τ's and trailing δ's'. Precisely this relation is expressed by $L \cdot \delta \leftrightarrows_{\tau} R \cdot \delta$.

3.22. **Remark.** The reader might wonder why we introduced these testers when after all the relation **R** can be read off from the graphs directly. However, in our motivating example, CABP, the proposed implementation is not given as a graph, but as a rather complex process term. To draw the graph is of course possible, but we saw in Section 2 that it involves a lot of work, and most of it is in fact redundant. The tester equation 3.20.4, on the other hand, encapsulates any redundant edge as soon as possible. That way, we can keep the amount of work feasible. In Section 4, we will actually carry out this calculation.

3.23. LEMMA. *Let* $g_i, h_i \in \mathbf{G}$ $(i=1,2)$.
Suppose:
i) *communication is trijective*: $C|\bar{C} = C°$;
ii) $g_i \sqsubseteq h_i$ $(i=1,2)$;
iii) $\alpha(g_1) \subseteq C$, $\alpha(g_2) \subseteq \bar{C}$.
Then $g_1 \| g_2 \sqsubseteq h_1 \| h_2$.

PROOF. First note that condition ii) implies that $\alpha(h_i) \subseteq \alpha(g_i)$, and hence condition iii) implies $\alpha(h_1) \subseteq C$, $\alpha(h_2) \subseteq \bar{C}$. Next, recall that trijectivity implies that $C, \bar{C}$ and $C|\bar{C}$ are disjoint. The upshot of all this, is that each trace in $g_1 \| g_2$ (or $h_1 \| h_2$) can be uniquely decomposed into traces in g_1 and g_2 (h_1 and h_2), i.e. we can establish atom by atom where it comes from.

So if a path $\pi: r(h_1 \| h_2) \xrightarrow{\sigma} \cdot$ can be lengthened to $\pi': r(h_1 \| h_2) \xrightarrow{\sigma} \cdot \xrightarrow{\sigma'} \cdot$ we can find the unique labels $\sigma_1, \sigma_2, \sigma'_1$ and σ'_2 of the (possibly non-unique) paths $\pi_i: r(h_i) \xrightarrow{\sigma_i} \cdot \xrightarrow{\sigma'_i} \cdot$ that 'caused' π'. In any case, there exist paths $r(h_i) \xrightarrow{\sigma_i} \cdot$ that can be lengthened to $r(h_i) \xrightarrow{\sigma_i} \cdot \xrightarrow{\sigma'_i} \cdot$.

Moreover, each path $r(g_1 \| g_2) \xrightarrow{\sigma} \cdot$ 'originates' from paths $r(g_i) \xrightarrow{\sigma_i} \cdot$ also labeled σ_i. Now $g_i \sqsubseteq h_i$ implies that each such path $r(g_i) \xrightarrow{\sigma_i} \cdot$ can be lengthened to $r(g_i) \xrightarrow{\sigma_i} \cdot \xrightarrow{\sigma'} \cdot$, and therefore each path $r(g_1 \| g_2) \xrightarrow{\sigma} \cdot$ can be lengthened to $r(g_1 \| g_2) \xrightarrow{\sigma} \cdot \xrightarrow{\sigma'} \cdot$ as was to be shown. □

3.24. THEOREM. (Modular Assembly Principle, or MAP).
Let $M_i, N_i \in \mathbf{M}$ $(i=1,2)$. *Suppose*:
i) *communication is trijective*;
ii) $M_i \models N_i$;
iii) $\alpha(M_1) \subseteq C$, $\alpha(M_2) \subseteq \bar{C}$.
Then $M_1 \| M_2 \models N_1 \| N_2$.

PROOF.
$|M_1 \| M_2| \sqsubseteq |N_1 \| N_2|$: This follows directly from Lemmas 3.19.i and 3.23.
$!N_1 \| N_2! \sqsubseteq !M_1 \| M_2!$: Suppose, as always, a path $\pi_M: r(!M_1 \| M_2!) \xrightarrow{\sigma} \cdot$ can be lengthened to $\pi'_M: r(!M_1 \| M_2!) \xrightarrow{\sigma} \cdot \xrightarrow{\sigma'} \cdot$, and consider a path $\pi_N: (!N_1 \| N_2!) \xrightarrow{\sigma} \cdot$. There are three cases:

1. π_N passes through the loopy node of $!N_1 \| N_2!$. In that case the result is trivial, because in a loopy node one can construct any trace one likes.
2. π_N does not pass through the loopy node, but π_M does. This contradicts the fact that $!N_1! \sqsubseteq !M_1!$ and $!N_2! \sqsubseteq !M_2!$, because for entering a loopy node in the merge, one of the components has to go through a barred edge,

thereby entering a loopy node itself.

3. π_M and π_N do not pass through loopy nodes. In this case the proof of Lemma 3.23 works, using the observation that when π'_M enters the loopy node in $!M_1 \| M_2!$ we can choose to continue this path in that component that caused the loopy node and hence has a loopy node itself. □

3.25. Recall that barred edges are supposed to be redundant, i.e. we intended them to occur in a context in which they can not communicate. So if we encapsulate we expect all barred edges to disappear. Consequently, the resulting graphs should be robust. As was to be expected, this is the case in our motivating example, CABP:

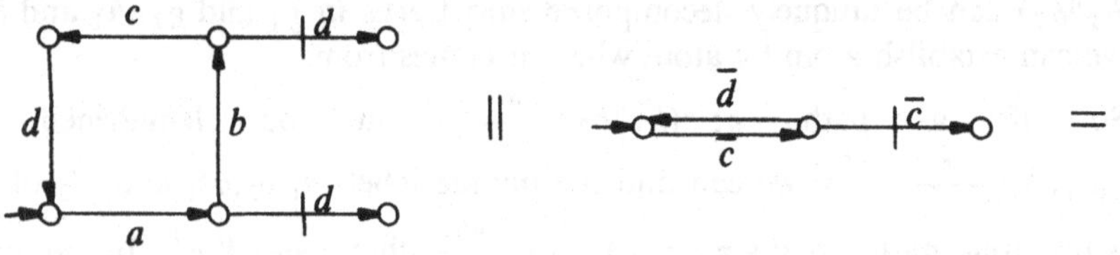

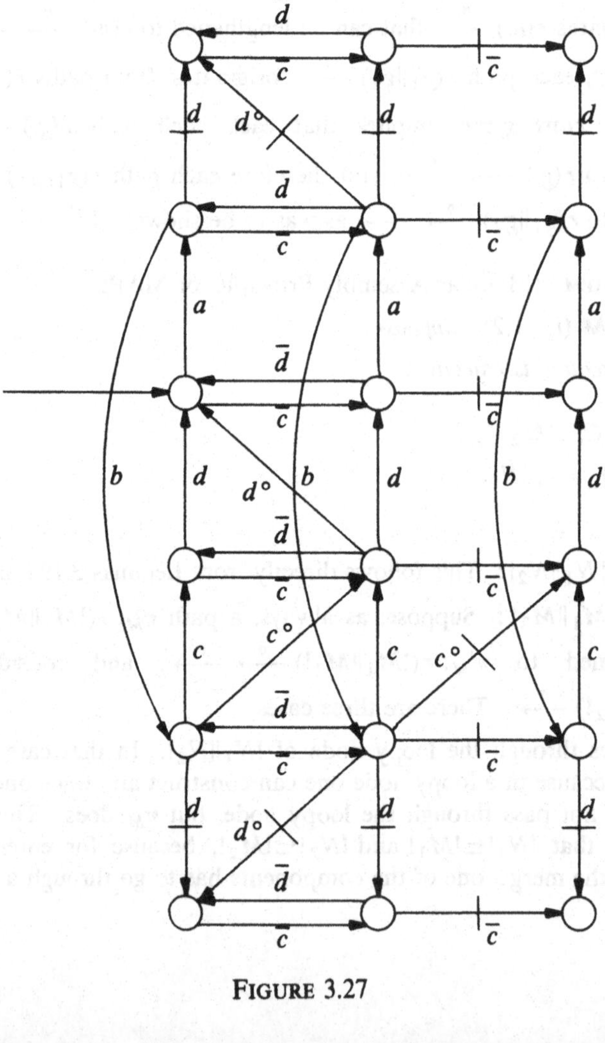

FIGURE 3.27

$\partial_{\{c,\bar{c},d,\bar{d}\}}(CABP) =$

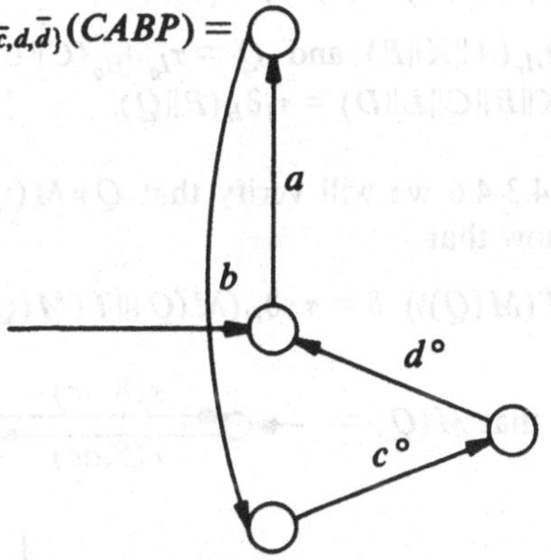

FIGURE 3.28

3.26. THEOREM. (RObustness Principle, or ROP). *If $g \models h$, and both g and h are robust, then $\tau \cdot g \cdot \delta = \tau \cdot h \cdot \delta$.*

PROOF. Robustness means that $|g| = !g! = g$ and $|h| = !h! = h$. So $g \models h$ boils down to $g \trianglelefteq h$ and $h \trianglelefteq g$.

Now define a relation $\mathbf{R}$ on $N(g) \times N(h)$ by putting $n\mathbf{R}k$ if and only if a word $\sigma \in A^*$ exists such that $\exists \pi$: $r(g) \xrightarrow{\sigma} n$ and $\exists \pi'$: $r(h) \xrightarrow{\sigma} k$. Then, if $n_1 \mathbf{R} k_1$ and there is a path $n_1 \xrightarrow{\sigma'} n_2$ in g, then $h \trianglelefteq g$ implies that there exists a path $k_1 \xrightarrow{\sigma'} k_2$ in h, and so $n_2 \mathbf{R} k_2$, for $r(g) \xrightarrow{\sigma * \sigma'} n_2$ and $r(h) \xrightarrow{\sigma * \sigma'} k_2$.

The same holds with g and h interchanged. In other words, g and h are τ-bisimilar, except possibly for their end node labels. I.e., $\tau \cdot g \cdot \delta = \tau \cdot h \cdot \delta$. □

4. A VERIFICATION OF CABP

4.1. In this section the calculations alluded to in Section 3.22 will be carried out. In Section 4.3 through Section 4.6 TEP is applied to $C \| L \| D$, in Section 4.7 through Section 4.10 it is applied to $A \| K \| B$, and in Section 4.11 an algebraic reformulation of Section 3.25 follows.

4.2. NOTATION. In Sections 1.3 and 2.2 we named some subsets of A:

$$H = \{r(d,p), s(d,p) \mid d \in \mathbf{D},\ p \in \{2,3,5,6,7,8\}\}$$

$$I = \{t(d,p) \mid d \in \mathbf{D}, 1 \leqslant p \leqslant 8\} \cup \{ik, jk, kk, il, jl, kl\}$$

$$H_P = \{r(d,p), s(d,p) \mid d \in \mathbf{D},\ p \in \{2,3\}\}$$

$$I_P = \{t(d,p) \mid d \in \mathbf{D},\ p \in \{2,3\}\} \cup \{ik, jk, kk\}$$

$$H_Q = \{r(d,p), s(d,p) \mid d \in \mathbf{D},\ p \in \{6,7\}\}$$

$I_Q \quad = \{t(d,p) \mid d \in \mathbf{D},\ p \in \{6,7\}\} \cup \{il, jl, kl\}$

We defined $P = \tau_{I_P}\partial_{H_P}(A \| K \| B)$ and $Q = \tau_{I_Q}\partial_{H_Q}(C \| L \| D)$ and noticed that CA1,2,5,6 $\vdash \tau_I\partial_H(A\|K\|B\|C\|L\|D) = \tau_I\partial_H(P\|Q)$.

4.3. In the Sections 4.3-4.6 we will verify that $Q \models M(Q)$. According to TEP (3.20), it suffices to show that

$$\tau\cdot\partial_H(Q\|T(M(Q)))\cdot\delta = \tau\cdot\partial_H(M(Q)\|T(M(Q)))\cdot\delta \qquad (*)$$

Recall that $M(Q) =$ 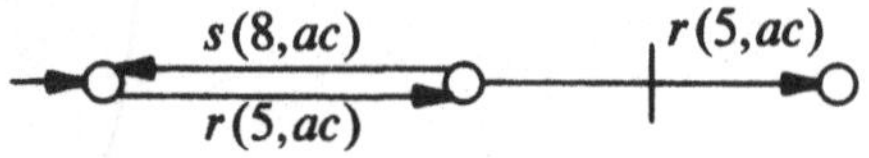

and $T(Q) = T(M(Q)) =$ 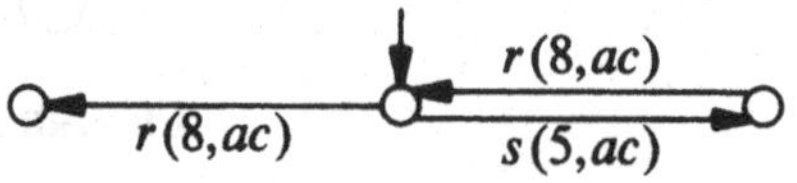

In order to calculate $M(Q)\|T(M(Q))$ we need some notation for the barred $r(5,ac)$-edge of $M(Q)$. We choose $r(5,ac)\cdot\Omega$, inspired by Section 2.2, where barred edges were introduced to denote '$r(5,ac)$, followed by some unidentified process'. More formally, barred edges communicate and are encapsulated like their unbarred counterparts. In an earlier version of this paper we used the notation $r(5,ac)\cdot\chi$, thus suggesting that the barred edge is followed by chaos. This is not exactly true: in an implementation the barred edge is followed by a definite, albeit unspecified, process. At any rate, it should be possible to eliminate all Ωs.

4.4. We will abbreviate:

$5 = s(5,ac)$, $\bar{5} = r(5,ac)$, $5° = t(5,ac)$,

$8 = s(8,ac)$, $\bar{8} = r(8,ac)$, $8° = t(8,ac)$,

$T_1 = T = T(M(Q))$, $T_2 = \bar{8}\cdot T_1$,

$M_1 = M(Q)$, $M_2 = 8\cdot M_1 + \bar{5}\cdot\Omega$.

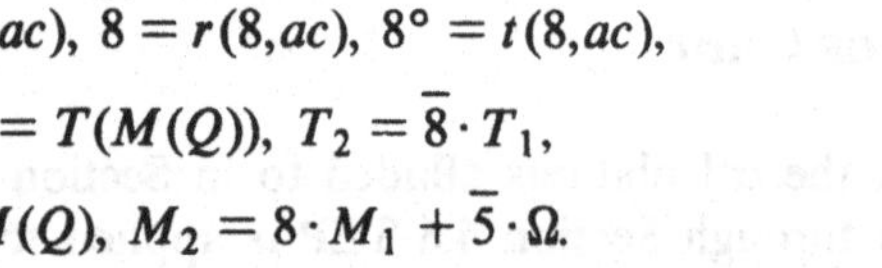

FIGURE 4.1

So:

$$T_1 = 5 \cdot T_2 + \overline{8},$$
$$T_2 = \overline{8} \cdot T_1,$$
$$M_1 = \overline{5} \cdot M_2,$$
$$M_2 = 8 \cdot M_1 + \overline{5} \cdot \Omega.$$

Hence

$$T_1 \| M_1 = 5 \cdot (T_2 \| M_1) + \overline{8} \cdot M_1 + \overline{5} \cdot (T_1 \| M_2) + 5^\circ \cdot (T_2 \| M_2)$$

and

$$T_2 \| M_2 = \overline{8} \cdot (T_1 \| M_2) + 8 \cdot (T_2 \| M_1) + \overline{5} \cdot (T_2 \| \Omega) + 8^\circ \cdot (T_1 \| M_1).$$

Consequently

$$\partial_{\{5,\overline{5},8,\overline{8}\}}(T_1 \| M_1) = 5^\circ \cdot \partial_{\{5,\overline{5},8,\overline{8}\}}(T_2 \| M_2)$$

and

$$\partial_{\{5,\overline{5},8,\overline{8}\}}(T_2 \| M_2) = 8^\circ \cdot \partial_{\{5,\overline{5},8,\overline{8}\}}(T_1 \| M_1).$$

Therefore

$$\partial_{H_Q}(T_1 \| M_1) = 5^\circ \cdot 8^\circ \cdot \partial_{H_Q}(T_1 \| M_1).$$

So

$$\partial_{H_Q}(T_1 \| M_1) = (5^\circ \cdot 8^\circ)^\omega.$$

So the right hand side of (*) reduces to $\tau \cdot (5^\circ \cdot 8^\circ)^\omega \cdot \delta$.

4.5. In order to investigate $Q = \tau_{I_Q} \partial_{H_Q}(C \| L \| D)$, we will need quite a lot of notation. First we abbreviate:

$$5 = s(5, ac),$$
$$6_b = s(6, b) \quad (b = 0, 1),$$
$$7_b = s(7, b) \quad (b = 0, 1, e),$$
$$8 = s(8, ac),$$
$$\overline{5}, \overline{6}_b, \overline{7}_b, \overline{8} = r(\cdot, \cdot),$$
$$5^\circ, 6^\circ{}_b, 7^\circ{}_b, 8^\circ = t(\cdot, \cdot).$$

Next, we need names for all states of the processes involved:

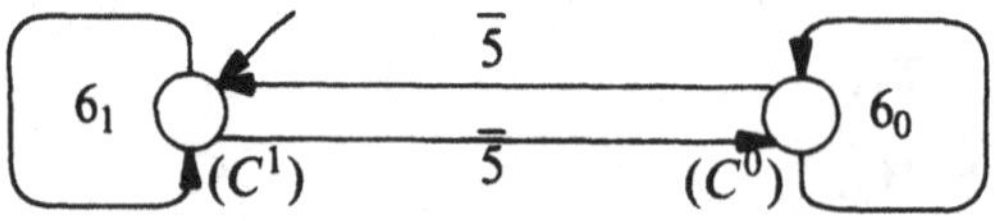

FIGURE 4.2

C: $C = C^1$

$C^b = \overline{5} \cdot C^{1-b} + 6_b \cdot C^b$

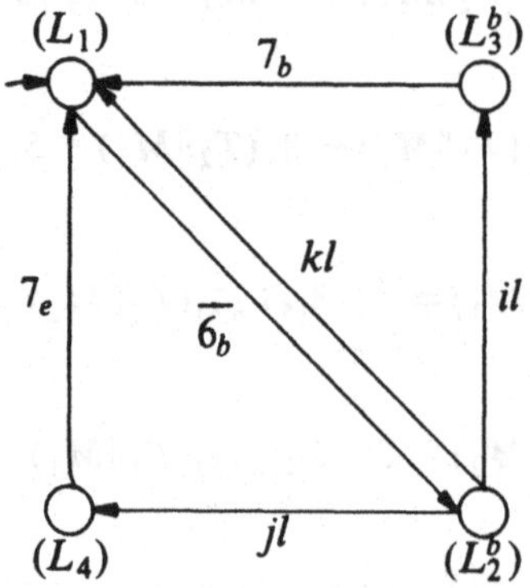

FIGURE 4.3

L: $L = L_1$

$L_1 = \overline{6}_0 \cdot L_2^0 + \overline{6}_1 \cdot L_2^1$

$L_2^b = il \cdot L_3^b + jl \cdot L_4 + kl \cdot L_1$

$L_3^b = 7_b \cdot L_1$

$L_4 = 7_e \cdot L_1$

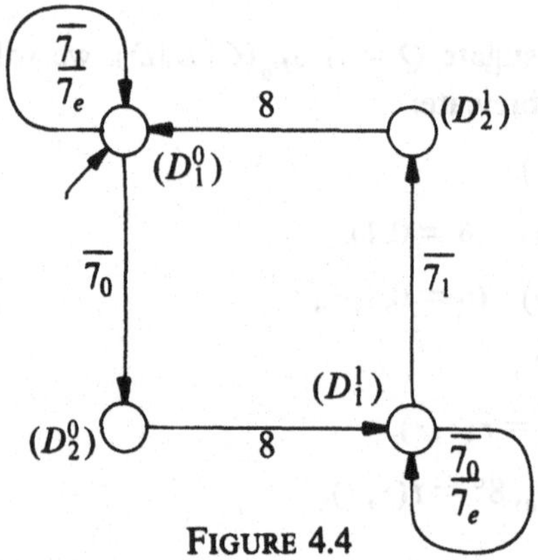

FIGURE 4.4

D: $D = D_1^0$

$D_1^b = \overline{7}_b \cdot D_2^b + (\overline{7}_{1-b} + \overline{7}_e) \cdot D_1^b$

$D_2^b = 8 \cdot D_1^{1-b}$

Finally, we introduce names for some relevant composite terms:

$$Q_{1,b,i} = \partial_H(T_1 \| C^{1-b} \| L_i^{(1-b)} \| D_1^b)$$
$$Q_{2,b,i} = \partial_H(T_2 \| C^{b} \| L_i^{(1-b)} \| D_1^b)$$
$$Q_{3,b,i} = \partial_H(T_2 \| C^{b} \| L_i^{(b)} \| D_1^b)$$
$$Q_{4,b,i} = \partial_H(T_2 \| C^{b} \| L_i^{(b)} \| D_2^b)$$

where $b = 0,1$, $i = 1, \ldots ,4$ and (b) is either b or blank, as appropriate.

4.6. CLAIM. $\partial_H(T \| Q) = \tau \cdot (5° \cdot 8°)^{\omega}$.

In Subsection 4.6.6 this will be deduced from a number of auxiliary claims:

4.6.1. CLAIM. $\partial_H(T \| Q) = \tau_{I_Q}(Q_{1,0,1})$.

PROOF.

$$\begin{aligned}
\partial_H(T \| Q) &= \partial_H(T \| \tau_{I_Q} \partial_{H_Q}(C \| L \| D)) \\
&= \partial_H \tau_{I_Q}(T \| \tau_{I_Q} \partial_{H_Q}(C \| L \| D)) && \text{by CA4} \\
&= \partial_H \tau_{I_Q}(T \| \partial_{H_Q}(C \| L \| D)) && \text{by CA2} \\
&= \tau_{I_Q} \partial_{H_Q}(T \| \partial_{H_Q}(C \| L \| D)) && \text{by CA7} \\
&= \tau_{I_Q} \partial_H(T \| C \| L \| D) && \text{by CA1 and CA5} \\
&= \tau_{I_Q} \partial_H(T_1 \| C^{1-0} \| L_1 \| D_1^0) \\
&= \tau_{I_Q}(Q_{1,0,1}) \quad \square
\end{aligned}$$

4.6.2. CLAIM. $\tau_{I_Q}(Q_{1,b,i}) = \tau \cdot \sum_{i=1}^{4} 5° \cdot \tau_{I_Q}(Q_{2,b,i})$.

PROOF.

$$\begin{aligned}
Q_{1,b,1} &= 5° \cdot Q_{2,b,1} + 6°_{1-b} \cdot Q_{1,b,2} \\
Q_{1,b,2} &= 5° \cdot Q_{2,b,2} + il \cdot Q_{1,b,3} + jl \cdot Q_{1,b,4} + kl \cdot Q_{1,b,1} \\
Q_{1,b,3} &= 5° \cdot Q_{2,b,3} + 7°_{1-b} \cdot Q_{1,b,1} \\
Q_{1,b,4} &= 5° \cdot Q_{2,b,4} + 7°_{e} \cdot Q_{1,b,1}
\end{aligned}$$

We find that $\{Q_{1,b,i} \mid i = 1, \ldots ,4\}$ is a cluster. Applying CFAR yields:

$$\begin{aligned}
\tau_{I_Q}(Q_{1,b,i}) &= \tau \cdot \tau_{I_Q}\left(\sum_{i=1}^{4} 5° \cdot Q_{2,b,i}\right) \\
&= \tau \cdot \sum_{i=1}^{4} 5° \cdot \tau_{I_Q}(Q_{2,b,i}) \quad \square
\end{aligned}$$

4.6.3. CLAIM. $\tau_{I_Q}(Q_{2,b,i}) = (\tau\cdot)\ \tau_{I_Q}(Q_{3,b,1})$. Here $(\tau\cdot)$ is $\tau\cdot$ iff $i \neq 1$.

PROOF.

$$Q_{2,b,1} = \partial_H(T_2 \| C^b \| L_1 \| D_1^b) = Q_{3,b,1}$$
$$Q_{2,b,3} = 7^\circ{}_{1-b} \cdot Q_{3,b,1} \quad \text{hence } \tau_{I_Q}(Q_{2,b,3}) = \tau \cdot \tau_{I_Q}(Q_{3,b,1})$$
$$Q_{2,b,4} = 7^\circ{}_e \cdot Q_{3,b,1} \quad \text{hence } \tau_{I_Q}(Q_{2,b,4}) = \tau \cdot \tau_{I_Q}(Q_{3,b,1})$$
$$Q_{2,b,2} = il \cdot Q_{2,b,3} + jl \cdot Q_{2,b,4} + kl \cdot Q_{2,b,1}$$
$$\text{hence } \tau_{I_Q}(Q_{2,b,2}) = (\tau^2 + \tau^2 + \tau) \cdot \tau_{I_Q}(Q_{3,b,1})$$

The claim is now easily derived. □

4.6.4. CLAIM. $\tau_{I_Q}(Q_{3,b,1}) = \tau \cdot \tau_{I_Q}(Q_{4,b,1})$.

PROOF.

$$Q_{3,b,1} = 6^\circ{}_{1-b} \cdot Q_{3,b,2}$$
$$Q_{3,b,2} = il \cdot Q_{3,b,3} + jl \cdot Q_{3,b,4} + kl \cdot Q_{3,b,1}$$
$$Q_{3,b,4} = 7^\circ{}_e \cdot Q_{3,b,1}$$

We find that $\{Q_{3,b,i} \mid i = 1,2,4\}$ is a cluster. Applying CFAR yields:

$$\begin{aligned}\tau_{I_Q}(Q_{3,b,1}) &= \tau \cdot \tau_{I_Q}(il \cdot Q_{3,b,3}) \\ &= \tau \cdot \tau_{I_Q}(il \cdot 7^\circ{}_b \cdot Q_{4,b,1}) \\ &= \tau^3 \cdot \tau_{I_Q}(Q_{4,b,1}) \\ &= \tau \cdot \tau_{I_Q}(Q_{4,b,1}) \quad \square\end{aligned}$$

4.6.5. CLAIM. $\tau_{I_Q}(Q_{4,b,1}) = \tau \cdot \sum_{i=1}^{4} (\tau\cdot) 8^\circ \cdot \tau_{I_Q}(Q_{1,1-b,i})$. $(\tau\cdot)$ is $\tau\cdot$ iff $i = 3,4$.

PROOF.

$$Q_{4,b,1} = 8^\circ \cdot Q_{1,1-b,1} + 6^\circ{}_b \cdot Q_{4,b,2}$$
$$Q_{4,b,2} = 8^\circ \cdot Q_{1,1-b,2} + il \cdot Q_{4,b,3} + jl \cdot Q_{4,b,4} + kl \cdot Q_{4,b,1}$$

So $Q_{4,b,1}$ and $Q_{4,b,2}$ form a cluster and (using CFAR):

$$\begin{aligned}\tau_{I_Q}(Q_{4,b,1}) &= \tau \cdot \tau_{I_Q}(8^\circ \cdot Q_{1,1-b,1} + 8^\circ \cdot Q_{1,1-b,2} + il \cdot Q_{4,b,3} + jl \cdot Q_{4,b,4}) \\ &= \tau \cdot \tau_{I_Q}(8^\circ \cdot Q_{1,1-b,1} + 8^\circ \cdot Q_{1,1-b,2} \\ &\qquad + il \cdot 8^\circ \cdot Q_{1,1-b,3} + jl \cdot 8^\circ \cdot Q_{1,1-b,4}) \\ &= \tau \cdot (8^\circ \cdot \tau_{I_Q}(Q_{1,1-b,1}) + 8^\circ \cdot (Q_{1,1-b,2})\end{aligned}$$

$$+\tau\cdot 8^\circ\cdot\tau_{I_Q}(Q_{1,1-b,3})+\tau\cdot 8^\circ\cdot\tau_{I_Q}(Q_{1,1-b,4}))$$

$$=\tau\cdot\sum_{i=1}^{4}(\tau\cdot)8^\circ\cdot\tau_{I_Q}(Q_{1,1-b,i})\quad\square$$

4.6.6. Summing up:

$$\tau_{I_Q}(Q_{1,b,i})=\tau\cdot\sum_{i=1}^{4}5^\circ\cdot\tau_{I_Q}(Q_{2,b,i})$$

$$=\tau\cdot\sum_{i=1}^{4}5^\circ\cdot(\tau\cdot)\tau_{I_Q}(Q_{3,b,1})$$

$$=\tau\cdot 5^\circ\cdot\tau_{I_Q}(Q_{3,b,1})$$

$$=\tau\cdot 5^\circ\cdot\tau_{I_Q}(Q_{4,b,1})=\tau\cdot 5^\circ\cdot\tau\cdot\sum_{i=1}^{4}(\tau\cdot)8^\circ\cdot\tau_{I_Q}(Q_{1,1-b,i})$$

$$=\tau\cdot 5^\circ\cdot\sum_{i=1}^{4}(\tau\cdot)8^\circ\cdot\tau_{I_Q}(Q_{1,1-b,i}).$$

Similarly, $\tau_{I_Q}(Q_{1,1-b,i})=\cdots=\tau\cdot 5^\circ\cdot\tau_{I_Q}(Q_{3,1-b,1})$. (**)

Hence $\sum_i(\tau\cdot)8^\circ\cdot\tau_{I_Q}(Q_{1,1-b,i})=\sum_i(\tau\cdot)8^\circ\cdot\tau\cdot 5^\circ\cdot\tau_{I_Q}(Q_{3,1-b,1})$

$$=\tau\cdot 8^\circ\cdot 5^\circ\cdot\tau_{I_Q}(Q_{3,1-b,1})=\tau\cdot 8^\circ\cdot\tau_{I_Q}(Q_{1,1-b,1}),$$

using (**) in both directions.

Consequently, substituting $1-b$ for b, $\tau_{I_Q}(Q_{1,b,1})=\tau\cdot 5^\circ\cdot 8^\circ\cdot\tau_{I_Q}(Q_{1,1-b,1})$. Similarly, $\tau_{I_Q}(Q_{1,1-b,1})=\tau\cdot 5^\circ\cdot 8^\circ\cdot\tau_{I_Q}(Q_{1,b,1})$. Hence both equal the unique solution of $X=\tau\cdot 5^\circ\cdot 8^\circ X$, which is $\tau\cdot(5^\circ\cdot 8^\circ)^\omega$.

So the left hand side of (*) in Section 4.3, being equal to $\tau\cdot\tau_{I_Q}(Q_{1,0,1})\cdot\delta$, equals the right hand side. This proves (*). $\square$

4.7. In Section 3.4 we introduced two modules $M(P)$ and M_P differing by one barred edge. For no specific reason, we choose to verify $P\models M_P$ in the next four sections. They will be rather similar to the last three.

According to TEP, it suffices to show

$$\tau\cdot\partial_H(P\|T(M_P))\cdot\delta=\tau\cdot\partial_H(M_P\|T(M_P))\cdot\delta. \qquad (*)$$

4.8. NOTATION. We will use abbreviations similar to those in Section 4.5, e.g. $2_{d,b} = s(2,(d,b))$. Incidentally $5, \overline{5}$ etc. have the same meaning as in Section 4.4, whereas T_1 etc. have not.

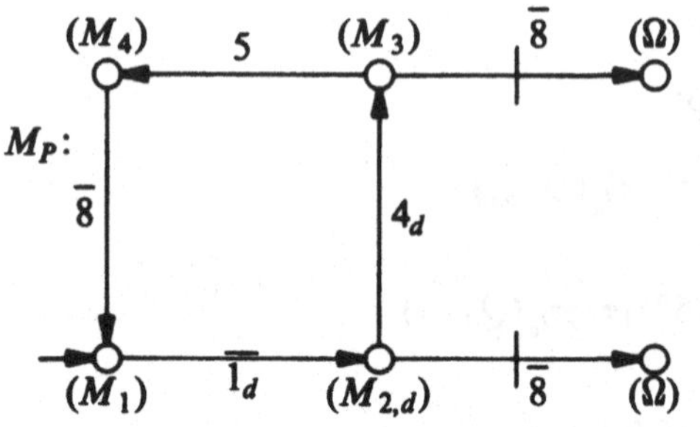

FIGURE 4.5

$$\begin{aligned} M_P = M_1 &= \sum_{d \in D} \overline{1}_d \cdot M_{2,d} \\ M_{2,d} &= 4_d \cdot M_3 + \overline{8} \cdot \Omega \\ M_3 &= 5 \cdot M_4 + \overline{8} \cdot \Omega \\ M_4 &= \overline{8} \cdot M_1 \end{aligned}$$

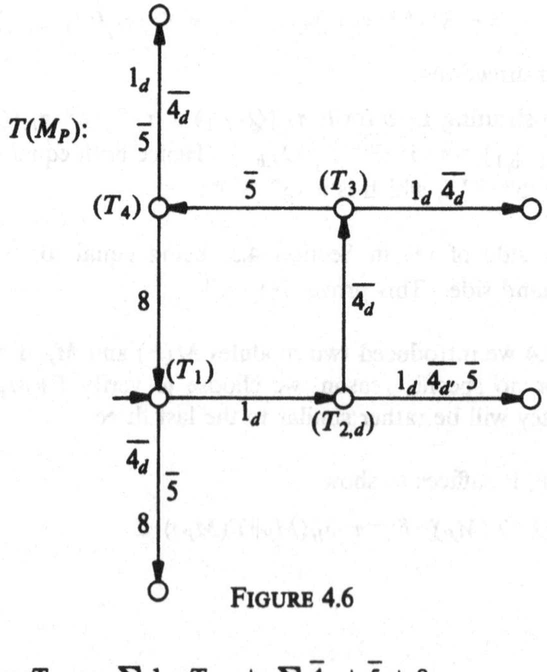

FIGURE 4.6

$$T(M_P) = T_1 = \sum_{d \in D} 1_d \cdot T_{2,d} + \sum_{d \in D} \overline{4}_d + \overline{5} + 8$$

$$T_{2,d} = \overline{4}_d \cdot T_3 + \sum_{d \in D} 1_d + \sum_{d' \neq d} \overline{4}_{d'} + \overline{5}$$

$$T_3 \;= \overline{5} \cdot T_4 + \sum_{d \in D} 1_d + \sum_{d \in D} \overline{4}_d$$

$$T_4 \;= 8 \cdot T_1 + \sum_{d \in D} 1_d + \sum_{d \in D} \overline{4}_d + \overline{5}$$

One easily sees:

$$\partial_H(T_1 \| M_1) \;= \sum_{d \in D} 1°_d \cdot \partial_H(T_{2,d} \| M_{2,d})$$

$$\partial_H(T_{2,d} \| M_{2,d}) = 4°_d \cdot \partial_H(T_3 \| M_3)$$

$$\partial_H(T_3 \| M_3) \;= 5° \cdot \partial_H(T_4 \| M_4)$$

$$\partial_H(T_4 \| M_4) \;= 8° \cdot \partial_H(T_1 \| M_1)$$

Therefore the right hand side of (*) in Section 4.7 reduces to $\tau \cdot (\sum_{d \in D} 1°_d \cdot 4°_d \cdot 5° \cdot 8°)^{\omega}$.

4.9. Like in Section 4.5 we repeat the relevant parts of Section 1.4:

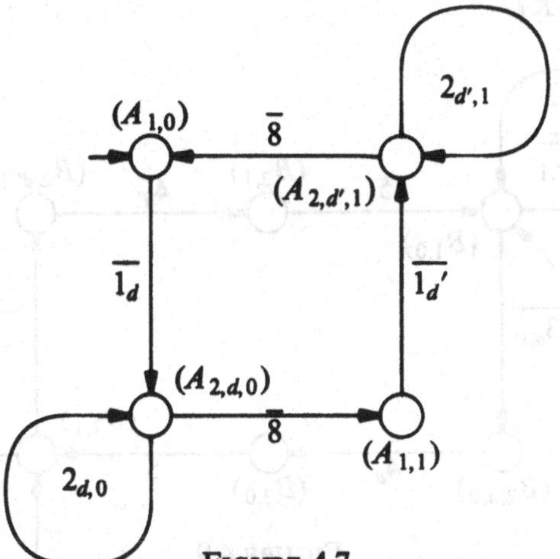

FIGURE 4.7

$$A: \quad A \;= A_{1,0}$$

$$A_{1,b} \;= \sum_{d \in D} \overline{1}_d \cdot A_{2,d,b}$$

$$A_{2,d,b} = 2_{d,b} \cdot A_{2,d,b} + \overline{8} \cdot A_{1,1-b}$$

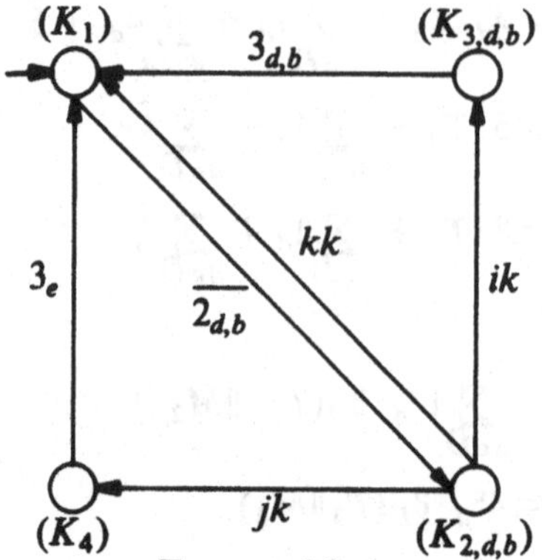

FIGURE 4.8

K: $K = K_1$

$K_1 = \sum_{d \in D, b \in B} \overline{2}_{d,b} \cdot K_{2,d,b}$

$K_{2,d,b} = ik \cdot K_{3,d,b} + jk \cdot K_4 + kk \cdot K_1$

$K_{3,d,b} = 3_{d,b} \cdot K_1$

$K_4 = 3_e \cdot K_1$

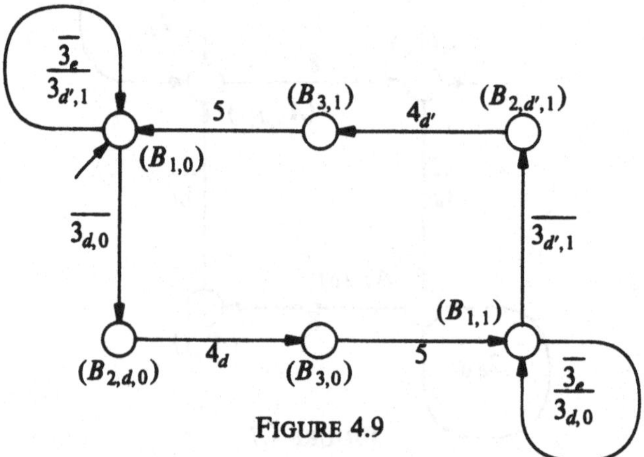

FIGURE 4.9

B: $B = B_{1,0}$

$B_{1,b} = \sum_{d \in D} \overline{3}_{d,b} \cdot B_{2,d,b} + \sum_{d \in D} \overline{3}_{d,1-b} \cdot B_{1,b} + \overline{3}_e \cdot B_{1,b}$

$B_{2,d,b} = 4_d \cdot B_{3,b}$

$B_{3,b} = 5 \cdot B_{1,1-b}$

Relevant composite terms are:

$P_{1,b,i,(d)} = \partial_H(T_1 \| A_{1,b} \| K_{i,(1-b,d)} \| B_{1,b})$

$$P_{2,b,i,(d'),d} = \partial_H(T_{2,d} \| A_{2,d,b} \| K_{i,(1-b,d')} \| B_{1,b})$$
$$P_{3,b,i,(d)} = \partial_H(T_{2,d} \| A_{2,d,b} \| K_{i,(b,d)} \| B_{1,b})$$
$$P_{4,b,i,(d)} = \partial_H(T_{2,d} \| A_{2,d,b} \| K_{i,(b,d)} \| B_{2,d,b})$$
$$P_{5,b,i,(d)} = \partial_H(T_3 \| A_{2,d,b} \| K_{i,(b,d)} \| B_{3,b})$$
$$P_{6,b,i,(d)} = \partial_H(T_4 \| A_{2,d,b} \| K_{i,(b,d)} \| B_{1,1-b})$$

where $b = 0,1$, $d \in D$, $i = 1, \ldots, 4$ and (x) means either x or blank, as appropriate.

4.10. CLAIM. $\partial_H(T(M_P) \| P) = (\sum_{d \in D} 1°_d \cdot 4°_d \cdot 5° \cdot 8°)^\omega$.

This will be deduced in Subsection 4.10.10.

4.10.1. CLAIM. $\partial_H(T(M_P) \| P) = \tau_{I_p}(P_{1,0,1})$

PROOF. Entirely analogous to Claim 4.6.1. □

4.10.2. CLAIM. $\tau_{I_p}(P_{1,b,1}) = \sum_{d \in D} 1°_d \cdot \tau_{I_p}(P_{2,b,1,d})$

PROOF. Straightforward calculations. □

4.10.3. CLAIM. $P_{2,b,1,d} = P_{3,b,1,d}$

PROOF. By definition. □

4.10.4. CLAIM. $\tau_{I_p}(P_{3,b,i,d}) = \tau \cdot \tau_{I_p}(P_{4,b,1,d})$

PROOF.

$$P_{3,b,1,d} = 2°_{d,b} \cdot P_{3,b,2,d}$$
$$P_{3,b,2,d} = ik \cdot P_{3,b,3,d} + jk \cdot P_{3,b,4,d} + kk \cdot P_{3,b,1,d}$$
$$P_{3,b,4,d} = 3°_e \cdot P_{3,b,1,d}$$

We find that $\{P_{3,b,i,d} \mid i = 1,2,4\}$ is a cluster. We apply CFAR:

$$\begin{aligned}\tau_{I_p}(P_{3,b,i,d}) &= \tau \cdot \tau_{I_p}(ik \cdot P_{3,b,3,d}) \\ &= \tau \cdot \tau_{I_p}(ik \cdot 3°_{d,b} \cdot P_{4,b,1,d}) \\ &= \tau \cdot \tau_{I_p}(P_{4,b,1,d}).\end{aligned}$$

This proves the claim for $i = 1,2,4$. It trivially holds for $i = 3$. □

4.10.5. CLAIM. $\tau_{I_p}(P_{4,b,1,d}) = \tau\cdot \sum_{i=1}^{4}(\tau\cdot)\, 4°_d\cdot\tau_{I_p}(P_{5,b,i,d})$. Here $(\tau\cdot)$ is $\tau\cdot$ if and only if $i=3,4$.

PROOF.

$$P_{4,b,1,d} = 4°_d\cdot P_{5,b,1,d} + 2°_{d,b}\cdot P_{4,b,2,d}$$
$$P_{4,b,2,d} = 4°_d\cdot P_{5,b,2,d} + ik\cdot P_{4,b,3,d} + jk\cdot P_{4,b,4,d} + kk\cdot P_{4,b,1,d}$$

Hence $P_{4,b,1,d}$ and $P_{4,b,2,d}$ form a cluster and (applying CFAR):

$$\begin{aligned}\tau_{I_p}(P_{4,b,1,d}) &= \tau\cdot\tau_{I_p}(4°_d\cdot P_{5,b,1,d} + 4°_d\cdot P_{5,b,2,d}\\ &\qquad + ik\cdot P_{4,b,3,d} + jk\cdot P_{4,b,4,d})\\ &= \tau\cdot\tau_{I_p}(4°_d\cdot P_{5,b,1,d} + 4°_d\cdot P_{5,b,2,d}\\ &\qquad + ik\cdot 4°_d\cdot P_{5,b,3,d} + jk\cdot 4°_d\cdot P_{5,b,4,d})\\ &= \tau\cdot(4°_d\cdot\tau_{I_p}(P_{5,b,1,d}) + 4°_d\cdot\tau_{I_p}(P_{5,b,2,d})\\ &\qquad + \tau\cdot 4°_d\cdot\tau_{I_p}(P_{5,b,3,d}) + \tau\cdot 4°_d\cdot\tau_{I_p}(P_{5,b,4,d}))\\ &= \tau\cdot\sum_{i=1}^{4}(\tau\cdot)4°_d\cdot\tau_{I_p}(P_{5,b,i,d}).\quad\square\end{aligned}$$

4.10.6.1. CLAIM. $\tau_{I_p}(P_{5,b,i,d}) = \tau\cdot\sum_{j=1}^{4}(\tau\cdot)\, 5°\cdot\tau_{I_p}(P_{6,b,j,d})$ for $i=1,2$. Again, $(\tau\cdot)$ is $\tau\cdot$ if and only if $j=3,4$.

PROOF.

$$P_{5,b,1,d} = 5°\cdot P_{6,b,1,d} + 2°_{d,b}\cdot P_{5,b,2,d}$$
$$P_{5,b,2,d} = 5°\cdot P_{6,b,2,d} + ik\cdot P_{5,b,3,d} + jk\cdot P_{5,b,4,d} + kk\cdot P_{5,b,1,d}$$

Again $P_{5,b,1,d}$ and $P_{5,b,2,d}$ form a cluster and, by CFAR:

$$\begin{aligned}\tau_{I_p}(P_{5,b,i,d}) &= \tau\cdot\tau_{I_p}(5°\cdot P_{6,b,1,d} + 5°\cdot P_{6,b,2,d} + ik\cdot P_{5,b,3,d} + jk\cdot P_{5,b,4,d})\\ &= \tau\cdot\sum_{j=1}^{4}(\tau\cdot)\, 5°\cdot\tau_{I_p}(P_{6,b,j,d}),\text{ as before.}\quad\square\end{aligned}$$

4.10.6.2. CLAIM. $\tau_{I_p}(P_{5,b,i,d}) = 5°\cdot\tau_{I_p}(P_{6,b,i,d})$ for $i=3,4$.

PROOF. Straightforward. □

4.10.7. CLAIM. $\tau_{I_p}(P_{6,b,i,d}) = \tau \cdot \sum_{j=1}^{4} 8^\circ \cdot \tau_{I_p}(P_{1,1-b,j,(d)})$.

PROOF.

$$P_{6,b,1,d} = 8^\circ \cdot P_{1,1-b,1} + 2^\circ{}_{d,b} \cdot P_{6,b,2,d}$$
$$P_{6,b,2,d} = 8^\circ \cdot P_{1,1-b,2,d} + ik \cdot P_{6,b,3,d} + jk \cdot P_{6,b,4,d} + kk \cdot P_{6,b,1,d}$$
$$P_{6,b,3,d} = 8^\circ \cdot P_{1,1-b,3,d} + 3^\circ{}_{d,b} \cdot P_{6,b,1,d}$$
$$P_{6,b,4,d} = 8^\circ \cdot P_{1,1-b,4} + 3^\circ{}_e \cdot P_{6,b,1,d}$$

We find that $\{P_{6,b,i,d} \mid i = 1, \ldots, 4\}$ is a cluster. Applying CFAR yields:

$$\tau_{I_p}(P_{6,b,i,d}) = \tau \cdot \tau_{I_p}(\sum_{j=1}^{4} 8^\circ \cdot P_{1,1-b,j,(d)})$$
$$= \tau \cdot \sum_{j=1}^{4} 8^\circ \cdot \tau_{I_p}(P_{1,1-b,j,(d)}) \quad \square$$

4.10.8.1. CLAIM. $\tau_{I_p}(P_{1,b,4}) = \tau \cdot \sum_{d \in D} 1^\circ{}_d \cdot \tau_{I_p}(P_{2,b,1,d})$.

PROOF.

$$P_{1,b,4} = \sum_{d \in D} 1^\circ{}_d \cdot P_{2,b,4,d} + 3^\circ{}_e \cdot P_{1,b,1} = \sum_{d \in D} 1^\circ{}_d \cdot 3^\circ{}_e \cdot P_{2,b,1,d} + 3^\circ{}_e \cdot \sum_{d \in D} 1^\circ{}_d \cdot P_{2,b,1,d}$$

Hence $\tau_{I_p}(P_{1,b,4}) = \sum_{d \in D} 1^\circ{}_d \cdot \tau_{I_p}(P_{2,b,1,d}) + \tau \cdot \sum_{d \in D} 1^\circ{}_d \cdot \tau_{I_p}(P_{2,b,1,d})$

$$= \tau \cdot \sum_{d \in D} 1^\circ{}_d \cdot \tau_{I_p}(P_{2,b,1,d}). \quad \square$$

4.10.8.2. CLAIM. $\tau_{I_p}(P_{1,b,3,d}) = \tau \cdot \sum_{d' \in D} 1^\circ{}_{d'} \cdot \tau_{I_p}(P_{2,b,1,d'})$.

PROOF. Analogous to Claim 4.10.8.1. □

4.10.8.3. CLAIM. $\tau_{I_p}(P_{1,b,2,d}) = \tau \cdot \sum_{d' \in D} 1^\circ{}_{d'} \cdot \tau_{I_p}(P_{2,b,1,d'})$.

Proof.

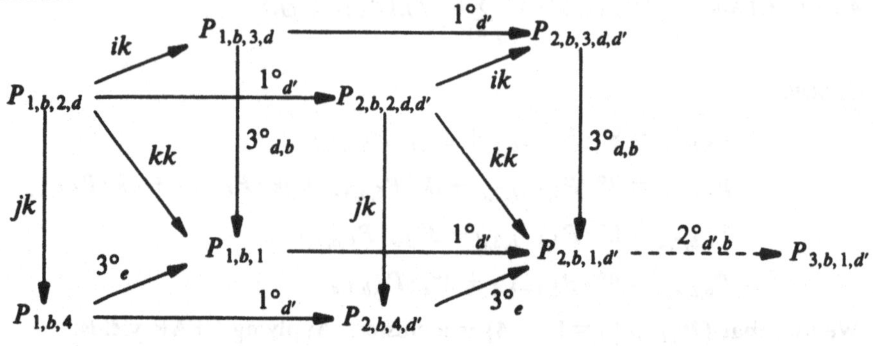

FIGURE 4.10

$$P_{1,b,2,d} = \sum_{d'\in D} 1°_{d'}\cdot P_{2,b,2,d,d'} + ik\cdot P_{1,b,3,d} + jk\cdot P_{1,b,4} + kk\cdot P_{1,b,1}$$

$$= \sum_{d'\in D} 1°_{d'}\cdot(ik\cdot P_{2,b,3,d,d'} + jk\cdot P_{2,b,4,d'} + kk\cdot P_{2,b,1,d'})$$
$$+ ik\cdot(\sum_{d'\in D} 1°_{d'}\cdot P_{2,b,3,d,d'} + 3°_{d,b}\cdot P_{1,b,1})$$
$$+ jk\cdot(\sum_{d'\in D} 1°_{d'}\cdot P_{2,b,4,d'} + 3°_{e}\cdot P_{1,b,1}) + kk\cdot \sum_{d'\in D} 1°_{d'}\cdot P_{2,b,1,d'}$$

$$= \sum_{d'\in D} 1°_{d'}\cdot ik\cdot 3°_{d,b}\cdot P_{2,b,1,d'} + jk\cdot 3°_{e}\cdot P_{2,b,1,d'} + kk\cdot P_{2,b,1,d'})$$
$$+ ik\cdot(\sum_{d'\in D} 1°_{d'}\cdot 3°_{d,b}\cdot P_{2,b,1,d'} + 3°_{d,b}\cdot \sum_{d'\in D} 1°_{d'}\cdot P_{2,b,1,d'})$$
$$+ jk\cdot(\sum_{d'\in D} 1°_{d'}\cdot 3°_{e}\cdot P_{2,b,1,d'} + 3°_{e}\cdot \sum_{d'\in D} 1°_{d'}\cdot P_{2,b,1,d'})$$
$$+ kk\cdot \sum_{d'\in D} 1°_{d'}\cdot P_{2,b,1,d'}$$

The claim is now easily derived. □

4.10.8.4. We can summarize Claim 4.10.2 and Claim 4.10.8.1 through 4.10.8.3: $\tau_{I_p}(P_{1,b,i,(d)}) = (\tau\cdot)\sum_{d'} 1°_{d'}\cdot\tau_{I_p}(P_{2,b,1,d'})$, where $(\tau\cdot)$ is blank if and only if $i=1$.

4.10.9. Summing up Claims 4.10.3 through 4.10.8 we find:

$$\tau_{I_p}(P_{2,b,1,d}) = \tau_{I_p}(P_{3,b,1,d}) = \tau\cdot\tau_{I_p}(P_{4,b,1,d}) = \tau\cdot\sum_{i=1}^{4}(\tau\cdot)\, 4°_{d}\cdot\tau_{I_p}(P_{5,b,i,d})$$

$$= \tau\cdot\sum_{i=1}^{4}(\tau\cdot)\, 4°_{d}\cdot\tau\cdot\sum_{j=1}^{4}(\tau\cdot)\, 5°\cdot\tau_{I_p}(P_{6,b,j,d})$$

$$= \tau\cdot 4°_{d}\cdot\sum_{j=1}^{4} 5°\cdot\tau_{I_p}(P_{6,b,j,d})$$

$$= \tau \cdot 4^{\circ}_{d} \cdot \sum_{j=1}^{4} 5^{\circ} \cdot \tau \cdot \sum_{k=1}^{4} 8^{\circ} \cdot \tau_{I_P}(P_{1,1-b,k,(d)})$$

$$= \tau \cdot 4^{\circ}_{d} \cdot 5^{\circ} \cdot \sum_{k=1}^{4} 8^{\circ} \cdot \tau_{I_P}(P_{1,1-b,k,(d)})$$

$$= \tau \cdot 4^{\circ}_{d} \cdot 5^{\circ} \cdot \sum_{k=1}^{4} 8^{\circ} \cdot (\tau \cdot) \sum_{d' \in D} 1^{\circ}_{d'} \cdot \tau_{I_P}(P_{2,1-b,1,d'})$$

$$= \tau \cdot 4^{\circ}_{d} \cdot 5^{\circ} \cdot 8^{\circ} \sum_{d' \in D} 1^{\circ}_{d'} \cdot \tau_{I_P}(P_{2,1-b,1,d'})$$

So if we denote $\sum_{d \in D} 1^{\circ}_{d} \cdot \tau_{I_P}(P_{2,b,1,d})$ by P_b then

$$P_b = \sum_{d \in D} 1^{\circ}_{d} \cdot 4^{\circ}_{d} \cdot 5^{\circ} \cdot 8^{\circ} \cdot P_{1-b}$$

and

$$P_{1-b} = \sum_{d \in D} 1^{\circ}_{d} \cdot 4^{\circ}_{d} \cdot 5^{\circ} \cdot 8^{\circ} \cdot P_b$$

So both equal the unique solution of $X = \sum_{d \in D} 1^{\circ}_{d} \cdot 4^{\circ}_{d} \cdot 5^{\circ} \cdot 8^{\circ} \cdot X$, which is $(\sum_{d \in D} 1^{\circ}_{d} \cdot 4^{\circ}_{d} \cdot 5^{\circ} \cdot 8^{\circ})^{\omega}$.

4.10.10. **Finally we are in a position to prove Claim 4.10:**

$$\partial_H(T(M_P) \| P) = \tau_{I_P}(P_{1,0,1}) = \sum_{d \in D} 1^{\circ}_{d} \cdot \tau_{I_P}(P_{2,0,1,d})$$

$$= P_0 = (\sum_{d \in D} 1^{\circ}_{d} \cdot 4^{\circ}_{d} \cdot 5^{\circ} \cdot 8^{\circ})^{\omega}. \quad \square$$

4.11. **In this section we will calculate $\partial_H(M_P \| M(Q))$. As the notations from Sections 4.4 and 4.8 collide, we have to rename some states. We choose to rename the states of $M(Q)$ to N_1 and N_2. So:**

$$M_P = M_1 = \sum_{d \in D} \bar{1}_d \cdot M_{2,d} \qquad M_4 = \bar{8} \cdot M_1$$

$$M_{2,d} = 4_d \cdot M_3 + \bar{8} \cdot \Omega \qquad M(Q) = N_1 = \bar{5} \cdot N_2$$

$$M_3 = 5 \cdot M_4 + \bar{8} \cdot \Omega \qquad N_2 = 8 \cdot N_1 + \bar{5} \cdot \Omega$$

Next we compute:

$$\partial_H(M_P \| M(Q)) = \partial_H(M_1 \| N_1)$$

$$= \sum_{d \in D} \bar{1}_d \cdot \partial_H(M_{2,d} \| N_1)$$

$$= \sum_{d \in D} \bar{1}_d \cdot 4_d \cdot \partial_H(M_3 \| N_1)$$

$$= \sum_{d \in D} \bar{1}_d \cdot 4_d \cdot 5^\circ \cdot \partial_H(M_4 \| N_2)$$

$$= \sum_{d \in D} \bar{1}_d \cdot 4_d \cdot 5^\circ \cdot 8^\circ \cdot \partial_H(M_1 \| N_1)$$

So we find that $\partial_H(M_P \| M(Q)) = (\sum_{d \in D} \bar{1}_d \cdot 4_d \cdot 5^\circ \cdot 8^\circ)^\omega$.

4.12. In the previous sections we established $P \models M_P$ and $Q \models M(Q)$. We apply MAP (Theorem 3.24) and find $P \| Q \models M_P \| M(Q)$. This implies that $\partial_H(P \| Q) \models \partial_H(M_P \| M(Q))$, which was shown equal to $(\sum_{d \in D} \bar{1}_d \cdot 4_d \cdot 5^\circ \cdot 8^\circ)^\omega$. The latter being robust, we may apply ROP (Theorem 3.26) and find that $\tau \cdot \partial_H(P \| Q) \cdot \delta = \tau \cdot (\sum_{d \in D} \bar{1}_d \cdot 4_d \cdot 5^\circ \cdot 8^\circ)^\omega \cdot \delta$ holds in the graph model. Since these processes are perpetual (never terminate), this implies $\tau_I \partial_H(P \| Q) = (\tau \cdot)(\sum_{d \in D} \bar{1}_d \cdot 4_d)^\omega$. This proves that CABP is a correct communication protocol.

REFERENCES.

1. J.A. BERGSTRA, J.W. KLOP (1989). *An Introduction to Process Algebra.* This volume.
2. J.A. BERGSTRA, J.W. KLOP (1986). Verification of an Alternating Bit Protocol by means of Process Algebra. W. BIBEL, K.P. JANTKE (eds.). *Mathematical Methods of Specification and Synthesis of Software Systems '85 Math. Research 31,* Akademie-Verlag Berlin, 9-23. Also appeared as CWI Report CS-R8404, Centre for Mathematics and Computer Science, Amsterdam, 1984.
3. J.A. BERGSTRA, J.W. KLOP (1984). *Fair FIFO Queues Satisfy an Algebraic Criterion for Protocol Correctness,* CWI Report CS-R8405, Centre for Mathematics and Computer Science, Amsterdam.
4. J. PARROW (1985). *Fairness Properties in Process Algebra - with Applications in Communication Protocol Verification,* DoCS 85/03, Ph.D. Thesis, Department of Computer Systems, Uppsala University.
5. A.A. SCHOONE, J. VAN LEEUWEN (1985). *Verification of Balanced Link-level Protocols,* Preprint RUU-CS-85-12, State University of Utrecht.
6. A.S. TANENBAUM (1981). *Computer Networks,* Prentice Hall.
7. F.W. VAANDRAGER (1986). *Verification of Two Communication Protocols by means of Process Algebra,* CWI Report CS-R8606, Centre for Mathematics and Computer Science, Amsterdam.

Index of concepts

Index of names

Index of symbols and notation

Printed in the United States
By Bookmasters